/!/	Exclamation mark (page 413)
/-/	Hyphen (page 418)
( )	Parentheses (page 425)
.	Period (page 428)
ᴠ	Quotation mark (page 431)
⟨;⟩	Semicolon (page 438)

comp	Correct faulty comparison of adjective or adverb. (page 401)
concl	Revise the conclusion of this essay. (page 107)
d	Use a more exact, appropriate, or effective word. (page 407)
def	Define your terms. (page 149)
det	Add specific details. (page 94)
div	Divide a word at the end of a line only between syllables.
dm	Revise the sentence so the dangling modifier has something to modify. (page 405)
emph	Rewrite to strengthen emphasis. (page 411)
ex	Add an example. (page 94)
fig	Revise the figure of speech to make it more effective. (page 414)
frag	Make this fragment into a complete sentence. (page 415)
fs	Revise this fused sentence. (page 437)
glos	See the glossary in Chapter 11 for the word marked.
ital	Underline to indicate italics. (page 453)
logic	Rethink this passage. (page 420)
lc	Use a lowercase letter. (page 387)
mng?	Clear up the meaning. (page 402)
mm	Revise the sentence to put the misplaced modifier where it belongs. (page 422)
mix	Rewrite to get rid of the mixed construction. (page 402)
no punc	Don't use punctuation here. (page 423)
¶	Indent for a new paragraph here. (page 425)
¶ *dev*	Develop this paragraph more fully. (page 453)
paral or ‖	Make these elements parallel in form. (page 383)
pass	Change passive voice to active. (page 427)
quot	Use quotation marks correctly. (page 431)
ref	Make pronoun reference clear. (page 434)
rep	Get rid of careless repetition. (page 436)
run-on	Revise this run-on sentence. (page 437)
semi	Insert a semicolon where needed. *Or:* correct the misuse of the semicolon. (page 438)
shift	Revise to correct the shift in tense or person. (page 442)
sm	Correct the squinting modifier. (page 445)

(continued back cover)

The Writer's Rhetoric and Handbook

The Writer's Rhetoric and Handbook

SECOND EDITION

Elizabeth McMahan and Susan Day

Illinois State University

McGraw-Hill Book Company

New York   St. Louis   San Francisco   Auckland   Bogotá   Hamburg
Johannesburg   London   Madrid   Mexico   Montreal   New Delhi
Panama   Paris   São Paulo   Singapore   Sydney   Tokyo   Toronto

THE WRITER'S RHETORIC AND HANDBOOK

Copyright © 1984, 1980 by McGraw-Hill, Inc. All rights reserved. Printed in the United States of America. Except as permitted under the United States Copyright Act of 1976, no part of this publication may be reproduced or distributed in any form or by any means, or stored in a data base or retrieval system, without the prior written permission of the publisher.

2 3 4 5 6 7 8 9 0   D O C D O C   8 9 8 7 6 5 4

ISBN 0-07-045424-8

See Acknowledgments on pages 497-503. Copyrights included on this page by reference.

This book was set in Caledonia by Bi-Comp, Incorporated.
The editors were Jim Dodd and Barry Benjamin;
the designer was Merrill Haber;
the production supervisor was Leroy A. Young.
New drawings were done by Danmark & Michaels, Inc.
R. R. Donnelley & Sons Company was printer and binder.

Library of Congress Cataloging in Publication Data

McMahan, Elizabeth.
    The writer's rhetoric and handbook.

    Includes index.
    1. English language—Rhetoric.   I. Day, Susan.
II. Title.
PE1408.M395   1984   808'.042   83-9850
ISBN 0-07-045424-8

In loving memory of Moose
1970–1982

Contents in Brief

Contents

(

*Conjunctions, Correlative • Conjunctions,
Subordinating • Conjunctive Adverb • Connotation
and Denotation • Contraction • Coordinating
Conjunction • Coordination • Correlative
Conjunction • Dangling Modifier • Dash •
Denotation • Determiner • Diction • Digression •
Doublespeak • Ellipsis Dots • Elliptical Construction •
Emphasis • Euphemism • Exclamation Point •
Expletive • Figures of Speech • Formal Usage •
Fragment • Function Words • Fused Sentence •
Generalizations • Hyphen • Infinitive • Informal
Usage • Interjection • Intransitive Verb • Irregular
Verb • Italics • Jargon • Levels of Usage • Linking
Verb • Logic • Misplaced Modifier • Modifiers •
Mood • Nominal • Nonrestrictive Clause • No
Punctuation Necessary • Numbers • Object •
Overburdened Sentence • Paragraph • Parallel
Structure • Parentheses • Participle • Participle
Endings • Passive Voice • Period • Personification •
Phrase • Point of View • Possessives • Possessives
with Gerunds • Predicate • Predicate Nominative •
Predicate Adjective • Predication, Faulty •
Preposition • Pronoun • Proper Noun • Qualification •
Quotation Marks • Redundance • Redundant
Prepositions • Reference of Pronouns • Regular Verb •
Repetition • Restrictive Clauses • Run-On
Sentence (Fused Sentence) • Semicolon • Sentence
Types • Shifts in Tense and Person • Simile • Simple
Sentence • Slang • Spelling • Split Infinitive •
Squinting Modifier • Subject • Subjunctive Mood •
Subordination and Coordination • Tense • Thesis
Statement • This and Which • Titles • Topic
Sentence • Transitions • Transitive Verb • Triteness •
Underlining • Underdeveloped Paragraphs • Unity •
Usage • Variety • Verb • Verbal • Word Division •
Wordiness*
Comprehensive Exercise

Preface

We have tried to follow our own advice in this book and write in a style appealing to students, our primary audience. Although the tone is sometimes light, the content is always serious. In this second edition we have provided a text balancing process and product orientation. We incorporate as much current composition theory as possible without burdening students with technical language or abstruse paradigms. Our purpose remains practical: to provide instruction that is pleasant to read and easy to understand. And we still aim to help students learn to write standard English that is clear, coherent, and concise.

PRACTICAL APPROACHES TO WRITING IMPROVEMENT

The content of *The Writer's Rhetoric and Handbook* is informed by our concern for pedagogy. The first eleven chapters, which constitute the Rhetoric, contain instruction in writing techniques. The remaining chapters make up the Handbook, which outlines the regulations governing standard English grammar and usage.

The Rhetoric

Our introductory chapter now contains more emphasis on audience and purpose, several additional invention strategies, and expanded advice on the composing and revising process. We have added a chapter on diction which stresses careful word choice; gives advice on connotative language, figures of speech, and usage levels; and provides suggestions for using a dictionary and avoiding sexist language. Chapter 3 on sentences now offers practice in imitating admirable and useful sentence models by professional writers. We have also expanded and strengthened the material on sentence combining.

Because sound organization is essential for clarity, we continue to devote considerable attention to patterns of development. We now have three chapters detailing methods for organizing essays according to seven rhetorical types, arranged from the simplest to the most complex. Argument and persuasion receive a good deal more attention in this edition. The explanation for each rhetorical type includes the following:

Invention ideas

Ways to introduce and conclude the essay

Appropriate transitional techniques

Sample essays and outlines written by students

Revision checklists for troubleshooting

Prewriting ideas for in-class practice

Essay topics designed to interest students of varying ages

Examples by professional writers illustrate good paragraph development, but as models for essays, we use student themes primarily—and lots of them. We have found that our students profit greatly by analyzing and editing each other's essays, discovering why one paper is successful, why another is less so. Our discussion questions are formulated to lead students to critical judgments.

The Special Skills Section

Chapter 8 on study skills, "Reading and Writing in College Classes," contains helpful advice on how to read textbooks, take notes, budget time, and pass tests—including essay examinations. Chapter 10 on researched writing covers library resources, précis writing, paraphrasing, and revising; it also provides documentation styles for all disciplines, as well as complete information following the style in the *MLA Handbook*. We now have in Chapter 11, "Practical Career Writing," valuable suggestions for writing effective letters, job applications, and résumés.

The Handbook

We limit our discussion of grammar to the concepts applicable to writing. Drawing on the most useful concepts from traditional, structural, and transformational grammar, we explain the system as simply as possible and illustrate the principles with sentence diagrams—a useful tool which lets students see how sentence elements function. We now call the chapter on mechanics, punctuation, and style the "Revising Index," because it contains—conveniently alphabetized— all the advice necessary for revising and editing a paper. The "Revising Index" is keyed to the theme correction symbols inside the front cover of this book. To the "Glossary of Usage," which reflects current standard English usage, we have added stern warnings against a couple of questionable habits that we have noticed in student writing lately.

Our suggested theme topics include over one hundred ideas for writing. Exercises—for prewriting, writing, and discussion—are interspersed throughout the book. There are three comprehensive exercises (one on sentences, one on grammar, and one on mechanics and style) at the ends of the grammar chapter and the Revising Index. These can be used as diagnostic tests and appear on duplicating masters in the Instructor's Manual.

Supplementary Materials

We have planned the Instructor's Manual as a resource book. Beyond suggesting answers for exercises and discussion questions and providing the answer key for *The Writer's Workbook*, the Instructor's Manual offers further ideas for classroom activities, suggested grading standards, diagnostic tests, and additional sample student papers on duplicating masters for in-class editing.

The Writer's Workbook is designed to provide extra practice and remediation for students who are not prepared for the level of difficulty the text exhibits. It includes exercises on thesis, sentence, and paragraph development as well as exercises that parallel the material in the Handbook.

ACKNOWLEDGMENTS

We want to extend warm thanks to the many people who have enabled us to improve this book—especially the composition specialists whose theories we have put into practice: James Kinneavy, Janice Lauer, Jacqueline Burke, Frank O'Hare, Linda Flower, Ken Macrorie, Winston Weathers, Donald M. Murray, Richard L. Graves, Sondra Pearl, Karl Taylor, Ronald Fortune, and Charles R. Cooper. We wish to thank our conscientious and helpful reviewers: Donald Morse, Donald Stewart, Earle Bryant, Mary Jane Dickerson, Thomas Martinez, James Willis, Norma Gaskey, and Richard Bullock. We would also like to express our warm appreciation to the McGraw-Hill editors and editorial assistants; Pat McCarney, our exemplary typist; to Robert Townsend of the ISU Milner Library; and to Nadine, Michele, Patsy, Mark, Sue, and Dan, our good friends and trusty assistants. We have also benefited from the loving support of our women's groups, who know more about rhetoric than they probably ever wanted to.

Elizabeth McMahan
Susan Day

The Writer's Rhetoric and Handbook

PART ONE
Writing Well

chapter One
Writing for Your Readers

In the *rhetoric*, which constitutes the first half of this book, we will refresh your memory about the whole writing process.[1] The last half of the text is a handbook, a reference guide which outlines the rules that govern standard English grammar and usage.

Standard English is the language as it is written and spoken by educated people. *Dialects*, which are varieties of language spoken by regional or foreign-born or minority groups, are often rich, colorful, and vigorous—but standard English is expected of college graduates. Virtually all the writing done by millions of people employed in white-collar jobs requires the use of standard English. By the time you finish reading this book you will understand what standard English really is.

COMMUNICATION IS THE GOAL

Writing is one of the most taxing jobs around, especially if you want to do it skillfully. But writing well is also one of the most useful crafts you can develop—essential, even—and valuable to prospective employers. You will greatly improve your chances of landing a good job if you can write clear, correct *expository prose.* That is the kind of writing we deal with in this book: not poetry or drama or fiction, but informative writing. And if you would like to consider a more immediate need, there is no honest way to get through college without being able to write. You simply cannot hope to get into law or medical school without a thorough knowledge of standard English. Whether

---

[1] *Rhetoric* is a broad, useful term that includes all the elements of writing—structure, style, diction, rhythm, tone—the entire writing process.

you plan to enter engineering, teaching, social work, or any business or professional career, you will have to write—memos, letters, reports, summaries, directions, analyses. As Richard Larsen points out, "In today's competitive market most employers place communication skills at the very top of their list of desirable employee traits."[2]

There is, as you may know, something of a national scandal over the general level of illiteracy in our country. Surveys have shown that many high school graduates are "functional illiterates"; that is, they cannot read signs or labels and cannot write a simple letter. More and more, it seems, people are finding it difficult to express themselves in writing. And the reason for putting words on paper in the first place is to communicate, to convey ideas, information, or impressions from your mind to the minds of your readers.

The truth is you need to be able to write. This book can help you learn to write well. We have tried to make the process as painless as possible, but writing is seldom easy because it requires precision. We struggle and sigh and squint and swear; we chew our nails, twiddle our thumbs, furrow our brows, and gnash our teeth—but eventually we write. And you can, too, if you are willing to work at it.

WHAT IS GOOD WRITING, ANYWAY?

What we consider good writing today would not necessarily have been admired a few hundred years ago when people put great stock in measured rhythms, rhetorical flourish, and elaborate words. Tastes change in language, just as in dress, but luckily not with such frequency and splash. There always remain common elements of good writing. Professor F. L. Lucas, a noted scholar, lists these basic principles as *honesty, clarity, brevity,* and *variety.*[3] His advice boils down to this:

1. Be honest: do not try to fake your ideas.
2. Be clear: do not puzzle your readers.
3. Be brief: do not waste your readers' time.
4. Seek variety: vary sentence length; work on liveliness.

Lucas mentions other attributes of effective writing: "Good humor, good sense, vitality, imagination." But if you can master the four essentials—honesty, clarity, brevity, and variety—you will be a competent writer.

[2] *College English*, **43** (Feb. 1981), 132.
[3] "On the Fascination of Style," *Holiday*, March 1960, pp. 11–21.

CLARITY IS THE KEYNOTE

Of the four characteristics of good writing listed by Lucas, the one that relates most directly to the goal of communication is clarity. When you write, you need to let your readers know at the outset what you are going to discuss and then discuss it. You need not attempt to dazzle them with multisyllable words and long, involved sentences. Graceful phrasing certainly contributes to good writing, but you must strive first for clarity. Work on refining the style after you are positive that what you have written cannot be misunderstood.

Try to coax someone to read what you have written before you submit the final draft. Molière tried his work out on the cook, Swift on his valet, to be sure that every word was perfectly clear. Very likely you have no cook or valet to perform this service, but impose on a friend or loved one. Ask your reader to call attention to sentences that do not make sense and any points that are unclear. Then revise those muddled sentences and add examples to clarify any weak points. You may have to retype a page or two, but do it and be grateful for having caught and corrected problems before going public with your work. Few readers will forgive a lapse of communication, and rightly so. As Lucas notes, it is ill-mannered to make your readers rack their brains trying to understand you. So make your writing clear. If possible, also make it graceful, make it persuasive, make it forceful. But primarily, make it communicate, and you will fulfill your chief duty as a writer.

WRITE IN YOUR OWN VOICE

Lewis Lapham, editor of *Harper's* magazine, complains: "I have found that few writers learn to speak in the human voice, that most of them make use of alien codes (academic, political, literary, bureaucratic, technical)."[4] Strive for a *human* voice when you write—your own. Many people produce on paper a kind of artificial language that writing specialist Ken Macrorie calls *Engfish*—a language much different from the kind people speak or the kind most professional writers use. Engfish is vague, wordy, roundabout, stuffy, pompous, jargon-ridden—hence, difficult to understand. For instance:

> Desiring to assume a proactive posture yet realizing some reactive measures are inevitable, the Council plans to put the by-laws, as adopted by the faculty, to task in an attempt to become a functional liaison between the Dean (including College office staff) and the larger College faculty constituency.

[4] "The Pleasures of Reading," *Harper's*, May 1975, p. 50.

Psychic powers far greater than ours are needed to divine the meaning from that sentence. Remember: clarity is the keynote of good writing.

Often Engfish also abuses the third person approach to writing. (Writing in the *third person* means adopting an impersonal approach by using *one, he, she, it,* or *they,* instead of the more personal *I, we,* or *you.*) Here is an example of third person Engfish:

> One can observe that athletics can be beneficial to the health of one who participates as well as entertaining for one who watches.

Put that sentence into English and you get:

> Athletics can be healthful for the players and entertaining for the fans.

Eventually you must master the third person approach without lapsing into Engfish. But unless the occasion requires strictly formal writing (see page 11), we suggest that you use the first person *I* or *we.* If you glance at a few of the samples of good writing included in this book, you will discover that most professional writers use *I* and *we* when expressing their own opinions, and many of them address their readers directly as *you.* If you do the same, you will find Engfish easier to avoid.

But take caution: the word *you* should always refer to the readers unless you intend to be funny. You may get an unexpected laugh if, in explaining how to prune a tree, you write, "Grasp your diseased limb firmly and saw it off immediately above the joint." Reserve this *indefinite you* for humorous writing in which no one will mind if you write, "The behavior of your average alligator tends to be torpid."

EXERCISE   **1-1**

Translate these sentences from Engfish into clear, straightforward English. You may have to guess at the meaning sometimes, but do your best. We will rewrite the first one to get you started.

1. The causal factors of her poverty become obvious when one considers the number of offspring she possesses.
   Translation: Her poverty is increased because she has so many children.
2. This writer's report enjoyed a not unfavorable reception by the Resource Center Committee.
3. The administrators have designated a period of time within which one must respond to charges carrying threats of disciplinary action.
4. The level of radiation in the immediate vicinity of the nuclear power plant was evaluated and found to be within acceptable danger parameters.

5. One realizes as one progresses through life that a great many statements of political figures are without substance or credibility.
6. The unacceptability of one's lifestyle can result in the termination of one's employment.
7. Police involvement in the conflict was considered to be an inhibiting factor to the peaceful progress of the protest.
8. It was with no little enthusiasm that one's peers inflicted various contusions and lacerations on members of the opposing affinity group.
9. One must recognize the enormous responsibilities that are to be assumed with an office of public trust.
10. It is the feeling of the committee that the established priorities in management-employee relations are in need of realignment.

Warming Up

If you have been conditioned to lapse into Engfish whenever you pick up a pen, try to break the habit through what Macrorie calls "free writing." A little practice should help you to achieve an easy, natural style. This linguistic limbering up involves nothing more than writing down thoughts as they run through your head, without bothering about coherence (how they hang together) or correctness. Set your alarm clock for ten minutes and write until it goes off. Just write. If your mind goes blank when you try it, start writing a record of your day's activities so far. Or look at some object across the room and describe it in detail. Or glance at one of the doodles in Figure 1-1 and write anything that comes to mind about its shape or significance.

Write, and write quickly. Get your pen moving rapidly across the page, and free yourself from inhibitions. After you have covered a page or so, read over what you have written and underline any phrases that you think are effective. Free writing serves the same purpose as calisthenics before a football game: getting warmed up, getting the kinks out, getting ready to write consciously but in a relaxed, natural, and effective manner. Here is what one of our friends came up with when we pressed her into service as a free writer.

Figure 1-1 Doodles for free writing.

Write about a doodle. Indeed. The very idea. Write for five minutes, ten minutes, without stopping? I've never done it before in my life, what makes these people think I can do it now. Ah well, why resist? So. Not to worry about punctuation, eh? Good thing. Not much complexity or creativity left at the end of the day. Well let's try the doodles. At least they're interesting. The first—a greeting, "hi," a little upside down perhaps a greeting from a trapeze artist, midswing. The second—a blood pressure, no EKG record—or someone's basal body temperature chart. The third a musical—what are those called?—signature? no, clef or something—one that doesn't know whether it's treble or bass—an Androgyne—

Free writing can also help if you are overcome by inertia, drawing a complete blank in your efforts to generate ideas to use in a paper. Instead of staring at the page as you think about your topic, start your pen moving. Perhaps imaginative, potentially useful material will flow from it. Later we are going to suggest a number of questions that you should ask yourself as you ponder your subject that will also help you come up with good ideas.

PREWRITING: THE THINKING PROCESS

The writing process begins long before you put pen to paper to labor through your first draft. And it does not end when you have completed that difficult but flawed first version. You will probably work through at least four stages before you complete your finished product. Do not attempt to rush the process. Many authorities believe that your subconscious mind will do some of your creating for you—even though you may not be actively concentrating on what you intend to write. So, start your thinking early enough to give your ideas time to germinate and grow.

In order to get the process going, though, you need to mull over three things:

1. **Your purpose:** Why are you writing?
2. **Your audience:**   For whom are you writing?
3. **Your topic:** What are you going to write about?

These questions are equally important, and your answer to one may well affect your responses to the others. In the actual writing process (which is often recursive—going back and forth—not linear—going straight from beginning to end) you can scarcely separate these elements because they are integral parts of the whole composition. But for purposes of discussion, we need to consider them one by one.

DETERMINING YOUR PURPOSE

Your purpose affects your whole approach to writing: how you begin, whether you state or imply your thesis, what specific details you choose, how you organize the material, how you conclude, as well as what words you select for each sentence. You must give thought to your purpose before you begin even the preliminary planning stage.

Ask yourself why you are exerting all this energy and straining your brain to do this piece of writing. It may simply be because your teacher or your boss told you to, but that is not a useful answer. Think beyond your immediate response. Consider the reason that makes writing worth doing. What do you hope to accomplish? Your aim may occasionally be self-expression, as in free writing or in a diary or a journal. More often, though, you will write for other people and for some definite purpose—usually *to inform, to entertain,* or *to persuade.* If, for instance, you decide to write to the library directors on your campus to complain because the building closes at five o'clock on Saturdays, you may write simply to vent your outrage in pure *self-expression.* Possibly you would write *to inform* them of the inconvenience this early closing causes. You could also write *to entertain* them with an account of your faltering social life in which Saturday night stretches before you vacant and lonely if you are severed from the solace of scholarship, barred from browsing through books and bibliographies. Probably, though, you would write *to persuade* them that the library should remain open on Saturday nights for the benefit of students with demanding courses, academic overloads, or part-time jobs. Obviously, with each change of purpose your whole letter would change—style, tone, content, virtually everything about it. So, keep your purpose firmly in mind as you plan and write your paper.

Should do all three

CONSIDERING YOUR AUDIENCE

You cannot easily determine why you are writing without also determining *who* is going to read what you write. Your audience may be a single person—your boss, perhaps, your history professor, your senator. Or you may sometimes wish to reach a larger audience—your city council, your composition class, the readership of some publication like your campus newspaper, *Time* magazine, or *Rolling Stone.*

If your purpose, for instance, is to inform, you need to think about how to present your information to your specific audience most effectively. You can see at once that the larger your audience, the more touchy the problem. If you are writing a letter to the editor of your local newspaper explaining the appeal of reggae music, you will be addressing people of all ages with assorted dispositions and prejudices. You need to choose your words carefully and present your information calmly, or you may end up with no readers at all.

If, however, you are writing a letter to the editor of *Rolling Stone* magazine, your verbal tactics would need to be different. Because your audience here would be primarily people who know a lot about popular music, you should omit background information explaining how reggae originated. You would write in a more conversational manner, using current slang and even music jargon, since your audience could be expected to understand the jargon and enjoy the slang.

Audience Analysis Checklist

In order to increase your abilities in evaluating your audience, ask yourself the following questions during the process of planning your paper.

1. How much will my readers already know about my topic?
2. Will they respond emotionally to my topic? Will I need to be especially careful not to offend them? If so, how?
3. Will they be interested in my topic? Perhaps bored by it? If they may be bored, how can I get them interested?
4. Will they be in agreement with me? Opposed? Neutral?
5. How well educated in general are my readers?
6. Do they fall into any particular age group?
7. Is it important to consider their race, sex, marital status, possible parenthood, or religion?
8. Do they identify with any political groups (like Republicans, Democrats, libertarians, socialists)?
9. Are they members of any public interest group (Moral Majority, Common Cause, National Organization for Women, American Civil Liberties Union, Sierra Club, etc.)?
10. How do they make their living? Are they rich, poor, middle-class?

Selecting Usage Levels

The nature of your audience and your purpose in writing will determine your *level of usage*—whether you use slang or contractions or six-syllable words. Certainly, if you write a letter to the editor of the *National Lampoon*, your word choice will be different from the language you would use to write a research paper for Economics 301. The letter to the *Lampoon* could be written on an *informal*, perhaps even *colloquial* (conversational), level, but the research paper would likely have to be *formal*. Formal, informal, and colloquial writing are considered appropriate on different occasions, just as you may have formal and informal clothes, plus your old blue jeans for around the house.

Formal Writing. Although formal writing is a lot less formal than it used to be, and there is not nearly as much call for it as there once was, it still has its uses. Many textbooks (not this one, though) are written in formal English, as are most scholarly articles and books and a few magazines. Most business communication still observes formal usage, but recently the use of *I* and *we* is replacing the strictly formal third person approach. Here are the main characteristics of formal usage:

1. No contractions (*do not,* instead of *don't; he will,* instead of *he'll*)
2. No slang
3. Third person approach (*one, he, she, it, they*); sometimes first person (*I, we*); no addressing the readers as *you*
4. No sentence fragments (look up *fragment* in the "Revising Index" if you do not know what one is)
5. A serious or neutral tone *a little humor would not hurt*

In strictly formal writing you may not be allowed to refer to yourself as *I.* Instead of writing (in the first person), "I find a discrepancy in these data," or "My findings differ from those of the County Board," you would be expected to write (in the third person), "One finds a discrepancy in these data," or "The findings of this writer differ from those of the County Board." Instead of "We can observe . . . ," you may have to write, "One can observe. . . ." Experienced writers can bring off this third person approach quite handily, and so can you with practice. F. L. Lucas, for instance, in discussing the need for brevity in writing, observes, "People who would not dream of stealing a penny of one's money turn not a hair at stealing hours of one's life," and he sounds graceful, even natural. In order to get the feel of writing in the third person, try changing the sentences in the following exercise from first person into the more formal third. The more you practice writing in third person, the more natural (and thus effective) your use of it will become when your purpose requires it.

EXERCISE   **1-2**

The following sentences are written using the first person (*I* and *we*) and the informal second person (*you*). Rewrite each sentence to eliminate every *you,* as well as all slang and contractions. Try to use the formal third person (*one, she, he, it,* or *they*). But if the sentence sounds stilted, go back to *I* or *we.* The use of first person is acceptable in much formal writing today.

1. The point I want to make is quite simple.
   Revised: The point is quite simple.
2. We hold these truths to be self-evident.
3. We must suppose, then, that the figures cited are OK.
4. It seems as if I should encourage you to be more exact.
5. You can't help expressing yourself, unless you live in a vacuum.
6. If you would hold the attention of your readers, you should cultivate a pleasing style.
7. We shouldn't make editorial decisions based solely upon our personal likes and dislikes.
8. The very people who most try your patience are often those who most want to please you.
9. If you attain high office, your responsibility to other people increases.
10. We could lack automobiles, banks, missiles, and computers, yet still be numbered among civilized peoples.

Informal Writing.   Much of the writing you will be called upon to do will probably be informal, which means ordinary, familiar, everyday writing. You can use *I* and *we* and address your readers as *you*. Contractions are fine. Slang is sometimes all right, but here you need to be especially aware of your audience. Even the genial F. L. Lucas, for one, considers slang "a kind of linguistic fungus; as poisonous, and as short-lived, as toadstools." So be wary. Remember, you do not want to put off your readers; you want to *communicate* with them. We personally like slang but realize it sometimes comes close to being an "in-group" language known only to those of a certain age or ethnic background. As a matter of courtesy, you should never use slang that your readers are unlikely to understand or that they may find offensive. By and large, your word choice in informal writing will consist mainly of those serviceable, everyday words that everyone uses all the time. Here are the main characteristics of informal usage:

1. Contractions are allowed.
2. Slang is sometimes acceptable if your audience will understand it and not be offended by it.
3. First person approach (*I, we*) and use of *you* to refer to the readers are both all right—as long as *you* does indeed always refer to the readers.
4. Stylistically effective sentence fragments are usually acceptable, but consider your audience.
5. An informal, somewhat personal, often humorous tone is appropriate.

Colloquial Writing.   In colloquial writing just about anything goes because it approximates everyday speech. The chief characteristics are slang, sentence fragments, and perhaps even nonstandard constructions. The call for colloquial writing is extremely limited, but it comes in handy for reproducing actual speech in an otherwise informal essay. The following illustration is from Jodi Lawrence's piece on the late Colonel Sanders, of fried chicken fame:

"When they told me I was agoin' to get that Alger award, I went to the library fust thing to make sure Alger warn't some Red," Colonel Sanders states at luncheon in the Beverly Hills Hotel's Polo Lounge. His cheeks flush and he continues, "But the library didn't have no Alger books. Didn't even know who he was. I finally found some in a used-book store. Out of print books. Anyways, I got quite a collection of them Alger books now and they're real inspirin', real inspirin'. All the things I always believe in."

—"Chicken Big and the Senior Citizen," *West Magazine,* 12 Oct. 1969.

Lawrence was able to capture the Colonel's character far more effectively by reproducing his actual speech for us than she could by paraphrasing his statements in standard English.

Figure 1-2 Usage levels for all occasions.

Formal: One should not admit defeat too easily.
I shall not admit defeat too easily.
Informal: We shouldn't give up too easily.
I'll not give up too easily.
Colloquial: I'm not going to throw in the towel too easy.

Formal	Informal	Colloquial (slang)
automobile	car	ride
comprehend	understand	dig
depart	leave	split
residence	house	crib
offensive	unpleasant	gross
exhausted	tired out	wasted
dejected	sad	down
hyperactive	jittery	wired
intoxicated	drunk	sloshed

DISCUSSION EXERCISE   1-3

In order to be able to adopt an appropriate level of usage in your own writing, you need to become familiar with the characteristics of formal, informal, and colloquial usage. After studying the chart in Figure 1-2 (which shows how word choices may differ on each level), read the paragraphs that follow. Pay particular attention to word choice, and try to determine the usage level of each passage by asking yourself the following questions about each one. Be prepared to support your answers with specific examples from every paragraph.

1. Are there any noticeably formal words?
2. Do you find any slang?
3. Are most of the terms familiar, everyday language?
4. Does the writer use *I* or *we* or the more formal third person?
5. Are there sentence fragments?
6. Are there contractions?
7. Does the usage level of each example seem appropriate for the content?
8. Can you identify the tone in any of the selections?

(1)

By the time I entered college in the autumn of 1932, the Great Depression had slid to its nadir. I remember how the iron benches under the elms in front of the courthouse and the wooden ones in the treeless, gravelly municipal park where the bandstand stood were occupied all during daylight by the unemployed of our town in Colorado. Sometimes these able men, disabled by inaction, held bitter symposia to discover why their decent lives had become ignominious; shouting and gesticulating, they inveighed against the Government, berated Wall Street, denounced the vile, mysterious forces that had closed down mines and mills and put an end to building, and had subjected them and their blameless families to the indignities of the soup kitchen.

—Jean Stafford, "Souvenirs of Survival," *Mademoiselle*, Feb. 1960.

(2)

We'd go to school two days sometimes, a week, two weeks, three weeks at most. This is when we were migrating. We'd come back to our winter base, and if we were lucky, we'd get in a good solid all of January, February, March, April, May. So we had five months out of a possible nine months. We started counting how many schools we'd been to and we counted thirty-seven. We never got a transfer. Friday we didn't tell the teacher or anything. We'd just go home. And they accepted this.

I remember one teacher—I wondered why she was asking so many questions. (In those days anybody asked a question, you became suspicious. Either a cop or a social worker.) She was a young teacher, and she just wanted to know why we were behind. One day she drove into the camp. That was quite an event, because we never had a teacher come over. Never. So it was, you know, a very meaningful day for us.

—Cesar Chavez, interviewed by Studs Terkel in *Hard Times: An Oral History of the Great Depression*, 1970.

(3)

There are blustering signatures that swish across the page like cornstalks bowed before a tempest. There are cryptic signatures, like a scrabble of lightning across a cloud, suggesting that behind is a lofty divinity whom all must know, or an aloof divinity whom none is worthy to know (though, as this might be highly inconvenient, a docile typist sometimes interprets the mystery in a bracket underneath). There are impetuous squiggles. . . . There are humble, humdrum signatures. And there are also, sometimes, signatures that are courteously clear, yet mindful of a certain simple grace and artistic economy—in short, of style.

—F. L. Lucas, "On the Fascination of Style," *Holiday*, March 1960.

(4)

O Lord our God, help us to tear their soldiers to bloody shreds with our shells; help us to cover their smiling fields with the pale forms of their patriot dead; help us to drown the thunder of the guns with the shrieks of their wounded, writhing in pain; help us to lay waste to their humble homes with a hurricane of fire; . . . for our sakes who adore thee Lord, blast their hopes, blight their lives, protract their bitter pilgrimage, make heavy their steps, water their way with tears, stain the white snow with the blood of their wounded feet! We ask it, in the spirit of love, of Him Who is the Source of love, and Who is the everfaithful refuge and friend of all that are sore beset and seek His aid with humble and contrite hearts. Amen.

—Mark Twain, from "The War Prayer" (published 1923).

(5)

Tony "Big Bear" Stagg sticks his derringer into his neat little holster, which is in one of his cowboy boots. It's tough getting down there below his stomach, which has ballooned up even larger of late, and the sweat runs off his shiny forehead. Still he manages gracefully. Like Sidney Greenstreet's, his fatness is imperial, swaying regally as he cruises a room, pops his gum, swivels his head, checking out the turf. . . . His smile is cockeyed, ambivalent, warm yet utterly distant; his teeth and eyes shine promises at once charming and dangerous.

"Hey," says Tony, "you like these boots? I got these boots for the Bicentennial, baby. You see, 1776. Nice, huh?"

Nice indeed. Blue leather and white stars and the American Eagle looking up at you like Marlon Brando in *Julius Caesar*. Tony is wearing a western jacket and safari hat. His Volkswagen, wild in the streets, features giant eagles on the front framed by huge white numbers against a blue backdrop: 1776–1976.

—Robert Ward, "The Mt. Kisco Sting," *New Times*, 4 March 1977.

Choosing a Tone

Both your purpose and your audience will determine the appropriate *tone* for what you are about to write. Tone is that quality which reveals your attitude toward your subject or your audience—or both. Primarily, tone involves choice of words and selection of details, but all aspects of style may be involved—usage levels, sentence structure, organization, even punctuation. If, for example, you feel your point will best be made by making your readers laugh, you will use a *humorous* tone, as did Dereck Williamson in describing bicycle riding when he was a kid:

There were three popular ways of stopping a bike—"coaster brake," "hand brake," and "hitting something." Less popular methods included accidentally sticking your foot in the front wheel or clamping hard on just the front hand brake, which made you do a tight little somersault over the handle bars.

Another rather sloppy way to stop was to get your pantcuff caught between the front sprocket and the chain, causing a sudden shift of weight to starboard. You slowly fell off the bike and scraped along the ground. The bike, still attached to your leg, jarred around on top of you until an axle bolt stuck in your ear.

—"The Mudbacks," *Saturday Review*, June 1971.

The following paragraph by Horace Sutton is also *light* and *humorous* in tone, but may be further described as *sarcastic*.

> It is perfectly clear to anyone who has tried it that you can't live in New York. Enough foxholes have been excavated in the city's streets to shelter all the divisions that took part in the Normandy offensive. If you're coming to town, don't bring your car, come in a tank. The barricades erected to keep the citizenry from falling into the trenches would humble the most valiant efforts of the street mobs during the fever days of the French Revolution. And cars caught in the web bellow in frustration. . . . It's quieter in the parks, but a stroller in those sylvan glens after dark has as much chance as a Chihuahua in the African veld.
>
> —"You Can't Live in New York," *Saturday Evening Post,* 11 March 1961.

In both the previous examples, the tone is easy to detect and describe. But tone may not always be so clear-cut. Most everyday writing is done in a *neutral* tone which is difficult to describe in more exact terms. Here is a typical example written by William Zinsser. We might call it *polite, straightforward,* perhaps *persuasive,* but that is as close as we can come to a precise description.

> Today there is so much verbal bloatage in the American air that you can hardly hear a plain declarative sentence. Yet simplicity is a virtue in writing, not something to be ashamed of and embroidered with pretty stitches. The writing that we most admire over the years—the King James Bible, Abraham Lincoln, Thoreau, E. B. White, Red Smith—is writing that has the strength of simplicity.
>
> —"Why Johnny's Teachers Can't Write," *New York Times Magazine,* Nov. 12, 1978.

Tone always depends to some extent upon how the words are received by the readers. Remember that the tone of your voice does not carry over to the written word. A neutral tone may be the best tone for most writing. But before you write, consider your audience and your purpose and choose a tone that seems appropriate.

Tempering Your Tone

Although you may on occasion want to make your audience angry about something—injustice, poverty, ignorance—you always want to avoid making them angry at you. Your purpose in writing is to persuade them to agree with you. Therefore, try to adopt a tone that will not antagonize your readers needlessly. You may sometimes *want* to write abusively when you feel abused, but try to resist the temptation. You will only annoy your readers. Mark Twain never published a line or even mailed a letter until his gentle wife Olivia had cleared his prose. You can begin to see why if you read his famous letter to the gas company.

Hartford, February 12, 1891

Dear Sirs:

Some day you will move me almost to the verge of irritation by your chuckle-headed Goddamned fashion of shutting your Goddamned gas off without giving any notice to your Goddamned parishioners. Several times you have come within an ace of smothering half of this household in their beds and blowing up the other half by this idiotic, not to say criminal, custom of yours. And it has happened again to-day. Haven't you a telephone?

Ys

S L Clemens

Needless to say, Olivia did not let that one pass. Twain revised his correspondence daily as his rage subsided, until he produced a temperate version that would not invite a libel suit. Try to do the same with your own writing. Adopt a tone that will allow you to be convincing, not offensive.

WRITING EXERCISE   **1-4**

Compose your own brief letter of complaint in a tone you think will be effective in addressing each of the following audiences:

1. The management of your favorite athletic team or movie theatre
2. The editor of your local newspaper
3. The gas company

Choose your own purpose. You may want to vent your outrage in pure self-expression, as Mark Twain did. Or you may want to inform your audience about some matter in which they have failed you. Or you may want to persuade your audience that they must do something about your complaint. If so, be sure to specify what needs to be done.

Indicate at the top of the page both your audience and purpose.

ANALYZING THE EFFECTS OF AUDIENCE, PURPOSE, AND TONE

Notice the extensive changes that occur in the following short passages as we write every one on the same topic—the lack of vegetarian fare in the Snack Shop—but change the purpose each time.

In the first group of examples, our audience is the Director of Food Services in the Student Union.

1. Purpose: to inform

Although the food served in the Snack Shop of the Union is appetizing and economical, the menu offers only a single entree, a grilled cheese sandwich, that is suitable for a vegetarian to eat. An expanded menu would better serve the needs of all students.

2. Purpose: to entertain

Even a toasty, golden-brown grilled cheese sandwich becomes a loathsome thing if the hungry person is trying to choke one down for the twenty-seventh day in a row. Our friends munch contentedly on a whole array of sandwiches—hamburgers, reubens, ham and turkey combinations, hot pastrami—while we vegetarians chew sullenly on our same old grilled cheese.

3. Purpose: to persuade

While the food served in the Snack Shop of our Union is appetizing and economical, the menu offers little variety for vegetarians. Besides your tasty grilled cheese sandwich, could you perhaps also offer egg salad or fried egg sandwiches? We would especially appreciate your adding a salad bar, which should prove popular with many of your patrons and thus profitable for you as well.

Now notice what happens when the topic remains the same but the *audience* changes. This time we will address ourselves to fellow vegetarians in a letter in the student newspaper.

4. Purpose: to inform

Every day we eat lunch in the Snack Shop of the Union because it's the closest and the cheapest place. And every day we end up ordering the same thing—a grilled cheese sandwich—because that's the only vegetarian item on the menu. We're astonished that at a university the size of ours the food service takes no account of vegetarians' preferences.

5. Purpose: to entertain

When we trudge over to the Snack Shop for lunch—exhausted from our morning classes, perishing for some wholesome food—we're confronted by a menu offering nothing but a disgusting array of dead animals: dead cow on a bun, dead pig on rye, dead fowl on a roll. We starving vegetarians must make do with a barely edible slice of imitation cheese grilled between two pale pieces of greasy balloon bread. We could get a more nutritious and tasty meal by munching grass out on the quad.

6. Purpose: to persuade

Vegetarians, unite! Our reasonable requests have so far produced no changes in the meat-laden menu at the Union Snack Shop. In order to convince the food service people that a substantial number of vegetarians are potential customers, we need to state our appeal collectively. Stop by the Food Services office next time you're in the Union and tell the manager that we need a salad bar.

DISCUSSION EXERCISE   1-5

1. In the first group of examples, addressed to the Director of Food Services, what details change when the purpose becomes to entertain rather than to inform? Can you tell why? What differences do you notice in word choice? Do you find them appropriate? Why?
2. What different details do you find in the third passage? Why are they introduced? Why do you think the terms *appetizing, economical,* and *tasty* appear?
3. Can you describe the tone of the first three passages? What is the level of usage in each?
4. In the second group of passages, addressed to fellow vegetarians, the words chosen to describe the meat sandwiches in example 5 are quite different from those used in example 2. Can you explain why?
5. Consider the descriptions of the grilled cheese sandwich in examples 2 and 5. Can you account for the differences? Would a nonvegetarian find example 5 amusing, do you think? If not, why?
6. How has the level of usage changed in the second group of examples? Is the change appropriate?
7. Try to describe the tone of each of the last three passages.
8. If you examine all six passages, you will notice that the most pronounced changes occur when the purpose becomes to entertain. What significant difference can you observe when you compare the passages aimed to inform (1 and 4) with those designed to persuade (3 and 6)?

The paragraph below was written by a student as advice for her peers. Rewrite the passage for each of the audiences listed, making any changes that might be appropriate.

1. Your local parent-teachers' association
2. The Lost Souls Motorcycle Club
3. Employees of the Department of Internal Revenue

Once you've firmly implanted in your mind the fact that you are definitely going to quit smoking, you must start observing the situations in which you smoke, and try to eliminate these situations. For example, go down to the cafeteria to eat lunch later than usual so you won't have time to light up before running to class. Chew a stick of gum or your fingernails. Just don't light up. That would defeat all of your effort, and remember, you don't need or want cigarettes any more! A good idea is to put aside the money you would normally spend for cigarettes and go out and celebrate after you've accomplished your goal.

THINKING TOWARD A THESIS: INVENTION

Probably the most difficult part of the writing process is planning what to say. If we could always do free writing, the task would be an entertainment. But seldom are we given such latitude when we write. Usually we are restricted by topic and length and sometimes even by the time available to do the job. The chief engineer wants a three-page report on the drilling core samples from the Gulfport well—today. The principal requires lesson plans of specified length and content—submitted a week in advance. Your history professor allows only fifty minutes to complete four essay questions. Even letters to the editor are often limited to 350 words. Standard freshman compositions can seldom be longer than 500 words and may have to be even shorter if written in class. You must face up to the necessity of limiting your approach and deciding what points to cover before you write.

While you are struggling to come up with a workable thesis, you may at the same time be generating ideas for its support. All the pondering, speculating, collecting, reflecting, judging, and sorting that go on during the planning process seldom gets done in an orderly step-by-step fashion. Often the stages are interchangeable or concurrent. By the time you arrive at a good central idea you may also have produced a wealth of concrete details to incorporate into the paper.

Narrowing Your Topic

Suppose you have been asked to write 500 words on conservation. You could dash off a paper on conservation in general without pausing to think. But probably it would be an essay that only a loved one would willingly read. You will earn a wider audience (and a better grade) if you focus on some aspect of conservation and cover that in detail. You need to find an approach—your thesis—and dredge up facts and illustrations to support this central idea.

Finding a Point

Your thesis should clearly state the *point* you want to make about your subject. If, indeed, your topic is conservation, you need to narrow it considerably for a 500-word paper. You might decide to write just about protecting wildlife. But even that is far too broad an idea to cover in a brief essay. You could then limit yourself to one endangered species—say, seals. But now, ask yourself, what *about* seals? What is the *point* you want to make? You could assert that seals should be protected from industry by international treaty. Or you could argue that slaughtering baby seals is inhumane. Or you could insist that people should not buy any product made of sealskin in order to keep industry from finding seal killing profitable.

> *REMEMBER:* **Your thesis should be a complete sentence which makes a point about your subject.**

Unsuitable thesis:	Drugs
Unsuitable thesis:	Drug abuse
Workable thesis:	Drug abuse occurs with perfectly legal prescription drugs.
Workable thesis:	Excessive use of alcohol constitutes the number one drug abuse problem in the United States.
Unsuitable thesis:	Marriage
Unsuitable thesis:	Marriage contracts
Unsuitable thesis:	A number of people are writing marriage contracts today. (Makes no point.)
Workable thesis:	A marriage contract can make a union less risky by clarifying the expectations of each partner before the ceremony.

Asking a Question

If your topic involves research, you will find it helpful to begin by asking yourself a thesis *question* instead of making a statement. You might start out by asking yourself, "How is our present high divorce rate changing our traditional ideas about marriage?" By the time you have done your reading and are ready to write, you will want to work out the answer to that question in a regular thesis statement. This might be something like, "Our high divorce rate is changing our ideas about lifelong fidelity, about parent-child relationships, and about the stigma of divorce." Probably when you present this idea in the introduction, you will want to make it more general: "Our high divorce rate is changing our ideas about marriage." You do not need to list your main points when giving your readers the thesis unless your paper is uncommonly long. After all, they are going to read the rest of the paper. But the thesis statement that you use *as a guide for yourself* should be as specific as you can make it.

Sharpening Your Thinking

You will discover that nothing reveals fuzzy thinking as effectively as making yourself write out your idea for the paper in a single sentence. As E. M. Forster puts it, "How do I know what I think until I see what I say?" If it turns out that your thinking *is* fuzzy, do not try to hide it from yourself. If you cannot get your thesis down clearly in a sentence, face up to it: you need to think some more. Do not go any further until you are able to see a single, clear, workable idea expressing the main point of your paper. You will be spared grievous, often unconquerable problems later in the process if you devise a good thesis statement before you begin writing.

Here are some acceptable thesis statements for various types of papers:

1. Many Americans spend too much time in front of their television sets, living only vicariously. (In your paper, this thesis might appear in a livelier form, like, "Turn off the TV and turn on to life!")
2. College students would benefit more from their education if people did not enroll in college before the age of twenty-five.
3. On a sunny summer morning last year, I realized that I was ultimately alone.
4. The perfect omelet is fluffy, light, delicately browned, and even attainable if the cook follows five practical guidelines.
5. In Shakespeare's *Hamlet,* Ophelia's insanity and suicide represent what would have happened to Hamlet had he been female.

Notice that each statement makes a point clearly and concisely. You may want to use one of these sentences as a guide as you strive to construct your own thesis.

Unifying Your Ideas

Once you have decided on a clear, concise thesis statement, you need to make sure that every idea in your paper relates directly to that thesis. If you have chosen to write an essay denouncing the brutal bashing of baby seals, do not toss in a tirade against killing whales. A brief mention in your introduction of other endangered species would be fine, but in the body of your paper stick to seals.

(For advice about thesis placement in the paper itself, see Chapter 4, pages 104 to 105.)

EXERCISE   1-7

Some of the numbered sentences below are workable thesis statements for an essay of about 500 words, but some need to be made more specific. Pick out the successful ones, and indicate what is wrong with the losers. See if you can make every one into a reasonably good thesis.

1. Television commercials are an outrage.
2. Freedom and independence carry with them responsibilities and consequences.
3. I'm going to describe the dying flowers and yellowing leaves outside my window.
4. My dog and my boyfriend are much alike.
5. I learned not to worry when I was sixteen.
6. Thousands of Americans go through the vicious cycle of eating until they are overweight and then dieting until they reduce.
7. The predominant views on capital punishment are very controversial.
8. The purpose of this paper is to compare and contrast the Catholic schools and the public schools.
9. Do you feel cheated because you can't grow a beard?
10. Making a lemon pie is easy.

SEARCHING FOR IDEAS

Deciding what to write about is easier for some people than for others, and many times part of the inventing is done for you. If you are assigned a paper, for instance, on some new development in deaf education, your general subject is already specified. But you must still decide what particular development you want to discuss, as well as how to approach that topic. If you consider a number of possibilities, you are more likely to come up with a good one than if you just adopt the first reasonable idea that comes to mind. We can provide several techniques to help you manage the thinking process that precedes the actual writing of your paper.

Pose Yourself a Problem

As John Dewey observed, "Thinking is a problem-solving activity." Some people find that they can generate ideas for writing most successfully by first thinking of a problem related to the topic. The solution to that problem then provides the material for the paper.

Brainstorming. How do you decide what the problem is? By brainstorming: that is, by jotting down every idea that comes to mind as you try to think of a problem related to your topic. One of our students, Grace Pennington, wanted to write about the donating of body organs because her brother needed a kidney transplant. She asked herself: What could be a problem about donating body organs? Her brainstorming went like this:

Donor banks — How do they work?
Expense?
How is donating done??
Laws concerning it?
Technical aspects?
Who donates? Why?
~~Expense~~
Why doesn't everybody?

With that last question Grace discovered her problem: the need to change the attitudes of people emotionally unable or unwilling to consider donating organs.

Grace then directed her thinking toward solving the problem of how to change people's attitudes. What arguments could she use? More brainstorming:

Why are people opposed?
 religious attitudes — body
 sacred — "Temple
 of God"

Don't know how
Know how it??
to go about it??

(Forms available
in Drivers
Licensing Bureau
in Illinois)

 Self-concepts tied in w/
 physical body
 (mutilation) — afraid they
 might not be truly
 dead??

How do
you go about
it??

 procrastination — people put
 off making decision?
 (But that may be
 emotionally caused!)

How to get people to change?
— Counter religious argument:
 once dead, body not
 sacred any more —
 "dust unto dust"
— Counter mutilation idea:
 once body is dead, the
 self ceases to exist —
 or goes elsewhere

Eyes
of
corpse
closed!
(exterior not noticeably
damaged by removing
organs anyway)

(clothing covers incisions)

- Argue that saving another's
life is more valuable
than ~~false~~ vanity
        in ˰conclusion
- Argue˰ that we should try
to overcome our emotional
~~attachment to our bodies~~
opposition to donating organs
so that others may live!
(and some may enjoy fuller
lives)

⌐Think of suffering alleviated,
lives saved —

    Cite examples —
    (my brother) blind, heart
    ~~disease~~ victims —
    children

        more
- Get˰ real examples (maybe
    from article on donating)

Eventually, Grace went to the library and located articles providing statistics on the need for donors and heartwarming examples of real people whose lives had been saved or enriched by organ transplants. She used these human examples as a means of countering the negative emotional response—fear of donating—with a positive one—joy of giving.

Her final paper was structured this way:

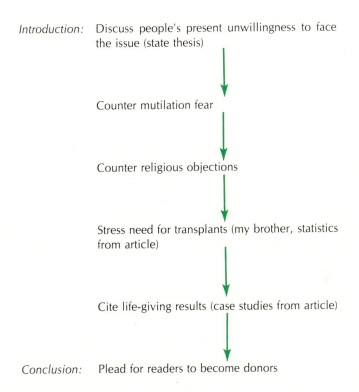

Thesis: People must be encouraged to understand and change negative emotional attitudes toward donating vital organs for transplants.

Introduction: Discuss people's present unwillingness to face the issue (state thesis)

Counter mutilation fear

Counter religious objections

Stress need for transplants (my brother, statistics from article)

Cite life-giving results (case studies from article)

Conclusion: Plead for readers to become donors

Ask Yourself Questions

If posing yourself a problem to solve only seems to complicate the problems you already have, you might want to try instead the journalistic method of gathering information. Reporters collect data for news stories by asking *who? what? when? where? how?* and *why?* about their subjects. All these questions may not be relevant to your essay topic, so try asking yourself variations like these:

What makes it important?
What are the consequences of it?
What can be done about it?
What point can I make about it?
How can I make this point?
How does it affect people?
Why am I interested in it?
Why should other people be interested in it?
Why am I going to write about it?
Who would be interested in this topic?
Who is my audience?

After you have jotted down all of your answers, go over the list and try to come up with a thesis: a one-sentence statement of the point you want to make about your topic.

Ask Others Questions

Once you have settled on a thesis, continue brainstorming: search your mind for any kind of information you can think of pertaining to your main idea. Talk to other people about your topic; ask whether your ideas make sense to them; see what information they can add. Write down every notion that you collect, whether it seems important or not. You can eliminate any items that prove irrelevant, and you may end up altering your thesis slightly to suit the available facts.

Try Keeping a Journal

Many professional writers keep journals or notebooks in which they jot down impressions, responses, descriptions, the germs of ideas—anything that might be used in developing a finished piece of writing. If you decide to keep a journal in which you record more than brief notes, try to make the entries involve you in thinking, preferably in *analysis*. Instead of merely recording, "I went to a movie tonight," make an effort, instead, to examine your response to it. How did you feel when you saw it? Why did you feel this way? What things in the movie provoked this response? Or, if you are having difficulty in some course this semester, try to describe how you feel about the problem. Why do you feel that way? What can you do about it? Or perhaps you learned a new word today. Look up and record its dictionary definitions. What did it mean in the context in which you encountered it? Write a few sentences in which you use the word yourself.

This kind of writing practice is good for you whether or not the ideas ever turn into finished papers.

Try Focused Free Writing

You could also try doing focused free writing in order to get started brainstorming about a topic. If you are considering writing a letter to persuade your legislators to increase the penalties for drunken driving in your state, you might generate some good ideas by free associating on paper—just reeling sentences out of your mind as you think about the issue and recording them rapidly, like this:

> So many social drinkers these days—it's no wonder we have a problem. People are afraid they may be the ones caught if penalties are made as severe as they should be. But the deaths are needless and tragic—something must be done. Would stiffer penalties actually decrease the number of drunken drivers? Public transportation would help in our town—but how to get it? How about revoking licenses for first offenders? Surely that's not unreasonable, and it would get the person convicted off the road, for a while at least. What about repeat offenders? Is a jail sentence too harsh if the drinker has maimed or killed someone? Would a sure-fire jail sentence act as a deterrent?

After you have covered a page or two, you should be able to reread your musings and glean at least a couple of ideas worth developing.

Let Your Mind Rest

Some writing specialists are convinced that your subconscious mind can work for you if given a chance. Start the planning process early to allow for periods during which you are not consciously thinking about your topic. Let the ideas incubate. If the theory is correct, you may achieve a breakthrough when a valuable insight matures in your subconscious mind and suddenly surfaces.

BRINGING ORDER OUT OF CHAOS: OUTLINING

Now, go over all your scribblings again. You need three or four main ideas to support your thesis, and you also need an equal number of minor points (details, examples) to support or illustrate each of your main ideas. On another sheet of paper, sort out your thoughts into major and minor points. Then decide which ones are the best ones to use. Look for patterns of similarity: you may discover several minor points that are related. If so, think up a major heading to cover them.

After you have chosen the main ideas and their supporting details, you then have to decide in what order to present them. If there is no chronology (time order) involved or no steps in a process, begin with a fairly important and interesting point to get your readers' attention. End with your strongest point to leave your audience feeling that you have said something worthwhile.

If you will then put Roman numerals beside your main points and capital letters beside your supporting details, you will perceive instantly that you have just put together an outline. The agonizing invention process is practically over: all that remains is to write, rewrite, and edit the paper.

COMPOSING THE FIRST DRAFT: THE WRITING STAGE

In order to understand thoroughly the process of putting words together into sentences, sentences together into paragraphs, and paragraphs together into a unified composition, you need to study the remaining chapters in the rhetoric portion of this text. But we can offer here a bit of general advice about the best way to get through the actual writing.

Sondra Pearl reports that poor writers go over and over each sentence as they try to get through a first draft. By struggling for the right word and the best sentence construction at this stage, they lose momentum and have difficulty maintaining a flow of ideas. Certainly choosing the exact word and devising effective sentences are both crucial to writing well—but not during the rough draft. Try to get through the first writing of your essay as rapidly as possible. Do your *rewriting* later.

You might profitably give some thought to environmental influences before you begin to write. Where do you do your best writing? at a desk? lounging in bed? in an easy chair? stretched out on your stomach on the floor? What do you write with most comfortably? pen? pencil? typewriter? When is the best time of day—or night—for you to write? Do you write most effectively with music blaring? in total silence? with the TV on? Naturally, you will be unable to choose your perfect writing situation when asked to write in class or at work. But given the opportunity, try to select surroundings that suit your writing habits.

REWRITING THE ROUGH DRAFT: THE REVISING STAGE

Take care to allow time for your rough draft to "cool off" before you begin revising. You will be better able to detect faulty sentences, ill-chosen phrases, lapses in thinking if you give your brain time to rest after that feverish burst of creative activity. You need to be at the height of your powers when you rewrite.

If you have not yet achieved an effective introduction or a forceful conclusion, you must now apply yourself to that task—with or without inspiration. If you still need a title, consult our advice on "Title Tactics" in the "Revising Index."

Drag out your dictionary and your thesaurus and be sure that every word you have used in your essay is precisely the right word and that all are correctly spelled. Be sure that every sentence is as stylistically effective as possible—especially the first and last sentence of each paragraph. And take care to attach fragments to the sentences preceding or following them, unless you are using a fragment on purpose to gain emphasis.

Pay attention as you reread the paper to make certain that your paragraphs are fully developed with plenty of convincing concrete details and clear transitions between ideas. Be sure that you have not strayed from your outline and taken any little side trips with only a passing relationship to your thesis.

Most important of all, be positive that the whole paper makes sense. Read it aloud so that your ear will catch any careless repetition of words. And, if possible, read it aloud to someone else—preferably someone sharp—who can tell you whether what you have said is entirely clear and convincing.

Revising Checklist

Read the paper one more time primarily for content, checking to be sure that:

1. Every sentence is truly a sentence: no accidental fragments or mixed constructions
2. Every paragraph has a topic sentence and is fully developed
3. Every idea is related to the thesis
4. Every transition is easy to follow
5. Every idea is perfectly clear

Revise accordingly and type or recopy the paper.

CORRECTING THE FINAL VERSION: THE EDITING STAGE

When you go over your paper this final time to correct any careless errors, you must look only at the words themselves and at the punctuation: pay no attention to meaning.

Some people read backwards—from the bottom of the page toward the top, from right to left—in order to avoid getting distracted by the content. We have a friend who cuts a thin rectangular slit (about two inches long and half an inch wide) in the middle of a three-by five-inch notecard. By passing the card slowly across each line, he forces himself to look at no more than two or three words at a time. Use whatever system works for you, but *do* proofread.

Careless errors can be funny and Freudian, like this one from a student discussing the public reaction to social changes in the twenties: "Ladies' skirts finally rose so high that the pubic was shocked." But careless errors are usually witless and annoying, like repeating a word needlessly (*and and*) or leaving off an *s* and producing an illiterate construction: "The record were lost." Such mistakes do nothing to encourage admiration for the brilliance of your observations—no matter how keen or well stated. So, watch the little things, too. Do not write *probable* if you mean *probably,* or *use to* for *used to,* or *then* for *than.* Check possessives to be sure the apostrophes are there—or not there in the case of *its.*

As Jessica Mitford cautions, "Failure to proofread is like preparing a magnificent dinner and forgetting to set the table, so that the wretched guests have to scramble for food as best they can." Be polite: proofread. Your grade may depend on it.

Proofreading Checklist

Reread the paper, paying no attention to content but checking to be sure that:

1. No words are left out or carelessly repeated
2. No words are misspelled (or carelessly spelled—*use to* for *used to*)
3. No plurals are left off
4. No apostrophes are omitted for possessives or contractions
5. No periods, dashes, commas, colons, or quotation marks are left out or used unnecessarily

Make the necessary corrections. Remember that a neatly typed paper has a psychological advantage. It suggests to your readers that time and effort went into the preparation, that it was not simply tossed off at the last minute. Make corrections neatly and retype any page that looks like a disaster area.

PROOFREADING EXERCISE   1-8

We have deliberately riddled the following student paragraph with fifteen errors to let you discover how good you are at proofreading.

Eating poses another problem for lefthanded people. When a table
is set the glass is placed above the spoon on the right side Left-handed
people have to reach over thier food to reach the glass. That doesnt
sound like much of a problem but if the diner is wearing long sleeves,
than the chances are good that the the sleeves will brush over the food.
Knocking elbows is a way of life for Southpaws. Unless they are put at
the end of the table. They are always banging elbows with the right-
handed person next to them, for some reason the left-handed person is
always blamed. Just once why can't the right-handed person be blamed
for sitting next to a left-handed person, an causing the bruised elbows.

From Caterpillar to Butterfly: Revising and Editing in Action

In order for you to see how the revising and editing process might
look, we are including a sample paragraph in three stages. The paragraph appeared in a student essay contrasting the television series
Family with life in a real family. The audience was the student's
classmates, the purpose to inform.

Rough Draft Version

Mrs. Lawrence, the mother in Family, has a lot more time to
pursue her own interests and activities than my mother does. She
wears nice clothes around the house, while my mother's house
dresses are out of date. My mother doesn't have the opportunities
to get away from it all that Mrs. Lawrence seems to have.

Instructor's Comments

A good beginning but not a well-developed
paragraph. Add specifics — details,
examples, illustrations. What kind of
"interests and activities" does Mrs. Lawrence
pursue? What do "nice clothes" look
like? What sort of "opportunities" does
your mother lack? As you revise, try
to choose descriptive words that will
convey your ideas more precisely.

(Titles of TV programs should be underlined; titles of individual episodes go in quotation marks.)

First Revision

trite, wordy

Can you avoid this repetition?

Good details!

(?)

Proofread! combine?

A bit wordy!

Don't stack punctuation

Kate Lawerence, the mother in Family, is constantly boggling my mind. The woman never does housework. She has so much time on her hands that she practices the piano at least hours a day, putters in their garden, and still has time to take night classes toward a masters degree in music. If, on a rare occasion, she is found doing housework, Mrs. Lawrence is always wearing nice fitting clothers (her pants always have pleats), and she is never seen exerting too much energy. I cannot remember a time I saw her sweat! The most amusing detail in her perfect life is the fact that her telephone cord is two feet long! If my mother tried talking on such a phone, she'd strangle herself trying to scrub the floor at the same time! How often my mother, while wearing her tacky housedress she bought at Woolworth's in 1968, has looked at Mother Lawrence and wondered, "How does she do it?" Her traumatic experiences of moving to the guest house after a fight with her husband, Doug, would have no equal parallel in our household. If my mother ever got that upset, she would have to move out to the garage. There is no other place to go.

Does this need to be a complete sentence?

Don't tell your readers that something is amusing; let them see for themselves.

best word?

Whose? ambiguous pronoun reference

redundant

Good revision! Details are now plentiful and specific. Try to tighten the syntax in your final revision. Clarify the pronoun reference and be sure to proofread carefully!

weak reference

"a fight" would only be one "experience"

Second, Edited Revision

Kate Lawrence, the mother in <u>Family</u>, constantly boggles my mind. She has so much free time that she not only practices the piano at least three hours a day and putters in her garden, but also takes night classes toward a masters degree in music. If, on a rare occasion, we see her doing housework, Mrs. Lawrence is always wearing nicely fitting clothes (her pants always crisply pleated), and she never exerts enough energy to perspire. And somehow in her perfect life she manages to make do with a telephone cord that's only two feet long! If my mother tried talking on such a phone, she'd strangle herself trying to scrub the floor at the same time. Often my mother, wearing a tacky housedress she bought at Woolworth's in 1968, must gaze at Mother Lawrence and wonder, "How does she do it?" Poor Kate Lawrence's most traumatic experience—moving to the guest house after a fight with her husband—would have no parallel in our household. In a similar situation, my mother would have to move out to the garage. There is no other place to go.

Instructor's Comments

Excellent job! Your sentence combining and reorganizing to avoid that slight repetition make a big improvement. Fine proofreading, too. Congratulations!

chapter Two
Choosing Words Wisely

Language, as described by Norman Cousins, is "the currency of communication."[1] He is pleased that "our linguistic capital" is being constantly enriched by the addition of new words. But others who write about the state of the language are far from happy. Newsweek reports that "Along with almost everything else, language is said to be slipping out of control in America. Inflation has eaten away our words; the bureaucrats in Washington churn them out by the millions, but they mean less and less."[2] Since people use language for thinking, as well as for communicating those thoughts, the charge that words are losing meaning is a serious matter.

In this chapter we encourage you to become conscious of words—to consider their meanings, to enjoy their sounds, to respect their importance. The only foolproof way of improving your vocabulary is through reading. You are, of course, constantly poring over textbooks, but try to find time to read other things as well. Your library has a comfortable browsing room in which all the latest newspapers and popular magazines are readily available. Make use of them. Relax and read. You will absorb the nuances of language as if by osmosis if you continually read the work of good writers.

IMPROVING YOUR COMMAND OF WORDS

If you are going to become skillful in choosing words precisely, you need a dictionary large enough to provide reliable help. Abridged

[1] "A Growing Wealth of Words," *Saturday Review* (March 1981), p. 7.
[2] "The Syntax Revolution," *Newsweek* (8 Dec. 1980), p. 91.

"pocket-sized" editions are fine for carrying to class when you have to write a paper or take an essay test, but a small dictionary will not do for the thoughtful work you must devote to revising any writing that needs to be polished and perfect.

Choosing a Dictionary

Barbara Currier Bell, writing in the *New York Times*, suggests that you will do well to buy a hardcover (rather than paperback) collegiate dictionary and lists the five most widely recommended:

American Heritage Dictionary, New College Edition
Funk & Wagnalls Standard College Dictionary
The Random House College Dictionary
Webster's New Collegiate Dictionary, 8th Edition
Webster's New World Dictionary, 2d College Edition

She then provides the following guidelines for choosing a dictionary:

1. **Readability.** This is one aspect of a dictionary not usually given top billing, but it is critical. You should not be embarrassed about paying attention to such "unscholarly" matters as typographic design, format and illustration.
2. **Clarity of definition.** Clarity matters more than other aspects of definition for the college student because so often the word to be looked up is abstract or general.
3. **Etymology.** The histories of words record essential dimensions of meaning. Etymologies encourage you to appreciate the organic quality of words, the way each one takes on a life of its own, and the extent to which that life is linked with others.
4. **Usage level.** Usually, concern centers on "good" language and "bad." Those who prefer a prescriptive approach either want to see only "good" words in the dictionary or, if all sorts are included, to have usage level stressed. Those on the descriptive side want to include as many words as possible and to play down usage level.
5. **Front-matter.** This can make or break you in your use of the dictionary as a learning tool. It is the instruction manual, telling you how the dictionary is put together. It also includes articles on the English language, the structure of languages in general and ours in particular, and on language usage.[3]

After you have acquired the dictionary you prefer, keep it handy and consult it often. But first, you need to learn how to use it.

[3] "A Few Words on Choosing Your Dictionary," *New York Times* (25 July 1982), section 12, p. 10.

Using Your Dictionary

For some reason, myths abound concerning dictionaries. Many people believe that the first meaning listed for a word is the "best" one. Not true. The first meaning will often be the oldest meaning; hence, it could be the least common one. The same thing is true of alternative spellings. Unless a qualifier is inserted (like *also* or *variation of*), multiple spellings are equally acceptable. And if the dictionary does not list parts of verbs, you know that those spellings are regular: only *irregular* plurals and verb forms appear in dictionary entries.

The only way to find out how your dictionary handles these matters is to force yourself to read the explanatory notes—the "instruction manual" at the beginning. It is not the liveliest reading imaginable, but it can be rewarding. You might find out that you have been skipping some of the most interesting parts of the entry when you look up a word. Besides spelling, syllabification, part of speech labels, pronunciation (check the bottom of each page for an explanation of the phonetic symbols), and definition, the entry may also give you the word's etymology (history); convenient examples of how the word is used; usage labels like *archaic, slang,* or *colloquial;* and synonyms and antonyms. Most dictionaries also provide entertaining material in the back, like punctuation rules, pictures of the planets and stars, lists of abbreviations, common given names with their meanings, and even rhyming words.

EXERCISE   2-1

After studying the explanatory notes of your dictionary, look up answers for the following questions.

1. What purpose do the guidewords (at the top of each page) serve?
2. Underline the syllable that should receive the primary stress (main accent) in these words: pterodactyl, atavistic, lycanthropy.
3. What word or words does the middle syllable of *machismo* rhyme with?
4. For the pairs of words listed, indicate which is the preferred spelling or whether both are equally acceptable.

hiccup, hiccough	traveler, traveller
judgment, judgement	aesthetic, esthetic
czar, tsar	hippopotamuses, hippopotami

5. What is a Murphy bed?
6. What was George Orwell's real name?
7. What sea does the river Rhine flow into?
8. What is the plural of *Mr.?* of *Mrs.?* of *Ms.?*

9. What does the symbol £ mean?
10. What usage labels do you find for these words?   *slang*

enthuse	irregardless *— not acceptable*
snot	veep
finalize	rip off
anyways	prof

11. From what languages do the following words come?

gumbo	mongoose *Dry* *Southern India*
rhinoceros	toboggan *Polenesian*
algebra	taboo

12. How do you form the plural of these words?

    deer   hobo   ox *oxen*   alumnus *alumni*
    beau   soliloquy   parenthesis
    soliloquies

13. What word is an antonym (means the opposite) of *pungent*?
14. Where in the United States would you expect to hear the word *potlatch* used?
15. What is the British meaning for these words?

    lift   biscuit *cook or cracker*
    elevator

16. In what country would you expect to encounter these terms?

    bairn   begorra   billabong *Australia*
    Scotch   Irish

17. How does the meaning of the word *Catholic* change when spelled without a capital letter?
18. What is the literal (etymological) meaning of the term *astronaut*? *nautical star sailor*
19. What etymological ancestor (root) do these words have in common?

    cereal   create   crescendo   accrue   increase

20. What do the following foreign terms mean in English?

omnia vincit amor	raison d'être *— reason for being*
repondez s'il vous plait *RSVP*	tempus fugit *+ time flys*
de gustibus non est disputandum	

    their is no disputing about taste

21. What are six meanings for the abbreviation *MS*?
22. Some words change grammatical function when they change pronunciation, i.e., change the syllable receiving the main accent. What grammatical function may each of these words have?

    pro' ject, pro ject'   ab' stract, ab stract'
    re' cord, re cord'   con' tent, con tent'

23. What does the combining form *heli* or *helio* mean? What plant name is derived from it? What gaseous element? Does our word *helicopter* stem from it? *helium*

24. Read the synonymy (comparison of similar word meanings) under *gaudy* and explain the distinctions in meaning for the following synonyms: gaudy, tawdry, garish, flashy.
25. Write six sentences in which you use six different meanings of the word *set*.
26. Where would you look for the phrase *in the know?*
27. Where would you find 20/20?
28. What is the shared meaning element of the following words?

> leaven   innoculate   ingrain   imbue   suffuse

EXERCISE   **2-2**

1. Following are two dictionary entries for the same word. Read the entries carefully and make a chart of similarities and differences in the way they handle the following elements:

	Entry A	Entry B
Pronunciation		
Usage labels		
Parts of speech		
Examples of use in sentences and phrases		
Etymology		
Synonyms and antonyms		
Definitions		

Entry A

sil·ly (sil′i), *adj*. [SILLIER (-i-êr), SILLIEST (-i-ist)], [ME. *seli, sili* (with shortened vowel), good, blessed, innocent; AS, *sælig*, happy, prosperous, blessed (akin to G. *selig*, blessed) < *sæl*, time; sense development: happy—blessed—innocent—(deserving pity) —unworldly—foolish; cf. INNOCENT, CRETIN], 1. feeble-minded; imbecile. 2. having or showing little sense, judgment, or sobriety; foolish, stupid, absurd, ludicrous, etc. 3. [Colloq.], dazed; senseless, as from a blow. 4. [Dial.], helpless; weak. 5. [Archaic], feeble; infirm. 6. [Archaic], simple; plain; innocent. *n*. [Colloq.], a silly person.
SYN.—silly implies ridiculous or irrational behavior that seems to demonstrate a lack of common sense, good judgment, or sobriety (it was *silly* of you to lock the door); stupid implies a dull-wittedness or lack of normal intelligence or understanding (he is not *so stupid* as to believe that); fatuous suggests stupidity, inanity, or obtuseness coupled with a smug complacency (a *fatuous babbitt*); asinine implies the extreme stupidity conventionally attributed to an ass (an *asinine* argument). See also absurd.—ANT. wise, intelligent.

Entry B

sil′ly (sil′ĭ), *adj.*; SIL′LI·ER (-ĭ-êr); SIL′LI·EST. [ME. *seely, sely*, fr. AS. *sælig, gesælig*, happy, good, fr. *sæl* good fortune, happiness; akin to OS. *sálig*, adj., good, happy, D. *zalig* blessed, G. *selig*, OHG. *sálig*, ON. *sæll*, Sw. *säll*, Dan. *salig*, Goth. *sels* good, kind, L. *solari* to comfort, and prob. Gr. *hilaros* cheerful. Cf. CONSOLE, v., EXHILARATE, SELE season.] 1. a *Now Scot. & N. of Eng.* In need of compassion or sympathy; pitiful. b *Archaic*, Helpless; frail; feeble;—now only of animals; as, *silly* sheep. c *Scot. & N. of Eng.* Weak; sickly. d *Archaic*. Simpleminded; unsophisticated; ignorant.
2. *Obs.* a Lowly in station. b Mean; paltry; poor.
3. Rustic; plain; simple; humble.

>   A fourth man, in a *silly* habit.   *Shak.*

4. a *Orig. Scot.* Weak in intellect; destitute of ordinary strength of mind. b Lacking in sense; foolish; simple; fatuous; as, a *silly* woman.
5. Proceeding from want of understanding or common judgment; characterized by weakness or folly; unwise; absurd; stupid; as, *silly* conduct; a *silly* question.
6. Dazed, as by a blow; as, he was knocked *silly*.
Syn.—Dense, brainless, shallow, indiscreet. See FOOLISH.
Ant.—Grave, serious, thoughtful, intelligent, sage.

What differences do you think are accounted for by the fact that the first definition comes from a college dictionary and the second from a huge unabridged dictionary? What difference is accounted for by the difference between a dictionary of the American language and a dictionary of the English language?

Increasing Your Vocabulary

A weak vocabulary stunts your growth in several directions. You miss the point of whole paragraphs, or sometimes even of lectures, because the topic sentence has a key word whose meaning you do not know or misunderstand. There are nuances (shades) of meaning that you fail to express in your speech or writing because you do not have the necessary words. And worst of all, you may decide you are dim-witted because you cannot understand so many written and spoken ideas, when you could grasp those ideas easily if you knew enough words.

So what do you do? The best advice is the same advice you have been getting since third grade: read a lot and use the dictionary. But "Don't swallow the dictionary," cautions Mortimer Adler. "Don't try to get word-rich quick by memorizing a lot of fancy words whose meanings are unconnected with any actual experience."[4] We agree wholeheartedly. You do better to learn words by coming across them and looking them up than by learning from a printed list with definitions. Vocabulary lists give you words in isolation, and that makes them hard to remember correctly. A word you find in a sentence within the context of a paragraph is more likely to click in your memory and stay there.

Once a word's meaning has found a place in your mind, you need to make it feel at home there. You do this by using the word. If you use it and people look at you strangely (or put question marks in your margins), you know you have not quite got it down yet. Look it up again, and use it again. After a while, you will wonder how you ever got along without that serviceable word.

EXERCISE   2-3

Write each italicized word, followed by the meaning which fits the context in which it appears.

1. Timothy's fishnet T-shirt was almost *salacious*.
2. Sara said his scanty garb inspired *lascivious* thoughts.
3. She told him she thought his attire too *worldly* for a seminary student.
4. "You look as if you're trying to attract a *paramour*," sniffed Sara.
5. Timothy thought her objections were *ludicrous*.
6. He wondered if her motives were *pernicious* or if she was just puritanical.
7. She had the *temerity* to criticize his clothing when she herself was clad in skimpy shorts.
8. Timothy decided to dismiss the incident as a mere *bagatelle*.

---

[4] "How to Read a Dictionary," *Saturday Review* (13 Dec. 1941), p. 19.

9. When Sara suggested they should both put on more clothes and go get a pizza, Tim was *amenable*.
10. The pizza, unfortunately, was the worst they had ever tasted, positively *execrable*.
11. Eubie complained that he found the steambath *enervating*.
12. Melvin argued that steambaths are *salubrious*.
13. Eubie, feeling hot and *irascible*, shouted at Melvin.
14. "I don't care how *salutary* sweating is," he yelled.
15. "I think steambaths are *odious!*"
16. "You needn't be so *strident*," reproved Melvin.
17. Eubie, not wanting to *exacerbate* the quarrel, apologized to Melvin for shouting.
18. But Melvin, feeling *pugnacious*, pursued the argument.
19. "Don't you want to be *svelte?*" he asked.
20. "No, I have a *penchant* for plumpness," Eubie responded.
21. Frequently a popular politician is *lionized* by the press.
22. The senator from Mississippi is often *loquacious*.
23. We hope our elected representatives are always *sagacious*.
24. Sometimes, though, their speeches are *turgid*.
25. One angry senator urged *retribution* for an injury to our national pride.
26. A colleague then accused him of *jingoism*.
27. *Trenchant* arguments were put forth by both sides.
28. An irate senator made an *insidious* proposal that could lead to war.
29. But his arguments were *tenuous* at best.
30. The senators voted to engage in no *surreptitious* actions.

WRITING EXERCISE   **2-4**

Now write thirty sentences in which you use each of the italicized words above (or some form of each) in a sentence of your own.

Using Your Thesaurus

If you often find yourself asking everyone you meet to tell you that little short word that means something like *enthusiasm*, a thesaurus is just what you need. This book will probably come up with the word *zeal* faster than your friends can. A thesaurus does not define words; instead, it gives lists of synonyms. You might need a synonym if you can not think of the precise word you want or if you have used the same word three times already and are looking for a substitute.

Thesauruses, like dictionaries, are available both in large, hardbound versions and small, softcover volumes. In this case, a paperback will serve you nicely. Some are organized so that you locate your word in the index, which refers you to a numbered section of the book.

There you will find a handsome selection of synonyms and almost-synonyms. Others are published in dictionary form: you just look up a word alphabetically to find its synonyms. The alphabetized variety are far easier to use.

Remember, though, that synonyms are not always interchangeable. Never, we repeat, *never* use an unfamiliar word without looking it up in a collegiate-sized dictionary first to make sure it conveys the exact meaning you want. For instance, *fanaticism* is listed in the thesaurus under *enthusiasm,* but its connotations are quite different, and it would not fit in every context. A good dictionary will also clear up distinctions between familiar words (*marvelous* and *excellent, dishonest* and *sly,* for example).

Used in combination with a dictionary, a thesaurus can sharpen your word choice, build your vocabulary, and cure you of staring into space, saying, "It's right on the tip of my tongue."

EXERCISE   2-5

A thesaurus entry for the threadbare word *nice* follows. Using the dictionary if necessary, choose the best synonym to substitute for *nice* in each of the sentences below. (The capitalized words indicate other entries to look up to find more synonyms.)

nice, adj. pleasant, agreeable, amiable, lovely (PLEASANTNESS); precise, accurate (RIGHT); fine, subtle, hairsplitting (DIFFERENTIATION).

—From *The New Roget's Thesaurus in Dictionary Form* (1961).

1. Sandy's sentence provided a nice definition of "chauvinism."
2. We had a nice time at the party last night.
3. Joyce is usually a very nice person, but she always argues with Hal.
4. She took a course to learn the nice points of constitutional law.
5. Autumn has nice weather.
6. I hate these endless bridge-table battles over nice rules of bidding etiquette.
7. You look quite nice in your new fake leopard-skin pillbox hat.

FINDING THE RIGHT WORDS

Mark Twain once observed that the difference between the right word and almost the right word is the difference between the lightning and the lightning bug. Our language is full of synonyms—words that mean approximately the same thing, like *happy* and *glad.* But, as we just mentioned above, synonyms often have different shades of meaning, different nuances. Although a *feeling* is a *sensation*, the two words are certainly not interchangeable. Neither are *witty* and *funny*, nor *visible* and *apparent*, nor *utensil* and *implement*—even though each pair of words shares an element of meaning.

Be especially careful not to confuse words that sound alike but mean different things—like *uninterested* and *disinterested*—or you will mislead your readers. Sometimes, of course, the confusion can be amusing. We have a friend whose grandmother is continually crocheting Africans. And James Thurber confides that "Margaret, our cook, says one of her sons works into the incinerating plant where they burn the refuge; has had the job since the Armitage." "Another lady," he goes on, "told me of a young man who passed his civil service eliminations. As far as real estate values goes, she says there is a great disparagement. You begin to feel insane after an hour or so of this."[5] Indeed. These *malapropisms*, as such misused words are called, are often funny, but you want your readers laughing with you, not at you.

Say What You Mean

Sometimes the sense of a sentence becomes unclear because the writer somehow fails to pay attention to what often-used words mean. The following sentences *sound* all right—until you realize they are nonsense. A local police officer recently announced in print:

> We are trying to put some teeth into the law to help enforce narcotic abuse.

We can hope he does not actually intend to force all citizens to abuse narcotics. More likely he meant "to help *curb* narcotics abuse," but he said he intended to make drug abuse mandatory. One of our students made this observation in an essay:

> Many important factors are determined by the way one dresses: the person's personality, lifestyle, profession, age, and sex.

She could not seriously believe that changing one's manner of dress could also change one's "profession, age, and sex," but that is what she *said*. Another student wrote this puzzler:

> There are a variety of media under the classification of painting.

[5] "Look Out for Turkey Wort," *Atlantic* (Dec. 1980), p. 70.

That is a grammatically correct but meaningless sentence. We think the student may have intended to say that painters use different substances to paint with, like oils, watercolors, and tempera. But we are only guessing.

When you write, pay attention to the words. Be sure that each sentence means exactly what you want to say. Try also to make sure that you have said it in the best possible words.

EXERCISE   **2-6**

The following sentences are taken from real life—from signs, newspapers, police reports, and student papers. We did not make up a single one. Each includes some subtle or blatant misuse of language resulting from the use of words without regard for meaning. Point out what is wrong with each sentence, and then rephrase it accurately. You may need to rewrite some completely in order to repair them. We will revise the first one, which was taken from a sign in a parking lot.

1. Illegal Parking Will Be Towed Away At Their Expense.
   Revised: Illegally Parked Cars Will Be Towed At Owner's Expense.
2. I spent half an hour looking for a writing utensil.
3. The intoxicated individual exited the vehicle.
4. The senator's aide described Duckett's testimony as "extremely forthcoming" and said every question was answered.
5. My brother confides in me not to tell on him.
6. Myself and Officer Barrett and Officer Smith responded to the eighth floor by way of the stairwell.
7. These statements deduce that the firm could expect a loss in sales.
8. Today's society has been pilfered with a barrage of legalized drugs.
9. Despite the massive quantity of books in the world, it is possible to generalize them into three categories.
10. Let's not let the planning ahead foreshadow the current dilemma.

LOOKING FOR LIVELY WORDS

In large measure, finding exactly the right words in writing involves choosing interesting, specific language that will keep your readers' attention. As Paul Roberts once noted, most topics—except sex—are basically boring; thus, he cautioned, it becomes the writer's job to make the topic interesting. Even *Business Week* magazine advises, "Be precise, be lively."[6]

[6] "How to Polish Your Writing," *Business Week* (6 July 1981), p. 110.

You cannot escape the limp *to be* verb* a good bit of the time, but whenever you can, find a more forceful verb. James Thurber, in his essay "Sex Ex Machina," speaks of "a world made up of gadgets that *whir* and *whine* and *whiz* and *shriek* and sometimes *explode*" (our italics). The force of the verbs conveys the feeling of anxiety produced by machine-age living. In his essay "A Hanging," George Orwell describes a dog that "came *bounding* among us with a loud volley of barks, and *leapt* round us *wagging* its whole body, wild with glee at finding so many human beings together." The verb *leapt*, plus the italicized verbal adjectives, enable the reader to visualize the energy and excitement of the dog. Thomas Heggen, in the introduction to *Mr. Roberts,* writes, "Surely an artillery shell fired at Hanover *ripples* the air here. Surely a bomb dropped on Okinawa *trembles* these bulkheads." These verbs produce precisely the effect he wants in the two sentences: the suggestion of being touched, but only barely touched, by events far away.

Be Specific and Vivid

There are, of course, other stylistic elements operating to make the preceding examples effective. But if your writing is colorless and tiresome, you need to work on vivid specific details. Mention the name, the time, the taste, the color, the smell, the place, the position, the size, the shape, the texture, the number whenever possible. Instead of writing, "We got into the car," try "All four of us piled into Herman's Honda."

To be sure you have the idea, let us give you examples of words that move from general to specific:

move	run	sprint	
vehicle	car	sedan	Jaguar
animal	dog	Collie	Lassie

Instead of writing, "Lester laughed," try to express the *way* he laughed. Did he chuckle, giggle, cackle, chortle, snigger? Your thesaurus can help you find the exact word.

Have fun with the following exercise; pile on the modifiers if you feel so inclined. But when you write for an audience, take care not to lapse into *purple prose*, like this:

> More devastating than cancer, accidents, and war, divorce has become the cyanide of society! With its misguided machete cutting a jagged, tetanus-covered swath through our emotionally crippled culture, divorce goes unchecked.

* The *to be* verb appears most commonly in these forms: *am, was, been, is, are, has been, had been, can be, could be, should be, shall be, will be.*

That writer's prose goes unchecked! His sentences are vivid and imaginative, all right, but his excessive enthusiasm provokes laughter instead of agreement. Make your own writing lively and precise, but keep the imagery within reason.

EXERCISE   **2-7**

In order to limber up your imagination, try rewriting the following dull sentences by substituting vivid, precise words for any general or lackluster terms. Here is an example:

Dull: Seymour was up late last night trying to finish typing his term paper.
Specific: Seymour sat hunched over his typewriter, pecking away doggedly until three o'clock in the morning, trying to finish his paper on the mating habits of hippopotamuses.

1. My friend, who exercises as a hobby, studies at night in order to have his afternoons free for sports.
2. That cat is behaving in a most peculiar fashion.
3. Some person had removed the very article I needed from the magazine in the library.
4. She came into the room, removed her shoes, and sat down.
5. The man I went out with last night is a real character.
6. The meat was not very good, and the salad was even worse.
7. Hearing someone make even slight noises at a symphony is distracting.
8. She and I have just been out driving around in her new car.
9. The woman left her office, walked hurriedly to the store, and made a purchase.
10. Near the window was an attractive plant in an interesting container.

Use Descriptive, Sense-Related Details

Words that convey precise descriptive details add both clarity and vitality to your writing. First, consider your purpose. Do you want to arouse an emotional response in your readers? Or are you trying to convey a word picture, without emotion but sharp and clear as a photograph? Your choice of words and details will differ according to the effect you want. Before you begin writing, look—really *look*—at what you plan to describe. Maybe you will want to smell and taste and touch it as well. Then try to record your sense impressions: the exact shapes, the lights and shades, the textures, the tastes, the sounds, the smells. Do not include everything, of course, or you may overwhelm your readers. Carefully select the details that suit your purpose in order to give your audience a sharp impression of what you are describing. Then search for the precise words to convey that picture.

Sometimes you may write a whole paragraph of description, as Mark Twain does in this passage from Eve's diary:

> I *had* to have company—I was made for it I think—so I made friends with the animals. They are just charming, and they have the kindest dispositions and the politest ways; they never look sour, they never let you feel that you are intruding, they smile at you and wag their tail, if they've got one, and they are always ready for a romp or an excursion or anything you propose. . . . Why, there's always a swarm of them around—sometimes as much as four or five acres—you can't count them; and when you stand in the midst and look out over the furry expanse it is so mottled and splashed and gay with color and frisking sheen and sun flash, and so rippled with stripes, that you might think it was a lake, only you know it isn't; and there's storms of sociable birds, and hurricanes of whirring wings; and when the sun strikes all that feathery commotion, you have a blazing up of all the colors you can think of, enough to put your eyes out.
>
> —"The Diary of Adam and Eve" (1893).

Frequently you will include a sentence of description in a paragraph devoted mainly to some other purpose. Dorothy Parker slips in a fine sensuous detail when she notes, "His voice was as intimate as the rustle of sheets." Kaye Northcott employs a telling visual detail when she observes, "The conventioneering police chiefs sat straight as night sticks in the spartan Dallas meeting hall. . . ." Larry King uses physical description to give us information about character: "He had a firm handshake and a wide mouth that often smiled when his eyes did not." And Katherine Anne Porter conveys the oppressive atmosphere of a courtroom this way: "The place was as dismal and breathless as a tenement fire escape in August." She goes on to describe the judge as "a little old gray man with pointed whiskers and the face of a smart, conspiratorial chipmunk."

Remember that good descriptive details will enliven almost any kind of writing. Get into the habit of observing closely and then presenting your observations through appeals to the senses.

OBSERVATION EXERCISE   2-8

In order to sharpen your sensory perceptions, we want you to practice observing with great attention to detail. In groups of three to five, go out on the campus during your composition class period and station yourselves at some busy place—like the coffee shop of the Student Union, the checkout counters of the book store, or the circulation desk of the library. Elect one person to take charge of making a list of at least one hundred details observed by the group. The first twenty-five or so will be easy, but after that you may have to concentrate harder. Remember that you should record all types of sensory details: sight, sound, smell, even taste and feel, if appropriate.

WRITING EXERCISE   2-9

Choose one brief experience that has a sensuous association for you—something like this: a person walks by wearing the same perfume you wore in eleventh grade; or you pet a dog that looks just exactly like old Spot, your devoted companion all through grade school; or you hear a special "golden oldie" on the radio. Write a descriptive paragraph in which you lead up to or develop that brief experience; then make a transition and discuss your remembered associations. Try to make the remembered details as vivid as those in the recent experience.

Avoid Clichés

When you are struggling to enliven your writing with vibrant language, be careful about jotting down the first phrase that comes to mind, for it will likely be a *cliché*, a phrase we pick up because it sounds perfect and then use over and over until it loses its force. The person who coined the phrases *cool as a cucumber, rugged individualist, ship of state,* or *frontiers of knowledge* deserves real credit. But if you use any of these worn out expressions, you will draw sighs from your readers, not praise. Remember that the single word *fine* is preferable to the tarnished phrase *worth its weight in gold.* Here is a list of some currently popular clichés that you may be tempted to use. Try to resist the temptation.

acid test	doomed to failure
at this point in time	first and foremost
ballpark figure	history tells us
bottom line	in this day and age
burning questions	last but not least
crystal clear	untimely death
cutting edge	

Use Your Imagination

Try to come up with some original *figures of speech*—analogies, metaphors, similes—to give zest to your writing. If you set your imagination loose, you can think of imaginative comparisons that will give your writing greater interest and clarity. Ralph Waldo Emerson in the last century remarked, "New York is a sucked orange"—an observation full of insight, phrased with great economy. Kurt Vonnegut, Jr., more recently described New York as "a sort of polluted lake on which splendid vessels bob. Many people can't even afford water wings, so an awful lot of drowning in untreated sewage goes on." Such comparisons are a form of *analogy*, a useful method of comparing something abstract (like the quality of life in a city) to something concrete (like a sucked orange or a polluted lake). Here is a simple but effective analogy from J. F. Kobler: "Like really good tomatoes, performance standards in each department must be home grown."

When Melvin Maddox declares in *Time* magazine that "Launching a new repertory company with Strindberg is a little like christening a ship with a bottle of cyanide," he suggests that Strindberg can be a loser with modern audiences. Certainly his *simile* (a comparison with *like* or *as*) is more interesting than just telling us that Strindberg is no longer popular. Maya Angelou observes that for black people some changes "have been as violent as electrical storms, while others creep slowly like sorghum syrup." Notice how forcefully Barbara Ehrenreich conveys the hazards of smoking when she asserts that the "medical case against smoking is as airtight as a steel casket." Brigid Brophy uses a *metaphor* (an implied or suggested comparison) to assert her belief that monogamy is a confining relationship: "At present, monogamy is the corset into which we try to fit every married couple—a process which has on so many occasions split the seams that we have had to modify the corset."

Sometimes you may use a metaphor or simile and then enlarge on the point in the next sentence, as Zora Neale Hurston does in her introduction to *Mules and Men* (1936): "The Negro offers a featherbed resistance. That is, we let the probe enter, but it never comes out. It gets smothered under a lot of laughter and pleasantries." This construction, called an *extended metaphor*, is as effective in expository prose as it is in poetry.

One thing you need to be wary about is the *mixed metaphor*, the comparison that fails to compare accurately, like this choice one from the *Nashville Tennessean:* "I may be just a little grain of salt crying in the woods, but I deplore this kind of thing." Just try to visualize that image and you can see the problem. Better no metaphor at all than one that is confused. And remember that figures of speech should clarify your meaning through comparisons that increase your reader's understanding.

EXERCISE   2-10

Write an extended simile or metaphor. Finish one of these statements with an item from our list below or fill in the blank with a concrete object of your own choice. Then write several more sentences, expanding the comparison further.

1. My room looks like _____ .
2. My mind is like _____ .

3. My friend's personality is _____ .
4. Kissing my lover is like _____ .
5. Failing an exam is like _____ .
6. Time is like _____ .

disco music	a buzzsaw
the inside of my purse	a bulldozer
a hot poker game	a fast train
an old boot	a 1957 Chevy
a K-mart blue-light special	a mirror
strawberry-banana jello	a greased pig
cottage cheese	a rearview mirror
a standard-transmission car	a thunderstorm
a brick wall	a slow baseball game
Twinkies	a picnic
a Picasso	a traffic jam
a peanut butter and jelly sandwich	

Here are a couple of student responses to this exercise to give you the idea:

My mind is like a cast iron safe. Whatever I put in it stays, always there. But when I need it, I forget the combination.

My friend's personality is like the contents inside the pocket of my winter jacket in spring. He's a crumb. He reminds me of an empty candy wrapper. Upon first meeting him, you would think he was full of personality, but once you get to know him, you find out there's nothing there.

Be Cautious about Connotations

Words are symbols with *denotative* meanings—the actual concrete property or abstract quality referred to—and *connotative* meanings—the emotional responses stimulated by associations with the word. The term "mother," for instance, *denotes* a woman who gives birth to a child, but the term often *connotes* warmth, love, security, and comfort. Most of our words have connotations in varying degrees—some so strong that the words should be considered "loaded." Whether you choose to refer to the President as a "statesman" or as a "politician" may well reveal your political affiliation. Consider the connotations of these pairs of similar words:

smut	pornography
mob	gathering
cur	pup

smog	haze
egghead	intellectual
prudish	chaste
jock	athlete
pennypinching	thrifty
foolhardy	courageous

Writers' attitudes are transparently revealed by whether they choose from the strongly negative words on the left or the more favorable words on the right.

We do not mean to suggest that you should avoid choosing words with strong connotations. Your writing would be lifeless if you did. But you must be aware of the hidden messages you convey with strongly connotative words or you run the risk of producing unfortunate sentences like this one:

Lori cherishes her siblings.

The word *sibling,* used primarily by social scientists to suggest objectivity, lacks all associations of warmth. That sentence would be more successful if written this way:

Lori cherishes her brothers and sisters.

The word *siblings* works fine, though, if you change the context:

Lori bickers constantly with her siblings.

Because ignoring connotations can produce regrettable effects, try to become sensitive to the emotional associations that some words carry. Your dictionary will help you.

EXERCISE   **2-11**

Using connotative language, rewrite each of the following neutral sentences in two ways: first, with a protaxpayers slant, and second, with a progovernment slant.

1. A group of citizens circulated a petition stating that property taxes should be lowered.
2. The Internal Revenue Service requested that an indigent citizen pay taxes on her winnings in Las Vegas.
3. A taxpayers organization offered objections to the salary raise granted to legislators.

AVOIDING UNCLEAR LANGUAGE

As you search for the right word, be cautious about words that sound impressive but have vague meanings. Avoid elevated language if you can say the same thing clearly and plainly without it. People who write "semantic and quantitative symbolizations" when they mean "words and numbers" are probably trying to impress their readers with their knowledge. But such *bafflegab* (from *baffle,* meaning "to confuse," and *gab,* meaning "talk") destroys clear communication.

In an article calling for "simple, direct prose that says precisely what you want it to say in the fewest words," *Business Week* magazine condemns bafflegab and provides the following examples, plus "translations":[7]

Bafflegab: Consumer elements are continuing to stress the fundamental necessity of a stabilization of the price structure at a lower level than exists at the present time.

Translation: Consumers keep saying that prices must go down and stay down.

Bafflegab: The finance director claimed that substantial economies were being effected in his division by increasing the time interval between distribution of data-eliciting forms to business entities.

Translation: The finance director said his division was saving money by sending fewer questionnaires to employers.

You get the idea. Try to avoid those monstrous new phrases that creep into the language via the federal bureaucracy, the educational establishment, the social sciences, and the computer people—phrases like "an increased propensity to actualize" (meaning "likely to occur"), "to restructure one's external/internal reward system" (meaning "to take a cut in pay"), "to facilitate the availability of funds" (meaning "to raise money"), and "sociologically compatible behavioral parameters" (meaning who knows what).

Be Careful about Jargon

Language used within a trade or profession that is understood perfectly well among that specialized group but not by outsiders is called *jargon.* Bridge players, for instance, mean something entirely different by *rubber, dummy,* and *slam* than the rest of us do. A computer programmer could remind a colleague that four bytes equal a word and be perfectly understood. No tennis fan would be confused if

[7] "How to Polish Your Writing," *Business Week* (6 July 1981), pp. 106–107.

a player called a let ball at 15-love. Before using jargon, consider your audience and your purpose. If your readers will find the terms familiar, and if these words help make your meaning clear, by all means, use them. If not, find more common terms, or else define the jargon (in parentheses following the word, as we often do in this text).

Watch Out for Doublespeak

Usually both jargon and bafflegab obscure meaning accidentally. But sometimes people conceal meaning deliberately to avoid saying something unpleasant, unpopular, or sexy. These intentional smoke-screens are called *euphemisms*, and some of them are quite innocent. Rather than say bluntly, "He died of cancer," we say, "He passed away after a lingering illness." It takes the shudder out and cloaks the whole grim business of dying in a soothing phrase. Undertakers (or "funeral directors," as they prefer to be called) sometimes carry euphemism to grotesque extremes, like calling the room where the body lies "the slumber chamber." A writer for *Newsweek* avoided calling a public figure "stupid" by saying instead that he suffered "profound alienation from the life of the mind."

Such indirect language seems amusing, but people also use an objectionable kind of euphemism, called *doublespeak*, to mask realities that ought not be concealed. A former President of the United States simply declared a false statement "inoperative" and thus avoided having to admit that he had lied to the American people. The CIA substitutes the vague phrase "terminate with extreme prejudice" for the ugly word "murder." The Pentagon refers to weapons designed to kill people as "antipersonnel implements." Instead of "bombing," the Air Force speaks of "protective reaction strikes." Such transparent attempts to make sinister happenings sound inoffensive are dangerously misleading.

These deceptive euphemisms are becoming widespread in our society. The National Council of Teachers of English recently conferred its annual Doublespeak Award on the nuclear power industry for coining these phrases:

an "energetic disassembly"   (meaning an explosion)
a "rapid oxidation"   (meaning a fire)
an "abnormal evolution"   (meaning an accident)

Police officers are no longer taught to aim to kill; now they aim "to neutralize the adversary." The faculty of an elementary school in Brooklyn, New York, was asked to use the following euphemisms for parent interviews and on report cards (we quote from the principal's instructions[8]):

Harsh Expression	Euphemism
(Avoid)	(Use)
1. Lies	Shows difficulty in distinguishing between imaginary and factual material
2. Cheats	Needs help in learning to adhere to rules and standards of fair play
3. Steals	Needs help in learning to respect the property rights of others
4. Is a bully	Has qualities of leadership but needs help in learning to use them democratically

If more and more individuals insist on the honest use of language, perhaps this deceptive trend can be reversed. At least you in your own writing can be truthful both in what you say and in the way you say it.

Be Wary of Profanity

There is still some debate about another kind of euphemism. Many people consider it euphemistic to substitute socially acceptable terms for frank and forceful four-letter words. You should, ultimately, consider your readers. You do not want to make them angry; you want to communicate with them. Different people are shocked by different things, but all of us are offended by something. To some people violence is the ultimate obscenity; to some racial prejudice is obscene; to some the sight or sound of four-letter words is obscene. We could argue about whose concept of obscenity is the most valid, but that would hardly help you avoid offending your readers. You need to size them up for yourself. Before you lapse into using four-letter words for emphasis, try to decide whether your readers will find them forceful or merely offensive. And when in doubt, leave them out.

DISCUSSION EXERCISE   2-12

We found every one of the following examples of bafflegab and doublespeak in print. Try to explain what you think these sentences mean. We have supplied some hints to help you along and will translate the first one to get you started.

1. The city budget proposes spending money for "effective confinement and extinguishment of unwanted and destructive fires."

---

[8] Abridged from Terrence P. Morgan, "Public Doublespeak," *College English,* Oct. 1974, p. 194.

Translation: The city budget proposes spending money for fighting fires.

2. The same city budget plans to "schedule adherence with emphasis on hitting checkpoints within the targeted time" for the city buses.
3. The new economic statistics "validated the essentiality of the President's struggle to cut the inflation rate."
4. "I cannot conceive of any scenario in which that could eventuate."
5. This product "does not appear to directly affect the integrity of the feto-placental unit."
   (*Hint:* That was taken from an advertisement describing for doctors a new abortion-inducing drug.)
6. "If we find the reasonable probability of repayment is slipping away from us, then, we'll have to respond in terms of extension of future credit."
   (*Hint:* Your banker might say this to you as a warning.)
7. All students need "experiential educational options that will maximize the personal value of their educational experience."
   (*Hint:* The director of a placement service wrote that.)

AVOIDING SEXIST LANGUAGE

In choosing words you should also be aware that some of your readers may be offended by sexist language. *Sexist* (a word coined by analogy with the now familiar word *racist*) means stereotyping females and males according to traditional roles. Linguists and psychologists agree that English reflects a male orientation that is ingrained in our society.

The He or She Dilemma

As it is sometimes awkward to repeatedly say *he or she, his or hers,* or *him or her,* the British Parliament decreed long ago that *he, his,* and *him* would include both sexes. That may sound reasonable, unless you are female or unless you have encountered William F. Buckley's extension of this principle. Buckley assures us: "The phrase 'will appeal to adventure-loving boys' is not an exclusionary phrase because the word 'boys' in this case means not only boys but also girls."[9] Most of us can at once see the injustice of that assertion because we have not been conditioned to accept *boys* to mean *girls,* as we have been to accept *he* to mean *she.*

[9] "Give the Lady an Inch," *Daily Pantagraph* [Bloomington], 13 July 1974, Sec. 1, p. 4, col. 4.

The Generic Man

To add to the difficulty, we also use the generic, or general term, *man* to mean both sexes, which sometimes leaves women out entirely (see *man/person* in Chapter 14). In his powerful novel *Invisible Man*, Ralph Ellison showed us that such invisibility lies at the heart of the problem of attaining true equality in society. And it does, as surely for women as for racial minorities. Consider, for instance, that famous declaration, "All men are created equal." We might assume that meant women also—but *did* it? At the time those words were written women were not allowed to vote and were held by law to be the property of their fathers or husbands. We can be certain that the word *man* does not always include women; thus its meaning is often ambiguous.

The All-Male Audience

Some writers—even recent ones—sound as if they are speaking to both sexes but in reality address themselves only to males. They give themselves away in subtle ways, usually through references to *wives*, which women never have. Here is Larry L. King writing about Bob Jones University: "By Jones' guidelines . . . the Bible is easier to offend than Maria Callas. Indeed your wife can offend the Book for you by wearing slacks or merely by griping."[10] In our local newspaper a reporter, reviewing supposedly for the whole community a summer theatre production, concluded this way: "Put the wife in the car and come out to spend an enjoyable evening in the park." We wonder whether the wife could not get into the car by herself—or whether she declined to go and had to be put in the car like the cat or the groceries.

Try the Plural

Probably the most useful strategy for eliminating male orientation in language is to write in the *plural*. Instead of writing

The applicant should mail *his* credentials promptly.

try

Applicants should mail *their* credentials promptly.

[10] "Bob Jones University: The Buckle on the Bible Belt," *Harper's*, June 1966, p. 53.

Both sexes really are included in the plural pronouns, *they/them/ their*. We are taught so early to write in the singular that we do so even when we *mean* the plural. For example, you may read

> The motorist must keep his eyes on the road.

What the writer really means is that *all* motorists must keep *their* eyes on the road. Writing in the singular is not an easy habit to break, but you can if you put your mind to it.

If you must write in the singular (and sometimes you may need to), go ahead and use an occasional *he or she* or *his or her*. The double pronoun has recently become standard usage again and really is not all that cumbersome—as long as you use it sparingly (see *he or she*, Chapter 14). Remember, if you can write what you want to say just as well in the plural, the problem disappears altogether. And once the problem disappears, women appear—no longer kept invisible behind the generic *man* and the masculine pronoun.

EXERCISE   2-13

See if you can eliminate all the sexist language from the following sentences without changing the meaning or causing awkwardness. We will do the first one for you.

1. Man must work in order to eat.

   Revised: One must work in order to eat.
               A person must work in order to eat.

2. Anyone with a brain in his head can see the dangers of utilizing atomic reactors.
3. The citizen may pay his water bill by mail or at the city hall.
4. The gregarious dog is man's best friend, but the more aloof cat keeps his own counsel.
5. He who laughs last laughs best.
6. "As long as man is on earth, he's likely to cause problems. But the man at General Electric will keep trying to find answers" [advertisement for GE].
7. Clyde was patched up by a lady doctor who stopped her car at the accident scene.
8. Gertie's mother is a computer repairman for IBM.
9. The hippopotamus is happiest when he is half submerged in mud.
10. The American pioneers loaded their wagons and moved their wives and children westward.

chapter Three
Writing Effective Sentences

Helen Hunt Jackson once wrote to her mentor, Thomas Wentworth Higginson, "I shall never write a sentence, so long as I live, without studying it over from the standpoint of whether you would think it could be bettered." An admirable aim for a writer. We urge you to take an interest in polishing each sentence to perfection. This chapter offers techniques to help you in composing as well as in revising your sentences.

PRACTICE WITH MODELS

Professional writers often consciously work at perfecting sentence structure by imitating eloquent passages from their extensive reading. Writers as diverse as Ben Jonson, Robert Louis Stevenson, Abraham Lincoln, Winston Churchill, and Somerset Maugham all practiced during their apprentice years by copying and imitating selections from accomplished stylists.

Classical rhetoricians knew the value of imitation centuries ago; composition specialists are once more recommending the technique. William Gruber attests that for his students, "The act of imitation became a tool to achieve individual freedom; instead of stifling personalities, it liberated them." But even if you do not intend to practice sentence modeling, you should still study this section carefully; it contains crucial information about devising effective sentences.

To begin model imitation, you should select a sentence or short paragraph you admire (or one that we have chosen for you) and copy it

---

[1] " 'Servile Copying' and the Teaching of English Composition," *College English*, 39 (Dec. 1977), 491.

precisely—right down to the commas, semicolons, dashes, and periods. Next, examine the model to discover how it is put together in order to discern its form. What are the linguistic devices that shape it? Does it use balanced phrases or clauses in series? Does it depend upon deliberate repetition of some word or element? Does it employ an inventory of details or examples? Does it marshal ideas one after another in order to achieve a point at the end? You are to discover the form and imitate it in a similar sentence using your own words and subject matter. Then, write ten more sentences just like it, changing the ideas each time. Hard work, we know, but in order to achieve a lasting effect upon your own prose you must reproduce each model repeatedly—just as you would practice a melody while learning to play a musical instrument.

In the following simple example, Michael Kernan describes the celebrated conductor, Leopold Stokowski:

> Again he clapped, the dry-handed clap that by now commanded instant attention.

The basic elements of that sentence can be illustrated this way:

> Again _____ , the _____
> that _____ .

Notice that part of the effectiveness of Kernan's sentence depends upon the deliberate repetition of the word *clap*. Try to include that repetition when you imitate the pattern. You might come up with a sentence like this:

> Again the warning system failed, the predictable failure that finally cost human lives.

Perhaps you noticed that imitation reverses the usual composing process in which writers begin with an idea and then try to find the best way to say it. But as Richard Graves points out, "Even though the activity seems alien, it is nevertheless valuable—like the batter swinging a weighted bat or the long-distance runner practicing with weights."[2] When you work with models, you are exercising your language faculties.

Although you must always be precise in copying the model, you need not always reproduce its structure as exactly as we did in our illustration. The important thing is to get the *feel* of it—to capture any distinctive features such as deliberate repetition, emphatic pauses,

---

[2] "Levels of Skill in the Composing Process," *Composition and Its Teaching,* Richard Gebhardt, ed. (Urbana IL: NTCE, 1979), p. 32.

symmetrical phrasings, or reversed patterns. No need to worry if you have no idea what makes phrases symmetrical or a pattern reversed: the beauty of imitation is that you can master an impressive rhetorical technique without even knowing the fancy name for it.

ACHIEVING VARIETY AND EMPHASIS

In order to become a competent stylist, you need a wide assortment of sentence structures at your command. First, you must be able to write good, everyday sentences, but then you must also be able to come up with impressive sentences to give variety to your writing and emphasis to your important points.

Loose Sentences

Most of the time people do not pay much attention to sentence structure as they write. They begin with their main idea and add details until they reach the end of the thought, where they put a period and start in on the next one. These everyday sentences—like the one we just wrote—are called *loose* (or *cumulative*) sentences and make up the bulk of most writing. The following loose sentence by George Orwell is ordinary in structure but remarkable in its specific details:

> He was a Hindu, a puny wisp of a man, with a shaven head and vague liquid eyes.

Here is another loose sentence, this one written by Philip Roth, illustrating a more complicated structure:

> Baseball was a kind of secular church that reached into every class and region of the nation and bound us together in common concerns, loyalties, rituals, enthusiasms, and antagonisms.

WRITING EXERCISE 3-1

Carefully copy Orwell's sentence. Now write ten of your own imitating this model. Try to choose details as effectively as Orwell does.

Periodic Sentences

Unlike loose sentences, which begin with the main idea, *periodic* sentences build to a big finish by saving the main idea until the end, just before the period. You can see the difference in these examples:

Cumulative: Seymour made the honor roll while holding down a part-time job and playing the lead in *Hamlet.*

Periodic: While holding down a part-time job and playing the lead in *Hamlet,* Seymour made the honor roll.

Cumulative: The students here are mostly moderates, though not all.

Periodic: The students here are mostly, though not all, moderates.

Cumulative: Our first consideration must be the preservation of our environment, even though preventing pollution costs money.

Periodic: Even though preventing pollution costs money, our first consideration must be the preservation of our environment.

E. B. White wrote the following periodic sentence to stress the impact of an emotion:

The memory of how apprehensive we were at the beginning is still strong.

Notice how the statement becomes limp if we turn it into a loose sentence:

The memory is still strong of how apprehensive we were at the beginning.

A more common type of periodic sentence involves putting the modifiers at the beginning and saving the main idea for the final clause, as Lewis Thomas does here:

If the earth were otherwise, and all the dying were done in the open, with the dead there to be looked at, we would never have it out of our minds.

You can see that you could not effectively use that unusual structure often. Save periodic sentences to achieve variety, to emphasize a point, to round out a paragraph, or to conclude an essay.

WRITING EXERCISE 3-2

Copy exactly the sentence by E. B. White; then write ten sentences of your own in imitation of it. Do the same using Dr. Thomas's sentence as a model. Notice that in White's statement the main idea ("the memory") appears at the beginning, but we are kept in suspense until the end to find out what about it (that it "is still strong"). With Dr. Thomas's somewhat less emphatic sentence the suspense lasts only until the final clause.

Balanced Structure

Another way to make your sentences emphatic and clear is to use *balanced* (or *parallel*) structure. Balanced sentences depend upon deliberate repetition—sometimes of the same words, always of the same grammatical structures: phrases, clauses, sometimes whole sentences.[3] We all remember Lincoln's "of the people, by the people, for the people," even if we have forgotten the rest of the famous Gettysburg address. Precisely balanced sentences are frequently memorable, always impressive. Virginia Woolf repeats the same adverb, changing only the verb each time to achieve this fine sentence:

> One cannot think well, love well, sleep well, if one has not dined well.

When we take away the specific verbs and remove the balanced elements, just consider the loss:

> One cannot function properly if one has not had a good dinner.

Mark Twain balances short independent clauses (simple sentences) for a comic effect in this line spoken by the first-person narrator of "A Dog's Tale":

> My father was a St. Bernard, my mother was a collie, but I am a Presbyterian.

In order to emphasize her astonishment at being favorably impressed upon meeting a famous woman she expected to dislike, Nora Ephron repeats almost exactly the same sentence three times:

> I did not expect to find her charming, and I did not expect to find her canny, and I certainly did not expect to find her moving. All of which she was.

---

[3] If you are hazy about the differences between phrases and clauses, remember that a clause has both a subject and a verb, and a phrase does not have both.

Phrases: having lost my head
             to lose my head
             after losing my head
Clauses: after I lost my head
             I lost my head
             that I lost my head

Infinitive and gerund phrases can have a subject but will not have a finite verb:

[The negatives to be developed] are on the desk.
[The film being shown] is a classic.

Each bracketed phrase functions as the subject of its sentence. The subject within the phrase is underlined.

Of course, Ephron changes each time the important adjective at the end (*charming, canny, moving*), but notice how emphatic the word *certainly* becomes when she uses it to interrupt the established pattern in the third repetition. The sentence fragment ("All of which she was") that follows the much longer statement is effective for similar reasons: its brevity is unexpected and its structure is reversed. The most common sentence pattern in English is

subject → verb → complement

but Ephron's fragment presents instead

complement → subject → verb

We will have more advice for you later about ways to achieve emphasis through variety, but first you should practice writing sentences that are balanced through deliberate repetition.

WRITING EXERCISE   **3-3**

1. Copy Woolf's sentence exactly; then, changing the subject matter, write three similar ones of your own, beginning (as she does) with the formal third person pronoun, *one*. Then, using different subject matter, write three sentences employing the less formal first person pronoun, *I* or *we*. Do the same thing yet again, but in your last three sentences begin with the highly informal second person pronoun, *you*.
2. Copy Twain's sentence precisely. Then, following his model, write two sentences of your own: one serious, the other humorous. You will, naturally, need to find appropriate subject matter in order to achieve the desired effect.

Practical Patterns. Nora Ephron's pattern of pointed repetition and reversal, although forceful, is perhaps too dramatic to be useful in everyday writing that would be required in reports, case studies, proposals, business letters, and the like. Here is a more practical sentence composed by Richard Lloyd-Jones that achieves the same emphatic purpose with admirable grace:

The point, however, is not so much discovering the new but noticing the old.

The ability to write such sentences in which you emphasize an idea through contrast with another is essential to good writing.

Another practical use of balanced structure involves putting items in series, but not necessarily with the dazzle of the models by Woolf, Twain, and Ephron. Here is a sentence from George Orwell that illustrates this fundamental technique:

> At each step his muscles slid neatly into place, the lock of hair on his scalp danced up and down, his feet printed themselves on the wet gravel.

Orwell's sentence seems less emphatic than those previous models because the elements in series here, while balanced, are not *precisely* balanced. Notice, though, that the key grammatical elements follow exactly the same pattern (pronoun/noun/verb):

his	muscles	slid
the	lock	danced
his	feet	printed

WRITING EXERCISE   3-4

1. Copy carefully the sentence by Richard Lloyd-Jones. The structure is essentially this:

   The _____ , however, is not _____
   _____ but _____ .

   First, write five sentences following this model, beginning with "The issue" or "The problem" or "The reason." Then follow the model five more times specifically *stating* your point, your issue, or your problem, like this:

   The major problem with grade inflation, however, is not that inept students are receiving passing grades but that good students are no longer receiving due recognition.

2. Copy Orwell's sentence exactly. Then write five sentences with the same basic structure using your own subject matter. The pattern of balanced elements is the thing you need to reproduce. After you have written those sentences, write five more copying the model, but this time insert the conjunction *and* after the second comma (before the last item in series).

Balance in Paragraphs.   Once you become skillful at maintaining balanced structure, you can use the technique to good effect in separate sentences by repeating the same grammatical structure in each sentence. As this cumulative balancing involves building to a climax, you will not be able to use it often, but the results are impressive if well done. Here is Pastor Martin Niemoeller, a Lutheran minister, explaining how he ended up in a Nazi concentration camp during World War II:

> In Germany, the Nazis first came for the Communists, and I didn't speak up because I wasn't a Communist. Then they came for the Jews, and I didn't speak up because I wasn't a Jew. Then they came for the trade unionists, and I didn't speak up because I wasn't a trade unionist. Then they came for the Catholics, and I didn't speak up because I was a Protestant. Then they came for me, and by that time there was no one left to speak for me.

Notice that the pattern Niemoeller repeats is basically just this:

_____ , and _____
because _____ . Then. . . .

Each sentence is attached to the previous one with the same connective, *then*. The eloquence derives from the simplicity of the deliberate repetition and, of course, from the force of his meaning.

In a structure somewhat more complicated, Maya Angelou repeats balanced introductory clauses, each beginning with *because*, in order to emphasize the reasons she formerly undervalued the virtues of her race:

> Because Southern black people move slowly, I was quick to think they did not move at all. Because many Southern black people speak in black English, I had taken too lightly the wisdom of their words. Because Southern black Americans had employed a gargantuan patience, I had not fully appreciated the splendor of their survival.

(For an example of balanced sentences as a means of achieving coherence between paragraphs, see page 102.)

WRITING EXERCISE 3-5

1. Copy Niemoeller's paragraph exactly. Then choose appropriate subject matter and write one of your own just like it in structure. Try to match his simplicity of language and make your ideas build to a climax as he does.
2. Copy Angelou's paragraph carefully. Then, using your own subject matter, write a paragraph that follows her model. Be sure to begin each sentence with the same word, and try to end your last sentence with a phrase as resounding as Angelou's "the splendor of their survival."

Deliberate Repetition

We have, of course, been discussing deliberate repetition since the beginning of this chapter in our advice about balanced structure. But occasionally you may want to repeat the same term for emphasis, as H. L. Mencken does with *some* in his definition of a puritan as "someone who fears that somebody, somewhere, somehow might be happy." Katherine Anne Porter, a master of deliberate repetition, here writes of her response to a bullfight:

> But this had death in it, and it was the death in it that I loved.

You have only to remove the repetition to see its value:

> But I loved the death that this had in it.

One caution, though, about repeating words: be sure that the word deserves emphasis and be doubly sure that you have repeated it on purpose.

Breaking the Pattern

Several times we have mentioned that you can achieve emphasis by doing the unexpected. Part of the effectiveness of balanced structures depends upon their being different from the ordinary sentences that people write. Following are several less complex ways to gain emphasis by departing from the usual patterns.

Try a Short Short Sentence.   Really short sentences—from two to six words—are easy to write and catch your readers' attention because they are abrupt. Notice how well John Hurt Fisher makes his point in the short sentence following one of normal length:

> Webster's dictionaries and the endless multiplication of handbooks and courses in English composition represent a desperate effort to prevent class distinction from revealing itself in language. And, of course, it has failed.

Jessie Birnbaum, writing in *Time* magazine, uses the same technique:

> Cavett's purpose was to ensure that I would suffer all the shocks, surprises, pitfalls, and confusions that afflict the host five shows a week. He succeeded.

Here Jane Howard reverses the procedure and puts her short sentence first—a single word, in fact—followed by sentences increasing in length:

> Dread. Now that's more like it. Dread comes closer to what makes a family a family.

Mark Twain uses yet another variation by putting three short, balanced sentences together in a series:

> The humorous story is American, the comic story is English, the witty story is French.

Remember that short sentences, like all emphatic constructions, will lose their impact if used too often.

WRITING EXERCISE   3-7

1. Copy Birnbaum's sentences precisely. Then, changing the subject matter, write two sentences of your own (a long one followed by a short one) imitating his. Use your second short sentence to reinforce—or contradict— the idea in your long sentence. Repeat the process ten times.
2. Copy Twain's sentence carefully. Think of something about which you have three things to say or something that you can divide into three parts. Then write three short, balanced clauses of your own in imitation of Twain's. Repeat the process ten times.

Use *Ands* to Separate a Series.   Most of the time people use commas to separate items in a series, as Mark Twain does in this sentence:

> Drays, carts, men, boys, all go hurrying from many quarters to a common center, the wharf.

Twain's brisk sentence is perfect for the bustle he is describing. If you would write a more stately sentence, a sentence that will be arresting because it is unusual, try replacing the usual commas with *ands* as William Faulkner does in defining the duty of a serious writer:

> It is his privilege to help man endure by lifting his heart, by reminding him of the courage and honor and hope and pride and compassion and pity and sacrifice which have been the glory of his past.

Here is a less lofty example from Rachel Carson:

> A child's world is fresh and new and beautiful, full of wonder and excitement.

The simplicity of Carson's language and sentence structure perfectly convey the qualities of innocence she describes.

WRITING EXERCISE 3-8

Copy Carson's sentence exactly. Then write a sentence of your own with the same structure. When you choose your subject matter, try to select something that merits emphasis. If you love music, you might write this:

> The first symphony is joyful and vibrant and sensuous, laced with counterpoint and arpeggios.

If you are an environmentalist, you might come up with something more like this:

> The American coyote is threatened by drought and starvation and poisons and rifles, hunted for bounty and faced with extinction.

Be sure that the elements connected by *and* following the comma are balanced in structure. Repeat the process ten times.

Experiment with the Dash. Because the end of a sentence is an emphatic position, you can use a dash there to good advantage. You can tack on an afterthought, as Kenneth S. Lynn does in this sentence:

> For one thing, he *looked* as if the world were his oyster—partly because he was eating so many of them in cream sauce late at night.

The dash is most useful for reinforcement of ideas or for elaboration, as Elizabeth Hardwick employs it here:

> That's what revision is—learning how to write.

And Colin Fletcher here:

> After all, there had been no drama—no ferocious snarling, no skirmish in the dust, no sudden slaughter.

And Martin Gansberg:

> He stabbed her a third time—fatally.

You can also produce considerable emphasis by interrupting the normal flow of your sentence with material set off by dashes, as George F. Will does:

> The trial allowed—indeed, required—a jury to pick between numerous flatly incompatible theories spun by credentialed "experts."

Using dashes to set off material in midsentence can simply be a handy way of sneaking in a definition or some other crucial piece of information, as Milton Friedman does:

> The real interest rate—the difference between the nominal rate and the rate of inflation—has averaged about 3 to 4 percent over long periods.

Like short sentences, dashes lose their effect if used too often. Do not become so enamored of this deft mark of punctuation that you sprinkle your pages with them.

WRITING EXERCISE   3-9

1. Copy Hardwick's sentence precisely. Then write ten of your own. Begin with a simple statement which needs explaining and use a dash to emphasize your explanation.
2. Copy Will's sentence with care. Then think of different topics and write ten like it, interrupting with intensifiers set off by dashes, as he does.
3. Copy exactly Friedman's sentence. Write ten of your own just like it, inserting between dashes a brief definition or some qualification of the idea in your main statement.

CUMULATIVE EXERCISE   3-10

If you want to be an adept writer, you will profit from imitating models as much as possible. Here are additional sentences for you to practice on. By now you know the instructions: carefully copy the model sentence; then think of your own subject matter and write ten sentences of your own like the model in structure.

Because model imitation is taxing work, we suggest that you do only one or two groups of sentences at a time. You will likely exhaust your powers of concentration and invention if you stay at the task too long. The exercise may require several weeks to complete.

1. Violence is immoral because it thrives on hatred rather than love.   (Martin Luther King)
2. Whenever something is gained, something is lost.   (Carll Tucker)
3. He learned fast, kept well, and we were satisfied.   (E. B. White)

4. All of the children had their own table in a small parlor and ate just what the grownups had: Kentucky ham, roast turkey, partridges in wine jelly, fried chicken, dove pie, half a dozen sweet and hot sauces, peach pickle, watermelon pickle and spiced mangoes.   (Katherine Anne Porter)

5. The refrigerator was full of sulfurous scraps, dark crusts, furry oddments. (Alice Munro)

6. His grey flannel shirt stuck to him, his heavy shoes were dusty. (Katherine Anne Porter)

7. But as I studied the salmon around the world I could only wish that more people thought about this: a world in which salmon cannot live may be a world in which mankind cannot live either.   (Anthony Netboy)

8. When a man wantonly destroys one of the works of man, we call him "vandal." When he wantonly destroys one of the works of God, we call him "sportsman."   (Joseph Wood Krutch)

9. It is sober without being dull; massive without being oppressive.   (Sir Kenneth Clark)

10. For so long as these laws stand, we will not be able to live—indeed, many of us will not want to live—as citizens in a free society.   (Thomas Szasz)

TRY SENTENCE COMBINING

Now that you have practiced forming sentences by following models, you need to boldly strike out and compose your own sentences, relying on the intuition you now have for putting words, phrases, and clauses together with skill and style.

Using Coordination and Subordination

Throughout our discussion of balanced structure, we were offering advice about *coordination*—linking similar structures together. But excessive coordination without the sophistication of deliberate structuring is far from effective. In fact, when small children talk, they tend to string simple sentences together using primitive coordination, like this:

> We got hats and balloons and Buffy got presents and Angie was late and we had cake with candles and ice cream and I blew my balloon up big and. . . .

So it goes, on and on and on, with little variety, few modifiers, and no distinction between important ideas and passing details.

By the time we reach the third grade or so, we learn to put our sentences together in more complicated patterns which depend upon *subordination,* as well as coordination. Subordination involves tucking less important ideas into dependent (or subordinate) clauses and small details into phrases. Thus our major ideas are usually expressed in *independent* or main clauses, where they receive proper notice. (If you are in doubt about what makes a clause dependent or independent, consult pages 360–365.

Most of this subordinating of details and ideas into phrases and clauses we do automatically. For instance, what if we wanted to incorporate into a single sentence the following ideas?

> I baked a cake.
> I did it this afternoon.
> It fell.
> It was flat.

Scarcely giving the matter a thought, we would write:

> I baked a cake this afternoon and it fell flat.

But we would then tighten up the sentence this way:

> The cake that I baked this afternoon fell flat.

In that revision, we subordinated the unimportant idea of the cake's being baked (after all, how many ways are there to cook a cake?) by slipping that information into a dependent clause:

> [that I baked].

Types of Sentences.   In order to explain a few ways to achieve a pleasing variety in your sentence structure, we need to remind you of the terminology you learned in seventh grade to describe the four basic types of sentences: simple, compound, complex, and compound-complex. (If your memory is fuzzy on these terms, look up *Sentence Types* in Chapter 13, the "Revising Index.")

Remember that *compound* sentences are nothing more than simple sentences attached by a conjunction or a semicolon:

> Our dog Bowser fancies himself a mighty hunter, but he has yet to catch so much as a butterfly.

You can get more variety out of *complex* sentences because you can move the clauses around, like this:

> Although our dog Bowser fancies himself a mighty hunter, he has yet to catch so much as a butterfly.

Although he has yet to catch so much as a butterfly, our dog Bowser fancies himself a mighty hunter.

Our dog Bowser, who fancies himself a mighty hunter, has yet to catch so much as a butterfly.

Even the simple sentence has considerable potential for variety. You just change the basic pattern, which in English is *subject,* then *verb,* then *complement:*

> *subj.   verb   compl.*
> Bowser fancies himself a mighty hunter.

You get a variation by phrasing a question:

> *verb   subj.   verb   compl.*
> Does Bowser fancy himself a mighty hunter?

But consider what a rousing sentence you get by putting most of the complement at the beginning:

> *compl.   subj.   verb   i. obj.*
> A mighty hunter Bowser fancies himself.

Take care with that last variation. You get a lot of emphasis because the pattern is seldom used. Make sure the content deserves the attention.

Fashioning Good Sentences.   Whenever you discover while revising that you have written two, perhaps three short sentences beginning with the same word—or with a pronoun referring to that word— you may do well to combine the sentences. If you find yourself repeating a word unnecessarily, consider sentence combining to get rid of the problem. You have a number of techniques at your disposal. We will begin with some extremely simple ones.

I. You can compress a simple sentence into a single word.
   A. **As an adjective:**
      Doris bought a motorcycle.
      It is maroon.
   Doris bought a maroon motorcycle.
   B. **As a compound adjective:**
      Fred is cleaning his yard.
      His yard is cluttered with trash.
   Fred is cleaning his trash-cluttered yard.

C. **As an adverb:**

Becky argued with Brad.
It was a brief argument.
Becky argued briefly with Brad.

D. **As a participle** (a descriptive modifier ending in *-ing* or *-ed*):

(*-ing*)　　Sam stirred the soup.
present　It was boiling.
Sam stirred the boiling soup.
(*-ed*)　　High in the oak tree is a squirrel's nest.
past　　The squirrels have abandoned it.
High in the oak tree is an abandoned squirrel's nest.

E. **As a gerund** (a naming word ending in *-ing*):

Many people have taken up a fad these days.
They do exercises.
Exercising has become a fad with many people these days.

II. You can embed a sentence as a phrase.

A. **A prepositional phrase:**

Larry sets tile.
He does it with great skill.
Larry sets tile with great skill.

B. **An appositive phrase:**

Dr. Cooley is a pioneer in transplant surgery.
He is a famous heart specialist.
Dr. Cooley, a famous heart specialist, is a pioneer in transplant surgery.

C. **A participial phrase:**

(*-ing*)　　The movie I saw on TV was a sentimental tear-jerker.
　　　　　Lassie was its star.
The movie I saw on TV starring Lassie was a sentimental tear-jerker.
(*-ed*)　　The announcement looked foreboding.
　　　　　It had a black border.
The announcement, bordered in black, looked foreboding.

D. **A gerund phrase:**

Marty is trying to learn Italian.
He is finding it difficult.
Learning Italian is difficult for Marty.

E. **An infinitive phrase:**

The test will be given on Tuesday.
It is designed to measure proficiency in writing.
The test designed to measure proficiency in writing will be given on Tuesday.

III. You can embed clauses using *who, whom, whose, which, that, when,* or *where.*

A. **Who:**

People often drive automobiles carelessly.
Many joggers think these people are trying to kill them.
Many joggers think people who drive automobiles carelessly are trying to kill them.

B. Whom:
      Nadene is the person I want to invite.
      I like her.
Nadene, whom I like, is the person I want to invite.

C. Whose:
      Mickey is the one I want to invite.
      I enjoy her company.
Mickey, whose company I enjoy, is the one I want to invite.

D. Which:
      Clyde won a pet python.
      He was not allowed to keep it, though.
Clyde won a pet python, which he was not allowed to keep.

E. That:
      Everything was lost in the fire.
      I owned all of it.
Everything that I owned was lost in the fire.

F. When:
      Our jeans were drenched.
      We got wet when the basement flooded.
Our jeans were drenched when the basement flooded.

G. Where:
      The Campus Cafe is a congenial place.
      Calhoun works there.
The Campus Cafe where Calhoun works is a congenial place.

Accomplished writers often use several of these techniques in crafting a graceful, sophisticated sentence. With practice you can soon be doing the same—phrasing and rephrasing each sentence until you strike the perfect combination of sound and sense, of economy and fluency.

But remember. **Achieving clarity remains the most important consideration in writing expository prose.**

Do not get so enthusiastic in your use of subordination that you try to compress too much into a single sentence and thus obscure the meaning.

Below are ten groups of short statements for you to use in practicing sentence combining. We devised these sentence groups by taking apart excellent sentences composed by professional writers (who are identified each time in parentheses). The original versions appear in the instructor's manual. After you have finished the exercise, perhaps your teacher will allow you to compare your sentences with those of the experts.

Combine each group into a single sentence. Then try to turn that sentence into a complex sentence. Select the most important idea and put that in the main clause. Then, after eliminating any *needless* repetition of words or ideas, subordinate the less important details as single-word modifiers, phrases, dependent clauses. You can, of course, use repetition deliberately for emphasis. If you think a group contains two equally important ideas, write a compound-complex sentence. Try to end up with a sentence you are proud of.

We will do the first one to be sure you have the idea.

1. In Europe the medieval peasants were in bad shape physically.
   They were distracted by war.
   They were weakened by malnutrition.
   They were exhausted by the struggle to win a living.
   Their portion of land was always inadequate.
   The soil was ever less fertile.
   They were easy prey for the Black Death.

Your first version might come out like this:

> In Europe the medieval peasants were in bad shape physically—distracted by war, weakened by malnutrition, and exhausted by the struggle to win a living since their portion of land was always inadequate and ever less fertile; they were easy prey for the Black Death.

Not bad. That sentence is perfectly respectable. But if you continue to look for repetition and for ways to further combine the structures, you might turn out a finished product like this (which happens to be quite close to the original sentence by Philip Zeigler that we hacked to pieces):

> In Europe the medieval peasants—distracted by war, weakened by malnutrition, exhausted by their struggle to win a living from their inadequate portion of ever less fertile land—were physically an easy prey for the Black Death.

2. The sun is that friendly lamp in the sky.
   It is a familiar lamp.
   It provides us with warmth and daylight.
   It provides night-light, too, for that matter.
   The night-light is its glow reflected off the moon.

(Albert Rosenfeld)

3. Hitler used to live in Munich.
   He began his rise to power there.
   He carried a riding whip always.
   It was heavy.
   It was made of hippopotamus hide.

(Alan Bullock)

4. There is a tiny beetle.
It lies dead in your path.
It was a living creature.
It once was struggling for existence like yourself.
It was once rejoicing in the sun like you.
It once knew fear and pain like you.

(Albert Schweitzer)

5. The Globe theatre was rebuilt.
The new building was located in a disreputable borough.
This borough was officially named The Clink.
It was famous for its profusion of brothels.
It also had many tenements, theatres, and prisons.

(from *Life* magazine)

6. English is a relatively uninflected language.
In English we need to pay attention to the conjugation of the verb.
And we need to pay attention to the number of the noun.
We need to consider the degree of the adjective.

(Mortimer Adler)

7. Male giraffes live in bachelor herds.
They live in these herds until they are fully grown.
They are fully grown at about seven years of age.
By then they are 17 to 19 feet tall.
They weigh a ton or more.

(George W. Frame)

8. J. B. Gurdon is a scientist at Oxford University.
He inserted the nuclei of human cancer cells into frog eggs.
The frog eggs were immature.
The human cell nuclei responded in dramatic fashion.
They swelled in size to as much as a hundredfold.

(Caryl Rivers)

9. Sonar eyeglasses are designed to help blind people.
These glasses have three disks mounted in the bridge.
The disks send and receive ultrasound.
Ultrasound is sound pitched extremely high.
It is pitched so high that it cannot be heard.

(Jacqueline Harris)

10. My theory is this.
The lake waters continue to recede.
The competition for food daily grows more keen.
The trout leave the cool depths.
I suspect they normally dwell in the depths.
They range out in search of food.
They try to avoid the ever-narrowing proximity with the bass.

(Robert Traver)

CULTIVATE EDITING SKILLS

All along we have stressed revising as one of the most important parts of the writing process. Now we have for you some concrete advice—tips for tidying your sentences, pointers for polishing your prose.

Revise for Wordiness

When you revise, try to make your writing clean, clear, and concise—within reason, of course. You need not be as abrupt as Calvin Coolidge. Grace Coolidge had to miss church one Sunday, and when her husband returned she asked him what the sermon was about. "Sin," he replied. Pressed to explain what the preacher said about sin, President Coolidge replied, "He was against it." That is concise, all right, but Mrs. Coolidge no doubt hoped for more.

Mostly you need to guard against just plain lazy wordiness. In *Provincial Letters* (1657) Pascal wrote, "I have made this letter longer than usual because I lack the time to make it shorter." And Hugh Henry Brackenridge observed in *Modern Chivalry* (1792), "In order to speak short on any subject, think long." Nothing will annoy readers more than having to waste their time plowing through a cluttered paragraph because you neglected to spend your time cleaning it up. Be diligent and prune your prose. Take out all the unnecessary words. Sentences like the following are bound to irritate any reader:

> It is believed by a number of persons in this country that the young people of today do not assume as much responsibility toward society as it might be hoped that they would. (33 words)

You can say the same thing better with fewer words:

> Today many believe that our young people assume too little responsibility toward society. (13 words)

Eliminate Redundancies. Be on the lookout for a special kind of wordiness called *redundancy,* which means saying the same thing twice—like *most unique.* Because the word *unique* means "without equal," you cannot legitimately qualify it. Such phrases can sneak by because they often sound quite grand. But pay attention to meaning, and you will notice that the following familiar phrases[4] all repeat the same idea:

---

[4] We borrowed this list from "Expressions to Avoid in Proposal Writing," *Academe* (March 1980), p. 116.

absolutely essential	green in color
audible to the ear	join together
circle around	necessary essentials
combine together	period of time
complete absence	point in time
completely unanimous	reason is because
continue on	refer back
example to illustrate	small in size
few in number	summarize briefly
general consensus	true fact

Avoid Needless Repetition. Deliberate repetition, as we have pointed out at length, can be one of your most effective devices, but careless repetition may offend your readers as much as wordiness. Ineffective repetition is often the result of thoughtlessness, as in this student's sentence:

> Walking up to the door, I came upon the skeleton head of a cow placed next to the door.

That is too many *to the door* phrases. Just changing the first phrase solves the problem:

> Walking up to the house, I came upon the skeleton head of a cow placed next to the door.

Be sure to eliminate any word or phrase that you have carelessly used twice.

EXERCISE 3-12

Sharpen your editing skills by tidying the following littered sentences. Try to keep the same meaning but eliminate all unnecessary wordiness. We will show you how with the first one.

1. It has been in the most recent past that many different groups of citizens have joined together in completely unanimous protest against the concept of nuclear war.

   Revised: Recently many groups have joined in unanimous protest against nuclear war.

2. It is my desire to be called Ishmael.
3. There is a general consensus that the paper which is judged to be the most original should be awarded the prize.

4. By and large a stitch sewed or basted as soon as a rip is discovered may well save nine times the amount of sewing necessary if the job is put off even for a short time.
5. Let me cite an example to illustrate the problem.
6. We finally selected a desk that was small in size and grey in color.
7. The participants who engage in polo playing seem to be few in number.
8. It is absolutely essential that we do something about the complete absence of members of minority groups among the members of this important committee.
9. The reason that I think we should postpone our decision on this problem is because this problem is a complex matter.
10. There was a feeling, at least on my part, based upon a number of true facts that I had been reading, that the food that we buy at the supermarket to eat may be poisoned with food additives.

Change to Active Voice. If your writing is generally lifeless, turgid, and wordy, the *passive voice* may be the culprit. The passive construction (in which the subject is acted upon instead of doing the acting) is less economical than active voice in conveying the same information:

Passive: Because patriotism was lacking in their hearts, the battle was lost by the mercenaries.
(14 words)
Active: Because their hearts lacked patriotism, the mercenaries lost the battle.
(10 words)

That is not many extra words, we grant, but if you add only a couple of unnecessary words to each sentence in a paper, you will seriously pollute your prose.

Even when not wordy, the passive leaves out information—sometimes essential information. Take this typical concise passive construction:

The prisoner was fed.

That is not an objectionable sentence. Nobody is perishing to know who fed the prisoner. But consider the same sentence with only one word changed:

The prisoner was beaten.

At once we want to know *by whom?* By the sheriff? By one of the deputies? By a guard? By a fellow prisoner? There is no way to tell from the passive construction. In his article "Watergate Lingo," Richard Gambino observes, "The effect of the habitual use of the passive is to create an illusory animistic world where events have lives, wills, motives, and actions of their own without any human being responsible for them."

Notice that the *habitual use of the passive* is treacherous. We do not mean that you should never use the passive voice. Sometimes it is the best way to convey information. You would likely choose the passive, "The President was elected by a comfortable majority," rather than the active, "A comfortable majority elected the President." No reader will be troubled by not being told who elected the President because everyone knows that the voters do the electing.

EXERCISE   3-13

Rewrite the following passive sentences in the active voice and eliminate any wordiness. We will get you started by doing the first one.

1. An empty disposable lighter is used by folksinger Utah Phillips to store kitchen matches in.

   Revised: Folksinger Utah Phillips stores kitchen matches in an empty disposable lighter.

2. Several disposable lighters were lost by Seymour last week.
3. It is probable that matches should be used by people who often lose things.
4. Matchbooks have been found to be more versatile than disposable lighters by some people.
5. No opportunities to become electricians, locksmiths, and engineers are offered by disposable lighters.
6. How many matches are left in a book can be easily seen by the match-user.
7. Let our daily bread be given to us this day.
8. It was stated by the author in the introduction that several approaches to grammar would be discussed.
9. Several secondary sources were studied in order to gain additional information for my paper.
10. The demand for shirts bearing alligators has been artificially stimulated by advertising.

Practice the Passive.   Despite all our warnings against habitual use of the passive, we are aware that writers in a number of jobs and in some academic disciplines are expected—even required—to use the passive voice. If you are taking courses in education, corrections, or any of the hard sciences (chemistry, biology, physics, and the like), you must learn to write gracefully in the passive voice. It can be done. But you will need to practice diligently.

Proceeding from the pen of an accomplished writer, the passive voice is not in the least objectionable. Jessica Mitford, for one, employs the passive so skillfully that you never notice its presence:

> Today, family members who might wish to be in attendance would certainly be dissuaded by the funeral director.

That sentence will not be noticeably improved by making it active voice:

> Today the funeral director would certainly dissuade family members who might wish to be in attendance.

In order to help you perfect your use of the passive, we have collected some useful and fairly simple sentences as models. If you must become a practitioner of the passive, you would do well to work this exercise twice, thinking of different material to use the second time.

WRITING EXERCISE 3-14

Copy each sentence carefully. Then, choosing subject matter from your academic major, write five sentences imitating the structure of each the originals. Work on them a few at a time. Do two or three, take a break, then come back and do some more. We will do the first one.

1. Certain things were not mentioned.   (Jane O'Reilly)

Imitations: Synthetic fertilizers were not unknown.
Pesticides were not advised.
Crop rotation was not used.
Early harvesting was not recommended.
Organic methods were not tried.

2. The entire body of a tarantula, especially its legs, is thickly clothed with hair.   (Alexander Petrunkevitch)

3. All others, except apprentices, are excluded by law from the preparation room.   (Jessica Mitford)

4. The poor are slated to take the brunt of the federal budget cuts.   (Barbara Ehrenreich)

5. The SKIP option can be used in input and output statements.   (J. S. Roper)

6. The emphasis is generally put on the right to speak.   (Walter Lippmann)

7. This could be done either by the accumulation of observed evidence or by mathematics.   (Sir Kenneth Clark)

8. But—poor little thing—the boundary ought in its turn to be protected.   (E. M. Forster)

Repair Flawed Sentences

Richard Graves believes that revising faulty sentences requires "a higher level of skill than sentence combining."[5] Certainly many people have difficulty in seeing their mistakes. Yet nothing is more important in the editing process than discovering sentence flaws and correcting them.

Balance Coordinate Elements.

You know about balancing elements to produce impressive sentences, but the technique is also fundamental to all good writing. If you by chance put together a sentence involving two similar elements or a series of them, your readers *expect* these similar parts to be balanced (or parallel). Such a structure may occur whenever you join parts of sentences with any of the coordinating conjunctions (*and, but, or, for, nor, yet, so*).

Consider the problem first in this simple example:

Clyde likes *to swim* and *water skiing.*

Your readers expect those italicized parts to sound alike, to be balanced in construction, like this:

Clyde likes *to swim* and *water ski.*

with *to* understood before *water ski;* or

Clyde likes *swimming* and *water skiing.*

Now look at a more typical example—the kind of sentence you are likely to write in a hurry and should work into balanced structure when you revise:

The plan is not workable: it delegates a dangerous amount of power to the government, and because it is unconstitutional.

That sentence contains three clauses in series, all of which should be balanced. The first two are both independent clauses (subjects are underlined once, verbs twice):

the plan is not workable
it delegates a dangerous amount of power to the government

Fine so far. The clauses do not have to be precisely parallel as long as the basic pattern (in this case *subject* → *verb* → *complement*) is the

[5] "Levels of Skill in the Composing Process," p. 32.

same. The trouble comes in the third clause, which is not independent but dependent (beginning with the subordinating word *because*):

> because it is unconstitutional

Probably the easiest way to revise the sentence is to make all three clauses independent by dropping the subordinating word *because:*

> *Revised:* The plan is not workable: it delegates a dangerous amount of power to the government, and it is unconstitutional.

You could also make both the second and third clauses dependent, and hence balanced, by adding another *because:*

> *Revised:* The plan is not workable because it delegates a dangerous amount of power to the government and because it is unconstitutional.

Usually there are several ways to restore balance to sentences, all of which are equally good. In order to increase your editorial skills, try your hand at repairing the following faulty sentences.

EXERCISE 3-15

The following sentences were written by students whose grasp of parallel structure was less than perfect. We want you to restore the balance. Do not aim for impressive, emphatic sentences in this exercise. Just try to produce good, clear, everyday sentences.

First, read each sentence and decide which parts need to be parallel. Look for elements in series and phrases or clauses connected by coordinating conjunctions (*and, but, or, for, nor, yet, so*). Then, change the part that is irregular so that its grammatical structure matches the structure of the coordinate parts. We will do one first to show you the technique.

1. Politicians face the difficult tasks of solving urban problems and how to find the money without raising taxes.

Here you need to balance the two grammatical structures connected by *and*—*solving* urban problems and *how to find* the money. The easiest way is to make *how to find* sound like *solving*—that is, use *finding:*

> *Revised:* Politicians today face the difficult tasks of *solving* urban problems and *finding* the money without raising taxes.

You could also make both elements begin with *how to:*

> *Revised:* Politicians today face two difficult tasks: *how to* solve urban problems and *how to* find the money without raising taxes.

2. This group is knowledgeable about lane conditions and choosing the proper bowling ball.
3. Roommates tell each other everything—even about grades or who they have a crush on.
4. In the movies all college men are portrayed as single and having other attractions, such as money, good-looking, and a great personality.
5. Progressive education teaches children to be open-minded, self-disciplined, and how to do logical thinking.

Straighten Out Confused Sentences

Some sentence errors are impossible to categorize as anything other than messed up. And they are the worst kind because they make no sense. These semantic disasters are sometimes called—for lack of a better term—*mixed constructions.* They apparently result when the writer begins to say something one way, loses track in the middle, and finishes another way. Nobody knows how they actually happen because the students who write them are more surprised than anybody when confronted with these prodigies. These are the kinds of sentences that make readers do a double take—we shake our heads, rub our eyes, and read them again, hoping for a better connection. But we never get it from mix-ups like these:

> When students have no time for study or moral training also breeds a decadent society.

> The first planned crime will tell how well a boy has learned whether or not he is caught to become a juvenile delinquent.

Those are pretty hopeless cases. They need to be scrapped. You will lose more time trying to patch up a troublesome sentence than you will by backing off and beginning in a different way. Take that last example. It needs a completely different beginning—something like this:

> *Revised:* Whether or not he is caught in his first planned crime may determine whether a boy will become a juvenile delinquent.

Occasionally a confused sentence can be easily revised, like this one:

> When frequently opening and closing the oven door, it can cause a soufflé to fall.

All you need to do to correct that one is scratch out the *when,* the *it,* and the comma:

> *Revised:* Frequently opening and closing the oven door can cause a soufflé to fall.

These mixed constructions seem to reflect varying degrees of illiteracy, but we imagine they usually result from nothing but sheer, unpardonable carelessness. For this reason, we urge you to edit carefully. Pay close attention so that these linguistic misfortunes will not slip by you.

EXERCISE   **3-16**

Try to straighten out the following mixed constructions. Some of them cannot be easily patched up: you need to back off and begin in a different way. We will revise the first one.

1. Sherry, hoping to find a job that interests her, and so she doesn't have to type.

   Revised: Sherry is hoping to find a job that interests her—one that doesn't involve typing.
   Revised: Sherry is hoping to find an interesting job in which she doesn't have to type.

2. The Rites of Spring festival has been postponed because of too many students are sick with the flu.
3. Marijuana users should stop being made into criminals.
4. Only through constant study will achieve academic excellence.
5. In time of crisis must be handled with cool judgment.

WRITING EXERCISE   **3-17**

Write a paragraph entitled "How I Relax." When you revise, check for active voice, conciseness, specific details, concrete examples, vivid word choice, and balanced structure.

COMPREHENSIVE DISCUSSION EXERCISE   **3-18**

On pages 117–118 you will find five paragraphs for analysis. Examine the construction of the individual sentences within these paragraphs.

1. What words in paragraphs b and c do you consider especially vivid? What specific details make the passages appealing?
2. In paragraphs a and e do you find any deliberate repetition of either words or structure? For what purpose is this repetition used? Emphasis? Tone? Clarity? Elegance? Is it effective?
3. Discuss the stylistic effect of Lawrence's long and short sentences in paragraph e. In paragraph d, what does Twain achieve by using the short sentence at the end?

chapter Four
Writing Proficient Paragraphs

Defining the term "paragraph" is next to impossible unless you understand the southern term "mess," a unit of measure meaning "just the right amount of something"—as in "a <u>mess</u> of black eyed peas," "a <u>mess</u> of fried chicken." Once you understand this word, we can explain that a paragraph is a mess of sentences about a single topic. Occasionally, though, for rhetorical reasons a paragraph may be a single sentence. You see how tricky a simple definition can get.

THE BASIC PARAGRAPH

Scarcely anyone is likely to ask you to *define* a paragraph; the important thing is to be able to *write* one that is unified, coherent, and complete. The average paragraph runs from about 100 to 150 words—somewhat longer perhaps in formal writing, considerably shorter in newspaper stories where the small type in narrow columns requires frequent breaks to ease eyestrain. Some special kinds of paragraphs—like introductions and conclusions—also tend to be shorter than average, but we will tell you about those after we have laid down some guidelines for writing solid, basic paragraphs.

Make the Topic Clear

Every paragraph you write is going to be *about* something: it will describe something, question something, demand something, define something, reject something. Your first duty as a writer is to let your readers know what your paragraphs deal with. You do this by using a *topic sentence* in each one. The topic sentence tells what that group of sentences is about; it unifies the ideas within the paragraph. Every idea, each detail, in the paragraph should then relate to the idea set forth in the topic sentence. And, as Mark Twain cautioned, "When in doubt, throw it out."

If, for instance, you decide to write a paragraph about the undeserved reputation of dogs, you may use this topic sentence: "Far from being one's best friends, dogs tend to be slow-witted, servile, slobbering beasts seldom deserving of their board and keep." Next you need to trot out examples of slavish spaniels and doltish Great Danes you have known in order to convince your readers that dogs make wretched companions. But if you then observe, "Cats are pretty contemptible also," you need a new paragraph. Or else you need to toss that bit of evidence out as being beside the point, the *point* being whatever idea you committed yourself to in the topic sentence. You can, of course, broaden the topic sentence if you decide cats are essential to your argument. You can expand the topic sentence to read something like this: "Both dogs and cats are exceedingly disagreeable creatures to have around the house." Now the way is clear to discuss all the skittish cats of your acquaintance as well as those loutish dogs in a comparison and contrast paragraph.

Remember: **The topic sentence should state the main idea of the paragraph, and all details and descriptions should relate to that main idea.**

DISCUSSION EXERCISE   4-1

Choose the most appropriate topic sentence from the list preceding each of these paragraphs. Explain why you rejected the other three choices as topic sentences.

    a. African bees are quite interesting.
    b. Life in Africa is hard for a bee.
    c. Africa is full of killer bees.
    d. Killer bees in Africa should be exterminated.

1. _____

_____. Nectar and pollen are sometimes scarce, and the landscape abounds with animals and people who think nothing of knocking over a beehive for its honey. The African honeybee (Apis mellifera adansonii) has evolved, therefore, with a hypersensitivity to disturbance and a tendency to launch disconcerting mass attacks against potential enemies who come too near its nests.

           —Ed Zuckerman, "The Killer Bees," *Rolling Stone*, 28 July 1977.

    a. America's exports and imports are not balanced.
    b. America imports enough fishmeal from Chile and Peru to meet the protein requirements of the Peruvian population for an entire year.

    c. While America absorbs protein from the underdeveloped countries, it does not return it as protein-rich food.

    d. Colonialism is perpetuated in the pattern of America's economic practices.

2. _____

_____. In fact, most of our food exports go to the wealthy areas—Europe, Japan and Canada. We currently ship three times more agricultural products to Europe than to Latin America and Africa *combined.* Of the ten leading U.S. agricultural exports, four—hides, tallow, cotton, and tobacco—are not edible at all, and of the remaining six, only two are high in protein—nonfat dry milk and soybeans. Most of the soybeans go to Japan, Western Europe and Canada, where they are fed to livestock. As for the one million tons of protein imported annually by the rich nations from the poor nations, much if not most of it comes from the soil of the underdeveloped world and goes into the mouths of European livestock in the form of high-protein seed meals like that made from African peanuts.

                —Frances Moore Lappe, "A Vegetarian Manifesto," *Ramparts,* June 1973.

    a. The notion of land reform is not new.

    b. The small farmer is more American than the huge corporate farmer.

    c. Land in this country is too expensive for most people to buy.

    d. Urban dreams of the good country life have focused national attention on "the country."

3. _____

_____. The basic idea dates back at least to 1776. The country's founders did not want the land to be held by a few very large and rich owners. Yet, despite the American Revolution and two centuries of strife, a few very large and rich owners still predominate. In rural counties, the top 20 landowners—less than 1 percent of the people—own 20–50 percent of the land. They run farms owned by corporations and other absentee landlords. Twenty-four corporations—energy companies and railroads—own or control mineral rights to over 122 million acres, or about 1 out of every 16 acres in the continental U.S.

                —Judith Strasser, "Grapes of Wrath: 1977," *New Times,* 1 April 1977.

Put the Topic Sentence in the Best Place

You do not always have to make the topic sentence the first one in the paragraph. Accomplished writers sometimes put their topic sentences in the middle or at the end of a paragraph as a matter of style. You should become familiar with the various ways of positioning topic sentences so that your writing will exhibit a pleasing variety.

At the Beginning. If you place each topic sentence at the beginning of its paragraph, your readers can grasp the outline of your essay just by glancing at the topic sentences, an arrangement that makes for clarity and easy reading. This is the best way to position the topic sentences whenever you write to inform or to explain, as in writing directions, term papers, essay examinations, and on-the-job reports.

Most paragraphs start out with the topic sentence followed by examples, details, or explanations, like this one (we italicize the topic sentences in the examples in this section):

> *Among his colleagues at the Public Broadcasting Service, Moyers' obsession for the texture of language is a matter of legend.* Moyers revises. He edits. He revises again, tuning even the most functional introductory sentence until it resonates. You don't watch a Bill Moyers PBS special as much as you listen to it.
>
> —Ron Powers, ''Where Have All the News Analysts Gone?'' *TV Guide* (Oct. 4, 1980).

Here is another example from James Thurber developed the same way:

> *The basic trouble, of course, is the astounding fact that the offspring of man have not developed the ability to be self-sustaining until their parents are practically worn down and in the grave.* The guinea pig is on his own the second he is born—even has his eyes open, leaps from the womb to the nearest carrot or lettuce leaf. Dogs are raising families of their own before the first anniversary of their birth; and so it goes among all the known species of animal except man, whose young are practically no good at all until they have wobbled around the house for almost a quarter of a century!
>
> —''Look Out for Turkey Wort,'' *Atlantic* (Dec. 1980).

At the End. Any time you develop a paragraph using inductive reasoning (gathering specific evidence and examples from which you draw a conclusion), the topic sentence will quite naturally come at the end, as in this example:

> In my mother's sun-belt apartment building, where the cost of utilities is included in the rent, air conditioners hum steadily, even when open windows would do the trick. ''Why not?'' they say. ''The landlord's paying for it.'' City housing agencies around the country will tell you that the way to get tenants to conserve is to individually meter apartments. *It is amazing how much less of anything people require when they have to pay the bill.*
>
> —Bernard Sloan, ''The Money Message,'' *Newsweek*, 6 Sept. 1982.

You can also place your topic sentence at the end as a means of achieving variety and emphasis, as Norman Cousins does in the next example:

I had a fast-growing conviction that a hospital is no place for a person who is seriously ill. The surprising lack of respect for basic sanitation; the rapidity with which staphylococci and other pathogenic organisms can run through an entire hospital; the extensive and sometimes promiscuous use of x-ray equipment; the seemingly indiscriminate administration of tranquilizers and powerful painkillers, sometimes more for the convenience of hospital staff in managing patients than for therapeutic needs; and the regularity with which hospital routine takes precedence over the rest requirements of the patient (slumber, when it comes for an ill person, is an uncommon blessing and is not to be wantonly interrupted)— *all these and other practices seem to me to be critical shortcomings of the modern hospital.*

—*Anatomy of an Illness* (1979).

Notice that Cousins' paragraph consists of only two sentences. His topic is implied in the short opening sentence but is not clearly stated until the very end of the long second sentence, a masterfully balanced series, both informative and emphatic.

In the Middle.   Putting the topic sentence in midparagraph occasionally is another way to achieve variety and thus make your writing more interesting. In the next example, the topic sentence neatly links the sentences preceding it with the ones following:

Across the street from the Rayburn Building, the 57 employees of the Botanic Garden nurture and then deliver two plants every other month to the 535 congressional offices. ("Cut flowers are available in the spring," says one gardener.) *These botanic niceties, from a greenhouse costing taxpayers $1.2 million a year, are among the less expensive touches of congressional office decor.* In 1977, the House will spend $4,000 a member for furniture and furnishings, much of it custom-made. In addition, every congressman is allotted $27,000 to furnish and equip a District office; for carpets and curtains in their home-state offices, senators can spend $4,500.

—Robert Shrum, "The Imperial Congress," *New Times,* 18 March 1977.

Some Handy Variations.   Using a variation on this technique, Jack London put together a paragraph with the topic sentence in the middle, but with the same idea repeated for further emphasis at the end. This example is taken from his account of the San Francisco earthquake:

On Wednesday morning at a quarter past five came the earthquake. A minute later the flames were leaping upward. In a dozen different quarters south of Market Street, in the working-class ghetto, and in the factories, fires started. There was no opposing the flames. There was no organization, no communication. *All the cunning adjustments of a twentieth-century city had been smashed by the earthquake.* The streets were humped into ridges and depressions and piled with debris of fallen walls. The steel rails were twisted into perpendicular and horizontal angles. The telephone and telegraph systems were disrupted. And the great water mains had burst. *All the shrewd contrivances and safeguards of man had been thrown out of gear by thirty seconds' twitching of earth crust.*

—"The Story of an Eye Witness," *Collier's Weekly,* May 1906.

You can do the same thing with a paragraph that has the topic sentence at the beginning. You can sum things up with a tidy sentence reiterating the idea of the topic sentence at the end, as Elliot Engel does with a clever twist here:

I've always been amazed at the nurturing emotional support that my wife can seek and return with her close female friends. Often the most intimate problems are shared and therefore diminished through empathy. Her three-hour talks with friends refresh and renew her far more than my 3-mile jogs restore me. *In our society it seems as if you've got to have a bosom to be a buddy.*

—"Of Male Bondage," *Newsweek* (June 21, 1982).

In the next example the topic sentence is stated at the beginning in general terms and reiterated at the end quite specifically:

The case of Chicago accountant Howard F. MacNeil is especially chilling. He was assessed $36,000 personally for the taxes of a corporation that had been one of his clients. MacNeil refused to be bullied into a "compromise" and the IRS, as it has the power to do, without any court proceeding, attached his bank accounts and posted signs around his house proclaiming "KEEP OUT—Property of the US Government." He lost his business and went into debt as he waited years for his case to come to court. *At the trial he was completely vindicated, but in the meanwhile the IRS had completely ruined him.*

—Blake Fleetwood, "The Tax Police," *Saturday Review* (May 1980).

This particular method of rounding out paragraphs gives them an admirable neatness that could become boring if you tried for it every time. Only occasionally will you want to produce such tightly unified paragraphs.

Remember: **All your paragraphs must achieve the simple, essential unity that comes from having every sentence relate to the idea in the topic sentence—even if your topic sentence is only implied.**

The Implied Variation.   Sometimes, especially in narrative and descriptive writing, you can get by without a topic sentence because all the details in the paragraph relate to an idea that is easily understood by your readers. Here is Studs Terkel giving us the words of Cesar Chavez:

> There was this young waitress again. With either her boyfriend or someone close, because they were involved in conversation. And there was this familiar sign again, but we paid no attention to it. She looked up at us and she sort of—it wasn't what she said, it was just a gesture. A sort of gesture of total rejection. Her hand, you know, and the way she turned her face away from us. She said: "Whattaya want?" So we told her we'd like to buy two hamburgers. She sort of laughed, a sarcastic sort of laugh. And she said, "Oh, we don't sell to Mexicans. Why don't you go across to Mexican town, you can buy 'em over there." And then she turned around and continued her conversation.
>
> *Hard Times: An Oral History of the Great Depression* (1970).

Notice that the paragraph has unity, even though the topic sentence is unstated. All the details support the implied statement, "One day I found out about discrimination firsthand." Certainly the paragraph would not be improved by adding that sentence. It is simply unnecessary.

DISCUSSION EXERCISE   4-2

From all but one of the following paragraphs, we have removed the topic sentences. Read the paragraphs; then find the topic sentence that belongs to each one and put it in the most effective place. Be prepared to explain *why* you chose that position. And remember: in one paragraph the topic sentence is implied. Choose from these topic sentences:

a. Vegetables simply do not taste as good as most other things do.
b. She accepted her status as an old woman, that is to say as a beast of burden.
c. There is no point.

(1)

Every afternoon a file of old women passes down the road outside my house, each carrying a load of firewood. All of them are mummified with age and sun, and all of them are tiny. . . . One day a poor old creature who could not have been more than four feet tall crept past me under a vast load of wood. I stopped her and put a five-sou piece (a little more than a farthing) into her hand. She answered with a shrill wail, almost a scream, which was partly gratitude but mainly surprise. I suppose from her point of view, by taking any notice of her, I seemed almost to be violating a law of nature. When a family is traveling it is quite usual to see a father and a grown-up son riding ahead on donkeys, and an old woman following on foot, carrying the baggage.

—George Orwell, *Such, Such Were the Joys* (1945).

(2)

A lead-pencil has a point, an argument may have a point, remarks may be pointed, and a man who wants to borrow five pounds from you only comes to the point when he asks you for the fiver. Lots of things have points: especially weapons. But where is the point to life? Where is the point to love? Where, if it comes to the point, is the point to a bunch of violets? Life and love are life and love, a bunch of violets is a bunch of violets, and to bring in the idea of a point is to ruin everything. Live and let live, love and let love, flower and fade, and follow the natural curve, which flows on, pointless.

—D. H. Lawrence, *Phoenix* (1936).

(3)

I bet two dollars and a dime Jimmy's folks never had a ol' rusty Buick propped up on Co'-Cola crates in the front yard, and that no Cah-tah ever drove the school bus or picked up pecans on the halves. They didn't whitewash old tires and half bury 'em in the yard and then plant zinnias in the middle. Likely they grew grass in the front yard, 'stead of them sweeping it down with a broom on Saturdays. And for all his being a "born-again" Christian, I expect ol' Jimmy never ate off an oilcloth depicting The Last Supper in twenty-four colors or owned a seventeen-inch statue of Jesus Christ that glowed in the dark.

—Larry L. King, "We Ain't Trash No More," *Esquire*, Nov. 1976.

(4)

Facts must be faced. And there isn't a single vegetable, hot or cold, that stands on its own two feet the way a ripe peach does, or a strawberry. (It is interesting to note that vegetables beginning with A are the most self-sufficient: artichokes, asparagus, avocadoes, which have really slithered out of the fruit kingdom by this time into the vegetable kingdom, no matter what the botanists say. But the further down the alphabet you go, through rutabagas, spinach, and turnips, the more hopeless they become, given all the butter and salt you've got.)

—Peg Bracken, *The I Hate to Cook Book* (1960).

Develop the Ideas Fully

The topic sentence states the main idea in each paragraph, but most paragraphs need more. To develop, or flesh out, that main idea, you supply facts, figures, examples, and illustrations—in short, *concrete details*—that pertain to your topic sentence. You say that riding motorcycles is dangerous; then you show how you know this to be true. Cite statistics, if you have them, to prove how many cyclists are maimed and killed each year, but never forget that specific examples can be far more convincing than impersonal numbers. Mention the broken noses, the split lips, the fractured femurs, the spurting arteries, the dislocated elbows, the splintered teeth, the crushed pelvises; and your readers may well be convinced of the risk.

Descriptive Details.   Descriptive details are usually intended to convey an impression—how something looked, smelled, tasted. They are especially common in eyewitness accounts of experiences, as in Edmund Wilson's vivid picture of Chicago during the great depression. (Topic sentences are italicized in these examples.)

> *There is not a garbage dump in Chicago which is not diligently haunted by the hungry.* Last summer in the hot weather when the smell was sickening and the flies were thick, there were a hundred people a day coming to the dumps, falling on the heap of refuse as soon as the truck had pulled out and digging in it with sticks and hands. They would devour all the pulp that was left on the old slices of watermelon and cantaloupe till the rinds were as thin as paper; and they would take away and wash and cook discarded onions, turnips, and potatoes. Meat is a more difficult matter, but they salvage a good deal of that, too. The best is the butcher's meat which has been frozen and hasn't spoiled. In the case of the other meat, there are usually bad parts that have to be cut out or they scald it and sprinkle it with soda to kill the taste and the smell.
>
> —"Hull-House in 1932," in *Travels in Two Democracies* (1933).

Factual Details.   You can use facts and figures if you have them, as Vincent P. Norris does in this informative paragraph:

> All told, ads cost us in 1972 more than $23 billion—which comes to more than $100 for every man, woman and child, or about $320 per household. That is almost seven times as much as we spent for books and plays, and it does not include the higher prices we are charged for advertised products, but only the cost of the ads themselves. If the higher prices (and monopoly profits) made possible by advertising were included, the cost per household would be much higher.
>
> —"Mendacious Messages from Madison Avenue," *Media and Consumer* (Sept. 1973).

Norman Cousins develops this convincing paragraph by recording facts:

> The history of medicine is replete with accounts of drugs or modes of treatment that were in use for many years before it was recognized that they did more harm than good. For centuries, for example, doctors believed that drawing blood from patients was essential for rapid recovery from virtually every illness. Then, midway through the nineteenth century, it was discovered that bleeding served to weaken the patient. King Charles II's death is believed to have been caused in part by administered bleedings. George Washington's death was also hastened by the severe loss of blood resulting from this treatment.
>
> —Anatomy of an Illness (1979).

Illustrations and Examples.   Most of the time we tend to use illustrations and examples to flesh out our paragraphs. Often a writer will use numerous examples:

When I get an idea for a poem or an article or a talk or a short story, I feel myself consciously draw away from it. I seek procrastination and delay. There must be time for the seed of the idea to be nurtured in the mind. Far better writers than I have felt the same way. Over his writing desk Franz Kafka had one word, "Wait." William Wordsworth talked of the writer's "wise passiveness." Naturalist Annie Dillard recently said, "I'm waiting. I usually get my ideas in November, and I start writing in January. I'm waiting." Denise Levertov says, "If . . . somewhere in the vicinity there is a poem then, no, I don't do anything about it, I wait."

—Donald M. Murray, "Write Before Writing," *College Composition and Communication* (December 1978).

In the next paragraph Mark Twain develops his idea by using a single illustration satirically:

Go to bed early, get up early—this is wise. Some authorities say get up with the sun; some others say get up with one thing, some with another. But a lark is really the best thing to get up with. It gives you a splendid reputation with everybody to know that you get up with the lark; and if you get the right kind of lark, and work at him right, you can easily train him to get up at half past nine, every time—it is no trick at all.

—"Advice to Youth," a speech delivered in 1894.

WRITING EXERCISE 4-3

1. Write a paragraph in which you organize examples, illustrations, or descriptive details deductively (from general to specific) beginning with your topic sentence, as does the student who wrote the following example:

For sanity's sake, off-campus living should be restricted to those with cars. IGA's grocery bags are not designed to endure the effects of a mile-long walk, and always choose to split and spill their contents in the street where the traffic is heaviest. The walk back from the laundromat is equally unnerving. Previously blue skies turn black immediately after the last of a dozen quarters have been fed to the dryers. The victim of another downpour has no choice but to borrow jeans from a roomie or suffer the embarrassment of staying home on a Saturday night. The bedraggled student at first finds the number of off-campus parties reassuring. After a few beers, however, the direction of home becomes distorted. The apartment is not equipped with the flashing lights of a high-rise dormitory. Frustration and weariness again get the best of the student. You can be sure, the next time you see a can of generic tuna in the middle of Willow Street or an argyle sock on Main, that student apartments are just around the corner.

—Wendy Wilson

2. Write a paragraph in which you organize descriptive details, facts, statistics, examples, or illustrations inductively (specific to general), concluding with your topic sentence, as the student does who wrote the following example:

> She sits at her vanity table, its marble top covered with bottles, jars, and tubes, and carefully polishes each long manicured nail, one by one. After the polish is dry, the long mane of ash blonde hair is swept up so that not even the slightest wisp is on the face. The liquid foundation is applied first, the small dots gently blended into the skin to a soft matte finish. The green almond-shaped eyes come next. After meticulous strokes of color and liner to the lids, and several sweeping brushes of mascara to the thick lashes, the eyes look like those of a majestic cat. High, shapely cheekbones seem to appear by magic as color and highlighter are applied and contoured. The lips, outlined and filled in with moist shining color, are shaped into a sensual pout. The final touch is pressed powder gently applied over the face to set the makeup and to absorb any moisture that might appear from the hot camera lights. One last glance, and voila! She is ready to face the camera.
>
> —Tammy L. Karlin

MAKE YOUR PARAGRAPHS HANG TOGETHER

If you want your writing to be clear and easy to follow, you must not let your readers get confused when you move from one point to the next or when you change the direction of your ideas. The things you can do to make your writing hang together, to make it *coherent*, are fairly simple, yet they can often mean the difference between a first-rate essay and a merely passable one.

Stay in the Same Tense

No matter how skillfully you weave your sentences together, you will lose that smooth coherence if you carelessly change tenses without good reason. You may write in either present or past tense, depending upon how you approach your material. This sentence, for instance, is written in present tense:

Moose-kitty *is twitching* his tail.

Past tense would be

Moose *was twitching* his tail.

or

Moose *had been* twitching his tail for fully five minutes.

There is a good bit of variety within the two tenses, which we will not go into now, but the thing to remember is this: pick either present or past tense and stay with it unless you have a reason to change. Here is an example of faulty tense switch:

> Moose *was* quietly *twitching* his tail, when suddenly he *pounces* on the dog next door. Poor Rover *yelped* and *ran,* while Moose *hangs on* like a broncobuster.

There is no call for the change from past to present tense. If Moose *was twitching,* then he also *pounced* and *hung on.* You can, of course switch tenses if you want to indicate a change occurring in time:

> Moose was *twitching* his tail alarmingly, but now he *is washing* his whiskers.

Just take care that you do not mix tenses without meaning to. (See *Tense* in the "Revising Index," Chapter 13, for a more detailed discussion.)

Use Transitions

The main principle of good coherence lies in providing transitions—posting verbal signs to show your readers that you are moving to another point. The indention of a new paragraph does this to a certain extent, but indenting could also mean that you are going to expand the same idea. And often your thought changes direction in the middle of a paragraph when organizing a contrast or when adding examples or noting exceptions.

So you need signals. These can be as pointed as "Next let us consider . . ." or "On the other hand, we must not overlook. . . ." That is pretty obvious, creaky transition, but it is better than no transition at all. A number of transitional words are neatly classified according to function in Figure 4-1. Take note of the different types of transitions illustrated, then tuck in a bookmark in case you get stuck and need a transition to help you over a rough spot.

Transitions between Paragraphs.
The transitions that you are most likely to notice are those that link ideas from paragraph to paragraph. Some of the more obvious ones are not at all difficult, but the more subtle ones require practice. We will begin with the easy ones and work up to the challenging ones.

The "Bob-Type" Transition.
An ultra-simple transitional device is recommended by Jessica Mitford in her memoir, *A Fine Old Conflict* (1974). This "invaluable writer's aid consisting of a double space

To move to the next major point: *too, moreover, next, in the first place, second, third, again, besides, in addition, further, likewise, finally, also, furthermore*
Examples: We can see *also* that the quality of most television programs is abysmal.
Furthermore, the commercials constantly assault our taste and insult our intelligence.

To add an example: *for example, such as, that is, in the following manner, namely, in this case, as an illustration, for instance, in the same manner*
Examples: The daytime game shows, *for instance*, openly appeal to human greed.
Soap operas, *in the same manner*, pander to many of our baser instincts.

To emphasize a point: *especially, without doubt, primarily, chiefly, actually, otherwise, after all, as a matter of fact, in fact, without question, even more*
Examples: The constant violence depicted on television, *in fact*, poses a danger to society.
Even more offensive are deodorant commercials, *without question* the most tasteless on TV.

To contrast a point: *but, still, on the other hand, on the contrary, nevertheless, contrary to, however, nonetheless, conversely, yet, although, granted that*
Examples: We abhor the violence, *yet* we cannot approve of censorship.
Although commercials may enrage or sicken us, they do, *after all*, pay the bills.
Granted that advertising picks up the tab, the deceptiveness of commercials remains indefensible.

To conclude a point: *consequently, so, accordingly, then, as a result, hence, in sum, in conclusion, in other words, thus, therefore, in short*
Examples: Soap operas *thus* contribute to the subtle erosion of moral values.
Commercials, *therefore*, are not worth the sacrifice of our integrity.
Television, *in short*, costs more than society should be willing to pay.

Figure 4-1 Useful transitional terms

between paragraphs" was perfected by her husband Bob. Mitford testifies that this conspicuous blank space was the only transition her lawyer husband ever used, and that it worked just fine for him. We think, though, it may be a trifle *too* easy. Unless you are a lawyer, use it with caution.

The Rhetorical-Question Transition. Another simple way to lead from one point to the next, from paragraph to paragraph, is to pose a rhetorical question and answer it, like this:

> How do we stop people from breeding? First, by not constantly brainwashing the average girl into thinking that motherhood must be her supreme experience. Very few women are capable of being good mothers; and very few men of being good fathers. Parenthood is a gift, as most parents find out too late and most children find out right away. So a change in attitude will help; and that seems to be happening.
>
> —Gore Vidal, "The State of the Union," *Esquire,* May 1975.

This device, useful though it is, will seldom work more than once in a paper. You must have others in stock.

The Short-Sentence Transition. Like the rhetorical question, the short-sentence transition must not be used often but comes in handy when you need it. You simply state briefly and graciously in advance what you intend to discuss next, like this:

> Europeans think more highly of Americans now than they ever did. Let me try to explain why.
>
> —Anthony Burgess, "Is America Falling Apart?" *New York Times Magazine* (7 Nov. 1971).

John Kenneth Gailbraith uses a slightly more formal version:

> Economics, foreign policy, the split in the party as it relates to racial equality, and some resulting questions of political style all require a special word. To these matters I now turn.
>
> —"Who Needs the Democrats?" *Harper's* (July 1970).

The Echo Transition. Sometimes you can get by without any clearly transitional word at all, if you will practice the echo method. This subtle technique also works within a single paragraph, but first let us show you how to touch on the idea from your previous paragraph as you introduce the idea for your next one. Sounds tricky, we realize, but it is worth working on if you want to write readable prose. The following examples will show you clearly how it works. In the first example, the final sentence of a paragraph by Frederick Lewis Allen explaining the fear of communism in the twenties is followed by the opening sentence of his next paragraph, which explains the reasons for the scare. (We have italicized the echoing words in all these examples.) Notice how *this national panic* refers back to *a reign of terror,* while at the same time leading into the new idea of some slight justification for the scare:

> It was an era of lawless and disorderly defense of law and order, of unconstitutional defense of the Constitution, of suspicion and civil conflict—in a very literal sense, *a reign of terror.*
>
> For *this national panic* there was a degree of justification.
>
> —*Only Yesterday* (1931).

Next is Horace Sutton's easy transition from a paragraph concentrating on the deafening city noise to his next paragraph suggesting possible relief:

> Reveille is celebrated in New York these frantic days by the *commencement of pneumatic drills.* If you live here you don't need an alarm clock.
>
> The only way to escape the *din of the asphalt bashers* is to move out or up.
>
> —"You Can't Live in New York," *Saturday Evening Post,* 11 Mar. 1961.

Pneumatic drills are, of course, one kind of *asphalt basher.* As in the previous example, the echo is sounded by using a synonym. You can, if you wish, repeat the very same word, as Michael Pousner does in ending a paragraph detailing urban blight and beginning the next one about the potential dangers that may result:

> Nowadays many cities contain block after block of empty stores, silent monuments to the epidemic of *business ripoffs.*
>
> Arson, street crime, *business ripoffs.* They add up to a far more widespread and much more potentially lethal contagion than that of the 60's.
>
> —"The New Urban Riots," *Newsweek,* 17 June 1977.

In the next example Katherine Anne Porter combines an echo with a regular transitional sentence to gain emphasis. She is writing about the peaceful protests preceding the execution of Sacco and Vanzetti in the twenties. The paragraph just concluding here delineates the frightening tactics of mounted police:

> I do not believe the police meant for the hoofs to strike and crush heads— it was just a very showy technique for intimidating and controlling a *mob.*

↘

This was not a mob, however. It was a silent, intent assembly of citizens. . . .

—"The Never-Ending Wrong," *Atlantic Monthly,* June 1977.

The Balanced Echo. Another skillful method of providing coherence involves echoing the same structure in the opening sentence of each paragraph. Mark Twain uses this device to perfection in the following example. Each of these balanced sentences heads a paragraph in Twain's original in which Eve is thinking about Adam:

I love certain birds because of their song; but I do not love Adam on account of his singing—no, it is not that. . . .

It is not on account of his brightness that I love him—no, it is not that. . . .

It is not on account of his gracious and considerate ways and his delicacy that I love him. No. . . .

It is not on account of his industry that I love him—no, it is not that. . . .

It is not on account of his education that I love him—no, it is not that. . . .

It is not on account of his chivalry that I love him—no, it is not that. . . .

Then why is it that I love him? Merely because he is masculine, I think.

—"The Diary of Adam and Eve" (1893).

We may question Eve's reasoning, but we can scarcely fault Twain's coherence. He uses a couple of variations to avoid monotony, but the sentences we omitted add the necessary variety to the complete version. Notice, too, that balanced structure adds emphasis as well as coherence. This is not your everyday transitional device, by any means, but it can be smashing on special occasions.

Transitions Within Paragraphs. While we are on the subject of coherence through parallel structure, we should mention that this can be an impressive technique within paragraphs as well. Here is Judy Syfers telling us in balanced sentences why she wants a wife. (We have italicized the deliberate repetition.)

I want a wife who will take care of *my* physical needs. *I want a wife who* will keep *my* house clean. *A wife who* will pick up after *my* children, *a wife who* will pick up after me. *I want a wife who* will keep *my* clothes clean, ironed, mended, replaced when need be, and ***who*** will see to it that ***my*** personal things are kept in their proper place so that I can find what I need the minute I need it. *I want a wife who* cooks the meals, a *wife who* is a good cook. *I want a wife who* will plan the menus, do the necessary grocery shopping, prepare the meals, serve them pleasantly, and then do the cleaning up while I do *my* studying. *I want a wife who* will care for me when I am sick and sympathize with *my* pain and loss of time from school. *I want a wife* to go along when our family takes a vacation so that someone can continue to care for me and *my* children when I need a rest and a change of scene.

—"Why I Want a Wife," *MS Magazine* (Dec. 1971).

Only twice does Syfers vary her basic pattern—in the third sentence and in the final one. The paragraph is tightly coherent because of the deliberate repetition which keeps our attention focused exactly where the writer wants it. But again, balanced structure is not something you can use all the time.

> *Remember:* **Your best chance of getting coherence in your paragraphs over the long haul involves keeping a clear continuity of ideas.**

You will also rely on deliberately repeated words and the echo of pronouns as they refer back to their antecedents. You may well work in one or more of the techniques used for coherence between paragraphs. Most of this echoing you do automatically, but you need to understand the process in case you have to patch up a paragraph some time.

In this next example, we have italicized the typical transitional devices and used boldface type to show the repetition of the key term *addict* and the pronouns that refer to it.

> *What to do about drug* **addiction?** I give you two statistics. England with a population of over fifty-five million has eighteen hundred **addicts.** The United States with over two hundred million has nearly five hundred thousand **addicts.** *What are the English doing right that we are doing wrong?* They have turned the problem over to the doctors. An **addict** is required to register with a physician who gives **him** at controlled intervals a prescription so that **he** can buy **his** drug. The **addict** is content. *Best of all,* society is safe. The Mafia is out of the game. The police are unbribed, and the **addict** will not mug an old lady in order to get the money for **his** next fix.
>
> —Gore Vidal, "The State of the Union," *Esquire,* May 1975.

Notice that the third and fourth sentences (both citing statistics) are approximately parallel in structure, which helps. And besides the repetition of the word *addict*, we get echoes from *England . . . English . . . they*, from *United States . . . we . . . society*, and from *doctors . . . physicians . . . who*. Even more subtle are the echoes from *content* and *safe*, words with a similar reassuring meaning. It is a nicely coherent paragraph, and you can do as well.

SPECIAL PARAGRAPHS

Not all of your paragraphs are going to conform to the advice we have been giving you about the length and organization of typical paragraphs. Most notably, *introductions* and *conclusions* have special requirements, as do brief *emphatic* paragraphs and *transitional* paragraphs.

Advice About Introductions

A friend once told Robert Benchley, the humorist, that introductions were easy if you knew how to start. All you had to do was type "the" at the top of the page, and the rest would come by itself. Next morning Benchley tried it. Tap, tap, tap, t-h-e. Nothing came. He thought, he fidgeted, he fretted, he chewed his nails and popped his knuckles. Finally, in exasperation, he typed "hell with it" and abandoned the project.

Unlike Benchley, you cannot afford the luxury of abandonment. But postponing the introduction until you have gathered momentum and are writing at the height of your powers is probably a good idea. You already know the main idea of your paper (otherwise you could not begin writing it), so scrawl your thesis statement across the top of that blank page and get going on the first section of your outline. Think about the introduction in spare moments. Solicit divine inspiration, if possible. Something appropriate will eventually come to you. Introductions need not be long. Two or three sentences leading up to the *thesis*, or main idea, of the paper will do nicely.

State Your Thesis. While drawing your readers' attention is an important element of introductions, their primary function is to let your readers know what that essay is about. You will not always need a bold statement of your thesis, but the more formal the writing, the more likely it is that you will need a straightforward statement. In the following introduction, George Crile, Jr., comes directly to the point:

> Today in the United States there is one profession in which conflict of interest is not merely ignored but loudly defended as a necessary concomitant of the free-enterprise system. That is in medicine, particularly in surgery.
>
> —"The Surgeon's Dilemma," *Harper's*, May 1975.

This whole introductory paragraph consists of only his thesis statement as the second sentence just concludes the idea begun in the first. It is pointblank, as introductions go.

Normally you will take several sentences to introduce your controlling idea. You can give a little background information or begin with some fairly broad remarks about your subject, then narrow the focus down to the specific idea covered by your thesis. This is the method used in the following introductory paragraph (we have italicized the thesis statements throughout this section):

> To her, tight jeans and no bra mean she's in style. To him, they mean she wants to have sex. So it goes among adolescents in Los Angeles, according to a survey by four researchers at U.C.L.A. Despite unisex haircuts, the women's movement, and other signs of equality between the sexes, *boys still read more sexual come-ons into girls' behavior than the girls intend.*
>
> —*Psychology Today* (Oct. 1980).

The article then presents other examples of dress and behavior that are often misinterpreted, just as the introduction promises. Be sure to give your readers at least the main idea of what your essay is going to be about somewhere near the beginning.

Get Your Readers' Attention.   If you are going to write skillfully, you need an introduction that will make your prospective readers eager to peruse your essay. You need to catch their interest at the onset. As a general principle, try to write an opening sentence that puts a picture in your readers' minds, as the writer does in this introduction:

> "Candid Camera" became so much a part of American culture in the 1960s that when a man hijacked a plane that producer Allen Funt was traveling on, the passengers stood up and cheered, assuming—incorrectly—that the hijacking was a stunt staged for television. After "Candid Camera's" seven-year run, CBS canceled it in 1967; *now Funt is not only developing new versions of the show but using old episodes to teach psychology and cure illness.*
>
> —"Smile, Allen Funt, You're a Star Again," *Newsweek*, 6 Sept. 1982.

The slapstick image of passengers applauding a hijacking is immediately engaging and clearly establishes Funt's celebrity. The last sentence tells the readers what the remainder of the article will be about, i.e., it states the thesis.

Find a Quotation.   Professional writers sometimes begin with a brief quotation that relates directly to the main idea of the essay. Beware of this technique unless you are a fairly skillful writer. The quotation must be gracefully connected to your opening sentence. If you can bridge the gap subtly, this type of introduction can be highly effective. Here is an example that begins with a quotation from a youth gang leader:

> "It's gonna be a hot summer, but it's always hot in the city."
> Speaking is "DSR," president of the Savage Nomads youth gang in the South Bronx. DSR wears a denim jacket with a skull painted on the back, chains on his belt buckle, and a tight-lipped grin on his face. When DSR speaks of heat, he is not talking about the weather. *He means the "Clockwork Orange" type of violence in which New York youth gang members dabble—arson, stick-ups, rape, even murder.* The violence is often unplanned, usually unprovoked, always senseless.
>
> —Michael Pousner, "The New Urban Riots," *Newsweek*, 27 June 1977.

Use Fascinating Facts.   You can begin an essay with facts and statistics—if you can find some real eye-openers like these:

> Every two-and-a-half minutes someone in the United States is robbed at gunpoint, and every forty minutes someone else is murdered with a gun. The weapons find their way into the hands of the criminals in a manner that almost nobody understands. Made in factories owned and operated by the most secretive industry in the country, the guns move through various markets and delivery systems, all of them obscure. Each year police seize about 250,000 handguns and long guns (rifles and shotguns) from the people they arrest. *Given the number of guns that the manufacturers produce each year* (2.5 million long guns and 4 million handguns) *the supply-and-demand equation works against the hope of an orderly society.*
>
> —Steven Brill, "The Traffic (Legal and Illegal) in Guns," *Harper's*, Sept. 1977.

Begin with a Question.   Another way to arrest your readers' attention is by asking a tantalizing question—or maybe a whole series of them, as does the writer of this introduction for a *Newsweek* article:

> Do Whitey Ford and Mickey Mantle *really* favor Miller's new Lite beer over all the others and hoist it off-camera as well as on? And how about Morris, the finicky cat? Does he dart for that other bowl of cat food once the floodlights fade?
> *Starting in mid-July, Whitey, Mickey, Morris and other celebrity hucksters better be prepared to back up their television-commercial claims by actually drinking, eating, or using the products they advertise— or answer to the Federal Trade Commission.*
>
> —"Say It's Really So, Joe!" *Newsweek*, 2 June 1975.

Notice how handy those rhetorical questions are for sneaking in the main idea. You pose a question, then answer it yourself, and you are off. But be reasonable: do not use something simpleminded (like "What is sorority life?" or "Were you ever so mad you could scream?") just because it provides an easy way to get started.

Try a Definition.   Another handy way to get started is by defining your subject, whatever it may be. The following introduction tells us some interesting facts about an unusual variety of sweet corn:

> The Indian and Hispanic people of Arizona and New Mexico eat blue tortillas, tissue-thin blue bread and a blue milk-drink. What gives these foods their color and much of their nutritional value is blue corn, a versatile corn that has been raised in the Southwest for centuries. The farmers who have cultivated it so long have developed it into an extremely drought-tolerant, disease-resistant corn that can be steamed, boiled or roasted in the milk stage, and ground into a delicious meal when mature.
>
> —Richard Flint, "Corn of a Different Color," *Organic Gardening,* Nov. 1982.

The remainder of the article provides useful information about planting, harvesting, and using blue corn.

State it very clearly

~~Imply~~ Your Thesis ~~Occasionally.~~   In narrative and descriptive essays your thesis idea is often so easy to grasp that you want to avoid stating it directly. Here is an example without a thesis statement—this time an anecdote, a real attention-getter:

> The room is dusty and ill-lighted, claustrophobic, the sort of room illegal operations are always performed in. Brenda is lying on the make-shift operating table, nervously fingering her shirt and the table edges. She is young, probably not more than nineteen, with rust-colored hair and freckles, and with small, tight breasts that rise gently from her chest. A needle is punched in just below the right nipple. Her arms flinch, she winces, but she says nothing. It's a long needle, three inches.
>
> —Al Reinert, "Doctor Jack Makes His Rounds," *Esquire,* May 1975.

That opening is so engrossing that you may be tempted to make a special trip to the library and read the rest of the article about illegal silicone injections to increase breast size.

Advice About Conclusions

Like introductions, conclusions ought to be forceful and to the point. Work especially hard on your last paragraph. Its effectiveness will influence the way your readers react to the whole paper. If you trail off tiredly at the end, they will sigh and feel let down. Avoid any sort of apology or hedging at this point. Do not end with a whimper. You want something climactic that does not overdo it.

In fact, if you are writing a short paper and have saved your strongest point for the end, you may not need a whole new paragraph in conclusion. The brief article in *Newsweek* about youth gangs ends with a paragraph speculating on the dismal future of DSR, the leader who was mentioned in the introduction (see page 106). The actual conclusion consists of the last sentence of the final paragraph (following the transitional word, *meanwhile*) and sounds a warning to the readers by echoing the phrase "hot summer" with which the essay began:

> As for DSR, he's starting to notice the obvious: casualties among gang members are about as high as those of frontline troops in Vietnam. He talks about getting a job "soon" and settling down a bit. Both goals are probably forever beyond his grasp. It is possible, though, that even DSR could be turned around if he knew he had a future beyond the Nomads. Meanwhile, it doubtless will be a "hot summer."

Restate Your Thesis Gracefully. If you have written something long and informative, like a term paper of ten to twenty typed pages, you will do well to summarize and restate your main idea. What you want, of course, is a tidy ending that reinforces the point you set out to make in the beginning. The writer of *Psychology Today*'s article on misinterpreting sexual signals (the introduction is on page 105) closes with a reinforcement of the thesis:

> The young people's ethnic backgrounds, ages, and previous dating and sexual experiences had almost no effect on their reactions. The girls' "relatively less-sexualized view of social relationships," the psychologists suggest, "may reflect some discomfort . . . with the demands of the dating scene"; women do, after all, have more to lose from sexual activity, facing risks of pregnancy and/or a bad reputation. The girls in the study were much more likely than the boys to agree with the statement, "Sometimes I wish that guys and girls could just be friends without worrying about sexual relationships."

The quotation at the end reflects the thesis idea (". . . boys still read more sexual come-ons into girls' behavior than the girls intend"), but does so in quite different terms and in a touching way.

Suggest Solutions. If you are writing analysis or argument, a useful closing device involves offering suggestions—possible solutions for problems discussed in the essay. This technique is valid only if you can come up with sound ideas for solving problems. Steven Brill ends his article about the traffic in guns (the introduction is on page 106) with some practical suggestions:

> All these small steps toward sanity are possible if we force the people who profit from America's free-wheeling gun traffic to be open, accountable, and fully responsive to law-enforcement needs. If we're going to continue to allow the RGs or the Smith and Wessons to make guns at all for civilian use, we ought to at least demand that they become partners in

the effort to curb the carnage their weapons cause. When we think of people murdered or robbed at gunpoint, we have to start thinking of brand names.

Try an Echo.   If you can bring it off, the technique of echoing some element from your introduction is an especially good one. It gives your essay unity. The *Newsweek* article about a new policy requiring people or pets who push products to actually use them concludes with a reference to the same celebrities mentioned in the introduction (on page 106):

> Most advertisers do not feel that the proposed regulations will cramp their style. In any event, it is unlikely to have much effect on Mantle and Ford, who are known to like their beer, and Morris seems honestly to savor 9-Lives cat food. But the rule could have posed a problem for Joe Namath, the nonpareil quarterback. Until recently, he did commercials for Beauty Mist Pantyhose.

Offer Encouragement.   Especially in process writing, you can fittingly close with a few words of encouragement for your readers. Tell them how delicious they will find the cheesecake if they follow your instructions to the letter. Or how rewarding they will find growing their own tomatoes, as Mark Kane does in this conclusion:

> When you shop for tomato seeds or plants this season, consider trying at least one new variety. There are hundreds to choose from and if you keep looking, one of them may find a home in your garden. Even if you find nothing to match your favorite, you'll have fun, and the pleasure of gardening is not just in the eating.
> —"The Tomato: Still Champion," *Organic Gardening,* (March 1982).

Conclusions are not all that difficult. Often they turn out weak because we write them last, when our powers are eclipsed. Treat your conclusion like your introduction: think about it off and on while writing the paper—during coffee breaks or whenever you pause to let your mind idle. Jot down anything promising that comes to you. And when you revise, concentrate on the conclusion, just as you will on the introduction.

Advice About Short Paragraphs

Introductions and conclusions tend to be shorter than body paragraphs but once in a while you may write a super-short paragraph— only one sentence long.

For Emphasis.   At once you can see that a single sentence used as a paragraph will be emphatic because it is unusual. It calls attention to itself by departing from the normal length for paragraphs. Michael Harrington begins his book *The Twilight of Capitalism* (1976) with this line set off as a paragraph:

> Western capitalism is in crisis.

He goes on to elaborate, of course, but the brevity of the single-sentence paragraph gives great impact to the statement.

You do not have to use an especially short sentence if your purpose is better served by a long one. Even a long sentence set off as a paragraph will command attention. Steven Brill makes a paragraph out of this sentence in order to emphasize a key point:

> It is sheer suicide that our police, our legislators, and the rest of us know nothing about how guns are being marketed: who's selling them and who's buying them, where and for how much.

Shorter statements are even more emphatic, but the technique works well either way. *But remember:*   You can not use this device often. Its whole force depends upon its being unusual.

For Transition.   If you are writing something long, you may need a short paragraph of pure transition—a sort of verbal bridge to get you from one idea to the next. In his article, "Mendacious Messages from Madison Avenue," in *Media and Consumer* (Sept. 1973), Vincent P. Norris cites figures to prove that more money is spent in this country on advertising than on higher education. Then he drops in these rhetorical questions, punctuated as a single paragraph:

> What did we get for our money? Who knows?

The next paragraph, then, begins speculation on that important question.

Keep in mind that setting off the sentence gives your transition more emphasis than just attaching it to the next paragraph. Most of the time you will want to be more discreet and tuck your transitions within the regular paragraphs.

PATTERNS OF DEVELOPMENT

The way you arrange details in each paragraph is up to you. Good writers use a number of patterns, usually without ever consciously thinking about the process. Most of these patterns, by the way, are the same ones people use (often more consciously) to organize complete essays. We are going to explain first how the patterns serve to organize individual paragraphs. In the next two chapters, we will discuss in greater detail how these patterns can be used to organize whole essays.

Descriptive Paragraphs

Usually authorities on writing suggest that you can organize descriptions spatially—top to bottom, left to right, near to far. True. You can describe your pussycat from nose to tail. But where do you include the texture of the fur, the stripes or spots, the color of the paws? And what about the meow? And the sinuous way the cat moves? Good description involves working a whole cluster of concrete details into some kind of spatial arrangement.

In this choice descriptive paragraph, Mark Twain takes his readers with him through the woods and into a meadow:

> Beyond the road where the snakes sunned themselves was a dense young thicket, and through it a dim-lighted path led a quarter of a mile; then out of the dimness one emerged abruptly upon a level great prairie which was covered with wild strawberry plants, vividly starred with prairie pinks, and walled in on all sides by forests. The strawberries were fragrant and fine and in the season we were generally there in the crisp freshness of the early morning, while the dew-beads still sparkled upon the grass and the woods were ringing with the first song of the birds.
>
> —*Mark Twain's Autobiography* (1924).

Dr. Jonathan Miller arranges details spatially in this description of the upper respiratory tract:

> The cough reflex is only one element in an elaborate system of respiratory protection. It is the most noticeable because it is such a strenuous action and because the cougher is usually aware of the stimulus which provokes it. But the surface of the respiratory tract is protected against quieter and more chronic threats as well. It is lined with cells, many of which are capable of pouring out a protective layer of mucus which smothers irritants and bacterial invaders before they have a chance to penetrate the living membranes. Other cells are equipped with mobile bristles whose concerted action wafts the mucus up to the mouth, where it can be swallowed or spat out. Chronic irritation may paralyse this microscopic escalator, which is one of the reasons why heavy smokers are so susceptible to repeated bronchial infection.
>
> —*The Body in Question* (1978).

Narrative Paragraphs

Since a narrative is simply a story, a narrative pattern is usually organized according to *chronology* (the order in which events happen). In writing a narrative paragraph your main concern will be choosing vivid, interesting details, as Peter Ustinov does in relating an incident from his days in the British army during World War II:

> There was, I remember, an odious procedure called kit-inspection. All one's kit had to be laid out in prescribed geometrical patterns, with the socks somehow arranged in square shapes, flanking the oblong greatcoat on top of the blankets. Now it is all very well for square people to have square socks, but once they have been worn by round people, they faithfully adopt the shape of the wearer. I did what I could to hammer them into the squareness demanded by military protocol, to no avail. The moment I left them alone, the wool expanded slowly into a voluptuous rotundity, and they lay there like buns on a breakfast tray. The sergeant-major entered my room in a fairly jovial mood, but when his eyes fell on my socks, I fancied I saw smoke emerging from his flared nostrils. He just had time before the appearance of the inspecting officer to promise me the direst punishments in the nastiest of manners.
>
> —*Dear Me* (1977).

Process Paragraphs

Another kind of writing that's easy to organize is the process paragraph. Any sort of how-to-do-it advice qualifies as a process. In organizing this material you mainly follow the steps in the procedure, but at appropriate points you may need to mention necessary equipment, amounts of ingredients, and elements of timing, and to warn your readers of any tricky places where things could go wrong. Here is a paragraph explaining how to transplant tomato seedlings:

> When you pot or repot a seedling, set it slightly deeper in the soil than it stood before. The buried portion of stem will strike roots. Even a light touch can damage the stem of young seedlings (a plant with only *one* or *two* true leaves), so hold them by a seed leaf. Transplant gently. Pick a cloudy day so the roots have an easier job of supplying water to the leaves. Take pains to water daily until the transplants resume rapid growth. Bury part of the stem, as you did in potting the seedlings, to force more roots. Tests in Texas showed that laying the stem in a shallow trench, so that only the topmost leaves of the plant were aboveground, resulted in higher, earlier yields.
>
> —Mark Kane, "The Tomato: Still Champion," *Organic Gardening* (March 1982).

Definition Paragraphs

A definition can be accomplished in anything from a couple of words in parentheses to an entire essay. Definition paragraphs are quite common and can be organized in various ways. Here is one by Gore Vidal. It begins with several sentences leading up to the actual definition, followed by a discussion of some grave implications of the term just defined:

> Fascism is probably just a word for most of you. But the reality is very much present in this country. And the fact of it dominates the world today. Each year there is less and less freedom for more and more people. Put simply, fascism is the control of the state by a single man or by an oligarchy, supported by the military and the police. This is why I keep emphasizing the dangers of corrupt police forces, of uncontrolled *secret* police, like the F.B.I. and the C.I.A. and the Bureau of Narcotics and the Secret Service and Army counterintelligence and the Treasury men—what a lot of sneaky types we have spying on us all!
>
> —"The State of the Union," *Esquire*, (May 1975).

Jessica Mitford offers a more extended definition in this paragraph:

> I first began to think of myself as a muckraker when *Time*, commenting in its press section on the Famous Writers School fracas, called me "Queen of the Muckrakers." I rushed to the dictionary to find out what I was queen of, and discovered that "muckraker" was originally a pejorative coined by President Theodore Roosevelt to describe journalists like Lincoln Steffens and Ida Tarbell, who in his view had gone too far in exposing corruption in government and corporate enterprise. Thus the *Oxford English Dictionary* says "muckrake . . . is often made to refer generally . . . to a depraved interest in what is morally 'unsavoury' or scandalous." (I fear that does rather describe me.) In the *OED* supplement of 1933, "muckraker" has come up in the world a little bit and is now defined as "one who seeks out and publishes scandals and the like about prominent people." And by 1950 additional respectability is conferred by *Webster's New International Dictionary*, defining "muckrake" as "To seek for, expose, or charge, esp. habitually, corruption, real or alleged, on the part of public men and corporations."
>
> —*The Gentle Art of Muckraking* (1979).

Classification and Analysis Paragraphs

Usually classification is a handy method of organizing whole essays, but occasionally you may use it as part of a paragraph of analysis. Paragraphs of analysis are extremely common, especially in book or movie reviews, syndicated political columns, literary criticism, or, for that matter, any writing that tries to explain a problem, a trend, a fad, a relationship, or an abstract idea. In the fourth and fifth sentences of the following example, Joan Didion classifies two types of national heroes. The paragraph as a whole analyzes the astonishing appeal of Howard Hughes as an American folk hero:

> Why have we made a folk hero of a man who is the antithesis of all our official heroes, a haunted millionaire out of the West, trailing a legend of desperation and power and white sneakers? But then we have always done that. Our favorite people and our favorite stories become so not by any inherent virtue, but because they illustrate something deep in the grain, something unadmitted. Shoeless Joe Jackson, Warren Gamaliel Harding, the *Titanic:* how the mighty have fallen. Charles Lindbergh, Scott and Zelda Fitzgerald, Marilyn Monroe: the beautiful and the damned. And Howard Hughes. That we have made a hero of Howard Hughes tells us something interesting about ourselves, something only dimly remembered, tells us that the secret point of money and power in America is neither the things that money can buy nor power for power's sake . . . , but absolute personal freedom, mobility, privacy. It is the instinct which drove America to the Pacific, all through the nineteenth century, the desire to be able to find a restaurant open in case you want a sandwich, to be a free agent, live by one's own rules.
>
> —"The Howard Hughes Underground," *Saturday Evening Post* (Sept. 1967).

In the next paragraph, Wayne Booth uses classification to organize his ideas for helping students write more interesting papers:

> As I try to sort out the various possible cures for those batches of boredom—in ink, double-spaced, on one side of the sheet only, please— I find them falling into three groups: efforts to give the students a sharper sense of writing to an audience, efforts to give them some substance to express, and efforts to improve their habits of observation and of approach to their task—what might be called improving their mental personalities.
>
> —"Boring from Within: The Art of the Freshman Essay," an address to the Illinois Council of College Teachers of English (1963).

And here is a paragraph of pure analysis by anthropologist Marvin Harris:

> Hindus venerate cows because cows are the symbol of everything that is alive. As Mary is to Christians the mother of God, the cow to Hindus is the mother of life. So there is no greater sacrilege for a Hindu than killing a cow. Even the taking of human life lacks the symbolic meaning, the unutterable defilement, that is evoked by cow slaughter.
>
> —*Cows, Pigs, Wars, and Witches: The Riddles of Culture* (1974).

Comparison and Contrast Paragraphs

One of the best means of organizing ideas in writing involves making comparisons and contrasts. Strictly speaking, we *compare* things that are basically alike and *contrast* things that are basically different, but the terms overlap. In making a *contrast*, we have to *compare*. There's no other way to point out the differences, i.e., the contrast.

Making a distinction between the two terms is not the important thing; knowing how to make distinctions by using comparisons and contrasts is essential. In our first example Gore Vidal contrasts two types of novels that are currently in vogue. His second sentence defines the two. Then he briefly discusses the first kind. With the transitional word *although*, he moves into a discussion of the second kind. His concluding sentence leads into a review of a novel of the second kind.

> Currently, there are two kinds of serious-novel. The first deals with the Human Condition (often confused, in Manhattan, with marriage) while the second is a word-structure that deals only with itself. Although the Human Condition novel can be read—if not fully appreciated—by any moderately competent reader of the late Agatha Christie, the second cannot be read at all. The word-structure novel is intended to be taught, rather like a gnostic text whose secrets may only be revealed by tenured adepts in sunless campus chapels. Last month, a perfect example of the genre was extravagantly praised on the ground that here, at last, was a "book" that could not, very simply, be read at all by anyone, ever.
>
> —"Paradise Regained," *The New York Review of Books* (20 Dec. 1979).

The following paragraph contrasts the differences between "street smarts" and rural savvy in an alternating pattern:

> The tools of the country lawyer are the friendly handshake, the homily and the quiet eloquence of a summation delivered in an elmshaded courthouse on a hot summer afternoon. The corresponding street skills are the judo throw, the wisecrack and the naked belligerence of an insult hurled from the back of a crowd at night. The country lawyer may pride himself on being able to look into a man's eyes and tell if he's a person of character; the street-smart politician can look at a man's mustache and tell if he's Greek or Armenian.
>
> —Jerry Adler, "So What Are Street Smarts?" *Newsweek* (7 June 1982).

Because the pattern of contrasts was set up earlier in the article, the paragraph is almost free from transitions; only the term *corresponding* provides a subtle transitional clue. But perfect continuity is maintained through balanced structure and the exactness of the contrasts: *tools* and *skills*, *look* and *look*.

Cause and Effect Paragraphs

As you can easily see, cause and effect writing is a kind of analysis. There are two ways to organize cause and effect paragraphs. Using one method, Adam Hochschild here *moves from a cause* (sexual segregation in his all-male prep school) *and speculates on the resulting effects:*

> Perhaps only the women who live with male prep school graduates can be the ultimate judges, but my own guess is that no one comes out of such an adolescence without some emotional crippling. It was not that we looked on women only as sex objects; it was that they were no kind of object at all. They didn't exist. Except on these rare weekends. Talking to a girl your own age was an *event,* like shaking hands with the president; it was analyzed and discussed and agonized over for months afterward. Should I have said this? Asked her that? To go from such an atmosphere to one in which you must live, study or work with women as equals each day requires a major adjustment, and I think some prep school graduates never made it.
>
> —"True Prep: The Ties That Bond," *Mother Jones* (May 1982).

In his next paragraph Hochschild employs the second method, which reverses the procedure. *Having discussed the effects* (of his all-male adolescent schooling), *he now ponders the causes:*

> I went to Pomfret about a decade too early. Today, it and almost all the other major prep schools are coed. Why did they hold out so long? Even longer, in fact, than it took most of them to become racially integrated? Ultimately, I think, these schools were set up with the same hope that is behind all institutions that are designed for men only, from armies to the Catholic priesthood: the hope that sexuality will be sublimated into competitive achievement. The appalling thing about this is that it works. I studied harder at Pomfret—sometimes six, seven hours a day, after classes—than I ever have elsewhere, before or since. But the price was too high, and I wish I had never had to pay it. I don't just mean the price in the dammed-up sexuality of those years, but in all the unexperienced gentleness, laughter and, for want of a better word, roundedness of life, which cannot exist to the full where one half of the human race is kept separate from the other.
>
> —"True Prep: The Ties That Bond," *Mother Jones* (May 1982).

DISCUSSION EXERCISE   **4-4**

1. The following paragraphs illustrate some of the methods of organizing paragraphs that we have just discussed. In order to become more familiar with these common patterns of development, study each paragraph and decide which of the following types it represents:

Descriptive	Analysis and classification
Process	Comparison and contrast
Definition	Cause and effect

Be prepared to explain how you determined your answer.

2. After you have determined the organization, point out the topic sentence of each paragraph (if there is one) and decide why the writer placed it in that position (or why it was only implied).

(a)

Fellow Americans, we are gathered here in the largest demonstration in the history of this nation. Let the nation and the world know the meaning of our numbers. We are not a pressure group. We are not an organization or a group of organizations. We are not a mob. We are the advance guard of a massive moral revolution for jobs and freedom.

—Asa Philip Randolph, "Why Should We March?" in *The Black Man and the Promise of America* (1963).

(b)

Down a piece, abreast the house, stood a little log cabin against the rail fence; and there the woody hill fell sharply away, past the barns, the corn crib, the stables, and the tobacco curing house, to a limpid brook which sang along its gravelly bed and curved and frisked in and out here and there and yonder in the deep shade of overhanging foliage and vines—a divine place for wading, and it had swimming pools, too, which were forbidden to us and therefore much frequented by us. For we were little Christian children and had early been taught the value of forbidden fruit.

—Mark Twain, *Mark Twain's Autobiography* (1924).

(c)

There is an approved method of dipping a brush into a paint can. Professional painters work from a half-full can and dip only a third of the bristle length into the can. Then they slap the inside of the can with the brush and withdraw the exact amount of paint, without spilling a drop. This method may be correct, but it's dull. Amateur painters prefer to brighten the day by using the Erupting Volcano Technique, wherein the paint flows steadily down the side of the can all day, gradually covering the village.

—Dereck Williamson, *The Complete Book of Pitfalls* (1971).

(d)

The humorous story is told gravely; the teller does his best to conceal the fact that he even dimly suspects that there is anything funny about it; but the teller of the comic story tells you beforehand that it is one of the funniest things he has ever heard, then tells it with eager delight, and is the first person to laugh when he gets through. And sometimes, if he has had good success, he is so happy that he will repeat the "nub" of it and glance around from face to face, collecting applause, and then repeat it again. It is a pathetic thing to see.

—Mark Twain, "How to Tell a Story" (1897).

(e)

When Adam went and took Eve *after* the apple, he didn't do any more than he had done many a time before, in act. But in consciousness he did something very different. So did Eve. Each of them kept an eye on what they were doing, they watched what was happening to them. They wanted to KNOW. And that was the birth of sin. Not *doing* it, but KNOWING about it. Before the apple, they had shut their eyes and their minds had gone dark. Now, they peeped and pried and imagined. They watched themselves: And they felt uncomfortable after. They felt self-conscious. So they said, The act *is* sin. Let's hide. We've sinned.

—D. H. Lawrence, *Studies in Classic American Literature* (1923).

(f)

The counter-cultural protest of the 60's, according to some sociologists, stemmed in part from the younger generation's discovery that the real world in no way conformed to those small-screen images [on television]. In any case, the social turbulence of that decade never invaded the tube. Prime time became congested with rural comedies like "The Beverly Hillbillies" and escapist fantasies like "I Dream of Jeannie" and "Mister Ed." The only whiff of reality was provided by the TV appearance of one-parent households. Nary a one, however, was the product of something so messy as a divorce. In "My Three Sons," Fred MacMurray played a widower. In "Family Affair," Brian Keith played a worldly bachelor who became a foster parent to three orphaned relatives. And to keep things familiar, there was usually a second authority figure around—a sagacious British butler, perhaps—to fill the role of surrogate mother.

—Harry F. Waters, "The TV Fun House," *Newsweek*, 15 May 1978.

WRITING EXERCISE

4-5

Choose one of the topic sentences below and write three paragraphs, each time using a different pattern of development. Choose from the following patterns, which get more challenging as you go down the list:

Descriptive detail

Example or illustration

Narrative

Process

Definition

Classification and analysis

Comparison and contrast

Cause and effect

1. Aristotle wrote, "The roots of education are bitter, but the fruit is sweet."
2. "One who has made a beginning has half the job done."   (Horace)
3. Racism is woven into the fabric of everyday life in the United States.
4. As Thoreau says, most people "lead lives of quiet desperation."

chapter Five
Cornerstones for Composing

As we saw in the last chapter, your short opening paragraph should let your readers know what your paper is about. But first you yourself have to decide. Usually your instructor will offer some suggestions for topics; there are more than a hundred in this textbook. Naturally you will pick one that interests you, if possible. But if nothing sounds exciting, force yourself. The first step is to arrive at a workable thesis—a main idea for the paper.

You do have things to say, opinions to voice, feelings to express, conflicts to work out. Using the invention techniques in Chapter 1 you will be able to come up with a writing idea, some details to work with, and even perhaps an idea about how to arrange the essay. After carefully working out the organization (Chapters 5 through 7 are designed to help with that task), you will construct a rough draft. Ideally this rough draft should be completed several days before the paper is due: you can revise with greater objectivity and renewed vigor if you and your writing have a little time to cool off. Remember also that you have to allow time for typing and proofreading the final draft. So get started at once, even though the deadline may seem a leisurely week away.

DESCRIPTION

Whatever you have to say, accurate and evocative description will help you say it. Descriptive detail, of course, adds liveliness, interest, and feeling to your essay—but it is not just a frill for special occasions. It is an integral part of all writing, for without description your reader may become lost in generality and abstraction. Imagine trying to tell someone how to find your apartment, what your best friend is like, or why you are depressed, using only abstract and general terms. You would not even attempt it. Your first impulse, in real life, would be to describe specific, concrete details: "There's a seedy cafe called the Joytime across the street"; "He has a pleasant expression even when he's paying his electric bill"; "The door handle broke off my Pinto again this morning," you would say. You must make use of your descriptive skills in all your writing, whether you are informing, persuading, entertaining, or expressing yourself to your audience.

EXERCISE   **5-1**

Turn back to Exercise 4-4 in Chapter 4. Find the descriptive detail in each sample paragraph there. Point out words and phrases that call forth mental pictures.

Technical Description

When you are writing in the world of work or when you are writing instructions, you will need to produce accurate technical descriptions. You need to set down clearly and objectively the details your readers will need to identify whatever it is you are describing. Here, for example, is a technical description from a drafting textbook:

> *Drawing paper* in the better grades contains a high percentage of rag stock, is tough and durable, and has a smooth, fine-grained, hard surface that will withstand frequent erasures. It is used primarily for precise graphical solutions and preliminary design layouts made with a sharp, hard pencil (3H to 6H). The drawing is not intended for reproduction.
>
> —B. Leighton Wellman, *Introduction to Graphical Analysis and Design* (New York: McGraw-Hill, 1966), p. 366.

This concise description covers what good drawing paper is, what its uses are, and what its uses are not. Notice that although the passage contains fifteen descriptive adjectives (almost 28 percent of the words), none of them is intended to be connotative, to arouse emotion. If the writer is a connoisseur who deeply appreciates fine paper, you would never know it.

Pretend that you are writing for a person unfamiliar with our surroundings—someone from the past, from another culture, or from another planet. Describe one of the following items carefully enough that the person would immediately recognize it and be able to pick it out from other objects. Choose one: an avocado, a bottle of mascara, a socket set, a mirror, a corn tortilla, a felt-tip pen, a rubber band, a card table, a paper clip. It is best to have the object before you as you write.

Compare your description with those by other students who chose the same object. Make note of similarities and differences in

1. Selection of details mentioned
2. Organization of the description
3. Choice of descriptive words

Imaginative Description

In contrast to technical description, imaginative description creates not only a visual or other sensory image but also an idea or emotion about the image. Thus, you will use more connotative language and will select only those details that reinforce the idea or feeling you want to convey. Here is a paragraph of description by Kaatje Hurlbut about a small statue (Eve) in her grandmother's living room:

> Sometimes I only considered Eve herself because of her loveliness. When the room was dim she gleamed in the shadowy corner; but when the sun came into the room in the morning she dazzled until she seemed to be made of light pressed into hardness. And the cleanness of her was cleaner than anything I could think of: cleaner than my grandmother's kid gloves; cleaner than witch hazel on a white handkerchief.

Notice that Hurlbut chooses descriptive details that give you an image of the child's fascination with the statue as well as the statue's luminous appearance.

In the following excerpt from a student essay, the writer uses descriptive details to characterize new wave music, especially in contrast to other musical styles and the worlds they reflect.

> The tight, driving beat of such groups as The Specials, B-52s, Roxy [1]
> Music, and other New Wave groups indicates a drive toward destruction and violence. Instead of an easy, flowing musical line that makes you want to bob your head and tap your feet, New Wave's fierce drum throbs and noisy, choppy guitar lines make you want to jump up and down and kick in your T.V. Even the romantic love songs of the New Wave trend

indicate the emergence of a rougher culture. Unlike the sentimental flow of most popular love ballads that stress roses, romance, and rendezvous, New Wave's fast, violently abrupt musical beat stresses driving, urgent physical release. It definitely underlines a New Wave of love, as well as of music.

New Wave music evokes a new wave life style. The bright, loud [2] colors of ripped shirts and skin-tight leather pants convey a sharp switch from the blue jeans and T-shirts of the rock 'n' roller. The spiked shoes and obnoxiously flamboyant make-up reflect the violence and boldness of the music itself, as do the heavy chained belts and safety-pinned cheeks. The mannerisms of the New Wave worshipper—crass, bold, daring—imitate the manners of the big city street punk.

—Beth Murphy.

WRITING EXERCISE   5-3

1. Make lists of contrastive words and phrases in Murphy's writing:

New Wave	Other
tight, driving beat	easy, flowing
fierce drum throbs	bob your head
noisy, choppy guitar lines	tap your feet

and so on.

2. Music is usually a challenge to write about because you must translate a primarily nonverbal medium into words. Write a paragraph or two describing your favorite kind of music or your favorite song. Consider using words that involve not only sound, but color, movement, and emotion.

The most imaginative descriptive writing you will likely do will be expressive—that is, you will describe your thoughts and feelings. Be sensitive to all the words at your disposal to denote emotional states. Choose the most specific one. If you write, "I felt terrible," question yourself closely: be more accurate. That vague sentence could mean anything from "I was humiliated" to "I had a stomach ache" to "Guilt overwhelmed me." Say which it was. Consider also the gradations and fine distinctions among feelings you may express. Are you restless, bored, enervated, or dead? Impressed, surprised, stunned, astounded, or shocked?

A student writer describes her (and others') feelings as beginning college freshmen in the following excerpt.

We packed our clothes, our stuffed animals, our stereos, our fris- [1]
bees, and our toothbrushes all into boxes and hauled them off to college.
As the luminous buildings that were to be our homes came into sight, the
butterflies in our stomachs began to stir. What had seemed to be ages
away was now the present. Our lives of secure dependence on our parents came to an abrupt end as we were left off in a world of strangers on
the college campus. Left in a daze after the parting hugs and kisses of
Mom and the bear hug from dear old dad, we sat and waited for something, someone to tell us what to do next . . . but no one did. We looked
around for something familiar to tell us we were still at home . . . but
nothing was there. We longed for our friends and lovers . . . but they
weren't there either. We were alone and frightened and undeniably on
our own. But somehow, we freshmen have made it through the school
year and have grown into independent young adults.

As we left for class on that first day of school, we wandered around [2]
looking as if we had just landed on an alien planet. We felt small, intimidated, and young among the upperclassmen, who seemed to know we
were the new crop of students. Bright, shiny new backpacks hung from
our shoulders. We stood in the middle of the bustle of students trying to
look nonchalant as we scoped out the path to our classes on the college
map we had pasted to the inside covers of our three-ring notebooks. Too
proud (or too shy) to ask anyone directions, we sometimes had to learn the
hard way that we were in the wrong class, classroom, or even building.

—Lisa Wandrey.

WRITING EXERCISE 5-4

List words and phrases from the Wandrey excerpt that reflect feelings. Then list
words and phrases that give details that help you visualize the scene.

Feelings	**Details**
secure dependence	stuffed animals
abrupt end	stereos, etc.
world of strangers	parting hugs and kisses

In the examples so far, we have seen descriptive writing used to
identify a product, to convey an idea about an object, to characterize a
kind of music, and to convey a feeling. The complete, unified student
essay below uses a description to define the word *peacefulness*.

I first realized how peaceful the night had become as I gazed out the [1]
frosty window to see the perfect flakes of snow drift slowly to the ground.
Outside the gentle wind carrying the snowflakes slowly down from the sky
was the only sound. Snowflakes dancing in the cold night air made the
only movements. I knew this would be the right time to take a quiet walk.

I was soon outside feeling the brisk air and tiny wet snowflakes softly [2] touch my face. The evening was silent except for the crunch of the new-fallen snow under my feet. Although I was alone, I felt a sense of tranquility overcome me as I stared at the beautiful winter scene. The snow-laden trees looked like white angels guarding the earth; a small snowman sat quietly watching the snow fall; the lonely streets were quiet, all the cars tucked away in their garages; no one else was about. The houses surrounded by snow gave off a warm and inviting glow, as I realized the air was turning even colder.

I finished my walk and entered my own home. A great breath of [3] warm air engulfed me as I walked through the door. The blazing fire reached out and invited me to come sit by it and warm myself. I felt I was in my own world, safe inside by the fire, but able to look out at the beauty of the first snowfall. The house was quiet except for an occasional crackle of the fire and my own steady breathing. The fire held me in a trance with its dancing warm glow until I slowly drifted off to sleep.

When I awakened, the fire had diminished and left a few glowing [4] coals still keeping me warm. The evening had turned into night, and the snow had stopped flowing from the cloudless sky. The whiteness outside the window lay cold and still, stretching for miles. I slowly climbed the stairs to my room. I got into bed and snuggled beneath the warm blankets. Soft comfort enclosed me. I will never forget the peacefulness I felt that evening and the harmony I felt later, as I lay staring out at the snowy night, falling into a tranquil dream.

—Lisa Birkett.

EXERCISE
                                                                    5-5

1. What senses (sight, hearing, taste, smell, touch) does the description appeal to? Order them according to their frequency in the essay.
2. Is *dancing* in the first paragraph the best word choice? What other words could be used here?
3. What images are repeated in the essay? Why?
4. What comparisons and contrasts appear in the description? Include similes and metaphors in your list.
5. Do the paragraph divisions in this essay make sense to you? What principle was Birkett using to decide where to indent?

WRITING IDEA

Write a three- or four-paragraph essay describing a solitary experience you once had. Try to convey, as Birkett does, the dominant feeling of the experience, whether it was positive, negative, or boringly everyday.

PATTERNS OF DEVELOPMENT

Your essay of description was most likely a narrative—that is, a story told from beginning to end. We will expand upon this form first, as it probably comes most naturally to you. But there are many other ways of arranging your ideas into identifiable groupings. In the following sections we offer you three of the seven traditional types of organization: narrative, process, and example and illustration. (In the following chapter we will cover the remaining four patterns: definition, classification and analysis, comparison and contrast, and cause and effect.) Once you have decided on your paper's purpose, you can choose which pattern of development suits it best, then look over the sample outlines and essays here, and finally please your readers and yourself with your clear, organized presentation. In most of your writing, you will find yourself combining the different patterns within one essay. We present them separately because they can easily be explained that way, but we will point out which ones are especially compatible.

Each pattern fits into one of two basic approaches: chronological and logical. Narrative and process writing use a *chronological* approach: you start at the beginning and stop at the end, telling events in the order in which they occur. The five other patterns are basically organized according to *logic:* items are grouped and put in order according to the ideas they develop and the relationships between those ideas.

NARRATIVE

If you have had the pleasure of knowing a good storyteller or the agony of knowing a terrible one, you already understand a lot about narrative. A poor narrator can make you yawn during a description of being kidnapped at gunpoint and locked up for three days in a sleazy pink motel. Or you can doze off in the middle of this person's account of a most impressive sexual experience. In contrast, great narrators can make a casually overheard exchange between a businessman and a waitress a perfect observation of how sexism manifests itself. Or they can make you smother your laughter so as not to miss the next detail of how they make toast in the morning. The difference between the two storytellers, as you can see, does not come from one's having more inherently interesting subjects than the other; the difference lies in the narrator's style and selection of detail. As you write narrative, keep in mind the image of someone you know who tells particularly good anecdotes, and try to imitate those good qualities.

When to Use a Narrative Pattern

You see narrative in its pure form whenever you read fiction. But that is not the only appropriate place for it. Every pattern of development is likely to include sections of narrative. For instance, a paper in which you attempt to persuade college students not to procrastinate will probably include somewhere a story of your own grim experience with procrastination, and in that story you should exercise all the narrative skills you are about to learn.

Narrative ties ideas to real, sensory, day-to-day experience: it binds the abstract to the concrete. That is why narration helps make all kinds of writing more interesting and meaningful. Do not hesitate to amuse your readers with a lively relevant story, no matter what kind of long essay you are writing. We must warn you that some experienced writers and teachers see no place for anecdotes in scholarly, formal writing, but most of your writing in this course, and in everyday life, will not be that formal.

How to Organize Narration

Not too many things can go wrong with straight chronological organization. Getting the events out of order is possible, but not likely. More probably you will digress, or wander off the main track, as you have noticed poor storytellers do. No one wants to hear a long digression about how Sharon won the "I Love America" essay contest in third grade if the narrator inserts this information just as the main story has left Sharon approaching the Mexican border guards with fifty pounds of marijuana in her knapsack.

Cases do come up in which a certain kind of digression—a *flashback*—is exactly what you want. A jump into the past can reinforce a mood, explain a character's motivation, or give background necessary for the reader's understanding of an event. J. D. Salinger's *Catcher in the Rye* is an example of a narrative that uses flashbacks. The main story takes place during just four days, but narrator Holden Caulfield associates these events with so many earlier events that, by the end of the novel, we know the major incidents of Holden's whole life. As a result, we understand his personality much more fully and respond more sympathetically than we would if Salinger had stuck strictly to the chronological sequence of events.

When faced with the temptation to go astray, how do you decide whether your tempter is an important flashback or a tiresome digression? Easily, if you have your goal firmly in mind. Ask yourself how much the proposed addition contributes to that goal, and give it space in direct proportion to its contribution. If the story about Sharon was intended to be an exciting, suspenseful tale of her smuggling attempt, then the irony of her childhood "I Love America" triumph should be mentioned just briefly. If, on the other hand, the narrative is meant to show the development of Sharon's political attitudes, then the writer should tell both the "I Love America" story and the smuggling story, linked with a transition. This process of choosing details is called *selection*, and a good storyteller does it all the time, both consciously and unconsciously.

Remember that your narrative goals do not always have to involve heavy, didactic revelations about the Meaning of Life or Human Nature. Your goal can be to tell an amusing, entertaining, exciting, unusual, or puzzling story; this kind of story can have an important point too.

Finding Your Story.   Storytelling is a fine old tradition still practiced among those who are not slaves to television. Most people have a stock of stories from their lives that they pull out and eventually tell to every new listener. A good storytelling session can be sparked with a leading question addressed to everyone in the group:

What was the happiest day of your life?
What was the most frightened you have ever been?
Who is your craziest relative?
When was the closest you ever came to going to jail?
What was the biggest lie you ever told?

Then people chime in with their tales. To find a subject for your narrative, you may try such a session with your classmates or friends. Notice that the leading questions above all deal with extremes—happiest, craziest, most frightened. This is natural, because the extremes are most memorable.

Facing the Blank Page.   Once you know your goal and what you are going to include in order to get there, you can no longer avoid writing a rough draft of the paper. And that means you will have to decide where to divide paragraphs. We admit that this is hard to do when you are writing a chronological sequence because everything seems to run together.

One hint is to look for breaks in the time sequence and try dividing paragraphs there. For instance, if your narrative concerns the problem of moving to a new apartment on Monday, discovering many cockroaches and no hot water on Tuesday, and fighting with the landlord and moving out on Wednesday, you might try dividing the paragraphs so you have one for Monday, one for Tuesday, and one for Wednesday.

Your action will not often divide itself tidily into Monday, Tuesday, Wednesday, or morning, afternoon, evening. If you do not have clear and even time breaks, look for other kinds of breaks. In narrative writing, sometimes the focus will shift from description of environment to description of character, from a character's inner thoughts to that character's outward action, from one character to another, from main story to flashback and back again, or from background material to action. These shifts of focus are possible places to divide paragraphs. Remember that a traditional paragraph within the body of an essay runs about 100 to 200 words long, so do not divide too often.

Writing dialogue into your narrative can help get you out of the paragraph division dilemma because you have to start a new paragraph with every change of speaker. Dialogue also gives the writing immediacy, like a play or movie, and can help develop characters by revealing their speaking styles.

Samples of Narrative Writing

The two student essays that follow are good examples of narrative writing. The questions after them will focus your attention on the techniques used. You may also refer back to these essays as you study narrative introductions, conclusions, and transitions.

The Change

I was driving my new red Corvette to school. It was beautiful, more [1]
beautiful than anything else in the school parking lot. I flew like the wind
with the knowledge that now the other kids wouldn't have any reason to
make fun of me, or call me names, or laugh at my worn-out clothes. I
could see them admiring my car, talking to me, maybe calling me up to
ask me over for a slumber party. "Hello, Cindy. . . ."

"Cindy? Cindy! Will you pay attention? If I catch you sleeping one [2]
more time in my class I'll send you to the office!" Miss Daniel's voice cut
through my dream. I heard giggles. "Do you know what we were talking
about?"

I was so certain the subject was square roots I could have staked my [3]
life on it. But I could not bear to say it in case I was wrong. I sat there
instead, letting her and the entire class become impatient at my stupidity.
A few more giggles floated up from the back of the room.

"We were discussing square roots." But the voice wasn't mine. It [4]
was Miss Daniel's, dripping icicles. "Tomorrow you can bring in a table
of approximate square roots of all the numbers up to one hundred."

I didn't dare look around me. I felt eyes on me from all over the class [5]
as it was. When the bell rang I would pick up my books and walk out of
class and I wouldn't cry. The bell rang. I picked up my books and dropped
them all over the floor. The giggles turned into laughs as the other children

left the room. Everything swam in front of me as I gathered my books and left the room. I cried into my locker for an eternity and was late for my next class.

The next morning in homeroom I started working on the square [6] roots. It wasn't nearly as hard as I thought, but it did take a lot of time. My best friend tried to help me but couldn't. By science class I was nearly done. I had worked on those square roots in every class except P.E. The only numbers I had left to do were ninety-five through one hundred. I was working hard on the last five when for some reason one of the boys in the class noticed what I was doing. He stood in front of my desk for a while looking down at me with a grin that made me wonder what he was thinking of.

Suddenly, he reached down and tore up my paper. All those num- [7] bers I had worked so hard to finish and were so close to being done were gone. I just sat there with my mouth hanging open. I couldn't believe that he had actually done that.

Without thinking, I yelled at him. "Just what do you think you're [8] doing? Do you think you have the right to tear up my paper like that? Just wait until we get to math class. Miss Daniel is going to drag you down the hall by the ear." This was something she was famous for.

He just stood there not believing that I had actually dared to say [9] anything. Usually I just took everything they did without a word. It was almost a game they played to see how much I would take without crying. I had never yelled before. I don't think any of them had really believed that I was able to speak in a voice above a whisper.

I was rather shocked myself. Not only at the fact that I had yelled at [10] him, but also at the fact that he hadn't struck me dead. As a matter of fact, he hadn't done anything at all. Maybe he couldn't think of anything to do.

I could hardly grasp that fact. That would mean that not only he, but [11] the others in the class, weren't put here on earth to make me miserable. They were just the same as me.

He was still standing in front of my desk when the teacher came in. [12] He went to his seat. I knew that from now on things were going to be different.

—Cynthia Fink.

Christmas Spirit

It had been one of those days when nothing goes right. I was due at [1] work at 8 o'clock, but I was ten minutes late because I overslept. When I finally arrived at K-Mart and punched in, I went straight to my regular post—the toy department. It was two days before Christmas and the department was a shambles. At 10 o'clock the front doors opened and the herd of customers stamping through the store caused me to think back to the time when I enjoyed Christmas. That was two Decembers ago, before I went to work for K-Mart.

Somehow the Christmas spirit had evaporated since that time, proba- [2] bly because I got just a little sick and disgusted when I had to put up the plastic trees with their cheap ornaments and "made in Japan" lights in the middle of September; when I went partially deaf from people yelling in my ears; when I became accustomed to hearing the same shrilling Christmas carols three times an hour over the public address system. No, Christmas didn't mean much any more, except more work and headaches.

I dismissed these thoughts temporarily when I saw an irate customer [3] heading my way. I adjusted my pre-tied tie, my plastic pocket protector with the red "K-Mart" printed on a Christmas tree background, and my plastic smile, and I was ready to meet her. . . .

She was a massive woman with a hint of beauty-salon culture. Her [4] perfectly coiffed wig perched on top of a make-up laden face that was beginning to turn red. "Can I help you, ma'am?" I asked, trying to get my plastic smile to stretch a little farther.

"Where are the Evil Knevil dolls?" she shrilled. "My son saw it on TV [5] and now he wants it for Christmas." I said we were sold out, and then came the deluge—Why don't you have it? Why don't you get more? How come this store never has anything I need? etc., etc.

After a few similar confrontations it was time for lunch, but my [6] stomach was tied in so many knots I couldn't eat anything, so I went back to work after fifteen minutes.

The afternoon was much the same as the morning. I was cursed, [7] shoved, yelled at, stepped on, and almost crushed when some idiot started a "blue light special" only three feet away from me. And I still had to finish my Christmas shopping that evening. I had just finished explaining to a man why we didn't sell firecrackers, when I felt a tug on my arm.

It was one of two kids I had been keeping an eye on for a while— [8] security told us to watch kids for shoplifting. He and his little sister had been looking at the "discount" counter, where we had all the cheapest toys. Before I even bent down to listen to him, I checked around for his sister, thinking he may be trying to divert my attention while his sister pocketed something. I didn't see her, and the boy also seemed to be looking around to make sure she wasn't around.

"Mister, do you think this would be a good present for my little [9] sister?" he said in a broken accent, holding up a bottle of soap bubble liquid. "I don't want her to know about it," he whispered before I could even answer.

He seemed to be so sure that she'd love it that I just agreed with him [10] and didn't say anything more. He stuck his hand in the pocket of his ragged jeans and pulled out a fistful of change, asking if he had enough money to pay for the soap bubbles. The bottle cost fifty-seven cents and he had forty cents, mostly pennies. "It looks like you'll have to try to find something else," I said. "You don't have enough money here." I'd seen this trick of picking up some extra money from some good-hearted soul before, especially at Christmas. He looked crestfallen and went back to find something else.

I watched him from the corner of my eye for a while as he looked at [11] other items, but always came back to the soap bubbles. I left the immediate area for a few minutes and when I came back he was still there, trying to find a cheaper gift. Somehow the kid struck me as different from most of the troublemakers we got in the toy department.

I went over to him and asked if he had found anything yet. He just [12]
shook his head and looked very disappointed. "Well, let's see how much
money you have again," I said. He dumped the change in with the two
dimes I had concealed in my hand. "Well, lookit here!" I said, "I must
have counted wrong before—you have just enough for those soap bubbles." His smile spread out to his ears again, and he headed for the
checkouts.

I followed him unobtrusively to see what he really spent the money [13]
on. He went through the line with the one item and a smile, then met his
sister outside. He kept the bag tightly clenched in his fist so his sister
couldn't see what he had bought for her with his last pennies.

Somehow the rest of the day went much better, and when I went to [14]
buy Christmas presents that night I looked for gifts instead of obligations.
For the first time in three years I had my Christmas spirit again, but I got
some really odd looks from my family when I came home with soap
bubbles.

—Larry DeBoever.

EXERCISE   **5-6**

1. Choose from each narrative a paragraph or two which seem to have especially vivid details. Note the details and tell what senses they appeal to:
   sight, hearing, taste, touch, smell.
2. Find examples of dialogue. Is it more effective than indirect description?
   Why? Find other places in the essays where dialogue could have been used.
3. Try to summarize each writer's goal.
4. Identify flashbacks and digressions and tell what, if anything, they contribute to the goal of the essay.
5. Find events which are condensed and summarized rather than told in detail.
   Why did the writer choose to condense?
6. Note how paragraphs are divided in each paper. Identify the principles each
   writer used in choosing where to start new paragraphs.

How to Introduce a Narrative Essay

The introduction to a narrative is usually quite different from
introductions to other common types of papers, in which stating your
thesis is important. In narrative introductions, your best plan is to hint
at your main point, focusing instead on preparing your reader psychologically for what is to come.

A good narrative introduction can do this in several ways. The
most obvious way is to give background the reader will need to understand the story. "Christmas Spirit" embeds necessary background information (that the narrator works at K-Mart's toy department) in the
opening scene.

In contrast, "The Change" does not open with any background as such. It jumps right into the narrator's daydream, and gives the reader the pleasure of discovering it *is* a daydream. At the same time, it builds the narrator's character and gives hints about her life situation to set the mood for the story. A poor storyteller would start "The Change" something like this:

> I was always a very shy, quiet child. Because I was so shy, my school-mates used to boss me around and make fun of me. I used to daydream to escape from it all. But one time I had an experience that showed me that I could be more assertive and people would respect me more. One day in school I was daydreaming about. . . .

This introduction offers lots of background in a boring way and practically slaps you with the main point of the narrative.

Inexperienced writers almost always need to cut the flab off narrative introductions. "Christmas Spirit" would be more spirited if the writer had cut the first sentence, which is a cliché. Besides, it does not really fit the situation; the story begins around 8 A.M., which is too early to say, "It had been one of those days."

Because openings are so difficult to write, though, we suggest that you go ahead and put down whatever you can bring yourself to write. Then go back to cut and revise after you have finished the rough draft. Be sure to check the first sentence or two to see whether they are better left off completely.

EXERCISE   **5-7**

1. Look at a published short story and identify the clues offered in the opening about the story's goal, mood, characters, setting, and background. Here is one for practice:

> "Reach in my purse and git me a cigarette without no powder in it if you kin, Mrs. Fletcher, honey," said Leota to her ten o'clock shampoo-and-set customer. "I don't like no perfumed cigarettes."
>
> Mrs. Fletcher gladly reached over to the lavender shelf under the lavender-framed mirror, shook a hair net loose from the clasp of the patent-leather bag, and slapped her hand down quickly on a powder puff which burst out when the purse was opened.
>
> —Eudora Welty, "Petrified Man," from *A Curtain of Green and Other Stories* (1941).

2. Identify the mood, setting, character, and goals implied in this introduction to a student's narrative essay:

> As we walked down the corridor, I could hear the screaming, the loud roaring and the mad laughter. The closer we came to the entrance, the louder this conglomeration of noise swelled in my

head. I slowly eased down the ramp, while others tugged and pulled at me to hurry on. Suddenly, bright flashing lights shone brightly in my face. The crashing and roaring was now above my head and as I looked up, I could see the deformed, twisted shape of the huge and massive "Chicago Loop," the most exciting roller coaster in the Midwest.

—Debbie Polzin.

WRITING EXERCISE 5-8

Pretend that you are going to write a narrative about a childhood incident. As an introduction, you have decided to describe briefly your own childhood character. Write the introduction in two different ways:

1. As though the main goal of your story is to be light and amusing
2. As though the main purpose of the story is serious

Be ready to point out the changes you made to alter the mood.

How to End a Narrative Essay

You may want to come right out and tell the reader your conclusions. "The Change" does this clearly. Note how the conclusion continues the mood of the paper by ending with a serious, determined statement.

"Christmas Spirit" relies a little more on understatement for its conclusion. It does not come right out and say, "The lesson I learned from this experience was . . . ," but it does get the point across in statements like, ". . . that night I looked for gifts instead of obligations." The ending also reflects the overall tone of the story: it has amusing touches but also underlying seriousness. The conclusion ties in with early statements in the paper about how "the Christmas Spirit has evaporated," which gives the paper a satisfying feeling of completeness.

The same advice goes for conclusions as for introductions: do not overstate. Do not express your main point in both the introduction and the conclusion, and do not repeat it over and over in the conclusion. Most readers prefer to derive the general theme themselves from the evidence you present; try not to deprive them of the pleasure.

EXERCISE 5-9

Here is the closing of the student essay whose introduction you read. See if it has the elements we have discussed here.

I could feel my legs getting ready to buckle beneath me. We walked away and sat down on the first bench we saw. Slowly I looked up and saw the gigantic, green creature once again. It seemed to be looking back, giving me a nasty grin.

"Are you all right?" he asked once again.

"Yes," I replied, standing up. I grabbed his hand and with confidence that I had never known before, I led him towards the roller coaster entrance.

"Let's ride it again!" I shouted.

—Debbie Polzin.

How to Hold a Narrative Together

Since narrative organization is basically chronological, the transitional words you use will usually refer to time: *then, after, when, during, meanwhile, later, earlier, before.* Their main purpose is to make time relationships between events clear. In a narrative, such transitions will probably come naturally, but there is one you have to watch out for: *and then.* In conversation, we usually join events in a story by saying, "Then . . . and then . . . and then." In writing, the repetition of this transition seems simpleminded. Surely you can think of something else.

How to Revise a Narrative Essay

Here is a handy checklist to refer to as you struggle to improve a rough draft written in the narrative pattern. You may want to exchange papers with another student and answer the questions about each other's rough draft.

1. Is my main goal clear in my mind?
2. Did I focus on events within narrow time limits in order to write more specifically?
3. Do the digressions and flashbacks serve a purpose?
4. Are the verbs correct? Past tense for past events ("I sneezed"), past perfect tense for past events that occurred even earlier than those I wrote in past tense ("I had sneezed"), and present tense for the thoughts and events happening now ("I sneeze"). (See *Tense* in the "Revising Index," Chapter 13, for more help.)
5. Does every paragraph contain specific details which appeal to the reader's senses and help build the response I want?
6. Are the body paragraphs divided according to a reasoned principle, not according to whim? Do most of them contain more than two sentences?
7. Does the tone in the introduction, body, and conclusion either stay consistent or shift for a reason (not changing accidentally)?

8. Is there dialogue that reflects character when appropriate? Is the dialogue punctuated correctly? (See *Quotation Marks* in the "Revising Index," Chapter 13, for help with punctuation.)
9. Are introduction and conclusion free from unnecessary padding?
10. Does the conclusion tie in with the introduction?

Ideas for Narrative Writing

Brief Prewriting Practice

1. Hold a storytelling session with two of your classmates. Use the longer paper ideas, which follow, for some ideas.
2. Choose fifteen minutes out of the past two hours and list as many details from that period as you can.
3. Write two paragraphs. In the first one, describe a certain smell, sound, or taste that has strong associations for you. In the second paragraph, describe in detail a specific memory you associate with the smell, sound, or taste.
4. Write a paragraph describing a classroom. Use specific details to convey one of the following emotions: peace, anxiety, depression, boredom, anticipation, suspense, joy. (Do not name the emotion in your description.)
5. Think of a conflict between two people: teacher and student, parent and child, employer and employee, man and woman. Describe the conflict first as though you were one of the people and then as though you were the other.

Longer Paper Ideas

1. I learned _____ the hard way.
2. I really liked my _____ , but I lost it.
3. Describe a misunderstanding of the world or of language you had as a child and tell how the misunderstanding was corrected.
4. Narrate a situation in which you fortunately or mistakenly followed someone else's judgment rather than your own; or narrate a situation in which you trusted your own judgment over someone else's.
5. Narrate an experience that led you to a new realization about yourself (or about someone else).
6. Tell the story of a tough ethical decision you once had to make and its consequences.
7. Write an account of your initiation into some element of the adult world of which you were unaware as a child or teenager. Examples: violence, hypocrisy, racism, sexism, sexuality.

PROCESS

Like narrative, process writing has an order set by time. Just as there are poor narrators and great narrators, some people have a knack for describing a process clearly and painlessly, while others could not be trusted to tell you how to get out of a telephone booth.

When to Use a Process Pattern

You make use of process writing whenever you put together a three-speed bicycle, make spinach soufflé, or take a final exam in psychology. These examples involve the most common form of process writing: a list of directions for how to do something. Process writing can also describe how something works: how a cigarette lighter lights or how yeast makes bread rise or how seeing-eye dogs are trained.

You have seen the victims of bad process writing: people who ride about with their pedals where their handlebars should be; who cheerfully pretend that what they wanted was spinach soup; who sit for hours mauling their grubby computerized answer sheets, trying to figure out what number their chewed-up pencils are. In the face of such ignorance, confusion, and even madness, there is still hope: you, at least, can learn to write clear step-by-step prose.

How to Organize a Process Paper

To write a process paper, you should make sure that all the different things are in there. First, an introduction is written. Next, the body of the paper is developed fully in several paragraphs. Near the opening of the paper, terms should be well-defined. The conclusion does not have to be very long—just long enough to tie it all up.

Before you give up, read on. The paragraph you just read is a sample of some truly miserable process writing. Jot down a list of five problems you see in it. Your list is likely to fit in with the following advice about how to do it right.

First, process writing involves a sequence of time and action, and that sequence is easiest to follow if it is in order. Do not jump around, like our sample does by telling you what to put in the opening *after* it brings up the body paragraphs. Problems of order make it absolutely necessary to write a scratch outline for process papers. This outline can be a numbered list of steps. You have to write the steps in the order that they should or do occur, which may not be the same order in which they happen to flit through your mind. When you have an outline, you can go back and fill in the steps in the right places, no matter when you think of them.

Second, think of *all* steps and write them down. Do not skip any. There exists a particularly deceitful practice among some cooks: when they give a friend a recipe for one of their specialties, they leave out some distinctive herb or spice. Thus, the friend's dish is never quite as tasty as the original cook's, and everyone is supposed to conclude that the original cook is specially gifted. Such dishonesty is not usually your motivation for leaving steps out of a process, but the omission can still sabotage your readers' efforts.

The third and biggest challenge in process writing is to explain each step fully. One weakness that you probably noted about our opening sample was lack of explanation. Here are five tips for explaining processes fully:

1. Define Terms. When you use a word that is unfamiliar to most of your readers, or use a common word in an unusual way, you should let your readers know what you mean. For example, in describing how to adjust a sewing machine stitch, you might advise the sewer, "Check the tension of the bobbin thread." Some readers might get frustrated looking for a thread that goes up and down and seems nervous. Two terms in that sentence need definition (unless you can be sure your audience is familiar with sewing machines). If you use a term that calls for a long definition (a paragraph or more), read the section on definition, pages 149–156.

2. Be Specific. In writing, you must learn to make yourself clear without all those gestures and grimaces you use in conversation. If you are *telling* someone how to wire a fuse box, you can say, "Strip the insulation off a short piece of the wire," hold your thumb and index finger about an inch apart, and everything is understood. But in writing, you have to change that "short piece" to "one inch," because when your reader is gaping at a twenty-foot length of wire, a "short piece" could reasonably be anything from half an inch to three feet— and you do not want to be responsible for three feet of stripped wire exposed in someone's basement.

3. Include Reasons. You could probably prevent someone from stripping three feet of wire if you explain that the stripped wire is used to make a little hook that fits snugly under a screw in the fusebox to make an electrical connection. Knowing the reason for stripping the wire would help the reader do it right. So *tell not only what to do, but why.* The same rule applies to descriptive process papers—the kind in which you describe a process without asking your reader to do anything but understand it. For instance, you may write, "The carburetor mixes gas and air," but it would be better to write, "The carburetor mixes gas and air to make the most highly combustible combination possible, so it can be easily exploded by the spark plugs." Telling why the carburetor mixes gas and air makes the process more intelligible and meaningful.

4. Include Don'ts.   If there happens to be a common (or uncommon but disastrous) mistake that people can make in pursuing the process you are describing, you had better warn your readers. Tell *why* it is a mistake, too (remember tip 3). For instance, "Do not stick your fingers in the fusebox unless you have pulled out the main fuse" is handy advice. You may even go on to explain, "or you are likely to electrocute yourself by touching live wires," to emphasize your point. Sometimes, as you can see, the *don't*s are as important as the *do*s.

5. Mention Possible Pitfalls.   People might follow your yogurt recipe meticulously and still end up with a batch that just will not yog (thicken). It would be a great comfort to these people if you mention that this problem might occur if the starter or culture used was old or if the cow the milk came from was given penicillin, which kills the bacteria that make yogurt thicken. Whenever things are likely to go wrong despite your careful directions, let your readers know about it. You may help save their sanity.

Finding a Subject.   Your best prospect is to describe a process that you happen to know more about than most people do. Do you know how to paste up a page in a newspaper? Do you have a foolproof method of washing the dog? Are you especially good at analyzing poetry, building picture frames, playing backgammon, or writing letters home for money? Do you happen to know why the sky is sometimes red at night? Make a list of your skills and interests. Surely you will find a process that will instruct or entertain your readers—or maybe do both.

Facing the Blank Page.   The paragraphs in your essay will probably be divided by steps and substeps in the process. Your decisions about paragraph division can be based on the suggestions we made in the previous section on narratives (see pages 127–128). Or your essay may be a presentation of several alternative methods of doing one thing, like one student essay advising small children "How to Get Rid of Your Peas." Its paragraph topics are:

Feed them to the dog under the table
Hide them under other food on your plate
Put them in your mouth, but quickly transfer them to your napkin

The last and most difficult task in process writing, as in so many areas of life, is to do it with grace, wit, and charm. Even very practical how-to books, like cookbooks, bicycle repair manuals, and textbooks are sometimes happily endowed with these qualities.

Grace is especially difficult to achieve in process writing because process writing lends itself to one of the clumsiest grammatical constructions ever to stultify a sentence: passive voice (see the "Revising Index," Chapter 13). Note in the sample at the beginning of this section that the "introduction is written" and the "body . . . is developed." Very stuffy. In this book, we use the informal "you" to address our readers, and you can probably get away with it too. It does help get rid of passive voice: "First, you write the introduction," "You develop the body by. . . ." You can also leave the "you" out: "First, write the introduction. . . ." We could make the tone formal by substituting "the writer" or "one" for "you." You may have to do this if your teacher instructs you not to use "you." Whichever you use, be consistent throughout the paper.

As you seek out and destroy passive voice in your writing, look for narrative possibilities. You can liven up your points by illustrating them with personal experiences. Imagine what this technique could do for a "Three Ways to Drive Parents Crazy in a Car" theme.

In the same way, using comparisons and contrasts can clarify as well as perk up your writing. For example, pastry recipes advise you to cut the lard into the flour until the lumps are the size of small peas. Almost any cook knows what a small pea looks like, so the comparison functions as a visual aid. Read the section on figures of speech in the "Revising Index." Keep an eye out for lively phrasing as you read the following process essay.

Ninety Eight Point Sick

Let's say that for whatever reason, you decide to call in sick next [1] Thursday. Perhaps you're dying to see the Phil Donahue Show, or your best friend is going to be in town then. Chances are if you request the time off, you'll be denied it. The only way to solve this dilemma, then, is to call in sick. Calling in sick need not be anxiety-inducing; it can be a painless start to a personal holiday. Planning your strategy in advance makes facing the boss the next day much easier. This is why excellent planning is essential for a credible illness alibi. After all, who wants to use paid sick days thrashing around in bed with the flu?

To insure a smooth-running alibi, a person should start feigning [2] illness at least one day prior to calling in sick. Complaining of nausea, headaches, or extreme fatigue will usually get the point across. If you're having lunch with your boss or with coworkers, make sure you don't gobble everything on your plate. Remember, you don't feel well. (If chicken noodle soup is on the menu, order it with hot tea.) Finally, before you leave the office make sure that all of your work is caught up. This way, no one will have questions the following day about your work; therefore, they will have no reason to contact you at home about it. One word of caution needs to be issued here: you may get so wrapped up in convincing everyone you're sick that you start believing it yourself.

Relax as you leave the office and head for home. The first part of [3] your mission has been accomplished. You are now free to have an enjoyable evening, alone or with a friend, especially when you can anticipate the enjoyment to be derived from not going to work the next day.

Before you turn off into the land of nod, set your alarm clock for just [4] a few minutes till starting time for work. As soon as your alarm goes off, head for the telephone and make your call to your boss. Don't worry about sounding too hoarse or groggy: it will only reinforce your illness alibi. Having completed the call to your boss, you are done with your dirty work. Fix that Bloody Mary, turn on Phil Donahue, or go back to bed till noon. It is your day, and it's just begun.

A person that has a truly sound illness alibi still has some follow-up [5] work to do. Don't let your happy, smug attitude shine through when you go back to the office. To give the appearance of having been ill, wear your least becoming color. For some this may be Pepto Bismol pink; for others it could be pea green or gravy gray. If you're a female who usually wears makeup, this is the time to forget it. You may also wish to bring some aspirin, cough drops, or similar medication to set on your desk as visible proof of your shaky health.

In the final stage, don't let your conscience bother you when co- [6] workers say with great sympathy that maybe you should not have come back to work so soon. Everyone deserves a piece of dessert now and then, and sometimes that just desert is a day off from work.

—Cindy McKinney

EXERCISE   **5-10**

1. What is the tone of "Ninety Eight Point Sick"? What audience would most enjoy the paper?
2. How do you know that the writer has sufficient knowledge about her subject?
3. What principle does the writer use to divide the paragraphs? Why is there a lapse of time between paragraphs 4 and 5?
4. What important *don't*s does the writer include?

How to Introduce a Process Paper

By the time your readers finish your first paragraph, they should know exactly what process you are about to describe. To open a "how-to" process paper, you may reassure your readers by giving your credentials—telling them why they should listen to *you* on this subject.

You also might mention the advantages of knowing how to do whatever you describe, as the writer of "Ninety Eight Point Sick" does.

Many times, the joy of a good descriptive process theme comes from satisfying curiosity. Wouldn't you like to know how a water tower works? Or how cornflakes are made? Or how people write letters in Braille? Stirring up curiosity and promising to satisfy it are sometimes good introductory tactics.

Another common element of process introductions is a list of materials involved. In a how-to paper, it is convenient for the readers to have all the necessary items named in one place. If they are going to follow your directions for washing the dog, for instance, they should be told to collect the soap and towels before they collect the dog; otherwise, the beast will bolt while they are gone. If you decide to include such a list, double-check to make sure you do not leave anything out.

WRITING EXERCISE 5-11

Write an introductory paragraph for a process theme on one of the following topics: How to Make Whole Wheat Bread, How Batteries Work, How to Make Your Sweetheart's (or Spouse's) Parents Approve of You, How to Train a Dog to Sit, How to Take Care of Your Records.

How to End a Process Paper

A really impressive closing is hard to come by, but we will mention a few ideas that may help. You can get specific about the advantages of knowing the process. Be sure that you are not just repeating the introduction, though. Or you can mention related or complementary processes that your reader might be interested in. For instance, if you have just taught your readers how to stir-fry vegetables in a wok, you may advise them that learning to make tempura is even more challenging. Or you can give your readers a few cheery words of encouragement. Just one warning: do not mindlessly insist that a process is "fun and easy" when you know it is not. You might lose your credibility. Try "difficult but rewarding" instead.

EXERCISE 5-12

What closing strategies are used in the conclusion of "Ninety Eight Point Sick"?

> **WRITING EXERCISE** 5-13
>
> Write a conclusion for the introduction you wrote in Exercise 5-11.

How to Hold a Process Paper Together

Because your process paper is most likely chronological, the transitions will refer to sequence: *first, second, third, next, then, finally, last*. It is common to number the steps or stages with ordinal numbers (first, second, third). Instead of numbering, you may prefer to make up labels for the different steps you describe. For instance, an essay on "How to Become Suicidal" might move from the Do-My-Friends-Really-Like-Me? stage to the I-Even-Bore-Myself stage, culminating with the My-Life-Is-Worthless stage. Another trick that keeps your readers with you is the echo transition: summarize each step briefly at the beginning of the following step. The transitional terms in "Ninety Eight Point Sick" keep the reader aware of the time relationships:

Paragraph 2: *start, finally*
Paragraph 3: *first part, now*
Paragraph 4: *before, as soon as, just begun*
Paragraph 5: *still*
Paragraph 6: *in the final stage*

How to Revise a Process Essay

Check your rough draft for these elements of a good process theme (or exchange papers with someone else).

1. Does the introduction make clear what process I am explaining? Does it list materials and working conditions if necessary?
2. Are the steps or stages of the process all here and in order?
3. Are terms defined?
4. Is each step explained fully?
5. Does the paper give reasons for the steps or stages?
6. If necessary, does the paper include *don'ts* and warnings about possible dangers?
7. Are most sentences in the active voice?
8. Did I use vivid comparisons?
9. Did I use narrative to support my points where appropriate?
10. Does the level of usage stay the same throughout? Are there shifts of person, like, "One should speak heartily to *one's* dog while bathing it; otherwise, *your* nervous dog might gnaw *your* arm"?

Ideas for Process Writing

Short Prewriting Practice

1. With a ruler and compass, draw a fairly simple diagram consisting of five lines or so, something like the one in Figure 5-1. Then write a set of directions telling a classmate how to draw your diagram. The object is to ensure that your reader draws the same diagram you did without ever looking at your drawing.

Figure 5-1 A fairly simple diagram.

2. Write a sample process outline for the theme "How to Alienate Your Roommate (or Spouse or Housemate)."
3. Find out and describe out loud how some simple familiar thing works (examples: soap, can opener, hand eggbeater, wart remover, or ballpoint pen).
4. Think of an everyday process that you would like to have automated. Describe in detail a fantasy machine that does this process.

Longer Paper Ideas

1. How to train an animal (examples: cockroach, dog, parrot, turtle, or cat).
2. How to get rid of a bad habit. Choose only one habit to discuss (for instance: nail biting, smoking, or interrupting others).
3. How to get rid of the blues.
4. How to fix a bad Afro, trim split ends, give a home permanent, and so on.
5. How to say no to a persistent man (or child or woman).
6. How to solve a specific kind of problem.
7. Think of some established process that could use improvement (grading, registration, income tax, or courtship, for example). Describe how a preferable substitute system would work.
8. How to clean a carburetor.
9. How to change a light switch.
10. How to build a successful campfire.

EXAMPLE AND ILLUSTRATION

Once you have a good thesis idea, the essay of example is a simple one to write. It can follow the old

Paragraph 1:   Introduction
Paragraph 2:   Example 1
Paragraph 3:   Example 2
Paragraph 4:   Example 3
Paragraph 5:   Conclusion

pattern that you probably are already familiar with; even in its fancier forms, this one is hardly a brain-teaser. Coming up with the examples will be your toughest task here.

When to Use Example and Illustration

We can propose three closely related situations in which examples (or illustrations, those longer narrative examples) are valuable. First, examples explain ideas. Look at the two versions of the paragraph below which explain a distinction between formal and informal English. First, without examples:

> Standard English adds the -*ly* (to adjectives) and uses the resulting adverbs rather freely as to position. But very informal—not necessarily substandard—English does not favor -*ly* adverbs before the verb or verb phrase. It prefers the other position (after) or some adverb not ending in -*ly*.

Got it? Probably not. Now try the same passage as it appears in Dwight Bolinger's *Aspects of Language*—with examples.

> Standard English adds the -*ly* [to adjectives] and uses the resulting adverbs rather freely as to position: *They left rapidly, They rapidly left.* But very informal—not necessarily substandard—English does not favor -*ly* adverbs before the verb or verb phrase. It prefers the other position (after) or some adverb not ending in -*ly*: instead of *He grew steadily worse, I promptly told him,* and *She's constantly complaining,* it will say *He grew worse and worse, I told him right there,* and *She's all the time complaining.*
>
> —*Aspects of Language* (New York: Harcourt, Brace, & World, 1968)

That passage does not seem nearly as difficult with the examples. The second valuable use of examples, a close cousin of the first, is to clarify a concept. This next passage proves conclusively that no one would ever understand linguistics without examples.

> In an elaborated [communication] code, the speaker and listener are acting parts in which they must improvise. Their standing with each other is such that neither can take much for granted about the other. Intentions and purposes have to be brought into the open and defined. What the speaker will say is hard to predict, because it is not about commonplaces but about something more or less unique, related less to some foreseeable role and more to him as an individual. He is wearing not a comic nor a tragic mask but his own face, and that is harder to put into words. An example would be that of a man told to do something by his boss and having to explain why it is impossible for him to comply.
>
> —Bolinger, *Aspects of Language*

We found the definition a little fuzzy until the end of the paragraph, where the concrete example gave us the flash of recognition we needed to understand the whole concept. In fact, we think if he had worked in the example first, we would not have been puzzled at all.

Finally, when you are trying to prove a point, you need examples to support your idea. If your friend Lynn comments to you on Jose's new romance this way, "Oh, Jose always gets tired of his girlfriends quickly," you can expect her to follow that up with stories of how he got bored with Brenda in three months, grew weary of Wendy in two, and lost interest in Liz in a record three weeks. That series of examples is not an airtight argument—the new romance could be a glorious change—but it does lend some credibility to Lynn's generalization. As a writer, you should sincerely believe your examples to be honestly representative when you use them to support a debatable point.

How to Organize an Essay of Example

Within the body of a simple essay of example, each example will be developed in a paragraph of its own, with the introductory or concluding paragraph (or both) making a general statement that ties the examples together, thus:

I. Introduction with thesis: I believe that it is impossible to find the perfect apartment in Bloomington.

II. My first apartment was perfectly located, but I quickly found it to be infested with cockroaches, waterbugs, and spiders.

III. My second apartment was beautiful and bugless, but it was four miles from work and the heating bill was $160 a month in the winter.

IV. My third apartment is cheap, bugless, and close to work. It has no windows, and the wallpaper is designed to look like paneling, but I think I'll stay.

V. Conclusions: When apartment-hunting in Bloomington, do not look for the perfect place: look instead for one with faults you can tolerate.

Each of those body paragraphs could be fully developed, we are confident, with horrifying descriptive detail.

A variation on this plain pattern would be appropriate when you have two or three minor examples and one big convincing illustration of your thesis. For instance, in your paper about how you seem to choose absent-minded boyfriends, you may want to mention Herb, who forgot your dates all the time, and George, who forgot your name, but you have a lot more to say about Jack, who last weekend forgot you were with him at the shopping mall and drove home, leaving you to search for him in thirty-seven stores. The illustration will make up most of the body of your paper, requiring several paragraphs for development, and the short examples will be placed in a paragraph (or paragraphs) before or after the illustration.

The order of your examples and illustrations is something else to think about. The apartment outline above is arranged according to time, like a narrative or process paper. If time is not important in your paper, though, you may consider placing your examples in order of importance, impressiveness, wittiness, outrageousness, or seriousness, putting the example strongest in that quality last so its impression will remain with your readers.

Although you will sometimes need to use transitional terms like *for example, as an illustration, in one case,* and *for instance,* many times the introduction to this type of essay clearly indicates to the readers that what they should expect is a series of examples, and there is no use continually reminding them of that fact. In such a case, you need transitional terms only when you desire to include a paragraph that is *not* an example.

The following student essay is a good sample of the pattern we have been describing. Notice that the writer here omits obvious transitional terms at the beginnings of paragraphs with no harm to coherence, but uses a couple of transitional sentences (paragraph 3, sentence 2 and paragraph 4, sentence 1) to keep the ideas flowing.

"Just a Minute!"

Have you noticed that some people lose all concept of time when [1] they say, "Just a minute"? A mere sixty seconds can expand into ten minutes, half an hour, and even longer in just a minute.

My son answers "just a minute" every time I tell him to take his [2] shower, go to bed, do his homework, or whatever else he doesn't want to do. I can almost hear him start saying it before I finish voicing my request.

He seems to believe that if it's really important, I will remind him again; and after three or four reminders, he'll finally get up and do what I first asked him half an hour ago. However, I have also observed that he uses "just a minute" when he has no intention of doing what I asked of him. This usually happens when he's outside playing and doesn't want to interrupt the game to take out the garbage.

"This won't take long. I'll run in the store and be out in just a   [3]
minute." I'm sure you have dealt with this type of person at some time. Count on driving around the block four times before finally finding a place to park. Then you can sit in your car another twenty minutes before she comes out of the store carrying a tiny sack. "Sorry I took so long," she explains, "but they were having a sale on toothpicks, and the check-out line was murder. The man in front of me bought half the store." The murder you're considering by now wouldn't even compare to her ordeal.

"Just a minute" can be an effective stall technique in the business   [4]
world, too. Your boss asks for the report that was due yesterday. You simply tell him, "I'll have it on your desk in just a minute." What you really mean is you forgot all about the report, but will start it immediately and have it finished in an hour or two.

Last week, I telephoned my doctor's office; the nurse asked me to   [5]
hold for "just a minute." After five minutes, I hung up. I figured she didn't know where the doctor was and by then had probably forgotten who I was and what my ailment was. If you're persistent and hang on long enough, she'll eventually get back to you, but chances are *you* might have forgotten why you called, having fully recovered while you were waiting.

As you can see, "just a minute" is rarely just a minute. So, beware of   [6]
the person who tells you, "Just a minute." You might have a long wait.

—Mary Lou Travers.

How to Revise an Essay of Example

Consider these questions when you are working your rough draft over into a polished product.

1. Is each example or illustration an honestly representative case? This is especially important if you are using examples to support a serious argumentative point.
2. Does the thesis, stated or implied, make some point about all the examples?
3. Does each example support, clarify, or explain the thesis?
4. Is each example or illustration long and detailed enough to serve its purpose? Are there any digressions?
5. Does each example include concrete and specific details?
6. Does the order of the examples have some reason to it?
7. Do I avoid repetitive transitions? Do transitions appear where the reader needs a guide to what to expect next?

WRITING IDEAS

1. Write an essay giving examples which either confirm or deny the truth of an old saying like "If at first you don't succeed, try, try again"; "The grass is always greener on the other side of the fence"; or "Don't change horses in the middle of the stream."

2. Explain your relationship with one of your friends by giving three examples.

3. Make a generalization about one of your personal quirks and provide supporting examples. For instance:

   I have the most boring dreams of anyone I know.

   Multiple choice tests drive me crazy.

   I get sick when I'm under stress.

4. Support a statement about a friend or a public figure with examples. For instance:

   Red Smith was an unusual sports writer.

   Bob Seger is a nontraditional rock 'n' roll star.

   My friend Bill is absolutely dependable.

5. Make a general statement about the society you live in and provide examples to support it. For example, the society I live in:

   is contradictory.

   is cruel.

   is humorous.

   encourages conformity.

   encourages individuality.

6. Argue for or against some change in the political or cultural status quo, using examples to support your point. For instance, you may argue for (or against) socialized medicine by giving examples of how it works (or does not work) in other countries.

chapter Six
Typical
Expository
Patterns

In this chapter we will describe four more patterns of development: definition, classification and analysis, comparison and contrast, and cause and effect. These patterns may seem difficult at first, but you may find it helpful to realize that you use them in your everyday reasoning processes. You define words, classify tasks, analyze problems, compare products, and, we hope, employ cause and effect reasoning when you decide on courses of action. Focusing on these patterns in writing may, in turn, refine the logic of your thinking.

DEFINITION

Among the most bothersome people in the world are those who, when you argue your point cogently and logically, fall back on the argumentative technique of sniffing and saying, "Well. You should have defined your terms." Unfortunately, sometimes they are right. You can either avoid communication with such people, or you can define your terms so brilliantly in the first place that you disarm them. Such brilliant definition skills are among the talents we will explain in this section.

When to Use a Definition

First, you should define any word if your readers probably do not know its meaning. The special vocabulary of certain vocations, hobbies, and social groups usually needs definition. Labeling someone an "oralist" can be quite misleading if your reading audience knows nothing of education for the deaf.

Second, you should define what you mean when any abstract, ambiguous, or controversial terms figure importantly in your paper. Some of the grossest miscommunications occur just because audience and writer do not share the same idea about what a word or phrase means, either connotatively (by its associations) or denotatively (directly). For example, *daddy, father,* and *old man* all denote "male parent"; the connotations, however, are quite different. Three English teachers can argue severely over how to write well if teacher A thinks that "good writing" is whatever communicates the writer's idea; teacher B thinks that "good writing" not only communicates, but does it with correct punctuation, grammar, and mechanics; and teacher C thinks that "good writing" not only is correct and communicates, but does it with sparkle, wit, and zing.

Third, you might define something not as a means to an end, but as a challenge in itself. You can devote several hundred words to investigating the nature or essential qualities of just one word or phrase. Remember those tiresome essays in the front of your high school textbooks: "What Is Social Science?" "What Is Economics?" "What Is Citizenship?" These are painful examples of extended definitions. We think you can make yours more amusing and interesting with a little practice and thought.

How to Organize a Definition

If you are defining a word because it is a specialized term, something quite brief will usually do. A one-word synonym sometimes does the job. In the last chapter we defined the word *yog* just by putting the word *thicken* in parentheses after it, and you probably experienced no confusion.

If there is no apt synonym, you can try the traditional three-part definition, which goes like this: (1) the *term* to be defined, (2) the *class* to which it belongs, and (3) *specific differences* to distinguish it from other members of its class. Sounds pompous, but examples will help:

Term	Class	Specific Differences
A *klutz*	is a *person*	who is invariably clumsy.
A *tent*	is a temporary shelter	that is made of canvas or nylon and is portable.
A *smooch*	is a *kiss*	of casual affection.

You can leave one-sentence definitions as they are, or you can expand the third part. Abstract, controversial, or ambiguous words often require more than one sentence of definition. You can extend the definition by enumerating specific differences in several ways. Consider this student's expanded definition of one meaning of the term *smooch* and how her techniques could be applied to other definitions.

> A smooch is a quick kiss. The lips of two people press together for a short time, just a second. The eyes close while the closed lips protrude and touch the other set of lips. Smooching is not limited to members of opposite sexes, for you can smooch with anyone. It is considered a sign of affection, not a sign of deep feeling but a gesture of pleasant emotion, like a warm smile. A smooch is a casual kiss that can be done anywhere and still be considered proper. A person mostly smooches with relatives and friends. More intimate kissing is experienced by lovers, although they occasionally smooch also; for example, a husband and wife may smooch before they go to work in the morning. Anyone can tell a smooch from an intimate kiss simply by length of lip contact.
>
> —Mary McMurray.

Expanding a definition can involve any or all of the following techniques:

1. **Give descriptive details.**   In the smooch definition, the writer describes the process in detail in the first three sentences. To expand the other one-sentence definitions above, you could mention that a tent is supposedly held up by a complex system of stakes, ropes, and sometimes aluminum tubing, but note that you think it's all held up by the camper's faith. Or you could say that a klutz is sometimes recognizable by permanent bruises in the shin area, left from bumping into coffee tables.

2. **Exemplify and narrate.**   The smooch paragraph gives examples of who might smooch and when. To define *klutz* at more length, you could tell an embarrassing anecdote from the hard life of your friend Cuthbert, the klutz. Or you can narrate how you managed to mutilate three perfectly sound tents in one summer (cleverly slipping in definitions of the three types of tents you ruined). Or you can define a slangy phrase, like *nothing to write home about,* by giving examples of instances in which it would be appropriate.

3. **Compare.**   A smooch, says our writer, is "like a warm smile." If you wanted to clarify a definition of *egotist,* you could say that egotists are like misers, keeping love and admiration, instead of money, all for themselves. You could expand the comparison, saying that both types of people are lonely, insecure, neurotic, touchy. This kind of comparison is effective when your reader has a better knowledge of the second term than the first—in this case, when your reader has a more vivid mental picture of a miser than of an egotist.

4. **Contrast.**   In this method you develop specific differences, showing distinctions between the term you are defining and other things somewhat like it. The smooch above is contrasted with the intimate kiss. You may warn

your reader that the klutz should not be confused with the *schlemiel,* who is clumsy in the area of personal relationships. Klutzes can be diplomatic and sensitive in spite of their physical clumsiness, but schlemiels have no concept of these delicate qualities. Or, in writing the tent definition, you may point out that when your readers survey the campground they should be aware that the temporary shelters with wheels, metal sides, and TV antennas are *not* tents.

Using an apt combination of those four techniques, you can write anything from a paragraph to an entire essay of definition. You can write three one-sentence examples of klutzy behavior and put them all in one paragraph, or you can devote an entire paragraph to each example and end up with a whole essay on "What Is a Klutz?"

Another kind of definition essay investigates the different meanings of one word or phrase. We could write an essay about the three definitions of good writing on page 150, expanding on the opinions of teachers A, B, and C and perhaps telling which definition we prefer. Or consider the early and more recent meanings of the word *straight* when applied to a person:

1. Honest and trustworthy, blunt, open (antonym: *crooked*)
2. Endorsing the morality, lifestyle, culture, and political ideas that currently prevail (antonym: *freaky*)
3. Exclusively heterosexual (antonym: *gay*)

Another common definition essay cites the origin and development of a word. For instance, the slang meaning of the phrase *to dig,* which became popular through Black English usage, is possibly derived from the African Wolof word *degan,* "to understand." You can look up a word in the *Oxford English Dictionary*, which will tell you the different meanings of the word from its first known appearance until its present use. You can trace a word's history just because you find it interesting, or you can do it to prove a point. Barbara Lawrence's "Four-Letter Words Can Hurt You" (*New York Times,* 27 Oct. 1973) traces the origins of obscene words and shows that they reflect men's historical low regard and even hatred for women.

EXERCISE 6-1

1. Identify weaknesses in the three-part definitions below and try to rewrite them with improvements.

Example: A shoe is an article of clothing worn on the foot.

Weakness:	The specific differences are not sufficient. This definition could also describe a sock or slipper.
Possible improvement:	A shoe is an article of footwear, usually made of leather or canvas with a hard sole, worn to protect the feet and/or keep them warm outdoors.

A hippie is a person who wears cheap, sloppy clothes.

Bleach is a substance used to make clothes whiter.

Insanity is a state of mind in which you can't tell truth from falsehood.

A hypocrite is one who acts hypocritically.

2. Find examples of descriptive detail and exemplification in the selection which follows.

From "The Soaps—Anything But 99 4/100 Percent Pure"

"Love," in the soaps, tends to be a kind of hospitalization [1] insurance, usually provided by females to male emotional cripples. In these plays, a woman rarely pledges herself to "honor and obey" her husband. She pledges to cure him of his alcoholism, to forgive his criminal record, paranoia, pathological lying, premarital affairs—and, generally, to give him a shoulder to cry on.

An expression of love, or a marriage proposal, in the day- [2] time shows, often sounds like a sobbing confession to a psychiatrist. In *Search for Tomorrow*, Patti's father, a reformed drinker, took time out from brooding over his daughter's illegitimate pregnancy to express his "love" for his wife. It consisted of a thorough—and convincing—rehash of his general worthlessness and former drinking habits. "I need you," he moaned. "That's all I want," she said.

In *General Hospital* Connie's neurotic helplessness proved [3] irresistible some weeks ago; Dr. Doug declared his love. They engaged in a weird verbal competition as to who was more helpless than whom, who was more scared than whom, who "needed" whom more than whom. Doug won. Connie would be his pillar of strength.

—Edith Efron in *TV Guide*, March 1965.

3. Write out one section of the "Three Meanings of Cool" outline using exemplification and narration, comparison, or contrast as a descriptive strategy.

Three Meanings of Cool

I. Introduction—My mother, my older sister, and I all mean different things when we say "cool."

II. The old-fashioned meaning.
   A. Example: "When I asked her to dinner, she acted rather cool."
   B. Means that she was not friendly (warm)—almost snooty.
   C. Has negative connotation.

III. The 1960s meaning.
    A. Example: "Keep cool, baby."
    B. Means lacking in display of emotion—not enthusiastic or excited—implies calm, equanimity, levelheadedness.
    C. Has positive connotations for most people who use it this way.
    D. Contrast with examples of "uncool"—giggling, getting visibly nervous, upset, or joyful.

IV. The 1980s meaning.
    A. Example: "The new Led Zeppelin record is cool."
    B. Has the most general meaning—anything pleasurable and stylish.
    C. Definitely positive connotation.
    D. Contrast with 1960s meaning: this one can apply to people and things that display strong emotion, while 1960s "cool" cannot.

V. Conclusion—Example of communication gap caused by the different meanings.

Introductions, Conclusions, and Transitions

As you see from the examples, definitions come in all sizes and serve many different purposes. How you introduce, conclude, and tie together a definition is so dependent on its purpose and length that we cannot give you an easy formula. Of course, a synonym or a one-sentence definition does not need an introduction or conclusion.

If you are writing an extended definition, you may want to state the need for a definition in the opening. For example, "Before we can identify the best living jazz musicians, we must agree on a definition of *jazz.*" Or, your thesis sentence can be a traditional, three-part, one-sentence definition which you proceed to expand. If you are going to clarify a little-known, misused, or slang term, you may provoke curiosity by using the term at the beginning, like, "When my friend Rusty comes over, I put my coffee table in the hall closet and lock the closet door. Rusty's a klutz." One student began an essay that gave her personal definition of *boredom* in this way:

> For me, boredom usually sets in during a three-day holiday weekend. This break comes over Labor Day just after school has started, and everyone but me treks home by bus, car, or train to spend the holiday feasting with relatives while I halfheartedly ponder how I'll spend my hours alone. The fact of staying cooped up at college on this long weekend hits me when I see the last suitcase or overnight bag sail into the elevator going "down."
>
> —Cindy Reynolds.

Tailor the transitions and conclusions to your length and purpose. You can borrow closing and transitional strategies from other patterns of development, especially narrative (pages 133–134), process (pages 141–142), classification and analysis (pages 165–167), and comparison and contrast (pages 175–177).

EXERCISE   6-2

Define the transitional techniques used by the writer of "The Soaps."

WRITING EXERCISE   6-3

Write a paragraph of introduction and a paragraph of conclusion using the outline of "Three Meanings of Cool."

How to Revise a Definition

Answer these questions about your own or a classmate's essay to see if your definitions are graceful and clear.

1. Did I avoid using *is when* and *is where* in sentences of definition? These phrases are not only inaccurate but awkward, as in these examples:

   Risible is when you laugh a lot.
   Geometry is where you do math related to lines and shapes.

2. Are there any circular definitions, that is, definitions in which the specific difference basically repeats the term? For example:

   Organized crime is an organization of criminals.
   A dietician is a person who studies diets.

3. Are the differentiating characteristics stated precisely? Phrases like *kind of small* can mislead a reader who has a different idea of small than you do.

4. Did I keep my common ground with my audience in mind? You have probably heard someone give a definition in terms that need defining themselves. Be sure that your definition is phrased in terms your readers know. For example, you would not offer the following definition to anyone but a group familiar with computer science:

   A compiler is a kind of master program that translates source code into object code.

Ideas for Definition Writing

Short Prewriting Practice

1. Write one-sentence, three-part definitions for the following: *magazine, flower, cream, anthropology, infancy, new wave music.*
2. Develop one of the definitions you just wrote for number one into a 100-word paragraph. Use one or more of the four strategies listed on pages 151–152.
3. Write a paragraph that defines a slang term.
4. Think of a subject that you know more about than the general reader. Choose a term from that subject area and define it. Examples:

Subject	Term
electricity	*ground*
used cars	*burned*
cooking	*boil, simmer, scald*

Longer Paper Ideas

1. Think of a word or phrase you use a lot, and define what you mean by it in different situations. Examples: *same difference, right on, you know, between a rock and a hard place, really, out of it.*
2. Define a certain type of person. Examples: *perfectionist, slob, chauvinist, intellectual, egomaniac, miser, life of the party, radical.*
3. Write about a term you feel is used in more than one way. Examples: *love, friend, materialism, hippie, ugly, interesting.*
4. For an audience of people from another culture, define *situation comedy, junk food, soap opera, human potential movement,* or another term that labels one of our cultural phenomena.
5. Trace the history of a word. Examples: *nice, gossip, happy, hashish, conservative, rhetoric, cute, assassin, curfew.*
6. Write the definition of an abstract concept. Examples: *beauty, alienation, eccentricity, power, happiness, progressive, mean.*

CLASSIFICATION AND ANALYSIS

These two kinds of papers are like gerunds and participles: most people have a hard time keeping straight which is which. It may help you to remember that in *classification*, you are taking *many* items and dividing them into a few groups, but in *analysis*, you are taking *one* item and dividing it into its component parts. If your subject is squashes, and you find yourself outlining three types of edible squashes, you are classifying; if you outline three parts of a squash plant, you are analyzing.

The reason we discuss the two together here (and the reason you get them confused) is that they are similar in some important ways. First, both are based on the logical process of division, and second, both are written using the same kind of organizational tactics.

When to Use a Classification or Analysis Pattern

These processes stave off confusion and chaos, in either your reader's mind or your own. Both types of organization impose or reveal order, and order makes things much more understandable and can be quite comforting. The kind of order you impose depends on who you are and what you are up to. If you are working on a political campaign, you are likely to *classify* people into Republican and Democrat or conservative and progressive; if you are a literary snob, you are likely to *classify* people into those who read Milton for fun and those who read trash; if you are an egotist, you are likely to *classify* people into the unsavory millions, the merely disagreeable few, and your own wonderful self.

When you *analyze* something, you make the whole thing more understandable by revealing and explaining its parts. Explaining a process, speculating on cause and effect, arguing a point, and interpreting literature require analysis. In fact, all the papers you write require analytical thinking. The analysis pattern we will discuss here is all-purpose; in other sections we go into more specific analytical skills.

Analysis is always a part of effective problem solving. Take this topic: Why is it so hard to study? Rack your brains to think of the component parts of your difficulty in studying. You may come up with three rather curable contributing factors, like: (1) I have not bought the textbook, (2) the light bulb in my desk lamp has been burned out for three months, and (3) I turn on the TV as soon as I get home from class. Then all you have to do is borrow a book, change the bulb, abstain from television and think up three more rationalizations. Eventually you may get to the heart of the problem, and you will owe it all to your powers of analysis.

How to Organize a Classification or Analysis Essay

As a rule, essays have three parts: the introduction, the body, and the conclusion. The body is the longest, most detailed part—the one that most puts your organizational skills to task—so we suggest that you deal with it first. Then, after you are warmed up, you can tackle a lively introduction, a unifying conclusion, and clear transitions to hold it all together. We follow this suggested order—body, then introduction, conclusion, and transitions—in our advice for writing papers here.

In planning a classification or analysis essay, first you need to decide on a subject—something that you can break down into groups or components. Here are just a few categories that lend themselves to analysis: objects (a vending machine), characters (Cinderella), ideas (humanism), organizations (the Quakers), processes (how people become cynical), events (any war), or problems (Why is it so hard to study?). Subjects for classification can be found in nature (Remember *cirrus*, *stratus*, and *cumulus*?); in media, especially advertising (How many distinct kinds of cigarettes are there, anyway?); and in humanity (different types of bores, for instance, who inflict themselves on others daily). Look at the Longer Paper Ideas on page 168 for more inspiration.

After you decide on a subject, choose a basis for division. You must do this carefully or your paper will be a disaster. Heed these warnings:

1. **Know the difference between useful and useless bases of division.** Classifying history teachers into those who wear black socks and those who wear dark blue socks is useless. There is nothing significant about the grouping because it has nothing to do with teaching. But classifying history teachers into those who use a lecture-and-question format and those who rely more on open discussion could be significant, as well as useful to a prospective history student, because it may reveal the teachers' philosophies and attitudes toward the subject and the students.
2. **The division should cover all the times and parts you claim it covers.** If, for instance, you know of many history teachers who are not strictly either lecture-and-question or discussion types, you cannot pretend they do not exist just to make your classification tidy. At least *mention* exceptions, even if you do not give them as much ink as you give the major divisions.
3. **The basis of division should not shift, and the divisions should have parallel rank.** This sounds like gobbledygook, but if you can find the faults in these outlines, you already understand it:

Types of Aardvarks	**Types of Recorded Music**
I. Introduction	I. Introduction
II. The Fuzzy Aardvark	II. Classical
III. The Hairless Aardvark	III. Easy listening
IV. The Friendly Aardvark	IV. The Rolling Stones
V. Conclusion	V. Conclusion

In the aardvark outline, the basis of division shifts: the first two types are divided according to physical characteristics, whereas the last type is defined by its personality. You can see the worry this causes: Can a hairless aardvark be friendly? Are fuzzy aardvarks ill-tempered? How much hair does a friendly aardvark have? The music outline displays a problem in rank. Although the Rolling Stones do represent a type distinct from classical and easy listening, the category is not parallel to the others: it's too small. It should be rock 'n' roll, or hard rock, or something like that, with the Stones used as an example.

4. **Ask yourself if you can handle the subject and its divisions in the number of words you want.** Whole books have been written on the types and qualities of heroes: if you only want a 750-word paper, maybe you should consider "Types of Heroes on Popular TV Shows" or "Eliot Rosewater's Heroic Qualities." Or if you have decided to analyze Eastern philosophy and list twelve characteristics to develop in a 500-word essay, you will be wise to analyze the appeal of "Sesame Street" instead. If you find that you will be able to devote fewer than fifty words to each type or part you list, that is nature's way of telling you to change topics, consolidate groups, or choose major divisions to develop fully, mentioning the minor ones briefly.

You should end up with a list of classes (if you are classifying) or a list of components, factors, or parts (if you are analyzing). From here on in, we will call these divisions "parts." These parts will be the main divisions of your paper. In a short essay, you will probably write a paragraph on each part. For example, an essay on "Three Irritating Argumentative Techniques" could include one paragraph on the "Yes, But" Interruption, one paragraph on Endless Equivocation, and one paragraph on Stony Silence.

Paragraphing. The length of each of the body paragraphs should usually be about the same. Classical, easy listening, and rock 'n' roll may seem fine as a list of types of recorded music until you discover that you know next to nothing about classical recordings, all you have to say about easy listening amounts to a series of snobbish cracks, and you could write page after page about rock 'n' roll. This situation means that you and the subject are not suited to each other. You do not need to *like* all the types equally, but you do need to know enough to write at some length about each of them. Listing name after name of classical composers will not fill the bill for good paragraph development either, for most readers will sense a lack of depth in your acquaintance with classical music.

One possibility to consider for producing interesting paragraphs is to use real or imaginary individual cases to reveal the characteristics of an entire group, like "Percival is a perfect example of the Intolerable Bore." The paragraph would go on to tell what Percival's favorite subjects are, how he manages to ignore the yawns of those around him, and what characteristics make him intolerable rather than merely agonizing or intermittently bearable.

It's handy if your subject divides naturally into parallel, meaningful items, and the items slip conveniently into patterned paragraphs of roughly equal length. It's not the most likely thing in the world, though. One problem that comes up often is the urge to devote whole paragraphs to subdivisions of one of the items. For example, take this scratch outline for an analysis of "The Contents of My Closet."

   I. Introduction

  II. Items that do belong there: clothing I wear regularly.

 III. Items that do not belong there
     A. Clothing I wear seldom or never
        1. Because it's not mine and I've never seen it before
        2. Because it's my donkey costume from my fourth grade Christmas pageant
        3. Because I hate it
     B. Miscellaneous
        1. Nonperishable: boardless Monopoly game, broken Vegematic, K-Tel record rack, etc.
        2. Perishable: Forgotten sack lunches, orange in raincoat pocket, etc.

In a case like this, it would be ridiculous to restrict your discussion of III to the length of II or to try to expand II (which is quite bland) to equal III arbitrarily. It would be better to give in to the urge to write one paragraph about II and two paragraphs about III. Just be sure to make clear in your transitions which paragraphs deal with major divisions and which with subdivisions, like, "The other category of items that do not belong in my closet includes miscellaneous unwearable objects."

After you know how you are going to develop the paragraphs, decide in what order to arrange them. The order in which you first thought of them is not necessarily the best. Your items might lend themselves to chronological order. The types of recorded music example, for instance, is ordered roughly according to date of composition, from earliest to most recent. An analysis of a machine or process may be ordered spatially—top to bottom, left to right, in to out. A classification of types of people, like gamblers, may be arranged numerically—from the group with the fewest members to the group with the most. Consider other arrangements by degree too: least important to most important, simple to complex, mildly irritating to totally disgusting. When you organize this way, it is traditional (except in business writing) to put the strongest item last for emphasis.

Sample Classification and Analysis Essays

Here are three good student essays which demonstrate some of the organizational tactics we have mentioned so far.

Drunks

It was about 1:00 when I finally got out of my apartment and headed [1] for what I anticipated to be a fabulous party. When I arrived I discovered, with extreme disappointment, that all the thirsty people there had sloshed down the entire evening's ration of beer. Consequently, by conversing (in a sober state) with drunks, I discovered three distinct types: the obnoxious drunk, the denying drunk and the depressed drunk.

I found the obnoxious drunk as I walked towards the stereo. He was [2] shouting at no one in particular until his eyes finally focused on me.

"Hello, schreetheart," he grunted, as he gave me a firm slap on the [3] back and slid his arm around my waist.

Obnoxious drunks are the type who live to be the center of attention. [4] They will disco on table tops and yell like banshees to get some recognition, even if the recognition is negative. This particular obnoxious drunk turned my stomach, so I moved on toward the quieter end of the room and proceeded to talk to a prime example of the denying drunk.

He was posed with his feet crossed and his arm casually propped [5] against the wall. I expected him to fall without the wall for support. My assumption was correct. When his hand left the wall to shake mine, he stumbled over his twisted feet and spilled his beer down his shirt front.

"Excuse me," he slowly mumbled, "someone must have tripped [6] me. I've been drinking since mid-afternoon, but really, *really* I'm not drunk."

The denying drunk will ramble on and on about how much he can [7] drink and how many times he has gotten sick from it. He drinks, he says, to have a good time but denies that alcohol has any effect on him. I propped this teetering soul back up against the wall and quickly escaped to join a quiet girl in the corner.

"Why are you sitting alone?" I asked. "Are you OK?" [8]

"Oh," she sniffed, "I'm just wonderful." [9]

"What's wrong?" I inquired. [10]

"Oh, it's my dumb boyfriend," she moaned, sloshing down the [11] remainder of her warm beer.

I should have thought twice before striking up a conversation with [12] this depressed drunk. She proceeded to tell me all her problems, from age twelve to the present. She was the typical depressed drunk, a perfect example of the type who talks for hours on end about nothing but her pitiful self. I was stuck playing the Dear Abby role with her for the remainder of the evening.

As a result of this experience, I have come to the conclusion that [13] going to parties can be enlightening if you happen to be sober. Examining a party environment without the interference of alcohol can give you a clear view of what alcohol does to some people. You are then better able to recognize the ones who would be safe to talk to and distinguish them from the ones you need to avoid.

—Sharon Sacchi.

World Champions

The Philadelphia Phillies are the current world champions of base- [1] ball, having won the 1980 World Series. But were they the best baseball team in 1980? It not, what made the champions the champions? What does it take to be the world champions of baseball?

First of all, and most obviously, talent must be considered as an [2] overriding factor. A team must have the players who can go out and perform well. They need players with specialized skills who can be called upon in crucial situations. The Phillies had players who came through when they were needed. Mike Schmidt, who hit a major league high of 48 home runs, gave the Phillies someone who could always be considered a real threat to put one over the fence. Steve Carlton, with a 24-9 record, provided the club with a pitcher that could be counted on to hurl a fine game. Tug McGraw was a dependable relief pitcher who consistently saved victories in the late innings. Del Unser delivered in clutch situations many times as a pinch-hitter. To be world champions a team needs players with capabilities such as these.

Secondly, luck also plays a part, a part bigger than most people [3] realize. Luck is a wind-blown home run that is pushed fair just at the last moment. Luck is a ground ball that takes a sudden hop over the infielder's head, allowing the winning run to score. Luck is also remaining relatively injury-free. To have a team of 25 players stay free from injuries over a 162 game schedule, through the playoffs and the World Series, is truly luck. Luck can also appear from a surprise source, such as a rookie brought up late in the season from the minor leagues. The Phillies had two rookies make major contributions on their drive to the championship. When their starting left fielder, Greg Luzinski, was hobbled by knee problems, the Phillies were forced to put a rookie, Lonnie Smith, in the line-up. Smith not only filled a spot in the batting order, but hit .339 and stole 33 bases en route to winning the National League Rookie of the Year Award. Marty Bystrom was with the club only a month, but what a contribution he made! Bystrom won five games without a loss during the final month of the season, when every game is vitally important.

Finally, the role of teamwork cannot be overlooked. By teamwork, I [4] do not mean that everybody gets along well all the time. The Phillies had some much publicized disagreements, but they managed to work as a team the minute they stepped out on the field. Teamwork is every person on the team knowing his role and accepting it for the betterment of the team. Keith Moreland had an excellent year at the plate, batting .314, but he realized his role was as a reserve and performed well when he was called upon. Teamwork is also a good mix of experienced veterans and eager youngsters. Players such as forty-year-old Pete Rose worked well with younger players like Smith and Moreland.

Many intangibles must combine for a team to become world cham- [5] pions. Who will be the 1981 world champions? I have no idea, but you can bet talent, luck, and teamwork will have a lot to say about the outcome.

—Randy Reinhardt.

Macho Lights

"Camel. Where a man belongs." At least that is what the advertiser [1] would like us to believe. The advertisement presents a rugged-looking individual leaning against his Jeep, taking a cigarette break from his hard work. The advertiser is trying to get us to buy Camel Light cigarettes by showing us that not only sissies smoke light cigarettes; they are also enjoyed by the most macho of men.

The picture in the ad focuses on a man who has been, for some [2] unknown reason, digging into a pile of rocks. The man is dressed in work clothes—soiled, worn khaki pants, a thick black leather belt, and a shirt with the sleeves rolled up to his bulging biceps and the buttons open to expose his hairy chest. His face is weather-beaten—obviously from working in this forbidding climate—and his hair is tousled. This man is no cream puff who constantly worries about his appearance. He has enough confidence and drive to be what he wants to be and (as we should believe) to smoke the cigarette that suits him.

The man is smoking a Camel Light while leaning against his vehicle. [3] He does not drive a Porshe or an M.G. like a spoiled rich kid might. This man drives a Jeep. What other automobile has a more rugged image than the work-horse of World War II? This Jeep is not for weekend recreation, either. It is obvious, by the battered condition the vehicle is in, that the man uses this four-wheel-drive titan for his tough jobs like digging rocks. This is not the kind of transportation that one must leave in some parking garage in the middle of town. No, sir. This guy has jockeyed the Jeep right up to the top of the pile of rocks that he is working on and there it sits, this testimonial to toughness.

The natural setting also emphasizes the man's toughness. The rocks [4] that the Jeep is resting upon are heavy, jagged boulders. It would take a Herculean effort to move stones of that size unassisted, but this man can take on the world—and he smokes Camel Lights. The scene is in a desert. Working hard under those conditions would demoralize the average individual.

The brand name and slogan are printed in bold type, not written in [5] wimpy delicate style. The advertiser does not fool around with catchy jingles or cutesy sayings. The slogan is quite blunt. At the bottom of the ad we are given the details: "Camel Lights. Low tar. Camel taste." The information is straightforward and to the point—the way every real man should be.

The most convincing part of the ad, though, is found in the lower [6]
left-hand corner of the page. A small white box contains the message:
"Warning: The Surgeon General Has Determined That Cigarette Smoking
Is Dangerous to Your Health." Cigarette smoking has been linked to such
diseases as lung cancer, heart disease, and tuberculosis. It takes a real
swashbuckling kind of guy to flirt with death so heedlessly.

"Camel. Where a *man* belongs."   [7]

—Bob Petkoff.

EXERCISE   **6-4**

1. Identify each paper as either mostly classification or mostly analysis.
2. See if you can make a brief three- to five-item outline of the body of each
   paper.
3. Can you identify the principle used by each writer to order the paragraphs—
   that is, why is the first item placed first, and so forth? Are there places where
   you think a change of order would be appropriate? Why?
4. List some of the methods of paragraph development (see Chapter 4) that are
   used in these essays.

How to Introduce a Classification or Analysis Essay

When you are working on a rough draft, you can just introduce the
paper with something like, "There are four kinds (or parts) of blah.
They are blah, blah, blah, and blah." That will get you started, but you
need to go back and tinker with it before you type it up. Here are some
techniques that can make your introduction more appealing.

Of course you should name the subject that you are classifying or
analyzing. You can make it more enticing by setting it in a context. In
"Drunks," the subject—types of drunks—is set in the context of a
narrative. Another context you might try is historical: either remote
history ("In the 1950s, few people criticized the nutritional value of
the American diet. Now . . .") or personal history ("When I was a
teenager, I lived on ice cream and potato chips and never thought I
would grow up to be a health food enthusiast. Now . . ."). Stating a
problem may set a good context for some subjects: "Affluent city
dwellers are faced with the dilemma of choosing what kind of housing
to live in: a rented apartment, a condominium, or a mortgaged house."

Another opening strategy you may use is to state the purpose or
value of your classification or analysis. A paper that begins, "As a
child, I was the victim of babysitting blues until I classified babysit-
ters into three types and learned to deal with each type differently,"
combines personal experience and statement of purpose.

You can list parts in the introduction if your paper is long. But if the paper is short, it may seem too mechanical to list them all and then go into them one by one. "World Champions," for example, wisely does not list talent, luck, and teamwork in the introduction. If you wish to surprise your readers with your clever division of items, listing them would defuse the surprise. In deciding whether to list or not, consider the length of your paper and the complexity of your analysis or classification.

WRITING EXERCISE 6-5

Practice writing introductions using these subjects: Qualities of a Perfect Picnic, Types of Misleading Advertising, The Problems of Lecture Classes, The Positive Side of Lecture Classes, The Ideal Essay Topic.

How to End a Classification or Analysis Essay

Closing your essay in the same way you opened it is a dreary idea. Your readers will think you cannot come up with anything else. If indeed you cannot, try these tactics.

Advise the Readers. Try to think of a way that your readers can put your analysis or classification to use, like, "If you recognize the third type of teacher in your classes next fall, drop the class immediately and save yourself headache and heartache." "Drunks" subtly advises the reader to try staying sober at a party sometime.

Look into the Future. Ask yourself, "What are the long-term implications of what I've said here? Will this classification or analysis hold true in the future? Why or why not?" The answers might give you something to say in your conclusion. "World Champions" uses this tactic.

Point Out Exceptions. Indicate areas in which your analysis or classification may be partial or incomplete. For instance, "I realize that several other factors, which I have not analyzed here, cause women to feel insecure about their appearance, but I am sure that the fashion industry is the main culprit." This makes you sound fair and reasonable, but insists on the importance of the points you did cover in the essay. Be careful, though, not to give the exceptions so much emphasis that you undercut your whole paper. "World Champions" suggests that the three qualities discussed are not the only ones that determine a team's success, but emphasizes that these are the essential ones.

Emphasize Relationships. You might point out, for instance, underlying similarities among parts (that all bores are basically insecure, for example). Or you might attempt to show how all the parts of your analysis work together to create a whole, as verse form, sound, word choice, and subject work together in poetry. The italicized word *man* in the "Macho Lights" closing ties together all the masculine imagery the essay has analyzed.

WRITING EXERCISE   6-6

Write practice closings for the topics in the exercise on page 165.

How to Hold a Classification or Analysis Together

The basic function of transitions in a classification or analysis paper is to remind your reader of the relation between parts or categories as you bring them up, paragraph by paragraph. The transitional words and phrases you use depend upon what principle of order you chose for the paragraphs. If you ordered your parts chronologically, you can use the "first, . . . second, . . . third, . . ." method. Here are the first sentences of three body paragraphs of such a paper:

> The first thing I noticed when he asked me to dance was his demoniac smile. . . .

> As we twirled around the floor, he revealed his second arresting characteristic: mindless chatter. . . .

> The music stopped, and Elbert's third personal quality, persistence, came to the fore as I tried to excuse myself from the room. . . .

Other chronological transitions are phrases like, "The *next quality* you encounter is . . ." or "*Later, another problem* emerges. . . ." "World Champions" uses simple paragraph transitions: "First of all . . ." "Secondly . . ." "Finally. . . ."

If you have organized the paragraphs according to degree, the transitions can be references to the degrees, like "The most urgent question is," "The most important part is," or "The simplest (or most complex or more dangerous or least alarming) type of student is. . . ." "Macho Lights" concludes with "The most convincing part of the ad. . . ."

Parallelism is another transitional device you may try. There's a smashing example from Mark Twain in Chapter 4 (page 102). Using another kind of parallelism, "Drunks" introduces each new type with the narrator's approaching the drunk and reporting a line or two of dialogue.

Just two more bits of advice: first, do not forget to indicate clearly when the topic of a new paragraph is a subdivision rather than a topic of equal rank (see page 160). Second, never use the old, tired phrase *last but not least* as a transition.

How to Revise a Classification or Analysis Essay

A quick check of the points below will help you perfect your paper. The first four concern problems in the planning stages, so start early enough to allow time for a real overhaul in case you trip up there.

1. Is the subject limited enough? Here are some examples:

Too Big	Better
People	Typists
Cars	Compact foreign cars
Sex	Sex in daytime TV commercials

2. Have you put that limited subject into a brilliant thesis sentence?
3. Do the parts overlap, shift in basis of division, or lack parallelism of rank (pages 158 to 159)?
4. Is the classification based on sufficient evidence or knowledge?
5. Are there too many or too few divisions (parts or types) of the subject? Too many divisions may prevent you from developing any of them fully, and too few divisions sometimes means your analysis or classification is too simplistic. One bad example is the "has/has not" kind of classification: "There are two kinds of people. The first kind has a sense of humor, and the second kind does not."
6. If you introduce subgroupings, are they clearly distinguished from larger groupings?
7. Is the style of both introduction and conclusion consistent with the style of the body? Is either the opening or the closing more formal than the rest?
8. Are *analysis* and *category* spelled correctly?

Ideas for Classification and Analysis Writing

Short Prewriting Practice

1. *Classification.* In outline form, classify the cartoons in the Sunday funny papers. Then do it again, using a different basis of classification.
2. *Classification.* Write a paragraph using an extrovert (or introvert) you know as a specific example of the general type.
3. *Analysis.* In a small group, exchange jokes with other students and discuss the elements that make the jokes funny.
4. *Analysis.* Think of a situation in which you procrastinated and make a list of factors which contributed to your procrastination.

Longer Paper Ideas

1. *Classification and analysis.* What types of TV shows are the most popular this season? Tell why you think each type is popular.
2. *Analysis.* Contemplate a magazine advertisement or an ad campaign (a series of related ads, like Seven-Up's "uncola" series). What emotions and thoughts is it designed to appeal to?
3. *Analysis.* Choose a hero you have had in your lifetime and analyze what qualities made this person your hero.
4. *Classification.* If you have ever been a salesperson, waitress, or waiter, how would you classify your customers?
5. *Classification.* Here are some more subjects that can be classified into types: neighborhoods, dreams, courage, happiness, freedom, intelligence, marriages, laughter, suicide, prison, students, teachers, tennis players, drinkers, pet owners, jokes, passions, fingernail biters.
6. *Analysis.* Describe the qualities of the ideal roommate, dinner date, novel, Saturday afternoon, parent, or child.
7. *Analysis.* Summarize an especially vivid dream you have had and analyze the relations its various elements (setting, people, events, and so on) have with your everyday waking life.

COMPARISON AND CONTRAST

When you think of what you are and then think of what you would like to be, you are practicing a common (though perhaps painful) type of comparison and contrast. If you are lucky, the process is mostly comparison, since in a sense *comparison* refers to pointing out similarities and *contrast* refers to pointing out differences. Usually, people use *comparison* to mean both processes.

Comparison is a kind of analysis. Probably you do it every time you make a choice between two things: two rhetoric teachers or restaurants, two sweethearts or shampoos. Logical comparison is the intelligent alternative to strategies like flipping coins.

When to Use Comparison and Contrast

Decision making is one way you use comparison inside your own head. In comparison and contrast writing, you will always reveal and explain the likenesses and differences between two comparable items. (*Comparable* means having some basic similarity: you would not choose to compare a banana and a wall, for instance.) You should do all this revealing and explaining for a purpose, though. Here are four possible purposes for comparing things:

1. **To convince your readers that one of the items is superior to the other,** or that you prefer it (going to the laundromat as compared with buying a washer-dryer)
2. **To explain something your readers probably *do not* know about** by comparing it with something they probably *do* know about (living in a commune as compared with living in a nuclear family)
3. **To show how two seemingly similar things or people are really different** in important ways (yourself as compared with your sister Delores)
4. **To show how two seemingly different things or people are really similar** in important ways (the education of a university student as compared with the manufacture of a tape recorder)

Whatever your purpose is, remember that when you are done, your reader should respond with an "Aha!" and not a "So what?" Brilliant organization will help bring the desired response, so read on.

How to Organize a Comparison and Contrast Paper

Writers organize comparison and contrast essays in three basic ways. The way you choose depends on your subject and on your purpose. Using the traditional rhetorical terms, we will label the three patterns for organizing the body of your paper: *case, opposing,* and *alternating.*

The Case Pattern. Say you have decided to write about two of your fellow college students, Alonzo and Barth, because they represent two extremes in attitudes toward school. If you want your reader to ponder two whole personalities, side by side, use the case pattern. You first write a character sketch of Alonzo as a student (Alonzo's case), and then a character sketch of Barth as a student (Barth's case). Your outline would look like this:

I. Introduction

II. Alonzo's case
   A. Morning routine
   B. In-class behavior
   C. After-class activities

III. Barth's case
   A. Morning routine
   B. In-class behavior
   C. After-class activities

IV. Conclusion

Notice that within the body paragraphs, the subjects get similar treatment in the same order (A, B, and C). You can present the two subjects with no reference to each other and let your readers come to their own conclusions about them. Or you can tie the two subjects together in the conclusion of the paper.

The Opposing Pattern.   If your purpose is better served by close point-by-point comparison and contrast, the case-by-case pattern does not give you enough opportunity to interweave the two subjects without a lot of repetition. In an opposing pattern, you put all the similarities between the subjects together and all the differences together. Opposing would be a wretched choice for the essay on Alonzo and Barth. Because the heart of this particular essay lies in the difference between two extremes, the similarities section would be skimpy and dull: it would basically say that both Alonzo and Barth are male university students. The opposing pattern is suited to subjects whose likenesses and differences are more balanced. For instance, you could probably write a good opposing outline about your two best friends, as they probably share certain qualities you like but also differ in many ways.

The Alternating Pattern.   If a case pattern separates your subjects too widely, and opposing throws your essay off balance, alternating is just what you need. In the alternating pattern, you interweave statements about both subjects and group those statements under general topics. The alternating pattern is probably the best choice for Alonzo and Barth. Here's how it looks:

I. Introduce Alonzo and Barth

II. Morning routines
   A. Details of Alonzo's life, 7:00 to 10:30 A.M., weekdays, contrasted with details of Barth's life, 7:00 to 10:30 A.M., weekdays
   B. Details of Alonzo's life, 10:30 to noon, weekdays, contrasted with details of Barth's life, 10:30 to noon, weekdays
   C. Alonzo's Saturday mornings contrasted with Barth's Saturday mornings

III. In-class behavior
  A. How Alonzo enters the classroom and prepares for class contrasted with how Barth enters the classroom and prepares for class
  B. What Alonzo does during lecture and discussion contrasted with what Barth does during lecture and discussion
IV. After-class activities
  A. Alonzo's supper in the dormitory cafeteria contrasted with Barth's Fritos, pretzels, and beer in the nearest bar
  B. Alonzo's study habits contrasted with Barth's study habits
  C. Alonzo's recreational activities (reading historical novels) contrasted with Barth's recreational activities (drinking, playing pinball, watching situation comedies on television)

The alternating pattern gives you plenty of opportunities to write balanced sentences like, "Alonzo leaves the lecture hall as though he were tenderly leaving a lover; Barth leaves the lecture hall as though he were narrowly escaping a wasps' nest." The most difficult task in organizing an alternating pattern is classifying the details into general groups for the body paragraphs, but the effort is usually rewarding.

Try this practical plan for deciding among the three kinds of organization. After you choose subjects for comparison, write the two subjects side by side at the top of a piece of paper. Under these headings, write pairs of details as fast as you can think of them: do not worry about whether the pairs are similarities or differences, or whether they overlap or repeat. This activity is called *brainstorming*. Write more pairs than you think you will ever need. Force yourself to be specific. Then, using this list of pairs, write scratch outlines following the case, opposing, and alternating patterns. Try all three; do not skip the alternating pattern just because it's hard to think up the general topics. In most cases, you will see right away which pattern is best for your subject and purpose. If the decision is not obvious to you, show the three outlines to a couple of your intelligent friends and let them choose.

Sample Comparison and Contrast Essays

Two examples of well-written comparison and contrast papers will illustrate how the task may be accomplished.

Two Armies

Previous to my entry into the Army in 1969, I had heard about all the [1] harassment that lower-ranking enlisted men received from commissioned and noncommissioned officers. I was, for that and other reasons, leery of induction, but had little choice in the matter, for I had been drafted. It did not take long to realize that much of what I had heard was true.

Upon arrival at the basic training center, I knew I was not going to   [2]
like being in the army. We were processed in and told it was time to get
haircuts. We were given a choice of military styles A, B, and C, with C
being the longest. I told the barber type C, and was disappointed to find I
had only one quarter inch of hair left when he had finished. After our hair
was cut, we were put to work on various details. Mine involved moving
rocks from one tree to another about twenty yards away. If anyone ques-
tioned the reason for performing one of these senseless functions, he was
made to drop down and perform push-ups while the drill inspector stood
there and watched. I could not believe we were being subjected to this
harassment and paid only ninety dollars a month. But as I stated before, I
had little choice.

I served my time reluctantly and toward the end of my second year I   [3]
noticed a definite change. It seemed the Army was lacking in manpower
and decided to encourage enlistments by making Army life seem a little
more desirable. New regulations forbid the creation of work for the purpose of harassment. Another stopped a person of higher rank from making
an underling do push-ups unless he did them too, and another even
relaxed the restrictions on the maximum length of hair. The military also
went as far as to give large increases in salary, depending on rank. For
instance, a person entering the Army now receives a starting salary in
excess of two hundred dollars a month.

Though I am quite sure I would never re-enlist, I am curious about   [4]
how Army life is now. I guess I'll never find out first hand, because, thank
God, my six-year commitment is up next month, and I will receive my
discharge papers.

—George Kohl.

New Theater

New styles of plays and productions in recent years have forced   [1]
theater architects to redesign the relationship of the audience to the stage.
One of the most prominent examples of the new designs is the arena
stage. Also called theater in the round, this kind of staging can be quite
intimate because the audience totally surrounds the playing area. In contrast, the traditional proscenium arch theater is usually larger and seats the
whole audience in front of the acting area, looking into a boxlike stage.
Although any theatergoer can easily see the differences between the two
arrangements, the necessary differences in scenic design, lighting design
and acting techniques are not as apparent but are crucial to the performance.

For the scenic designer, arena staging offers challenges not present in   [2]
a proscenium set. The setting in which the action takes place must be
indicated without the aid of large, high vertical scenic backdrops, in order
to keep the view clear all around. This restriction eliminates the use of
"flats" or artificial walls, which are employed on the traditional stage. But
instead, the designer for a show done in the round may concentrate on
smaller details like props, because the audience is usually quite close to
the stage. Also, when the audience is seated on all four sides, set pieces
must look presentable from all four sides. This requirement demands more

construction and finishing time than traditional stage sets, which only need one good side. Finally, because of the extra time and care required for each piece, scenery for an arena play is usually more simplified and more suggestive than for a proscenium presentation.

Lighting must also be designed differently for these two types of presentation. In an arena stage, lighting should look more natural because it can and must be focused on the stage from all directions. But since the play must also be seen from all sides, lighting problems are in some ways compounded. For example, in a proscenium setting, the lighting designer need not worry about the possibility of focusing lights into the audience, a common problem when staging in the round. Arena lighting must also strictly define the playing area in a pool of light, whereas the proscenium playing space is already obvious. Also, actors in the arena must be adequately lit from all four sides, unlike actors in a proscenium frame who are only seen from one side at a time. [3]

The actors, too, must alter their techniques to suit the circumstances. The most conspicuous difference is that acting on a proscenium stage requires a less natural style of movement. Certain techniques, like exaggeration of facial expression and gestures, must be used by actors in proscenium staging to make movements both believable and visible to the audience. Clearly, in an arena setting, where the actors are always facing away from some audience members, the need to display all actions toward one direction disappears. The more realistic movement, combined with the comparative intimacy of theater in the round, demands more truth and precision in stage action. This style, in turn, demands greater concentration from the actors, most of whom find concentration easier in the familiar proscenium theater, where the audience is farther away. Nevertheless, in spite of, or perhaps because of, these greater demands on their skills, some actors enjoy doing arena plays even more than acting on regular stages. [4]

Clearly, the differences between proscenium and arena staging are important in producing plays. The modern theater in the round is one in a long progression of possible methods of theatrical presentation, each of which has created new production problems as well as dramatic advantages. [5]

—Lynn Cooper.

EXERCISE 6-7

1. Identify the organizational patterns of "Two Armies" and "New Theater." Make a brief two- or three-item outline of the body of each essay.
2. Summarize the thesis and purpose of each essay. Which essay has a clearer thesis? Why?
3. Point out examples of parallel details in the development of paragraphs 2 and 3 of "Two Armies."
4. Identify how the writer of "New Theater" avoids tiresome repetition of key terms.

How to Introduce a Comparison and Contrast Paper

Like the classification and analysis introduction, the opening paragraph of your comparison essay should reveal the subject and set it in a context. The writer of "Two Armies" presents his subject in the context of his own experience, meanwhile gaining credibility on the subject. Recall the four possible purposes for using comparison and contrast: explaining the unfamiliar, showing one item to be superior, showing differences between seemingly similar items, and showing similarities between seemingly different items. You may want to state or suggest one of these purposes in your introduction.

If you intend to convince your readers of the superiority of one item over another, for instance, it will probably help to state briefly in your opening the terms of the controversy you are resolving: "Some people claim that fuzzy aardvarks are the best pets because of their cuddly, docile temperaments. Others say that fuzzy aardvarks are dull and bland, and these folks endorse the passionate, excitable hairless aardvark as a pet." Then, of course, you would go on to compare the two kinds of aardvarks and prove which is actually the superior pet.

If your paper is long and involved, you may want to indicate in the introduction how it is organized. Then your readers will know what to expect and will follow your points easily. The last sentence in the opening of "New Theater" leads the reader to expect sections on scenic design, lighting design, and acting. When you thus set up your terms of comparison, even if each term takes a different number of paragraphs to discuss, the readers will be able to keep everything straight in their minds.

EXERCISE 6-8

1. Analyze the writer's introductory techniques in the following introduction to a student essay. Consider (a) the writer's credibility, (b) the statement of subject, (c) how the context is set, (d) the statement or suggestion of purpose, and (e) the statement of basic similarities and/or differences.

> Aldous Huxley's *Brave New World* and George Orwell's *1984* are two of the most brilliantly written novels concerning mankind's self-inflicted destruction by technological advances. Both set in the future, the plots similarly develop technology and its misuses to a result of evil, not good. The ultimate evil is what happens to the human character. Each novel relies upon the elimination of human emotion as the determining factor in achieving power for the governing bodies. Huxley creates 16,000 identical twins through the use of biological technology; Orwell brainwashes a society through the use of mechanical technology.
>
> —Carla Barrows.

2. Find introductions of comparison and contrast articles in magazines and newspapers and analyze the introductory techniques listed in number 1.

How to End a Comparison and Contrast Essay

Your closing should briefly tie your subjects and your purpose together without repeating what you have already said in the body of the paper or in the introduction. To accomplish this feat, you can try out the tactics we suggested for classification and analysis papers: advise the readers or look into the future. These strategies often remind you of something you can reasonably say in the closing, like, "So do not let anyone sell you a hairless aardvark unless you want to spend the rest of your life at the mercy of your pet's whims."

Let us warn you about two ways of closing that seem quite tempting at two o'clock in the morning, but that usually weaken the paper. First, summarizing similarities and differences in closing a short paper (500 to 800 words) is not a good idea. Your readers remember them if you have written the paper adequately at all, and if you have not, a clear conclusion cannot pull the whole thing out of the fire. Second, the temptation to apologize may come after you have presented a strong case for the superiority of one item over the other. You get to the conclusion and panic, so you apologize repeatedly ("Well, this is just my opinion, others might feel differently," and so on) and insist on your ignorance until your readers are convinced of it. This tactic undercuts the purpose of your paper. If you express a strong opinion and support it in the body of the essay, do not back off in the conclusion.

EXERCISE 6-9

1. Write possible introductions and conclusions for comparison and contrast essays about the following subjects: nuclear energy versus solar energy; strict parents versus permissive parents; full-time school versus part-time school; taking a shower versus taking a bath.
2. Analyze the student writer's tactics in the conclusion to the essay on Orwell and Huxley:

> The fact that both novels give a pessimistic outlook on the future may also be a reason society takes their message seriously. Neither author saw any hope for human salvation. Neither novel expresses any hope for mankind. None of the characters in *Brave New World* or *1984* is able to change or bring about a change in the situation. This method is effective—had the novels ended happily, no one would consider them a warning. They would

simply have been considered entertaining but extremely fanciful
stories.

—Carla Barrows.

3. Find comparison and contrast conclusions in magazine and newspaper
articles and analyze the writers' tactics.

How to Hold Your Comparison or Contrast Together

Your transitions should tell your reader when you are comparing,
when you are contrasting, and how much. You will probably use the
comparative (*better, more, juicier*) and superlative (*best, most, juici-
est*) forms of adjectives and adverbs to show relationships between
your subjects. For example, here is the end of one paragraph about
morning routines and the beginning of the next about classroom behavior, from the alternating pattern paper we discussed earlier:

. . . Sprawled on his bed, Barth is only dimly aware that Saturdays even
have mornings.
  In classroom behavior, Alonzo again shows himself to be more alert,
but less spontaneous.

Barth's vague awareness is connected to Alonzo's alertness by the
comparative words—*only dimly, again, more, less.*

It's *even easier* to make transitions in papers using opposing and
case patterns. (Did you notice that graceful transition?) Here is an
example from a case comparison paper:

. . . Finally, at exactly midnight, Alonzo sets his alarm for 7 A.M., hops
into his neatly made bed, and falls instantly asleep.

  At the same time, Alonzo's neighbor Barth is at his liveliest. . . .

And here is a transition from an opposing comparison paper:

. . . As first-year students, Alonzo and Barth both take required courses
in history, math, biology, and English.

  But for Alonzo, not only courses are required: he requires academic
excellence at any price. Barth requires fun and recreation.

These examples make use of the *echo* technique of transition, in
which you make a word or phrase in the first sentence of a paragraph
echo a word or phrase in the last sentence of the previous paragraph.

Like a real echo, the word or phrase you use in the transition does not have to sound exactly like the word or phrase in the previous sentence; it should just remind your readers of what came before.

How to Revise a Comparison and Contrast Essay

Here are some basic points to check as you struggle to improve your rough draft (or a classmate's).

1. Do my two items have a logical basis for comparison?
2. Is my subject too big to handle in the number of words I want? (For instance, Good and Evil or Men and Women have a logical basis of comparison, but a writer would run into problems trying to compare them in 500 words.)
3. Do I know what my purpose is in comparing these two items?
4. Did I experiment with all the outline forms and choose the best one?
5. Did I give the points similar treatment; that is, if I pointed out A's durability, did I also point out B's durability (or lack of it)?
6. Did I take up comparable details in the same order for each item?
7. Did I explore all the pertinent points of comparison and contrast and eliminate points of comparison and contrast that were irrelevant to my purpose?
8. Did I consider using balanced sentences to emphasize some of the similarities and differences (see Chapter 3, pages 63–66)?

Ideas for Comparison and Contrast Writing

Short Prewriting Practice

1. Make up five sets of comparison and contrast items that would be suitable for 500-word papers, like pen and pencil, sweater and sweatshirt, or plastic pipe and lead pipe. Exchange lists with another student. Write comments next to each set—which you think would be most interesting, which most dull, which most difficult, which too broad, what special problems might come up, and so on.
2. Find a magazine which is basically written for men and one which is basically written for women. Make a brainstorming list of paired details about these publications. Then write down or discuss four or five different thesis statements a writer might choose from when comparing the women's magazine with the men's magazine.
3. Here are two versions of the same narrative about a man named Richard Cory. The first is a poem by E. A. Robinson, and the second is a song by Paul Simon. Using these as items for comparison and contrast, make a brainstorming list of paired details. Then practice organizing the details in case, opposing, and alternating patterns. Discuss the outlines in class. See if everyone can agree on which outline would be best to choose for the paper.

RICHARD CORY BY EDWIN ARLINGTON ROBINSON (1869–1935)

Whenever Richard Cory went downtown,
We people on the pavement looked at him;
He was a gentleman from sole to crown,
Clean favored, and imperially slim.

And he was always quietly arrayed,
And he was always human when he talked;
But still he fluttered pulses when he said,
"Good-morning," and he glittered when he walked.

And he was rich—yes, richer than a king—
And admirably schooled in every grace:
In fine, we thought that he was everything
To make us wish that we were in his place.

So on we worked, and waited for the light,
And went without the meat, and cursed the bread;
And Richard Cory, one calm summer night,
Went home and put a bullet through his head.

RICHARD CORY BY PAUL SIMON (1942–   )

With Apologies to E. A. Robinson

They say that Richard Cory owns
One half of this old town,
With political connections
To spread his wealth around.
Born into Society,
A banker's only child,
He had everything a man could want:
Power, grace, and style.

Refrain:
But I, I work in his factory
And I curse the life I'm livin'
And I curse my poverty
And I wish that I could be
Oh I wish that I could be
Oh, I wish that I could be
Richard Cory.

The papers print his picture
Almost everywhere he goes:
Richard Cory at the opera,
Richard Cory at a show,
And the rumor of his parties

And his orgies on his yacht—
Oh he surely must be happy
With everything he's got.

Refrain

He freely gave to charity,
He had the common touch,
And they were grateful for his patronage,
And they thanked him very much,
So my mind was filled with wonder
When the evening headlines read:
"Richard Cory went home last night
And put a bullet through his head."

Refrain

—"Richard Cory," by Paul Simon, copyright 1966, Charing Cross Music, Inc.

Longer Paper Ideas

1. Look up a description of your astrological sign and write about how your personality does or does not fit the description. Give plenty of examples.
2. Discuss one or more illusions that are presented as reality on television and compare the illusion with the reality as you know it.
3. Compare and contrast any of the following: two lifestyles you have experienced, two artists, two films, a film and the book it was based on, two people (two of your friends, two television characters, two of your fiances, your parents, a friend and an enemy), two LP's by the same artist, two cars you have driven.
4. Compare how you perceived some person, place, or situation as a child with how you perceive the same thing today.
5. Write about a situation in which you expected one thing and got another—in other words, in which the expectation and the reality were different. Many times, these situations are "firsts": your first day of school, your first roommate, your first spouse, your first health food restaurant.
6. Write about two things that you think most people mistakenly believe to be alike, but are really different in your opinion (existentialism and absurdism, common sense and practicality, men's fear of failure and women's fear of failure).

CAUSE AND EFFECT *Cause/Result*

Most people believe that things happen for reasons. Furthermore, most people cannot help trying to figure out those reasons. If you planted tomatoes last summer and got a luscious crop, and you plant tomatoes this summer and get none, you are not likely just to shrug your shoulders and say, "Well, whaddaya know, those tomatoes didn't grow this year," and go calmly about your business. No, you are much more likely to say, "Now how come those stupid tomatoes didn't grow?" and try to figure out the causes for their failure.

If they have any sense, people think about the effects, or consequences, of things too. For instance, if it has not rained in three weeks, and you keep putting off hosing down the tomato patch, you have to consider the effects of your procrastination.

Most of us do go around every day blithely analyzing causes and effects as though everything made sense. Whether it does or not is debatable, but you can certainly learn to write a paper that makes life *sound* reasonable.

When to Use a Cause and Effect Pattern

Cause and effect is a type of analysis, and you can concentrate on either causes or effects in your thinking and writing. Remember that a cause answers the question, Why? and an effect answers the question, So what? If your subject is being on probation and you write, "Why I Am on Probation," that is primarily a cause paper, and if you write, "What Being on Probation Does to My Life," that is primarily an effect paper.

Some subjects are safer than others for cause and effect writing. "Why I Love Grammar" and "The Effects of My Divorce" are fairly safe because they are so personal that if they sound reasonable and sincere, no one is going to argue with you. But things like, "Why the Grass Is Green" and "The Effects of the Civil War" require precision because they are objective and logically provable or unprovable. If you truly know why the grass is green, or if you concentrate on just two effects of the war and say so, these subjects are fine. Just remember that different types of subjects exist, and your analysis of each will be evaluated on slightly different grounds.

Try to choose a subject that will either amuse or instruct your readers. A well-written personal paper will almost always be of interest because people are curious and like to know what makes others tick. You can be instructive by writing about the effects of something unusual, fantastic, or frequently overlooked—things like intergalactic war, Pepsi addiction, or Tourette's syndrome. Or you can point out causes your audience might not be aware of for effects they are familiar with, like how a hangover develops.

How to Organize a Cause and Effect Paper

For the body of your essay you have four kinds of organization to choose from. We will first describe the most straightforward kinds, saving the complicated ones for later.

Single-Cause/Many-Effects. With this pattern, you can bring up the cause in the introduction, write a paragraph about each effect, and establish a conclusion on the end. Here is a diagram to show you how easy it is:

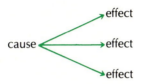

Of course, there is a catch. Those effects cannot be causally related to each other; that is, one effect cannot be a cause or effect of another. Here is a rough outline of a single-cause/many-effects paper:

I. Introduction: I went back to college after ten years of being a housewife. (Cause)
II. Negative effects
    A. My husband feels intimidated.
    B. My children are not perfectly clean.
    C. I no longer have time for my own reading.
III. Positive effects
    A. My husband is learning to deal with his children.
    B. My children are learning to deal with their father.
    C. I am learning to deal with my self.
IV. Conclusion

The writer wants to emphasize the positive effects, so she puts them in the stronger last position. Effects can also be arranged by topic instead of by the positive-negative method. You might arrange the effect paragraphs from the most obvious to the most subtle, from the unimportant to the earthshaking, from local to national to worldwide to galactic. Like most elements of writing, the arrangement is bound to be better if you think about it than if you do not.

Many-Causes/Single-Effect. The second kind of organization is just like the first, only flip-flopped:

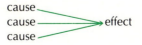

Once more, you have to be sure the causes are not causally related, and again you have to think about the order of the paragraphs. In this pattern, too, you can present the single item (the effect) in the introduction and devote a paragraph to each cause in the body. Here is an example of a speculative many-causes/single-effect outline:

 I. Introduction: What makes your engine overheat?
 II. A slipping fan belt or damaged water pump can reduce circulation of coolant.
 III. Using too-heavy engine oil can increase internal friction and cause heat.
 IV. A plugged-up exhaust system can retain hot exhaust gases.
 V. Conclusion
—Information from Herb Carrier, "How to Keep Your Engine Cool," *Popular Science*, Aug. 1967.

In that outline for a speculative paper, any *one* of the causes could be the culprit, but in the following outline, *all* the causes contribute to the final effect:

 I. Introduction: Why I flunked philosophy.
 II. I am not a good reader, especially of abstract material, and the text confused me.
 III. I was intimidated by the class discussion and neglected to ask questions to aid my understanding.
 IV. The class met at 8 A.M., and I overslept frequently.
 V. Conclusion.

The above outline is arranged from the most understandable cause (poor reading) to the most unreasonable (oversleeping).

Causal Chain.   The diagram for the third kind of organization is the most exciting:

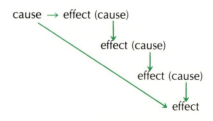

In this pattern, each cause has an effect, which then is a cause of another effect, which then is a cause of another effect, and so on in a series, just like life. Here is an example:

cause	You drink alcohol.
↓ ↓	
effect	Alcohol turns off your antidiuretic hormone (ADH, which makes your
cause	cells absorb water).
↓ ↓	
effect	Your body passes all the liquid you drink right through, instead of
cause	absorbing some of it (which is why you visit the bathroom so much
↓	while you are drinking).
↓	
effect	Your cells slowly dry up, including your brain cells, as the night wears
cause	on.
↓ ↓	
effect	In the morning, you have a headache, a dry mouth, and furry teeth, all
	of which are caused by thirsty cells: a hangover.

By looking at any sentence in the chain, you should be able to see that the item before it is its cause and the item after it is its effect. Also notice that there is a causal connection between the first and last items. (Drinking alcohol causes hangovers.) The ones close to each other are called *immediate* causes and effects, and the ones farther away are called *remote*.

This is all quite tricky. One outlining method we suggest is to write the first item at the top of a page, and under it write the *most immediate* (closest) effect you can think of. Then cover up the top item and pretend that the sentence you can see is the top item, and write down *its* most immediate effect. The reason we ask you to do such a silly thing is that concentrating on the last item you wrote, without looking above it, will help you stay in a chain instead of accidentally branching out into a many-effects type, a common accident which happens like this:

1. Two-year-olds are energetic and curious.
↓
2. Staying at home with a two-year-old can cause a person's nervous collapse.
↓
3. Two-year-olds can be the most amusing and charming people in the world.

If you are halfway awake, you will see that item 3 is not caused by item 2 but by item 1, and items 2 and 3 are not causally related. Item 3 could be something like, "A nervous collapse impairs a person's child-raising ability," which *is* causally related to the item above it: the two-year-old's energetic curiosity causes the parent's nervous collapse which causes impairment of child-raising ability.

You need to practice causal chains, because you will probably use them to develop paragraphs within the other three types of organization. For instance, paragraph II of the "Why I Flunked Philosophy" outline (page 182) might trace a series of events which led to the writer's poor reading skills.

Single-Cause/Single-Effect.   The fourth kind of organization is the easiest but the most uncommon. It is uncommon because most things just do not happen that way. Things usually have more than one cause and more than one effect. But sometimes a single-cause/single-effect pattern does apply to personal decisions or changes: one event can cause a drastic shift in your life or outlook. Here's a passage illustrating that type, related by a submarine commander:

> I think I can date the beginning of my conversion—for that, as you will see, is what it really is—to a precise event during the war. I had torpedoed an Italian merchant ship in the Mediterranean. She sank in less than three minutes, but they managed to get a lifeboat away. I surfaced to see if I could discover some information about my target. There were five men in the boat. Two of them were horribly injured, and one in particular, a lad of about nineteen, had had the side of his face blown away. We gave them what medical aid we could spare—and then a German plane came down at us and we had to dive in a hurry. Even during the depth-charging that followed, the face of that boy haunted me. It was no good telling myself that this was one of the inevitable accidents of war: this was something I personally had done to a young man on the threshold of life, the only life he would ever have. It was *my* act in firing that torpedo that had done it. The beastliness of war began to obsess me, and from that time on I could never fire a torpedo without feeling quite sick.
>
> —Edward Young, *The Fifth Passenger* (New York: Harper and Row, 1963), pp. 183–184.

Sample Cause and Effect Writing

Following are three examples of the techniques we have discussed so far. One is a cause and effect passage taken from a longer article, and the other two are humorous student essays which demonstrate more than cause and effect.

From "My Father's Farm"

> You shouldn't believe everything Dow says, he [my father] told us. [1] Just because they say so, that don't mean it's gonna work. You watch and after a while you'll see that the weeds'll get so they like the stuff. Then you'll have the same thing they had with that rat poison.
>
> The poison had been advertised as tasting so sweet no rat could resist [2] it. But some rats survived it and developed an immunity. They feasted on it and squealed for more. When cats caught and ate these superrats, however, they died because they were not immune to the poison. Soon

the corn cribs and barns, with no cats to defend them, were overrun by rodents with technology's finest toxin in their bellies.

The Old Man figured herbicides and pesticides would bring a similar [3] legacy. He was no scientist; he had dropped out of school after the eighth grade to work on the farm. But he knew nature. The weeds would mutate and endure, he predicted, and the chemicals would remain in the ground until they were siphoned up into next spring's grass and alfalfa. Then the cows would eat the poison and pass it along to people who drank their milk.

He was right, though not even scientists knew it them. [4]

—Howard Kohn in *Rolling Stone,* 28 July 1977.

What Do I Do Next?

I'm very proud to say that my first year of college was not for naught. [1] I learned a very important rule which will probably help me to survive these next three years. The rule is: continual procrastination of school work will lead to an early death. Putting studies off until the last minute is debilitating to the mental, emotional, physical, and social well-being of an individual. Bodies cannot withstand such torture, especially over an extended period of time. As I lie here on my hospital bed in the intensive care unit, I will attempt to relate my horrifying experiences that resulted from procrastination.

First of all, the college student's brain must take in information [2] quickly and in concentrated form. It is very difficult to keep facts straight when I hop from one book to another. In Children's Literature I had twenty rather time-consuming grade school books to read and analyze. Soon, the characters from *Charlotte's Web* appeared in my analysis of Greek mythology. Mix-ups like this didn't occur only in Children's Lit, but ran across a variety of subjects. Eventually, each course melted into one big blur, and I began to question which end was up.

After the mind is gone, procrastination begins to destroy emotions. [3] When I looked at my stack of overdue homework, I told myself that it wasn't as much as it seemed to be. So I tried being rational and wrote down exactly what had to be done. Unfortunately, there was more than I expected. All of a sudden I felt a chill as my blood froze in my veins. When I regained control of myself, I knew that I must start right away. I picked up a book, but someone walked in for a chat. My temper flared, and I said things to her that weren't at all pleasant. Soon, every little sound broke my concentration. I convinced myself that it was inconceivable to hope to get anything done. Everyone on the floor was sick of my complaining (which had become alarmingly frequent), so there was only one thing left to do. I called my mom long distance and cried for $2.10.

The rest of my body was crying, too. To put it mildly, I was a total [4] wreck. Late night studying put a terrible strain on my eyes. I found myself holding books two inches away from my nose. With all of the homework that had to be done, there appeared to be no time to sleep. I consumed quart after quart of coffee, but had to stop because I spent too much time shaking my way to the bathroom. I resorted to taping my eyes open with cellophane tape. The part of my body that was most affected by this ordeal was my right hand. After constantly writing index cards, English papers, and notes from various classes, it developed a severe case of writer's cramp, and a large callous emerged on my middle finger. For several days I could not uncurl my fingers.

The last effect I suffered from putting things off is undoubtedly the [5] worst. My social life became nonexistent. My (ex)friends and I used to eat a leisurely dinner, discuss the events of the day, and make plans for the evening. But soon, dining and talking became mere memories. If I had time for meals, I'd run to the cafeteria, shovel food in my mouth, and run back to my room. Phone calls were out of the question, and I couldn't allow any time for television. My (ex)friends finally realized the pressure I was under when I didn't show up to watch "Welcome Back, Kotter" or "All My Children." They were kind enough to leave me alone then, but I do wish they would bother me a little now. I knew that things were critical when I spent the weekend of the Rites of Spring Rock Festival in my room. I felt ridiculous walking through the quad after work with *Mike Mulligan and His Steam Shovel* tucked under my arm, seeing the quad filled with kids drinking and having a good time. They obviously weren't aware of the rapid approach of final exams. Or maybe they weren't procrastinators like me.

The doctor is releasing me in an hour. I hope that my experiences are [6] convincing enough that this disaster won't ever happen to anyone again. Take my advice—it isn't worth the mental, emotional, physical and social stress. I'm sure that my parents will be thrilled to know that after 36 weeks and $2800, their daughter has learned something. But I don't think I have time to tell them about it. I have to study for three tests and write two papers by Friday, then I have to. . . .

—Jean Allendorfer.

Writing Poorly

In the course of this dissertation I intend to illustrate the causes of [1] essays which are at once incongruent, incoherent, and ineffective. My introductory sentence has already confirmed my determination; I have weakened my essay fourfold by self-consciously and glaringly stating my intent at the outset. This technique, though one of the best, is just one in a multitude of rhetorical devices designed to turn any intelligent, well-thought-out argument into so much worthless scribbling. Many of these are so simple that they are overlooked, which helps to explain why so many essays are poor. Perhaps, by observing the mistakes I shall make in this essay, others may be able to avoid them. The causes of flawed essays, and poor writing in general, come in two varieties: mechanical and stylistic.

The mechanical variety comes in many forms. The most obvious of [2] these are speling erors. Spelling errors, if blatant enough, can lead the reader to question the principals the writer is attempting to proove and dimminish the arguement itself. Problems involving punctuation are also common. These can involve improper use of commas, and periods. My biggest punctuation problem is with semicolons; causing confusion when followed by a dependent clause. And worse, if followed with a fragment. Improper use of apostrophe's can also destroy a papers effectiveness by making the reader lose respect for the writer who wont learn (or look up) a few simple rules'. Sudden shifts in person may confuse readers so much that he will lose interest in what you are saying. On top of these errors, the serious writer will have to avoid graphic pitfalls in the actual writing writing of the essay, as well as avoiding writing sloppily or typing po rly. Careful proofreading will usually bring a few mechanical errors to light.

The second, and more evasive, source of fault is stylistic. Stylistic [3] mistakes are more difficult to notice and are much more diverse. For example, stating a point without specifics to back it up has many negative results. Impersonal construction may also hamper an argument. There are few problems in writing that are as subtle. Spontaneous alterations in tonal quality and connotation in the median of an argument generally screw up the reader and blow away the possibility of empirical judgment. As well as these flaws, there are other more insidious ones which can involve, in many cases, an abusive, sometimes abrasive, over-subordination of a complex sentence, which results in so many intertwined clauses that a reader, at least one of normal abilities, will become confused to the point of abandoning the original thesis, which has become completely obliterated. The opposite is equally true. Short, choppy sentences are disturbing. They make for jumpy reading. Varying sentence length is vital to good writing. Many writers who are able to avoid these mishaps dull their purpose by repeating themselves. Instead of offering support for a thesis, they merely repeat it under a cloak of semantics. Rather than develop, they just alter the words. Each sentence will appear slightly different from the last, and each may develop the point more fully, but at a snail's pace. At this slow rate of development, the reader will undoubtedly become bored. Careful revision is needed to correct most stylistic faults.

In conclusion, beginning a concluding paragraph by stating that it *is* [4] one is dull almost beyond equal. I should hope that, in this essay, I have provided a glaring example of what to avoid. If I have not accomplished this, then this conclusion will not bail me out now. Briefly, avoidance of the preceding pitfalls requires little more than caution. Careful proofreading and revision and a sound plan at the outset go a long way toward correcting such problems, particularly the type that thrive in a 3 A.M. Wonder, well known to anyone who has written for judgment.

—Frank P. Kelly.

EXERCISE   **6-10**

1. Identify the organizational pattern of the ''My Father's Farm'' excerpt.
2. Which pattern of cause and effect does ''What Do I Do Next'' follow?
3. What words and phrases set an informal style in ''What Do I Do Next''?
4. In the same essay, how are transitions made between paragraphs?
5. List some specific details and examples that make the procrastination essay lively.

6. The basic structure of "Writing Poorly" may be diagrammed this way:

cause: mechanical faults

effect: poor writing

cause: stylistic faults

Kelly also mentions specific *effects* one should avoid having on one's readers. List some of these effects.

7. Correct the flaws in either paragraph 2 or 3 of "Writing Poorly."
8. To get practice, write many-causes/single-effect, single-cause/many-effects, and single-cause/single-effect outlines for these subjects: nervousness before exams and speeches, a shortened workweek, student cheating, depression.

How to Introduce a Cause and Effect Paper

Since curiosity about causes and effects seems to be practically built in to people, you should not have too much trouble writing an appropriately seductive introduction. Anything that will get your readers to ask, "Why?" or "Why did you say that?" will do.

One way is to jolt them with an arresting statement of cause and effect right away. You could, for example, start the hangover paper we outlined earlier by saying, "When you take two aspirins with a glass of water to cure your hangover, the glass of water probably does you more good than the aspirin."

Another way to begin a cause and effect paper is to make a prediction. Then proceed to show the line of reasoning that allows you to make such a prediction. For example, you might begin a paper with, "If you put radial tires on your car, you will probably save $25 on gas next winter." Your readers will want to know how radial tires save gas, and so you tell them.

How to End a Cause and Effect Paper

When you are trying to bring your discussion to a close, you can fall back on one of the tactics we have discussed at length elsewhere: (1) advise the reader, (2) predict the future, or (3) summarize points (use this one judiciously). But there are some other closing strategies that fit cause and effect papers especially well.

Causes and effects have a tendency to branch out until the whole worlds of philosophy, science, and psychology are involved. Of course, you must prune that branching-out drastically in order to write a short paper (and keep your sanity). But in the conclusion, you are free to suggest some of the larger areas that your subject could branch into if you let it. This leaves your reader with something extra to think about. "My Father's Farm," for example, could close with a comment on the probable pollution of springs and rivers, as well as soil, by herbicides and pesticides. Or it could end in grim speculation on the global effects of such pollution. This is another closing tactic: leave your reader overwhelmed by the significance and import of your subject. (If your subject really is not overwhelmingly important, use this one only if you want to be funny.)

A less exciting but sometimes necessary function of the conclusion is to present causes and effects you did not discuss in the paper. If you write about only two causes of the Civil War, or only two effects of motherhood, you should probably point out in the closing that you have written about just the ones you find most interesting or important or personally relevant. You may name some of the others, too. This keeps you from sounding like a lamebrain who really believes that there were just two causes for the Civil War.

EXERCISE 6-11

1. Find a cause and effect essay in a popular news magazine (science and economics sections are good places to look). Does the conclusion summarize the points of the essay? Why or why not?
2. Can one sentence be enough to open or close a cause and effect essay? What conditions make such short paragraphs sufficient?
3. How would the opening and closing of a scientifically provable cause and effect paper probably be different from the opening and closing of a more personal or speculative cause and effect paper?

How to Tie a Cause and Effect Paper Together

The transitional words for this kind of paper have to do with cause and effect relationships, just as you might have suspected. Some handy terms are *thus, therefore, consequently, so, accordingly, then, as a result,* and *hence.* If you inspect samples of cause and effect writing, you will also find lots of paragraph transitions of the plain old "First, . . . Second, . . . Third," or, "One effect . . . Another effect . . . A final effect" type.

Because cause and effect relationships are so intricate, check over your transitions within paragraphs as well. Each sentence should have a clear relationship to the sentence before it. The transitional words mentioned above, therefore, will often appear within your paragraphs.

How to Revise a Cause and Effect Paper

Here are some tips that will help you in revision. Tips 2 through 8 concern errors in logic you should beware of. We discuss logical fallacies more completely in Chapter 7.

1. Am I sure my topic is safe? (You should feel very secure about your factual knowledge if you choose a "provable" subject.)
2. Do I assert that there is just one cause when I secretly know there are more?
3. Did I remember that just because event X happens before event Y, X does not necessarily cause Y? ("Everyone who drinks milk dies" is an example of this kind of logical fallacy.)
4. If I follow a causal chain, do I omit any links? Am I completely sure that no one could miss the right connection?
5. Do I attribute the wrong cause to an effect? (One way to do this is described in tip 3. Another is to think that just because two things happen together, they are causally related. For example, many great writers compose their works in the typewriter, but that does not mean that if you start composing in the typewriter you will become a great writer.)
6. Do I use transitional words to make clear the distinctions between immediate and remote causes and effects?
7. In a personal paper, do I rationalize? Am I half-unconsciously giving myself pleasant and kind motivations (causes) when the real ones are less admirable?
8. Am I aware of my own prejudices and do I refrain from presenting them as logic? ("She's single because no one asked her to get married," or "He must be uneducated because he uses the word *ain't*.")
9. Do I use the words *affect* and *effect* correctly? (Usually, *affect* is a verb and *effect* is a noun: "Your poem *affected* me. It was a burning *effect* somewhere around my kidneys.")
10. Did I correctly punctuate conjunctive adverbs? (Many causal transition words—*thus, therefore, consequently, accordingly, then, as a result, hence*—fit into this category. Look up *Semicolon* and *Comma Splice* in the "Revising Index," Chapter 13, for help.)

Ideas for Cause and Effect Writing

Short Prewriting Practice

1. Write one or two paragraphs in which you explain what causes some natural phenomenon. Examples: rain, dew, blue sky, twinkling stars, sweat, hiccups, the phases of the moon.
2. Make a list of twenty possible cause and effect topics, with five under each of these headings: personal life, science and technology, social trends, and politics. Compare your list with other students' lists. Each topic can be phrased as a question beginning with "Why" or "What effect."
3. In a small group, discuss major decisions in your lives. Investigate causes and effects of your decisions.

Longer Paper Ideas

1. Describe a failure you once had, and tell its causes or effects (or both).
2. Explain the causes (or effects) of any drastic change of opinion, attitude, or behavior you have undergone in your life.
3. Investigate the possible causes for any opinion, prejudice, interest, or unreasonable fear that you feel strongly.
4. "By governmental decree no one will be allowed to marry before the age of thirty." How will this statement affect personal relationships in our society?
5. Discuss the probable causes of any situation, practice, law, or custom that strikes you as unfair.
6. "All school attendance has just been declared voluntary." How will this change affect the schools?
7. A close friend of your own sex tells you that she or he is homosexual. What are your reactions? Why would you have these reactions?
8. A group of extraterrestrial beings visits Earth. On their planet, people are neither male nor female: each person is both. Using one of these beings as a first-person narrator, explain how their society differs from ours.

chapter Seven
Fundamentals of Argument and Persuasion

All the patterns you have learned so far can be used to persuade your readers or argue a point. You will combine many patterns of development that you already know when you write a persuasive paper, but you will also need some skills we have not talked about yet.

WHEN TO USE PERSUASION AND ARGUMENTATION

You already know when to use it: when you hope to get your readers to agree with you and maybe as a result to take some kind of action (like sending you some money or picketing city hall). Somewhere down inside, you have an opinion that you believe any reasonable person should agree with. This is your chance to set forth that opinion without interruptions—which is one of the delightful advantages of the written argument over the spoken.

Another advantage is that your writing will probably have two kinds of appeal: rational and emotional. *Argumentation* refers to logical appeals to reason: in a strict sense, an argument includes only facts, statistics, and rigorous reasoning. Its goal is truth. *Persuasion* refers to a form that makes use of moving appeals to emotion as well as reason. Its goal is agreement and perhaps action. In everyday language, the terms are used almost interchangeably, and most everyday argumentative writing involves the readers' emotions.

Find a Controversy

At the moment, you may think that you do not have an opinion for which you would mount the battlements of classical argumentative structure. You do have, though—a little prewriting activity will reveal at least one. Here are some approaches to finding an argumentative topic.

1. Think of an issue about which you have recently changed your mind. For example, you may once have thought that all husbands should be the breadwinners; now you do not necessarily think that is true. You are well enough acquainted with both sides of the issue to try to persuade others to believe as you do now.
2. Think of a conflict you have observed, read about, or experienced. For example, if you have been a waitress or waiter, you have no doubt had conflicts with customers. One way to develop a persuasive essay that stems from this conflict is to convince restaurant customers to alter their rude or unthinking behavior.
3. Think of any subject in the context of problems that are related to it. If you pick up a book, for instance, you may think of problems like censorship, sparse library funding, the high price of textbooks, widespread illiteracy. A few minutes' thought about the seashell you use as a paperweight may bring forth ideas about oil spills, commercialization of national seashores, endangered species, and boating accidents.

Jot down all the ideas you come up with using these invention methods: whichever one you use now, you may need the extras some day when your brain refuses to storm.

Do not exhaust your persuasive skills on an assertion that almost everyone already agrees with. This is a waste of time. For instance, "Children need love" is in the correct form for an argumentative thesis and could certainly be supported with reason and emotion but, unless handled with great originality, proves to be an empty exercise.

When you are assigned a research paper in one of your courses, keep the controversies of that field in mind. An argumentative research paper is usually more fun to organize and write and more interesting for your teachers to read than "Edgar Allan Poe led a very fascinating life" or "World War II had many causes." You can afford to write braver theses than *those*, especially if you adopt our constructive advice about how to approach the paper.

ARGUING FAIRLY: A QUICK LOOK AT LOGIC

Sound logic is the foundation of effective argumentation, so you need to know something about this intricate subject.

Examples of logical thinking and writing are not easy to come by. In fact, you have probably seen and heard so much bad logic that by now you have what Hemingway called a "crap detector" in your head, even if you do not know the correct term for each logical error (or *fallacy*) you detect. Here is a list of persuasive statements and assertions that violate some of the basic laws of logic. As you read each one, decide why the reasoning is faulty. Then read the analysis, which provides a high-sounding handle you can use to expose your opponent's faulty logic.

1. Podunk Community College should not require a freshman writing course. Harvard does not require a freshman writing course, and the students get along fine without it.

False Analogy. If students are admitted to Harvard, either they already know how to write or they are so well off it does not make any difference. Community college students come from much more varied educational and social backgrounds. The analogy is false because the two items do not have strong enough similarities to predict that what happens in one will happen in the other.

2. Everyone wants to get married someday. A good self-concept is important in attracting a husband or wife. Therefore, everyone should develop a good self-concept.

False Premise. Example 2 starts a logical statement with an assumption that is false: not *everybody* wants to get married. So even if the conclusion drawn is valid, the argument it is built on is not.

3. Suds 'n' Puds is a great restaurant: you can see how shining clean our kitchens are!

Distraction. Example 3 is called *distraction* because the readers' attention is drawn to the cleanliness of the kitchen (so they will not notice the powdered mashed potatoes, perhaps) instead of to the excellence of the food, which usually proves a restaurant great.

4. Ms. Bauer is an incompetent English teacher. She always wears blue jeans.

Ad hominem. Example 4 is called *ad hominem,* "against the person." Instead of pointing out faults in teaching techniques, it calls attention to things about the teacher *as a person* that are unrelated to her teaching performance.

5. Ms. Bauer is an incompetent English teacher. She's a wild-eyed radical in her educational theories.

logical error

Name-calling and genetic fallacy.   Example 5 does not deal directly with teaching performance, either. Instead, it uses *name-calling* and *genetic fallacy* to discredit the teacher. Descriptions like "wild-eyed" appeal instantly to people's prejudices, and that's name-calling. The suggestion that her ideas have their background in radicalism, and are therefore suspicious, illustrates the genetic fallacy: defamation of a person or ideas purely on the basis of their background. Another example: "I'm not surprised Al is in trouble. His father did a stretch in jail, you know."

6. Look at this fourteen-year-old child who has run away from home to hide her shame—pregnant, unwashed, friendless, penniless, at the mercy of our social service agencies. Can you still claim that sex should be taught in the classroom?

Appeal to pity.   You probably noticed several things wrong with example 6, not the least of which is its *appeal to pity.* In this shifty approach to argumentation, the writer gives such tear-jerking descriptions of the cruel opponents' victims that the reader would appear to be heartless to even think about faults in reasoning.

7. Suds 'n' Puds is a great restaurant: no one has reported a meal thrown at the waiter yet!

Appeal to ignorance.   Example 7 is called an *appeal to ignorance:* you argue that one thing is true just because its opposite has not been proved true. Really, Suds 'n' Puds could be a terrible restaurant that has polite customers who do not throw plates, or it could be a mediocre restaurant that no one gets very excited about.

8. Either we continue to build nuclear weapons, or we will fall prey to the Russians.

Either-or fallacy.   Ignoring alternative explanations sometimes takes the form of an *either-or fallacy,* like example 8. The writer pretends that only two choices exist and makes one of them look so grim that the reader is forced to choose the writer's preference—unless the reader is clever enough to see that the writer has ignored other alternatives.

9. It has been proven that all heroin addicts smoked marijuana in their youth. Therefore, smoking marijuana leads to heroin addiction.

Post hoc, ergo propter hoc. The oversimplification of cause and effect relationships in example 9 has the impressive name *post hoc, ergo propter hoc.* It means "after this, therefore because of this," if that helps you any. This fallacy assumes that if event Y happened after event X, then X must be the cause of Y.

10. All the teenagers who like punk rock display little enthusiasm for school and have dirty feet. Therefore, punk rock leads to dirty feet and lack of interest in school.

Concurrence fallacy. Closely related to example 9 is the *concurrence fallacy* in example 10. It assumes that just because X and Y happen at the same time, X is a cause of Y or Y is a cause of X.

11. History tells us that idealistic leaders are never effective.

Personified abstraction. Example 11 oversimplifies huge issues by blindly referring to a *personified abstraction.* "History" is personified because it is supposedly talking, but the writer can make it say anything he or she wants it to. For instance, the writer could say, "History tells us that idealistic leaders are the most effective," and that would sound just as impressive.

12. I don't have any children, but I take my niece and my neighbor's child to the zoo and the park every week or so. I can tell that children really love me.

Ill-Founded Generalization. This logical error occurs when a writer makes a general statement based on irrelevant, unrepresentative, or insufficient evidence. Two children who see you only weekly, who go on exciting excursions with you, and who receive your complete attention while with you are bound to love you. That does not mean that you are uniquely lovable to children in general—a fact which you would perhaps quickly discover if you lived full time with them. (This experience would also be likely to cure you of the *sweeping generalization,* "I love children.")

Any time you draw a conclusion from a collection of data, you make an *inductive leap*—at a certain point, you decide that you have enough specific cases or data to make a valid generalization. That is inherent in the inductive process. Just be sure to look before you leap.

13. All students who take earth science instead of physics are lazy. Susie took earth science instead of physics. Susie should be kicked out of school.

Non Sequitur.   The Latin name means "it does not follow." If, in example 13, the first premise is correct (and it's probably not; it's probably an ill-founded generalization), then you could conclude that Susie is lazy. But there is nothing in that line of reasoning that says lazy students should be kicked out of school: the conclusion does not follow.

14. Juan is an impressive speaker because he always touches his listeners deeply.

Circular Reasoning, or Begging the Question.   This problem occurs when the writer tries to support a claim by restating it in different words. You can tell example 14 is circular by considering this: Why is Juan an impressive speaker? Because he touches his listeners deeply. Why are Juan's listeners touched so deeply? Because he is such an impressive speaker. The very meaning of *impressive* includes the idea of touching someone deeply, intellectually or emotionally. What the writer is trying to prove in the second part of the claim is already assumed in the meaning of the first part.

This is tricky, so let's look at another one: "Essay exams should be abolished because they require writing skill." Really, this is saying, "Essay exams should be abolished because they are essay exams," because if they did not require writing, they would not *be* essay exams. The argument that this person probably wants to take up is whether writing skill should be required of students: in fact, "Writing skill should not be required of students" is the *hidden premise* in the original statement.

15. Drake says, "All students turn their papers in on time." Raythel says, "But I'm a student, and I turn papers in late." Drake says, "Then you're not really a student."

Equivocation.   Drake in example 15 is one of the most frustrating kinds of people to argue with. Such people change the definitions of the words they use whenever you bring up an objection. If Raythel lets Drake shift the meaning of "student" from "a person who goes to school" to "the *ideal* person who goes to school," sneaky Drake will probably switch back later and make generalizations about *real* students even though the original premise is true only for *ideal* students.

16. My political science teacher says that the new math is impossible for children to learn.

Appeal to the Wrong Authority. If the student in example 16 believes that the political science teacher's low opinion of new math strongly supports an argument against new math, the student is wrong. The political science teacher is an authority, but in a different field; the student needs a math teacher, preferably an elementary school math teacher, to give expert testimony on this issue.

You should also question the authority of your sources if they are dated. Of course, ten-year-old statistics do not apply to this year; but sometimes, twenty-year-old "facts" do not apply to this year either.

17. "No, you can't order a bacon, lettuce, and tomato sandwich with peanut butter instead of bacon! Then everyone would start wanting substitutions on their sandwiches!"

~Domino Theory~ **Slippery Slope.** This logical fallacy assumes that one instance will automatically lead to thousands of similar instances, and thence lead directly to chaos. And that is not necessarily so.

EXERCISE 7-1

Now, see if reading this section has sharpened your logical reasoning. Find and explain logical faults in the following examples.

1. This 1960 encyclopedia article proves that marijuana is addictive and causes fits of violence.
2. She is such a romantic; her ideas about social change just can't be taken seriously.
3. Poetry tells us that life contains more sorrow than joy.
4. X: "You always hurt the one you love."
   Y: "But I love someone, and I don't hurt her."
   X: "Ah, then you don't really know love!"
5. The last five times that I've worn my white painter's pants, something depressing has happened. I'm not going to wear those pants again!
6. Carlos Jones should not be elected secretary of our organization. He would have to keep minutes, and you know how terrible men's handwriting is.
7. Baggy jeans are disgusting because they make women look so ugly.
8. I think we should give our nephew books for Christmas. After all, everyone wants a large collection of books.
9. I think we should give our nephew a Void Banana album for Christmas. Doesn't he like those long-haired groups?
10. The United States is the greatest country in the world today. Look at all the great men who developed it: Washington, Lincoln, Jefferson, and so on.

EXERCISE   **7-2**

For more practice, collect letters to the editor from newspapers and magazines. No doubt you will find some real gems of illogical writing. Share them with your class. Which logical fallacies are the most popular?

WRITING EXERCISE   **7-3**

Write a humorous argument *for* an opinion you do not really agree with, using four or five logical fallacies as your main points. For inspiration, look at Figure 7-1, which shows how Alice Duer Miller turned the logical tables on the antisuffragists in 1915.

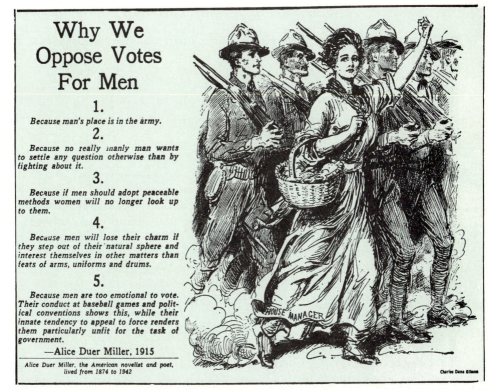

Why We Oppose Votes For Men

1.

Because man's place is in the army.

2.

Because no really manly man wants to settle any question otherwise than by fighting about it.

3.

Because if men should adopt peaceable methods women will no longer look up to them.

4.

Because men will lose their charm if they step out of their natural sphere and interest themselves in other matters than feats of arms, uniforms and drums.

5.

Because men are too emotional to vote. Their conduct at baseball games and political conventions shows this, while their innate tendency to appeal to force renders them particularly unfit for the task of government.

—Alice Duer Miller, 1915

Alice Duer Miller, the American novelist and poet, lived from 1874 to 1942

Charles Dana Gibson

Figure 7-1 Alice Duer Miller/Charles Dana Gibson/LNS.

CONSIDER CLASSICAL STRUCTURE

The discipline of rhetoric, as you may know, is based on the way a few sagacious Greeks gave long speeches to amuse and edify each other around 300 B.C. These people developed argumentation into an art. Their ideas on the organization of an argument make good sense and can be outlined thus:

I. Introduction
   A. Exordium — *an attention getting device*
   B. Exposition— *set a context*
   C. Thesis
   D. Plan of proof

II. Body
   A. Confirmation
   B. Refutation
   C. Concession

III. Conclusion
   A. Recapitulation
   B. Peroration

Some of that may, for good reason, sound like Greek to you. We will explain what goes into each part (in more modern terminology) directly after a discussion of the element that affects everything else: your readers.

THE AUDIENCE COMES FIRST

Your persuasive success utterly depends on your relationship to your audience. Consider carefully: who are you trying to reach in your essay? Some people will never change their minds on the subject you choose; they have decided their opinion and will stick to it no matter what. It is useless to include them when you define your audience. The appropriate audience is unfamiliar with your subject, undecided, or in disagreement but still open to change.

Who are they? Well, you really have to imagine them, using your experience of people and the world. If you plan to write a persuasive letter to your local newspaper, for example, you must think about the readers of that newspaper—what ideas they probably have about your subject, what they see as important and unimportant in life. The newspaper readers in our city, we imagine, are mostly middle- and upper-middle class full-time workers who value security, family life, and upward mobility. Most are conservative and Republican and go to protestant churches.

This analysis is important to anyone trying to sway our citizenry. If you were writing an editorial to convince this audience to walk, ride bicycles, and take buses to work instead of driving individual cars, you must be aware that most of your readers would be quick to dismiss certain arguments as crackpot. Thus, you might not mention that walking or biking back and forth from work would provide them with valuable time for meditation, for getting in touch with themselves—at least not in those terms. Instead, you would argue on the grounds of fewer traffic accidents, fewer exhaust fumes, more revenue to improve the bus lines due to higher ridership, and lower cost to each person.

You have limited your audience, not especially trying to appeal to minority segments of the newspaper's readership: the new young professionals who bring more cosmopolitan and liberal ideas when they move here, the university students, or the farmers in the large rural area the paper serves. If you happen to persuade them, that's great—but you need to aim at the majority as you understand them. (For further help in pinpointing the characteristics of your audience, review our Audience Analysis Checklist on page 10.)

You may choose to make up a more specific audience for a persuasive piece, and that will help you focus your purpose. For example, let's say you are arguing for the value of detective fiction. If you decide on an audience of avid novel readers who have never tried a mystery, your goal would be to convince them to read a few. If your audience is people who already read six mysteries a week, your purpose may be to provide *them* with persuasive arguments to justify their addiction. If you are writing for literary critics, you will attempt to prove that detective fiction is just as frequently artful in form, characterization, style, plot, and theme as accepted "legitimate" fiction is.

At no time should you suggest, in tone or content, that your readers are ignorant, unfeeling, or ridiculous. People dig their heels in when someone challenges not only their ideas but their personal worth. Choose an audience that you can respect, and let your respect for them show, even as you ask them to change their opinions or actions.

CONSIDER THE LIMITS OF REASON

Pretending that people's opinions and positions on issues are based on reason is ridiculous. We usually hold our positions because of our fears and prejudices and all the secrets of our anxious hearts. We cling to positions that are completely unreasonable because the alternatives are threatening.

So if you really want to dissuade someone from an erroneous opinion, you first must figure out what is threatening about your side.

You must soothe your readers' fears, reassure them, and decrease their anxieties until they are at least somewhat open to reason. The process of quieting your readers' qualms involves two parts: first, sympathetically restate your opponent's fears and give reassurance; and second, state a shared assumption or agreement as a starting point for your argument.

For example, let's say you decide you would rather take a two-year community college course in court reporting than go to the university and be an English major, as your parents want you to. This decision, you are aware, is likely to upset your parents. Using fear-reducing tactics, you might begin your announcement something like this: "I know you two think that going to the university is a great opportunity, one that you never had, and I realize that you're right. But I also realize that you want me to use my own judgment and that what you want most is for me to be happy." How can they disagree?

If indeed you can find no starting point of agreement, your argument will fail. You and your readers must share some principles. For example, an argument against nuclear warfare on the grounds that it will surely destroy the human race will not work on a person who perceives that our species has not done much to recommend itself for continuation. In this case, the basic assumption of the persuader—that the species should be preserved—and that of the reader—that its extinction may be an improvement—are hopelessly at odds.

HOW TO ORGANIZE A PERSUASIVE PAPER

Although the ancient Greek plan that we mentioned earlier is about 2300 years old, it still works well today. Now we will go through that multisyllabic outline and—using plain language—explain each section.

How to Introduce a Persuasive Paper

A well-developed persuasive essay will often turn out longer than your other essays did, especially if you include research. In a paper that approaches 1000 words, you can get away with two paragraphs of introductory material instead of just one. Sometimes you will need it. We have identified four introductory tasks that you can tailor to fit your paper.

Be Charming. In the *exordium* section, your first chore is to win the attention and goodwill of your readers. You can get attention by

telling an intriguing or humorous story, quoting a well-phrased comment on the issue, or using any of the other clever opening devices
you have learned so far. You win goodwill by avoiding pomposity and
showing concern for your readers. Present yourself as fair-minded and
genial. You also need to convince them that you know and care about
what you are saying by maintaining a self-assured tone and by stating
or suggesting your credentials—your qualifications as an authority on
the subject. *Don't appology for your position*

Be Informative. Sometimes the issue you are discussing involves words that your readers do not know; or words that are usually
general but that you are using in a specific way (like *argument* in a
rhetoric textbook); or words that are easily misunderstood or controversial in meaning (like *Romantic* in a literature paper). Define them
in the *exposition* section of your introduction.

Your readers may need other background material. If your issue
has not made the front pages, you may need to explain why there is a
controversy over it, how the dispute came about, who is on what side,
what the claims of each side are (in brief, of course), or why anyone
cares.

The introduction below, written by a student, sets the thesis in an
informative context.

> Coal-fired power plants annually pour about 53 million tons of sulfur
> and nitrogen compounds into the atmosphere, where they turn into highly
> corrosive acids. The resulting high-acid rain is destroying the life in hun-
> dreds of lakes and streams every year. Furthermore, one coal plant alone
> pours many tons of radioactive carbon-14 into the air. As world needs for
> energy increase, our coal supplies dwindle at an ever-increasing rate.
> Estimates show that the earth could be out of coal reserves as early as the
> year 2200. Nuclear power was once considered the gradual replacement
> for coal produced power. But public acceptance of nuclear power is now
> small because of the possibility of catastrophic accidents. Solar power is
> the logical alternative. According to a long-range plan for one of the large
> utility companies, "The Solar Power Satellite (SPS) is probably the most
> environmentally acceptable power-generating concept we've ever stud-
> ied" (G. Harry Stine, "Power Orbiter," *Omni,* April 1980).
>
> —Ted Giehl.

Be Straightforward. Being coy about your thesis is usually as
annoying as being evasive—however charmingly—about anything
else. It is helpful to tell your reader immediately what the issue is and
what you are persuading them to believe or do.

Be Organized. If your paper is long, you can tell your readers
how you plan to prove your points in the opening. For example, "Using the evidence of personal experience and the reports of two recent

experiments at major universities, I will show you that people can fly if they set their minds to it." This is a *plan of proof.* The following introduction to a student essay includes one.

> When I was a child, each Saturday morning the family room would become the social center of our household as my brothers, sisters, and I would all sit glued to the television set laughing hysterically as Moe, Curley, and Larry would poke each other in the eye or slap one another across the face. That was until our parents forbade us to watch "The Three Stooges" because what we viewed as funny Saturday morning often became reality at some other time during a typical sibling quarrel, when someone would get poked in the eye or slapped across the face.
>
> As seen through my own family situation, violence on television affected children ten years ago, and I believe that today it is an even more present and controversial issue. In this paper I will present facts, statistics, reasoning, and counterexamples concerning how violence on television affects children today.
>
> —Marianne Cullnan.

EXERCISE   7-4

1. In the above introduction to Cullnan's essay, find examples of the following introductory elements: winning attention and goodwill, defining terms, explaining the issue, and stating the thesis.
2. Find examples of introductory elements in essays from magazines and anthologies.

How to Organize the Body of a Persuasive Essay

Following the classical outline, we will divide our advice about the body of the paper into three parts: the *confirmation,* the *refutation,* and the *concession.*

Part One: Present Your Case.   The first part of the body, the confirmation, is the longest, for in it you present evidence that supports (confirms) your thesis, paragraph by paragraph. You can develop each paragraph in a different way (see Chapter 4, pages 111–116), but each should present one piece of evidence for your side. Whether you write from your own experience or rely on research, you will support your side through examples, cause and effect reasoning, and the logical processes of induction, deduction, and analogy.

Induction is the logical process of taking a bunch of data—cases, examples, instances, statistics—and coming to a general conclusion.

In a very simple form, this is probably how you know the sun rises every day: you have lived to see enough days that you can derive a general rule. That is an example in which you work from a series of exactly similar instances. Another example of induction takes more diverse data: a detective fiction fan comes home and considers these facts:

1. Her husband is gone.
2. On the kitchen table are his coffee cup, a wrench, the telephone, and the telephone book.
3. The coffee cup is still warm to her touch.
4. The phone book is open to the section from PIZZA to PRINTERS in the yellow pages.
5. Her husband intended to install a new washing machine that afternoon.

She concludes that her husband just went out a few minutes ago to buy plumbing supplies to hook up the washer.

Economist Lester Thurow uses case after case to inductively support his general conclusion that the economy is in bad shape:

> When the GNP data for the first quarter of 1982 are released, the American economy will be back to where it was in the first quarter of 1979. Unemployment is 9 percent and headed up. Thirty percent of our manufacturing capacity is idle. In the industrial heartland between Buffalo, N.Y., and Gary, Ind., it is no exaggeration to say that the Great Depression has been re-created in living color. In the last two years net farm income after correcting for inflation has dropped 44 percent. Think of the major American firms balancing on the edge of bankruptcy—Chrysler, International Harvester, Braniff. Entire industries—autos, savings and loans, rubber, trucking, housing, airlines—are awash in red ink.
>
> —Lester C. Thurow, "Hanging on a Cliff," *Newsweek,* 19 April 1982.

Deduction moves the other way. You begin with acceptable general principles—premises—and link them together to arrive at a conclusion, which is usually an application of the principles to a specific case. Knowing that your friend Clovis is undependable (a general principle you have derived through induction), you will not accept his offer to take back your nearly overdue library books. You are fairly sure you would find them in the back seat of his Chevy three weeks from now.

A pamphlet persuading students of the value of college English courses uses deduction in this paragraph:

> Another reason English may be for you is that it can enhance the quality of your life. Everyone has to make a living in some way, and each of us hopes and works for the best in that department. Yet making a living is not the same as living—most people realize sooner or later that a

career, while of great importance, can not be the whole of life. Literature has always sought to both delight and instruct its audience, to make sense of the world and human life in a pleasurable way. Acquaintance with literature can be the foundation for future enlightening encounters with, as Matthew Arnold put it, "the best that has been thought and said."

The passage asks the reader to take two general rules—that work alone does not make a fulfilled life and that literature is a fulfilling source of pleasure and instruction—and apply those principles personally (to an individual case).

Syllogisms and Enthymemes. In formal logic, the sentence "Clovis is undependable, so I won't let him take my library books back" is called an *enthymeme:* it does not state, but implies, one of its premises. It is an abbreviated syllogism. A *syllogism* is a series of three statements that provides a major premise, a minor premise, and a conclusion that follows from them. Here is the whole Clovis syllogism:

The person I entrust with my nearly overdue library books must be dependable.
Clovis is not dependable.
I should not entrust Clovis with my nearly overdue books.

The first premise is left out of the enthymeme because you assume that it is obvious and agreed upon by your listener.

A deductive argument which appears in this paragraph of student writing can be expressed in a syllogism.

I think one of the main problems with education today is the great emphasis that is placed on grades by parents and the job market. When hiring for a professional position, an interviewer seems unconcerned with what the student has actually learned and more interested in the interviewee's grade point average. As a result, the competition for good grades can become so intense that it actually defeats the academic goals of education. Students find themselves concentrating more on strategies to achieve high grades than on acquiring the knowledge the grades are supposed to represent. These strategies include taking "blow-off" courses, scheduling for "easy" teachers, skipping over reading material that they will not be specifically tested on, pumping professors for hints on upcoming exams, and, on the lowest level, obtaining test copies. Our energies and motivation are drained away from intellectual ambition and curiosity, diverted ceaselessly to the task of maintaining our GPAs. This is what we are rewarded for.

—Andy Neugebauer.

The syllogism underlying this argument can be expressed like this:

> Emphasis on grades makes students preoccupied with grade point averages.
> Real academic goals are not achieved by students preoccupied with grade point averages.
> Real academic goals are not served by emphasis on grades.

In an *analogy*, you take two situations that have strong similarities, and you predict that under the same conditions, what happens to one will also happen to the other. For instance, if you and your best friend share many interests, tastes, and habits, you are safe to advise your friend to take history from the teacher you find fascinating. Or if working at K-Mart made your friend suicidal last summer, you could reasonably dread working there next summer because you know it will dangerously depress you too. The following writer, arguing that sportswriters and editors unjustly ignore bowling, defends bowling by using an analogy with another spectator sport, baseball.

> Bowling may not be very lucrative but it has everything else. Action? A 20-point lead can be reversed with the roll of a ball. In the span of an hour and a half, four finalists are eliminated and a champion crowned. You can't tell me that this would be any less interesting to read about than a two-and-a-half-hour baseball game where the final score is 1-0.
>
> —Joseph M. Arena, "A Strike for Bowling," *Newsweek*, 28 June 1982.

The above explanations of induction, deduction, and analogy are deliberately straightforward and simple. Actually, there are many more ways to jumble logic than ways to get it right. Our minds really do not work like computers, and we muddle inductions, distort deductions, and twist analogies, accidentally most of the time and on purpose occasionally. That is why a whole section on logic preceded this section.

Now, back to the organization of the first part of your persuasive paper. If you can bring yourself to do a little research, you will have even more pieces of evidence to present on your side. You can get hard facts and statistics, which sound much better than "I think I read somewhere that nowadays half of the couples who get married end up getting divorced." You can also support your case with other writers' firsthand accounts of their experiences, the testimony of experts in the field, and reports of experiments and interviews, if you are willing to poke through some books and magazines. (You do risk finding out that your opinion is totally wrong, but we do not consider that a good enough reason to stay out of the library.)

PREWRITING EXERCISE   **7-5**

Decide, if you can, what your opinion is on each of the following statements. In a group, discuss why you feel the way you do. Then choose one of the statements and make a list of how you could go about defending or disproving it. Look at the descriptions of reference works on pages 267–270 to discover where you could find appropriate facts, statistics, and quotations by authorities. Also include in your list personal experiences and inductive, deductive, and analogous reasoning that supports your opinion.

1. Childhood is the most wonderful part of life.
2. Sex education should begin in junior high school.
3. Journalism can best be learned by doing it rather than studying it in school. (Substitute any other vocation for *journalism* if you wish.)
4. The pass/fail option in general education courses in college encourages students' intellectual laziness.
5. Overcrowding contributes to high crime rates.

Part Two: Undo Your Opponents.   In your research, or maybe just in discussing your paper at lunch, you will find out what the major opposing views are. Choose the most popular arguments against your thesis, and devote a paragraph or so to undermining each one. In terms of classical argumentation, this is the *refutation*.

Many refutations point out problems with their opponents' logic, as the following two examples do. The first, in a student paper, points out an unfair comparison between cars of the 1950s and modern cars.

> Another common misconception about modern cars is that they are lemons, constantly being recalled. The truth is that no one was around to do the recalling in the fifties. A good example of a lemon fifties car is the Edsel by Ford Motor Company. The Edsel was equipped with a gimmicky push-button automatic transmission that had a bad habit of going in reverse when pushed into DRIVE. A defect such as that would have demanded total recall today; however, nothing was done at the time. Today, one no longer buys without protection from the government and consumer agencies.
>
> —Steve Stepke.

Joseph Arena, the bowling fan, provides a refutation that simply rejects the opposing premise:

> Some say the reason bowling isn't covered by the print media is that the sport is a bore—just not exciting. Once you print the scores what else can you say? I don't buy that. After all, the number of people who bowl on a regular basis far exceeds the number who play tennis. I'm willing to

wager that plenty of these keglers would find bowling exciting to read about, too. ABC has been televising the P[rofessional] B[owlers] A[ssociation] tour for the past 21 years, and the program has been known to get higher ratings than the Masters golf tournament. Doesn't this say something about the enduring appeal of the game as a spectator sport?

—Arena, "A Strike for Bowling."

Other schemes for refutation involve accepting the opponents' line of thought to a certain point, but no farther. The following student's refutation in her essay against curving grades is of this type.

Teachers can come up with several arguments in favor of curving grades. Some feel that the exams they give are too difficult for grading on a regular scale. If this is the case, they should revise the exam to a more appropriate level, not curve the grades. Other teachers like to see competitiveness among their students. But many students choke under this type of pressure. They would probably do much better if they were judged individually.

—Anne Ryan.

Another example of limited acceptance of the opposing argument before refutation involves close attention to terminology or statistics:

The city council says that last week's meeting was their first one with the shopping mall developers. That's true—it was the first *meeting*. But the developers have taken the entire city council out to dinner, two by two, in the course of the last two months.

If you want to ridicule your opponents in this section, be sure that your chosen audience does not identify themselves with the opposition. If we were writing an antiracist essay, we would feel free to jeer at the excesses of the Ku Klux Klan—we would never include them in our target audience anyway. But remember our earlier advice about not alienating the very people you have chosen to persuade. Most people respond to a tone of sweet reason—especially those who were prone to disagree with you at the outset.

PREWRITING EXERCISE   7-6

Pretend that you are defending one of the following statements in an argumentative essay. For each, write three points that your *opposition* might bring up—points that you might need to refute. You may do this individually or in a group of classmates.

1. Government agencies protect us from harmful additives in our food.
2. Every family should consider abolishing Christmas gift-giving.

3. The government should discourage the use of private automobiles by heavily funding cheap, efficient public transportation.
4. The food industry purposefully misleads the public about the facts of nutrition.
5. A mother has a responsibility to stay home with her children until they are of school age.

Part Three: Concede Points Gracefully.   Sometimes our opponents do have points that are not illogical, ill-founded, untrue, or stupid. You can admit it in your *concession.* You can also explain why your opponents' good points are not good enough to sway you to their side of the controversy. For instance, you might write, "I agree with some critics of the custom of tipping who say that it just lets the restaurant owner get by with not paying the employees a living wage. But I do not believe that I should deprive an individual waitress of a tip just because I think the principles behind it are exploitative."

Modify the Three-Part Pattern.   If you find that most of the evidence on your side seems especially clear and persuasive when given in reply to the logical fumbles and fouls of your opponents, consider this variation. Expand the second part of the body (refuting the opposition) until it engulfs the first (presenting your side); that is, organize most of your paper around refuting your opponents' arguments. Your replies can be patterned after the comparison and contrast alternating organization (see page 170). Often people find such an argument quite persuasive because it has the appeal of a direct confrontation.

Sample Persuasive Essays

Here are two illustrations of persuasive techniques in student papers. After you study these essays, we will discuss conclusions.

Is Craft Dead?

We live in a technological society where most goods are mass pro-   [1]
duced on assembly lines by unskilled labor. Because of this, most people assume that craftsmanship, whether it be in making autos or building houses, no longer exists. It might be dead as far as the production of autos is concerned, but it is certainly not dead in the building of houses. In fact, the carpenter of today is actually a much better craftsman than his counterpart of fifty years ago. He is more intelligent, possesses more highly sophisticated tools, and if given the proper material, is capable of producing a home much better than those built in the past.

One of the ways these people wrongly support their view is by   [2]
pointing to fifty- and one-hundred-year-old homes which are still solid

and assuming that it is the craftsmanship which is responsible for their durability. "Homes in those days were well-built," they say. No doubt these homes were well-built, but what these people have done is confuse the quality of material used in the house with the quality of the craftsmanship. Since these homes have lasted for so many years, they wrongly assume that the craftsmanship was responsible. In reality, it's the quality of material which has allowed these homes their long life, not the craftsmanship.

Homes today could be built to last just as long as those old homes if [3] people were willing or able to pay the price. For instance, most people can no longer afford solid oak stairways, although they were once fairly common in older homes. Nor can they afford the high labor cost of employing a carpenter to build the stairway. Yet if someone can pay the high cost, there are still plenty of carpenters around capable of making those stairways. And not only would these carpenters know how to build them, they would probably do a better job than carpenters of old.

One thing the modern carpenter has which enables him to do a [4] better job than the old-time carpenters is access to much more highly sophisticated tools, tools which were unheard of even twenty years ago. Such tools as transits, power-mitre saws, laser beams, and powerplanes not only enable the modern carpenter to lay out a house better but also make more precision cuts on the lumber. Also, it is not uncommon any more to find carpenters with college degrees and carpenters with a solid knowledge of trigonometry and calculus. This knowledge would enable the carpenter to understand such matters as the amount of stress and strain pieces of lumber are able to take.

The problem of modern quality, then, really boils down to the prob- [5] lem of material, for the modern carpenter is just as capable of producing craftsmanship as the carpenter of fifty years ago, but only if given the proper material.

—Tom Zaffiri

The student whose paper appears below was presented with an imaginary dilemma, the basic elements of which she could not change, and asked to justify one decision or another—basically, whether or not to buy a stolen final exam under specific circumstances. She chose to argue for a decision she knew would be unpopular.

Cheating Who?

I had a difficult decision to make. Normally, choosing between hon- [1] esty and dishonesty barely requires thought. I try to be an honest person, but in my situation choosing to buy a black-marketed copy of an important math test forced me to be dishonest. As long as I understood how to work the required problems, I felt buying the test was not so unreasonable.

Before buying the test I weighed both sides carefully. I didn't want to [2] make a hasty decision, and I found a compromise I could accept. I devoted most of my studying time to the problems on the black-marketed test. After conquering them, I then reviewed the rest of the material until I had mastered it as well. Knowing I had put forth a good effort to study all that was required, I felt better about my decision. I hadn't cheated myself out of learning important math concepts that I would need in the future.

A comprehensive math exam ranks high in difficulty among exams in general. In a whole semester of an advanced math course, there are probably over one hundred types of problems. Out of those, the instructor selects around twenty for the exam. What a relief it would be to know exactly what types of problems would appear. Much of the tension and worrying that final exams cause would be remedied. When I bought the test, the aggravation of wondering how well or how poorly I would do on the exam was gone. I felt very confident about my math course, which gave me reassurance for my other final exams. [3]

Another reason for buying the test was the curve of our grades. Since almost all of my classmates had bought a copy of the test, they would naturally do well. The accumulation of high scores would push the curve way up, making it impossible for me to get a decent grade without a copy of my own. Math is one of my most important classes and one in which I must do well. Without a high score on the final exam and a good overall grade for the course, I would lose my scholarship and my means of finishing college. I was not ready to take that big chance; I could have lost too much. [4]

I realize my decision to buy a copy of the test was a dishonest one, and many people would not justify it. However, I could not afford to fail the exam or the course. The consequences of failing would affect my future in many ways. I could not afford the expense of college without a scholarship. Without finishing college, my chances of finding a good, satisfying job would be substantially lowered. [5]

Completing my college education sits at the top of my value list. My decision to buy the test assured me of a good math grade. I was also certain of being granted a scholarship. [6]

—Carol McKinstra.

EXERCISE   7-7

1. Analyze ''Is Craft Dead?'' in light of these questions: How convincing are the writer's arguments? Can you refute any of them? What audience would most likely be swayed by the essay? Are there examples of induction, syllogism, enthymeme, or analogy?

2. How does the writer of ''Cheating Who?'' win the attention and goodwill of her audience in the introduction (if, indeed, she does)? Give some examples of her careful word choice. What premises underlie her arguments? What is her tone? Does she include a refutation or concession?

3. Without changing the details of the imaginary situation in ''Cheating Who?'' write one of the following essays:
   a. An essay in which you, as the student, justify *not* buying the test.
   b. An essay in which you, as a fellow student, persuade the writer of ''Cheating Who?'' that she made a mistaken decision.

How to End a Persuasive Paper

If the paper is long, you can get away with repeating your major points. In fact, you may need to do this in a classically structured paper because the last thing you did before the closing was concede points. Before that you were blasting away at your opponents' points, so it has been quite a while since the reader concentrated on your main pieces of evidence. Sometimes it can be impressive, too, to list all your main points in a lump; the list can sound formidable.

Below is the conclusion of an essay concerning the 1969 occupation of Alcatraz Island by American Indians. The essay argues that the U.S. government, which had left the island abandoned for six and a half years, should turn the area over to the Indians to use in experimenting with new forms of society.

> By making Alcatraz an experimental Indian center operated and planned by Indian people, we would be given a chance to see what we could do toward developing answers to modern social problems. Ancient tribalism can be incorporated with modern technology in an urban setting. Perhaps we would not succeed in the effort, but the Government is spending billions every year and still the situation is rapidly growing worse. It just seems to a lot of Indians that this continent was a lot better off when we were running it.
>
> —Vine Deloria, Jr., "This Country Was a Lot Better Off When the Indians Were Running It," *The New York Times Magazine* (March 8, 1970).

In this conclusion, you can see the skeleton of Deloria's whole argument: its thesis, main points (recapitulation), and refutation.

Once you have your readers firmly on your side, you can, if you wish, call on them for support or action at the end of your essay. This is the *peroration.* Deloria, in the closing above, could have asked the Indians in the audience to join the group occupying Alcatraz; he could encourage all his readers to write their representatives in Congress on their behalf; or he could invite people to organize and hold demonstrations to put pressure on the government. The following conclusion urges consumer action:

> If enough of us stopped merely fuming to ourselves whenever we are offended by meretricious ads and began writing to the media about them, it might be a first step. Futile as our individual efforts might seem to us, if editors began receiving letters criticizing the ads in their publications, they might get the idea that we consumers—their audiences—do not believe that ads are sacrosanct. And although we may not now directly supply the bulk of their salaries, they know that without us they have no salaries at all.
>
> —Vincent P. Norris, "Mendacious Messages from Madison Avenue," *Media and the Consumer* (Sept. 1973).

How to Hold a Persuasive Paper Together

Your transitional words and phrases should identify the logical relationships between paragraphs. Avoid sneaky transitions to cover up a lack of logic rather than reveal logical process. Phrases like, "Any reasonable person would agree that . . ." are suspicious. Also avoid "Undoubtedly," "Certainly," "Any fool can plainly see," and "Even a five-year-old knows . . ."—messages that attempt to prove the truth of an assertion by insisting beforehand that it is true. As an overall guide, consult our list of transitional terms on page 99.

How to Revise a Persuasive Essay

The first thing you should do with your rough draft is attempt to read it through the eyes of your chosen audience. Putting yourself in their place, do you see anything that offends you, alienates you, or seems ill-supported? If so, change it.

The next thing you should do with your rough draft is to take it in your grubby, work-worn hand, turn to the logic section early in this chapter, and check the paper rigorously for each logical fallacy we list there. Search out and destroy every error in logic, even the ones you think no one else would notice. Then ask yourself these questions (some of which will overlap with the logic section):

1. Have I chosen an audience and analyzed it?
2. Have I got the facts straight?
3. Have I defined all the terms that are unfamiliar or unusual?
4. Is the thesis stated clearly somewhere within the first two paragraphs?
5. Are my generalizations fair?
6. Are the authorities I refer to reliable?
7. Are there pompous statements I can humanize? Are there single, long, clumsy sentences I can transform into two graceful, short ones?
8. Are the tone and level of usage appropriate for the subject and the audience I'm trying to sway?
9. Have I tried sympathetically to ease my audience's irrational anxieties?
10. Did I anticipate and deal with the main arguments against my thesis?
11. Did I refrain from overapologizing for having an opinion?
12. Did I refrain from putting an extra e in the word *argument*?

IDEAS FOR PERSUASIVE WRITING

Short Prewriting Practice

1. Choose some controversial subjects in class and stage brief informal debates between students. Discuss the debaters' persuasive techniques in terms of

appeal to reason and appeal to emotion.
2. Record deductions, inductions, and analogies you make in the course of an average day.
3. Write a paragraph or two using induction, deduction, or analogy to support an opinion you hold.
4. Make up a dialogue in which one person uses fear-reducing tactics to persuade another. Try one of these situations:

> A worker would like the boss to pay more attention to hazardous working conditions.

> A teenager would like her or his parents to do away with a set curfew.

> A student would like a teacher to throw out the grades on an unfair test.

Longer Paper Ideas

1. Partners in a marriage should (or should not) write their own detailed marriage contracts.
2. College teachers should (or should not) be formally evaluated by their students each term.
3. Think of one of our popular maxims, like "Honesty is the best policy," or "Love is never having to say you're sorry." Write about whether you consider the message truth or propaganda and why.
4. Informal education is (or is not) more valuable than formal education.
5. Communal living is (or is not) preferable to the nuclear family.
6. Argue for the alteration or abolition of one of our culture's rituals. Examples: traditional wedding ceremonies, funerals, high school graduation ceremonies, Christmas gift giving, proms, baby showers, presidential elections, dating, beauty contests.
7. Argue for public ownership of now privately owned services, such as electric companies, telephone companies, oil companies, railroads, airlines, or hospitals.
8. Argue for private ownership of now publicly owned services, such as the postal service.

PART TWO
Special Skills

chapter Eight
Reading and Writing in College

Classes The reading that transmits ideas into
your head is just as important as the writing process. You get
plenty of ideas from conversation, television, radio, and your
instructors' lectures, but the printed word offers you much more
range and variety—and time to think. Paul Harvey's words are
gone, off into space, after you hear them on the radio, but a
written editorial stays right there for you to reread, question, and
rethink.

Your college classes require much reading, and some people
continue reading regularly after college to satisfy curiosity or to
form educated opinions. In this chapter, we will recommend
intelligent schemes for dealing with reading and for managing
the chores every college student needs to do—studying, taking
notes, and taking tests.

BECOMING A CRITICAL READER

You have probably figured out by now that just because a statement is
in print does not mean it's honest or accurate. The logic section in
Chapter 7 provides some tools to help you correct writing that sounds
defective. Here we suggest that you develop a wary streak to use
when you read.

Cultivate a Questioning Attitude

Published writers are not the only ones who have prejudices,
biases, and quirks: we all have plenty, and we have to be vigilant as

we read. The education process bogs down unless you keep an open mind. You should not reject a new idea just because it conflicts with an opinion you presently treasure. As Mark Twain observed in his *Notebook,* "One of the proofs of immortality is that myriads have believed it. They also believed that the world was flat." Be willing to consider new ideas, examine them, think about them, and decide on the basis of the available evidence what is and what is not valid. You will be bombarded by facts and opinions from all sides. In self-defense you must try to distinguish the truth from the tripe. It's not easy.

Be Suspicious of Slogans

As you form the habit of questioning statements, the first ones to examine are epigrams and slogans. These prepackaged ideas are all neat and tidy, easy to remember, pleasant to the ear. We have been brought up on epigrams and have Ben Franklin to thank for a sizable number, like "A stitch in time saves nine" and "Early to bed and early to rise, makes a man healthy, wealthy, and wise." An *epigram* usually states a simple truth in a short, witty statement—but often epigrams cleverly disguise opinion as fact. For instance, we have always heard that "Home is where the heart is," yet George Bernard Shaw insisted, "Home is the girl's prison and the woman's workhouse." Clearly, the truth of both statements is debatable.

A *slogan* is a catchword or motto designed to rally people to vote for a certain party, agree with the opinions of a particular group, or buy a specific product. Bumper stickers reading "America—love it or leave it," or "America—change it or lose it" may inspire you, but do not consider them reasoned arguments. Your job as reader is to question opinionated statements: demand evidence and decide rationally which opinions are valid, which are empty propaganda, which are a mixture of both.

Consider the Connotations

More difficult to perceive than the bias of slogans is the subtle persuasion of *slanted writing.* But once you become aware of the emotional quality of many words, you are less likely to be taken in by slanted writing. Chapter 2 thoroughly discusses the difference between connotation and denotation.

Connotative language is not necessarily bad. In fact, without the use of emotional words, writing would be virtually lifeless. But you must be *aware* of connotations, both as you read and as you write. The rhetoric in the following passage by Theodore Roosevelt is first-rate.

He is speaking of the U.S. entrance into the Spanish-American war. The utterance has impact, conviction, persuasion. Let's examine how much connotative words lend to the writer's effect:

> If we stand idly by, if we seek merely swollen, slothful ease and ignoble peace, . . . then bolder and stronger peoples will pass us by, and will win for themselves the domination of the world.

Note that he says not "stand by" but "stand *idly* by." He fears we may seek "ease"—but not a well-deserved ease, instead, "*swollen, slothful* ease." The word "peace" alone would not serve: it is "*ignoble* peace." Notice, too, that the people who are going to "pass us by" and leave us with no world to dominate are "*bolder* and *stronger* peoples": we are subtly asked to envision not invaders slaughtering innocent hordes, but rather clean-limbed, fearless people inspired by an admirable vision of world conquest. Surely the piece deserves high marks as effective propaganda. But you as reader must be able to detect that the chinks in Roosevelt's logic are effectively plugged with rhetoric. See the either-or fallacy on page 195 for help if it is still not clear. Your best protection against propaganda is your ability to think—to examine the language and the logic, to sort out the soundness from the sound effects.

WRITING EXERCISE   **8-1**

Find examples of writings that pretend to be objective, but are really biased, in one of your textbooks, a newspaper, or a news magazine. Write an analysis of how the writing is biased—slanted word connotation, sloganeering, dubious sources, logical fallacies, or simple omission of relevant material.

EXPANDING YOUR STUDY SKILLS

In *How to Study* (2d edition, New York: McGraw-Hill, 1969), Clifford T. Morgan and James Deese analyze the most common difficulties students have when they try to study. These experts suggest that a study schedule can solve many such problems. Here is a summary of their advice.

Scheduling Your Study Time

As a typical student, you have probably run into the following troubles:

1. Even though you try, you do not study as much as you know you should.
2. You are disorganized and waste time when you finally sit down to study. You plan to do too much in too short a time.
3. It's hard for you to start studying; things keep interfering with getting down to work.

All three problems come from slipshod use of your time. You can sweat and stew for hours over a task that would take you fifty minutes if you were well-organized. A schedule for studying can help you make the best possible use of your time.

To help you develop a plan of your own, we have designed a sample schedule for a person who takes five college courses and works nineteen hours a week (Figure 8-1). Most of the study time is in one-hour blocks. Psychological research has shown that people work well when they work steadily for a period of time and then rest or change tasks. For studying, the best period of time is forty or fifty minutes of work followed by ten minutes of rest. A clear schedule takes the optimum work-and-rest cycle into account and thus makes your studying more efficient.

The study hours on the schedule are marked for specific subjects. That way, you will not waste time figuring out what to do, and you can plan in advance to have on hand all the study materials you need. You have probably experienced the frustration of finally settling down at the library to study only to find that you left an important notebook at home. Scheduling regular hours to study specific subjects will also help you avoid the vicious cycle of falling behind in one class as you cram for another.

Notice three more advantages of the sample schedule:

1. It gives less time to easy subjects and more to difficult ones. We have scheduled four hours of study for biology, but only two for the snap course, health.
2. It spreads out your studying. Research shows that you learn and remember better if you distribute eight hours of study over a week's time than if you study eight hours in a row.
3. It attempts to place studying at the best time possible for each course. In general, studying a subject close to its class period helps. For a lecture course, the best time to study is after class; for a recitation course, the best time to study is before class. Thus, we have scheduled time to study Spanish right before class and time to study health and economics, both lecture courses, directly after the class periods. The literature and biology classes are mixed lecture and recitation courses.

These suggestions may have helped you face the grim facts about studying: you have to do it, and it takes time. Once you get used to those ideas, it is possible to find satisfaction in developing your study techniques to sublime efficiency.

	Monday	Tuesday	Wednesday	Thursday	Friday	Saturday	Sunday
8:00–9:00		Economics class		Economics class			
9:00–10:00	Literature class	Study economics	Literature class	Study economics	Literature class	Study economics	
10:00–11:00	Biology class	Study biology	Biology class	Study biology	Biology class		
11:00–12:00	Study biology		Study biology				
12:00–1:00							
1:00–2:00	Study Spanish	Study Spanish	Study Spanish	Study Spanish	Study Spanish	Work	Work
2:00–3:00	Spanish class	Spanish class	Spanish class	Spanish class	Spanish class		
3:00–4:00							
4:00–5:00	Work	Health class		Health class			
5:00–6:00		Study health		Study health			
6:00–7:00							
7:00–8:00		Study literature		Study literature			Study literature
8:00–9:00							

Figure 8-1 Sample study schedule. This student works part time and carries five classes a semester. The gaps in the chart are for catch-up study, library time, or fooling around. When you make up your own schedule, be sure to make it consistent with your own preferences and habits. For instance, if you study well late at night, your chart will not be so empty at the bottom. Realize that you need room for flexibility, as you won't be able to follow your plan exactly week after week.

Analyze Your Study Habits

Research supports the idea that each of us has energy and alertness cycles of our own. Some find it exhilarating to hop out of bed at 7 A.M. to write an argumentative essay; others could not effectively sign their own names at that hour but are at their persuasive peak at six in the afternoon.

The factors involved in these peaks and valleys are too numerous to figure out scientifically, but if you pay attention to your own successes and failures you may learn valuable lessons. Try this system: whenever you have a particularly good or bad study session, take note of the following four variables.

1. **Time of day.** A study of California college students identified two peak learning periods occurring between 8 A.M. and 5 P.M. The students worked best between 9 and 11 in the morning and 3 and 4 in the afternoon. They were at their worst, as many of us notice in ourselves, right after lunch. You may or may not fit this pattern, but you probably have one of your own. Record the times of your best and worst study sessions and see if you can adjust your schedule accordingly.

2. **Your stomach.** Many people feel alert and zesty when they are a bit hungry. Others either suffer mentally-dulling physiological effects of hunger or else cannot concentrate on anything but a snack. If hunger does not make you feel perky, a high-protein morsel (peanuts, cheese, yogurt) may help.

3. **Your worries.** Letting worries interfere with your efforts is probably one of the most common syndromes. (Some people, though, are quite able to "throw themselves into their work" to escape their problems.) If worries get in your way, try fifteen minutes of meditation, yoga, or exercise; a brief talk with a friend; or even a page or two of free writing about your problem. Eventually you have to get down to work, no matter what is bugging you, but sometimes half an hour of self-therapy will save you hours of inattentive studying.

4. **Your setting.** Do your good study sessions happen at a clean, bare desk or among a sea of stimulating clutter? Sitting in the library or lying on the parlor carpet? What kind of music, if any, plays in the background? Do you prefer the tomblike atmosphere of 4 A.M. or the company of your fellow students turning pages and rattling typewriters? The differences among people are immense. Being sensitive to your own quirks will help you to design a study system that will work, as well as one that will help you avoid situations in which learning is depressingly hopeless for you.

Note-Taking

Two kinds of note-taking are usually called for in college: note-taking from lectures and note-taking from texts. Taking clear, well-organized notes can save you time when you study for tests, because writing plants the ideas more firmly in your mind, and if the material is tiresome, moving your pen can help you stay awake.

Our clever note-keeping system is designed for those read-the-book, listen-to-the-lecture, take-the-test courses that are so plentiful in your first years of college. We assume that you use a spiral or three-ring notebook and have a separate section for each of your subjects. This system integrates what you learn from books and what you learn from lectures by placing your notes on them conveniently next to each other: use the left-hand side for textbook notes and the right-hand side for lecture notes, as shown in Figure 8-2.

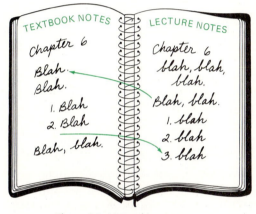

Figure 8-2 Note-taking system.

If you read the textbook assignment before the related lecture, you will have the backs of several pages filled with notes when you go to class. Take your lecture notes on the front of each of those pages, right across from the information you got from the book. If you read the text after hearing the lecture, do it the other way around. You can even draw little arrows to point out relationships between the two sets (when, for instance, your teacher brings up a different and better example of some general principle that the book discusses).

Lecture Notes.   Good lecturers start the class by previewing the topic or main points to be covered that day, and you can write these important items (and the date) at the top of the page. Your syllabus will often tell you what the topic of the day is.

Next you have to figure out the outline of the lecture—the main points and the details connected with them. Some lecturers list their main points on the blackboard, which makes it easy. Between main points, some of them pause, riffle their lecture notes, change their tone of voice, or use transitions like "The next solution has three drawbacks," in which case you can get ready to note down the solution and list three items under it.

Do not, of course, try to take down every word. Record only key words, and use abbreviations and symbols to save time (as long as you can be sure to remember their meaning later), like this note from an accounting lecture:

> Diff. in cost & selling price = *gross margin* or *profit gross*. Used to pay operating exp. Prod. cost = exp. matched w/sales rev.

As you read this note back to yourself, you reconstruct it in your mind this way:

> The difference between the cost and the selling price is the *gross margin,* or *profit gross*. This money is used to pay the operating expenses. The cost of the product is the expense that is matched with sales revenue.

You are in much better shape if you have read and taken notes on the relevant textbook assignment before the lecture. Then you will not furiously struggle to get down details from the lecture which also appear in the book. Writing down the main points more than once, though, will probably help you remember them.

If you do not have good lecturers, you may have to scribble down everything (except stuff like their son's piano recitals and their crummy jokes) and try to organize it later. In this case, it's good to have a three-ring notebook instead of a spiral, because it's easier to discard and replace pages.

Textbook Notes.   Taking notes from textbooks is much more comfortable. Writers usually provide headings and subheadings that tell you what the important concepts are. Many experts on study skills suggest that you look over a chapter's headings, subheadings, and emphasized type. Then jot down some questions that you suspect the chapter will answer. As you read the chapter, note the answers to the questions.

Here are the headings from a section of Elizabeth McMahan's *A Crash Course in Composition,* 2nd ed. (New York: McGraw-Hill, 1977):

Main heading:	A QUICK LOOK AT LOGIC
Subhead:	Avoid Oversimplifying
Italic type:	*either/or, false dichotomy*
Subhead:	Sweeping Generalizations

Here are some questions you might write before reading the text:

1. What does she mean by *logic?*
2. How quick is this going to be?

3. What is oversimplifying?
4. How are *either/or* and *false dichotomy* related to oversimplification?
5. What is one example of oversimplifying?
6. Where is the best place to sweep a generalization?
7. How do you know when a generalization is sweeping?

Some of these questions will turn out to be irrelevant (as well as irreverent), but they will give you a start on your thinking and note-taking.

If the book or article you are studying does not provide helpful headings, remember that a paragraph usually has a stated or implied topic sentence. Trying to find and note down these topics can be a healthy exercise. You will end up with a skeleton of the chapter or article, and as a result be able to see clearly how it's put together, what the logic underlying it is (just like looking at a human skeleton).

No bones about it, note-taking can really help you focus on the major, minor, and supporting points of a lecture or reading selection. Highlighting or underlining in your text will not do you as much good, as it does not require such a high level of involvement (psychologically or physically). If you will develop your note-taking skill, you will find that you can cut your studying time for an exam in half. Meanwhile, you will double the length of time that you recall what you learned (and that's what getting a college education is supposed to be about).

EXERCISE   **8-2**

1. Take lengthy notes on a single lecture by each of three teachers. Try to organize each set of notes into an outline of major and minor points. Which lecture was easiest to organize? Which was most difficult? Why?
2. Here are the headings from Chapter 6 of X. J. Kennedy's *An Introduction to Poetry*, 2nd ed. (Boston: Little, Brown, 1971). Make up study questions from them.

Chapter title:	Figures of Speech
Heading:	Why Speak Figuratively?
Heading:	Metaphor and Simile
Emphasized type:	*implied metaphor*
Heading:	Other Figures
Emphasized type:	*personification, apostrophe, understatement, overstatement, pun*

3. Make a list of headings like the one above, using one of your own future reading assignments from a textbook. Trade lists with another student and make up study questions for his or her list. After you get your list back, use the questions when you read your assignment, and report on their success or failure in helping you take notes and understand your reading.

Building Vocabulary as You Study

If you are a typical college student, your vocabulary could use enrichment. You are probably unfamiliar with the meanings of useful words like *esoteric, secular,* and *garish;* you can probably come up with just one meaning each for the words *pedestrian, sophisticated,* and *materialism.* And these are not oddball technical terms: they are used frequently in written English. Always follow the good advice in Chapter 2 about using your dictionary and thesaurus.

TIPS ON TAKING TESTS

Hardly anyone likes tests, and lots of intelligent people suspect that they do not even test what they claim to test; instead, they test how good you are at taking tests. But for many courses in college, your grades are likely to be determined by testing. In this section, we summarize some of the best advice we have heard, which can transform you into a calm, cool, and competent taker of tests.

Scoring High on an Objective Test

Objective tests consist of true-false statements, items to be matched, multiple-choice questions, fill-in-the-blank sentences, and any other grotesque devices teachers think up, as long as you are not required to write sentences. Often such tests involve writing A, B, C, or 1, 2, 3, or coloring in the right little stick with a number two pencil on a computer sheet.

Before the Test.   To prepare for an objective test, review the cleverly organized notes you took from your textbook and class lectures (see pages 224–227). There is no substitute for knowing the course material. You should have studied everything once already, before you begin to review for the test. If you have not, you need to work on your study habits. As you review, take notice of topics you do not remember clearly or in much detail; then reread the parts of your textbook that deal with those topics. Try making a list of special terms and their definitions. Making such a list, by the way, will help you on any kind of test.

One gimmick you can try is to squeeze the most important facts you need to know for the test onto both sides of *one* four- by six-inch index card. The process of choosing what to write on your card helps you to get all those pages of notes organized. Carry the index card around with you. You can stare sullenly at it while riding the bus or waiting in line at the grocery store or brushing your teeth.

Armed with a good night's sleep and a satisfied stomach (remember, these tests usually ask you to recognize fine distinctions, so you must be alert and keep your strength up), you are ready to take the test. Get to the testing place a little early, so you can sit and relax before the ordeal; you do not want your mind all muddled from rushing about. Be sure that you have a watch or that a clock is visible so you can schedule your time.

During the Test.   When you get the test, look it over. Check out what kinds of questions there are and how many of each, so you can get an idea of how long you should spend on each part. Then go back to the beginning and read the instructions very carefully. Filling out your answer sheet incorrectly can make your best efforts worthless.

Next go through the test and answer all the easy questions. This will help build your self-confidence and will get your mind in the right mood to tangle with the tough ones. Do not be too hasty, though. Read *all* the items in a matching list before you put down the answer to the first one.

After you have finished the easy questions, estimate how much time you can spend on each of the hard ones. For instance, if you have twenty minutes left and sixteen unanswered questions, you should puzzle over each one for only about a minute. This planning will keep you from wasting time racking your brains over one answer that you will never get, while slighting another that you *can* think out.

As you go through the test answering the hard questions, you may have the urge to change some of your earlier answers. One school of thought says you should always trust your first answer. This rule does not apply, though, when you have a perfectly good reason to change it, like having misread the question the first time or finding your memory now sharper on that point. Do not change your answers on a shaky basis, like panic. And do not keep going over and over them looking for teeny details you might have missed, or you will get greatly confused.

You are probably aware that not all teachers are skillful at making up objective tests, which are quite difficult to design. So you may encounter a test whose questions and answers you feel are ambiguous and confusing, even though you know the material. When you get the graded test back, discuss every ambiguous point with your teacher. You owe the effort to yourself and to the other students. If your grade is determined by tests, you must insist that the tests be clear and fair and that you are given the opportunity to learn from your mistakes.

Writing a Successful Essay Examination

The skills you need to write a good essay examination verge upon relevance. In other situations, too, you will sometimes have to come up with impromptu, one-draft writing (like memos, on-the-spot job forms, teacher evaluations).

Before the Test.   To prepare for an essay test, study your text and your notes, as you would for an objective test. The index card gimmick works here too. But remember that this time you do not just have to *recognize* all those facts; you have to *recall* them. A little more memorization of details and definitions might be a good idea. In the process, ponder possible essay questions and think about how you could organize your knowledge in writing.

During the Test.   When you get your test, survey it first. Look for instructions about how long each answer should be. Sometimes your teacher will ask for one- or two-sentence answers, sometimes for one well-developed paragraph, and sometimes for an essay of several paragraphs. These length differences are likely to be related to point distribution—for instance, on a mixed (both objective and essay) test, an essay may net a maximum of 30 points, while a short answer, no matter how clever, will provide a paltry 5 points.

If you have several short essays to write, immediately mark those questions that look most attractive (or least repulsive) to you.

The most unnerving thing about essay exams is lack of time. You can ease this problem a little by scheduling your time. Of course, you should distribute your time in proportion to the number of points assigned to each answer. Some teachers furnish a time schedule along with the test, but in other cases you are left on your own. If the written instructions do not assign points to questions, ask your instructor for the point distribution.

Here's a sample proportional schedule for an hour test worth 90 points on your grade:

$$\frac{90 \text{ points}}{60 \text{ minutes}} = 3/2 = \text{about 2 minutes for every 3 points}$$

	Points	Minutes
5 short identification items, 5 points each	25	15 (3 minutes each)
1 short essay (paragraph)	15	10
1 long essay	50	33
	90	58

This sample reveals how important time planning is. If you did not survey the test and make a schedule, you might probably be tempted to write for five minutes each on the identification items—and that extra ten minutes would really cut down on your time for the long essay, which has the most possible points.

After planning your time, plan your answers. Every test expert we consult agrees that the time you spend making a scratch outline of your essay is well worth it. Even though your answer may turn out shorter than it would be if you attacked the page immediately, your essay will be more pointworthy because of its clear organization and lack of sloppy repetition (which is sometimes suspiciously called *padding*).

As you plan, pay attention to the *verb* in the essay question: *list, explain, compare, evaluate, give examples*. Do what the verb tells you to do. If you are supposed to compare two kinds of cockroaches, a brilliant essay about cockroach habits simply won't do. And be careful not to miss a part of the instructions. If you are asked to *define* and *evaluate* five methods of cockroach extermination, and you just define them, you can expect only half credit for your answer.

In any course you may feel that you have a firm grasp of the general principles or trends or methods, but your teacher is not for a minute going to believe you do unless you follow up every general statement you make with a U-Haul full of specific details (names, dates, examples, quotations) that you have painstakingly memorized for this very purpose. Do not make the mistake of thinking that you need to know such "picky little stuff" only for objective exams. A mass of generalizations is boring and unimpressive to a teacher who is plowing through thirty essay exams over the weekend. A little life and color is certainly welcome (and likely to be rewarded) on those deadly Sunday afternoons.

In short, remember these three steps next time you must wrestle with an essay test:

1. Calmly survey the exam.
2. Schedule time according to point distribution.
3. Make a scratch outline of your essay.
   a. Do what the verb in the question tells you to do.
   b. Include lots of juicy details.

Sample Essay Exam Answers

To illustrate some common faults of essay exam writing, we are providing three sample answers (followed by analysis) to this question, based on material in Chapter 4:

In a short essay, discuss the placement of the topic sentence of a paragraph.

Answer A. The topic sentence states the main idea of the paragraph. It serves as kind of an umbrella that covers all the ideas that will be included therein. It may be placed at the beginning or end of the paragraph, whichever makes the paragraph more clear and interesting. All the details, examples, and reasoning in the paragraph should be clearly related to each other and to the topic sentence. A short topic sentence may be used infrequently to emphasize a point; a long, balanced topic sentence may also be effective. The paragraph should not wander off the topic sentence. Sometimes a topic sentence is not necessary at all, in which case you should leave it out.

Answer B. The topic sentence, or main point of the paragraph, is usually at the beginning in most writing. This placement makes the idea that the paragraph deals with clear to the reader right away. Then the supporting details and examples are easily understood, since the idea that unifies them is already in the reader's mind. This is why most topic sentences are near the opening of the paragraph. Closing with the topic sentence is a good idea too in certain situations. The supporting material may lead up to the main idea, or you may want to use the element of surprise that comes from not stating the point until the end. Placing the topic sentence at the end can also add variety to your paragraphs once in a while. A middle position may also add variety. Sometimes—not often—the center of the paragraph is just the right place for the topic sentence. You can also state the main idea twice if you want to, to emphasize and reinforce it. If no one could possibly miss the main point of the paragraph, you should not write in a topic sentence.

Answer C. The topic sentence of a paragraph usually appears at either the beginning or end; in a few cases, it may appear in the middle, twice, or not at all. The main idea you intend to expand in the paragraph may be made clear, and the outline of your expansion made easy to see, if you open with the topic sentence, as I did in this paragraph. A paragraph that depends on a series of details or examples to lead inductively to a general conclusion (the main point) lends itself to a topic sentence at the end. For example, you could list a series of outrageous building costs and close with the topic sentence, "Clearly, the governor spent too much on his mansion." This final placement would emphasize the general statement. Putting the topic sentence in the middle of the paragraph may be appropriate for a paragraph that begins inductively and then reflects on the main point. Stating the topic in different ways both first and last may clarify and unify a paragraph with a complicated or abstract main idea. Finally, the main idea of a paragraph of description or narration may be best left unstated—it should be clear from the details.

Analysis

Answer A was written by a student who was not quite desperate, but close. It only addresses the question specifically in two sentences: the others give a flurry of all the student knows about topic sentences and paragraphs, in a way that is disunified and, ironically, has no topic sentence.

Answer B is a great improvement. The student does have a grasp of the information the question asks for. The answer does survey the possible placements and gives some semblance of reason for each one. Still, some of those reasons are too vague, and some of the development shows signs of padding or lack of planning.

Answer C is a good one. It is obviously well planned, since the order of the discussion is predicted in the first sentence. It gives examples and intelligent reasons for the various placements. It devotes more space to the major placements than it does to the minor ones. The student is clearly in control of the material.

EXERCISE 8-3

1. Figure out a time schedule for taking the following tests:
   a. Test time: 50 minutes

	Points	Total points
10 short definition items	5 each	50
5 short essays	10 each	50

   b. Test time: 2 hours (120 minutes)

	Total points
15 true-false questions	15
20 multiple-choice questions	40
2 short essays (30 points each)	60
1 long essay	50

2. Here's a sample half-hour essay examination based on Scheduling Your Study Time (pages 221–223). Read the section again. Then plan your time and take the test without looking back to the section.

Short-answer essays (10 points each)
   a. List three advantages of setting up a study schedule.
   b. Identify the best unit of time for most college study and tell why it is good.
   c. When should you review for a recitation class? When should you review for a lecture class? Why?

Longer essay (30 points)
Summarize the studying problems that the writer identifies. From your own

experience, discuss whether that list of problems is true to life.

Analyze any difficulties you had with scheduling or planning your answers. Trade papers with other students and see how they handled the answers.

GETTING EXTRA HELP: USEFUL REFERENCE BOOKS

Laird, D. A., and E. C. Laird. *Techniques for Efficient Remembering.* New York: McGraw-Hill, 1960.

Miller, L. L. *Increasing Reading Efficiency,* 4*th* ed. New York: Holt, Rinehart, and Winston, 1977.

Morgan, C. T., and James Deese. *How to Study,* 3*rd* ed. New York: McGraw-Hill, 1979.

Robinson, F. P. *Effective Study,* 4*th* ed. New York: Harper, 1970.

Smith, G. L. *Spelling by Principles: A Programmed Text.* New York: Appleton Century Crofts, 1966.

chapter Nine
Writing about
Literature

Most college students find it fairly easy to talk with friends about books they have read. But when it comes to writing about literature—a story, novel, play, or poem—they are half-paralyzed, sure that they did not understand the work, or if they did, that they cannot express their thoughts about it in writing.

This chapter is designed to help such students. If you are one of them, the first thing to remember is that the rhetorical types we discussed in Chapters 5 and 6 (classification, analysis, comparison/contrast, and so on) can serve just as well for writing about the villain in Othello as for writing about your boss at McDonald's, and for analyzing the causes of Hamlet's indecision as well as for analyzing your own. Literary papers, like others, profit from clear purpose, well-developed paragraphs, logical organization, and impressive conclusions.

Of course our discussion in this chapter is limited; we cannot make you a literary critic in twenty-five easy-to-read pages. In a literature course, your instructor will expand remarkably upon the concepts we are about to introduce. Our purpose here is to provide you with ideas about where to start on a writing assignment concerning literature, and to give you specific suggestions about organizing traditional literary essays.

READING LITERATURE WITH SENSITIVITY

We hope you would never attempt to write a character sketch of someone you know only superficially. Nor should you start writing about a work of literature that you barely know. Just as a brief conversation gives you only incomplete understanding of a person, one quick reading of a poem may yield just a general impression—surely not enough to write an essay about.

Let's take the analogy further: when you try to get to know other people, you seek out repeated contacts with them; you observe how they dress, what kind of language they use, what gestures they favor; you try to figure out what brand of humor they enjoy, what they take seriously, what their beliefs are, what they imply without ever saying out loud; you search for patterns in their behavior that might explain what makes them tick. You can learn to approach a work of literature with the same attention to detail, subtlety, and pattern. Read the selection several times; be sensitive to connotations of words (see pages 51–52) and to sensory detail (see pages 121–124); let your imagination loose; bring your intelligence to bear on it. Formulate questions about it and try to dig out the answers. When you become intimate with the selection, you will no longer lack things to say about it.

Try Free Writing

Your writing about literature usually expresses your ideas and feelings about the work, but it also may be a way to *discover* those ideas and feelings. After a reading session, sit down and *free write* about what you just read—that is, keep your pen moving across the page, writing whatever pops into your mind without regard to correctness or coherence. Your beginning will probably be clumsy, but if you keep at it you are quite likely to write your way to an idea that is worthwhile. That idea, then, may serve as a focus for a more formal, organized essay.

EXERCISE   **9-1**

Consider the passage below, taken from a short story by Joyce Carol Oates. Write down as many statements as you can telling what you know about "the girl" in this passage—her age, personality, relationships with other people, appearance, class background, and so on. Tell what phrases or words led you to your conclusions.

The girl's heart is pounding. In her pocket is a pair of gloves! In a plastic bag! Airproof breathproof plastic bag, gloves selling for twenty-five dollars on Branden's counter! In her purse is a leather billfold (a birthday present from her grandmother in Philadelphia) with snapshots of the family in clean plastic windows, in the billfold are bills, she doesn't know how many bills. . . . In her purse is an ominous note from her friend Tykie *What's this about Joe H. and the kids hanging around at Louise's Sat. night?* . . . passed in French class. In her purse is a lot of dirty yellow Kleenex, her mother's heart would break to see such dirty Kleenex, and at the bottom of her purse are brown hairpins and safety pins and a broken pencil and a ballpoint pen (blue) stolen from somewhere forgotten and a

purse-size compact of Cover Girl Make-Up, Ivory Rose. . . . Her lip-
stick is Broken Heart, a corrupt pink; her fingers are trembling like crazy;
her teeth are beginning to chatter; her insides are alive; her eyes glow in
her head; she is saying to her mother's astonished face *I want to steal but
not to buy.*

—Joyce Carol Oates, "How I Contemplated the World from the Detroit House of Correction
and Began My Life Over Again," in *The Wheel of Love,* New York: Vanguard Press, 1970.

PARAPHRASING AND EXPLICATING

Paraphrasing means restating something in different words. A paraphrase is usually a brief and simplified version of the original work or
section of a work. Here is a poem by William Blake and its paraphrase:

Poem:

Her whole life is an Epigram, smack, smooth, & neatly pen'd,
Plaited quite neat to catch applause with a sliding noose at the end.

Paraphrase:

Her whole life is like a short, clever statement, precisely and carefully
planned to win approval, with a trap at the end.

It does not take a sensitive soul to see that the paraphrase re-
moves the poetry and spirit from the original. But the paraphrase does
show that the writer has a basic grasp of what is going on in the poem.
Before writing a literary paper, you paraphrase to make sure that you
understand the poem or passage on a literal level. In paraphrasing the
Blake poem above, for example, we looked up the words *epigram,
smack,* and *plaited,* even though we already had a general idea of
their meaning. Writing the paraphrase made us look more carefully.

Your paraphrase may actually appear in your paper to help the
readers when the passage you are discussing is especially complex. Or
you may include a paraphrase—really, a summary—of events in a
novel, play, or long poem in order to remind your readers of the
context of the passage you are discussing.

Paraphrase explains surface, literal meaning; *explication* expands
upon deeper meaning. Compare this brief explication of the Blake
poem with its paraphrase.

Explication:

The average woman's life consists of her efforts to be pleasant, attractive,
conventional, and inoffensive, in order to win approval from men. Like
the smoothness of precisely braided hair or the perfect control of neat

handwriting, these efforts are artifices, not natural or spontaneous. As such, they form a trap that ultimately restricts freedom completely. We can read the last line of the poem in two ways: we could see the noose as a trap (probably marriage) laid for a man by the woman's deceptive artifices, or we could relate the noose to the fate of the perfectly socialized woman herself, who ends up trapped in a confining and superficial life.

The explicator goes further than the paraphraser by identifying "smack smooth and neatly penned" and "Plaited quite neat" as images of conformity and artifice, identifying "her" as the average woman, giving possible interpretations of the last line, and suggesting that the poem's subject is female socialization. Such an explication lends itself to expansion and refinement: for instance, the writer could go more deeply into the associations of the word *epigram:* a statement that is short, witty, often amusing, but not to be taken too seriously or quoted too often. Or the explicator could explore the image of braided hair: how it is intricately arranged and controlled and has none of the flow, the free movement and variety of loose hair. A whole essay on this two-line poem appears on page 251.

In fact, most literature is so complex in meaning that it could generate whole essays and books of explication. The types of literary analysis in this chapter are really all interrelated forms of explication: choosing to grapple with just one type at a time helps keep you from being overwhelmed by the task.

EXERCISE   9-2

For each of the following passages, write a paraphrase and a brief explication. Compare yours with those of other students; discuss ways that the explications could be expanded or refined.

(1)

That summer when Father Eudex got back from saying Mass at the orphanage in the morning, he would park Monsignor's car, which was long and black and new like a politician's, and sit down in the cool of the porch to read his office. If Monsignor was not already standing in the door, he would immediately appear there, seeing that his car had safely returned, and inquire:

"Did you have any trouble with her?"

Father Eudex knew too well the question meant, Did you mistreat my car?

"No trouble, Monsignor."

"Good," Monsignor said, with imperfect faith in his curate, who was not a car owner. For a moment Monsignor stood framed in the screen door, fumbling his watch fob as for a full-length portrait, and then he was suddenly not there.

"Monsignor," Father Eudex said, rising nervously, "I've got a chance to pick up a car."

At the door Monsignor slid into his frame again. His face expressed what was for him intense interest.

—From J. F. Powers, "The Forks," in *Prince of Darkness and Other Stories* (New York: Doubleday and Co., 1947).

(2)

WHEN I WAS ONE AND TWENTY BY A. E. HOUSMAN

When I was one-and-twenty
  I heard a wise man say,
"Give crowns and pounds and guineas
  But not your heart away;
Give pearls away and rubies
  But keep your fancy free."
But I was one-and-twenty,
  No use to talk to me.

When I was one-and-twenty,
  I heard him say again,
"The heart out of the bosom
  Was never given in vain;
'Tis paid with sighs a plenty
  And sold for endless rue."
And I am two-and-twenty,
  And oh, 'tis true, 'tis true.

(3)

RICHARD CORY BY E. A. ROBINSON (See page 251.)

(4)

HAIR POEM BY SAINT GERAUD

Hair is heaven's water flowing eerily over us
Often a woman drifts off down her long hair and is lost.

FINDING A FOCUS FOR YOUR PAPER: WRITING APPROACHES

We will now offer you suggestions for organizing nine very common types of literary papers and illustrate them with excerpts from students' writing. We have tried to avoid using technical terms, but sometimes literary-analysis lingo is necessary; the terms are briefly defined. Remember that these definitions are condensed; check one of the reference books at the end of this chapter for a fuller definition before you start throwing a term around too freely.

As you write, frequently quote specific parts of the work you are analyzing. See page 286 in Chapter 10 for help in citing your sources.

Analyze a Character

Most students analyze characters in literature rather skillfully. Perhaps that is because well-drawn characters are like real people, and we respond to them with the expertise of a lifetime of knowing people. You must find some order for your insights to get them across to your readers clearly. Here is a respectable outline for a character analysis paper.

I. *Introduction.* Tell what character you will analyze and discuss this person's position in the work (major or minor). Clearly state a central idea about the character—an idea that serves as a thesis sentence. Suggest how you are going to organize your analysis (see a., b., and c. below).

II. *Body.* Describe the character's personality—drives, aims, ideals, morals, conscience, weaknesses, strengths—by analyzing what the person says, thinks, and does; what other characters say about the person; and what the author tells about him or her. You can organize it in one of these ways:[1]

   a. Organize around *central characteristics,* like narrow-mindedness, stupidity, and envy, and give examples from the work which bring out these characteristics.

   b. Organize around *central incidents* in which the character's traits are conspicuous. Remember to focus on the character development, not on plot, especially in your topic sentences. Show how these incidents help explain the character's behavior in other situations.

   c. Organize around the *chronological sections* of a work. This method is useful to show that a character changes from the beginning to the end of the work—from selfish to benevolent, from weak to strong, from innocent to disillusioned. Tell what qualities are emphasized in key scenes. This same method is useful to show how a character can undergo numerous enlightening experiences and *not* change, remaining selfish, ignorant, or weak to the end.

III. *Conclusion.* Here, if you want, you can discuss whether the character is believable, motivated, fully developed, or a stock character. (A stock character is a shallow one who appears repeatedly in literature and whom you instantly recognize, like "the loyal-but-not-so-bright side-kick," "the shrewish wife," or "the braggadocio.") Also—and most important—you should connect what happens to the character with the meaning of the whole work.

Here is an example of the introduction to a student paper concentrating on character change.

> In William Shakespeare's *Hamlet,* the title character is often thought of as a deranged and helpless young man who is poised on the very edge

---

[1]These ideas for organizing the body appear in Edgar V. Roberts' useful book, *Writing Themes About Literature,* which is listed as a reference at the end of this chapter. If you plan to take literature courses in college, you will never regret picking up one of these valuable books.

of sanity. Because of this, readers of the play sometimes overlook the fact that Hamlet is actually quite witty and possesses an active sense of humor. Throughout the play Hamlet uses this sense of humor to enable him to think when another man might be inclined to act. Hamlet's active and restless mind allows him privately to rationalize freely, while outwardly displaying his humorous side. But he eventually realizes that the time has come when he must act on his feeling. In the process, his sense of humor slowly disappears. Through the gradual diminishment of Hamlet's sense of humor, Shakespeare shows us both the loss of self-reflection that accompanies the demand for action, as well as the impending tragic set of circumstances that attends upon that action.

—Joseph Glasen.

Ponder the Point of View

Point of view is a more difficult approach than character analysis. Maybe the difficulty comes from our everyday use of the phrase "point of view" to mean "opinion" or "attitude," while that is not at all what point of view means when we talk about literature. Basically, point of view identifies who narrates the story and how. An added problem is that several different systems exist for naming the point of view of a work. We will untangle the varieties of point of view by defining four basic ones and listing considerations which will provide you with topics for paragraphs in your paper.

Omniscient (or Shifting) Point of View. The author is "all-knowing," can move at will into any character's mind, and can comment on the action freely. When the narrative viewpoint shifts from one character to another or to author comment, you need to identify the places where shifts occur. What are the advantages of the author's freedom to let you into several characters' minds? In one section of Lisa Alther's *Kinflicks,* the author presents alternately a mother's thoughts and then her daughter's thoughts as each decides to protect the other from knowing that the mother is dying. In this case, the shifts in point of view allow the reader some ironic insights into the mother-daughter relationship.

Dramatic (or Objective) Point of View. This is practically the opposite of omniscient. Instead of having access to all the characters' interior responses, the dramatic point of view narrates only external, observable things: action, facial expressions, gesture, speech. The dramatic point of view reminds you of watching a play; the work tends to be largely conversation.

In your paper, consider why the author chose not to let you into any of the characters' minds. In spite of such limitation, are there any clues to the author's own sympathies and philosophy? (For instance,

The Grapes of Wrath is written primarily from a dramatic point of view, but it includes many passages that reveal Steinbeck's own analysis of the story's events. Hemingway's short story "Hills Like White Elephants" is presented in purely dramatic form, enabling readers to consider objectively the implications of the moral dilemma with which the two characters are struggling.)

The next two points of view are both *limited omniscient;* that is, the reader has access to only one character's inner responses.

Central Point of View.   Most students find this point of view the easiest to identify. The story is told from the mind of a central character; no other character's interior responses are told directly. The author refers to the narrator in either first or third person (the main character is referred to as *I* or as *she* or *he*).

In a paper that concerns central point of view, your main consideration is how the character's personality affects the story. In Ken Kesey's *One Flew Over the Cuckoo's Nest,* for instance, narrator Chief Broom tells us that the room is filling up with thick white fog. But because we are aware that Broom hallucinates, we know that his account is not quite reliable: the room is not really foggy. A less obvious example is first-person narrator Jake Horner in John Barth's *End of the Road.* Horner has such a sense of humor that he makes us, the readers, see situations as funny which we would not normally find amusing, and which may in reality not be funny to anyone else involved. In some cases the narrating character does not understand the implications of what he or she is telling. Such a naive narrator—Huck Finn, for example—affects our response to both character and plot.

You may also try to discover whether the narrating character is a mouthpiece for the author, which is quite often true when the point of view is central. Consider, too, the character's relationship to the reader and how that affects the story. Jane Eyre, in Charlotte Bronte's novel, often turns from the action and addresses us directly: "Gentle reader, may you never feel what I then felt! May your eyes never shed such stormy, scalding, heart-wrung tears as poured from mine."

Peripheral Point of View.   Here, too, the story is told from a single character's point of view, but the character is a minor one. For example, Somerset Maugham's story "Rain" is narrated by a doctor who stays in the same rooming house as the story's main characters. To analyze peripheral point of view, you must consider the same things you would for a central narrator; in addition, you must ask yourself why the author chose a minor character rather than a major one to tell the story. Mystery stories are often told from the peripheral point of view. To keep you in suspense, the brilliant detective's loyal-but-not-so-bright sidekick tells the story, leaving the detective's thoughts veiled until the end.

The following introduction to a paper concerning point of view emphasizes the significance of the peripheral narrator's psychology.

> In "Death in the Woods," Sherwood Anderson relates the story of an old woman—her empty and difficult life and her bizarre death in the woods on a moonlit night. At first, the story seems to be primarily concerned with the old woman, but eventually a change that takes place within the narrator's mind also becomes significant. Thus, the story is about the old woman, but only as she appears through the eyes and the memory of the narrator. Her physical appearance changes because of the narrator's attitude. This remarkable illusion occurs in the death scene in the woods.
>
> —Ann Hein.

Concluding Your Analysis.　You could briefly compare the author's presentation with another alternative and show why the author's choice was preferable (if, indeed, it was). For instance, Holden Caulfield is the first person, central narrator of *The Catcher in the Rye*. If the story were told without access to his mind, the novel would be a less effective recounting of his thoughts instead of Holden's engaging interior monologue. The book would also lose the all-important elements of the readers' sympathy with Holden, since his thoughts, not his actions, are what make us like him.

Remember that always your conclusion should make clear how the element of the work you have been discussing influences the meaning of the whole—its theme.

Survey the Structure

In the essays you write for English class, the *structure* involves your division of ideas into paragraphs—visually defined parts. Similarly, in a work of literature the structure is the composition of parts: chapters, episodes, acts, scenes, interludes, climaxes, turning points, stanzas. (For a more specific discussion of the structure of poetry, see pages 246–249.) In writing about structure, you identify the plan of the work and then investigate the logical relationships between parts. The parts of the work are probably related in some or all of the four ways presented here.

Chronology.　Most traditional stories, novels, and plays are structured according to time: they begin at the beginning of a sequence of events and move right through to the end. Many also include flashbacks, which serve purposes like giving background or motivation at an appropriate place. And some are chronological, but they skip time:

Kate Wilhelm's novel *When Late the Sweet Birds Sang* covers the story of four generations of people by skipping long periods of time between sections.

Space.   Sometimes prose works are also organized according to setting: *The Grapes of Wrath*, for instance, moves from Oklahoma across the desert to California. Setting also functions structurally in works that establish patterns of events happening indoors and outdoors, upstairs and downstairs, in one household and another household. These patterns usually invite comparison between the characters, atmospheres, and events in the two locations.

Emotional Response.   Occasionally parts are arranged to draw an emotional response from the reader. Suspense is a common feeling that writers strive to build by leaving us with cliff-hanger endings to acts, scenes, or chapters. In Ross MacDonald's detective novels, for instance, chapters often close just as detective Lew Archer takes off in pursuit of another clue. Writers can arrange parts to build your sympathy or distaste for characters. John Fowles' *The Collector* provides an example: in the first part, a demented kidnaper tells how he imprisoned a young woman, and in the second part we hear the same story told again in the diary of the kidnaped woman. (Notice that in this case, structure and point of view are interdependent.)

The traditional structure of a play, story, or novel works this way:

1. Rising action, in which conflicts are introduced and the plot becomes complicated
2. Climax, in which conflicting elements clash
3. Falling action (or denouement) in which the loose ends are tied up and conflicts resolved

Many works follow this basic structure with additions and variations. Daphne DuMaurier's *Rebecca*, for example, has three or four climaxes. After each one, the reader expects falling action but instead finds more plot complication leading to yet another climax. And Mario Puzo, in *The Godfather*, always overlaps the falling action of one subplot with the rising action of another subplot, which keeps the reader turning pages.

Ideas.   Parts of a literary work may also be related by logic. For instance, the last two lines of a Shakespearean sonnet are set off from the rest, and they usually tie together or conclude all the ideas suggested in the first twelve lines. In Steinbeck's *The Grapes of Wrath*, Melville's *Moby Dick,* and Kurt Vonnegut, Jr.'s, *Player Piano*, there are interposed chapters that do not advance the central narrative of the novel but do expand and explain the ideas that the author suggests in the work as a whole.

Concluding Your Analysis. The conclusion will probably be evaluative. Does each part contribute something to the total effect and meaning of the work? Did each part make its contribution in the best place?

Develop Insights about Imagery

To use this approach you first must learn to identify *literary images*—passages or words that arouse your senses by implying or stating a comparison between two things. Imagery includes similes and metaphors (pages 49–50), and symbols (consistent patterns of images that carry more thematic weight in the work than other images). Here are some brief examples of images in poems:

the yellow fog that rubs its back upon the window-panes

—T. S. Eliot, "The Love Song of J. Alfred Prufrock."

I have it in me so much nearer home
To scare myself with my own desert places.

—Robert Frost, "Desert Places."

Like a long-legged fly upon the stream
His mind moves upon silence.

—W. B. Yeats, "Long-Legged Fly."

Eliot compares the fog with a cat; Frost compares a mental or spiritual state with a desert; Yeats compares a mind with a long-legged fly and silence with the still surface of a stream.

For a paper on imagery, narrow your subject to a pattern of imagery in the work (like nature imagery, color imagery, or religious imagery) or to a single motif (one image that is repeated, like the sea in James Joyce's story "Eveline").

In the body of your paper be sure to give plenty of examples of the imagery you have chosen. Analyze the associations that the image has for you: in Frost's "Desert Places," for instance, the desert has connotations of death, dryness, thirst, loneliness, extreme cold, monotony, the absence of growing things. You can probably see how these associations can apply to the inner state Frost is describing. And you can see why he says that his "desert places" scare him. Frost's image serves his purpose well: the whole poem, in fact, is a series of images of blankness and emptiness in nature, which Frost says is not nearly as terrifying as blankness and emptiness within himself.

In concluding your analysis, you might suggest how your image is related to other images or ideas in the work. Tell how it serves to illuminate theme or intensify reader response.

This concluding portion of a student paper aptly relates the imagery of Mary E. Wilkins Freeman's "A New England Nun" to character and theme.

> The images of Louisa's quiet little home and her serene lifestyle at first appear quite positive. The author gives no reason to suspect that Louisa feels at all victimized as she sits, at the story's opening, "peacefully sewing at her sitting-room window." Louisa has "almost the enthusiasm of an artist over the mere order and cleanliness of her solitary home." And surprisingly enough, Louisa Ellis has the refreshing capability to do things for her own enjoyment: using the good china every day, distilling her roses into perfume, and sewing fine linens. Louisa's life appears calm and tranquil, serenely cut off from the harsh, anxious world outside.
>
> It becomes clear, however, that Louisa is locked into a stultifying life, whether or not she realizes it. She seems incapable of being comfortable in the presence of Joe, her betrothed, and he apparently feels the same way: "Every time, sitting there in her delicately sweet room, he felt as if surrounded by a hedge of lace. He was afraid to stir lest he should put a clumsy foot or hand through the fairy web, and he had always the consciousness that Louisa was watching fearfully lest he should." It seems reasonable to infer that Louisa is frightened of sex. Many passages contain images of the whiteness and delicacy with which she identifies herself, and she more than once contrasts her belongings, "redolent with lavender and sweet clover and every purity," with the "indelicate" notion of Joe's "coarse masculine belongings . . . , disorder arising necessarily from a coarse masculine presence." Although Louisa's life is "smooth maybe under a calm, serene sky," it is also "so narrow that there was no room for anyone at her side." Choosing to keep her autonomy and her "delicate harmony," she has sold her chance for human companionship and physical love; both she cannot have.
>
> —Doris Dungey.

Relate Versification to Meaning

When you analyze a prose work, you look for meaningful patterns of structure, imagery, and character. When you analyze poetry, patterns again serve to reveal meaning. Patterns in versification may be of four types: examining a poem for all of them is sure to spark some new insights to write about.

Repetition of Sounds.   The most obvious pattern of sounds occurs in end rhyme. If the poem you are analyzing does have end rhymes, ask yourself if there is any significance to the rhyming words.

In Dylan Thomas's "Do Not Go Gentle Into That Good Night," for example, all the lines rhyme with either "night" or "day"—and those are the central images Thomas uses for death and life in the poem. Many other patterns of sound exist in poetry, perhaps affecting you more unconsciously than rhymes do. Look at the repetitions of sound which fuse this passage from Sylvia Plath's "Lady Lazarus":

There is a charge

For the eyeing of my scars, there is a charge
For the hearing of my heart—
It really goes.

And there is a charge, a very large charge,
For a word or a touch
Or a bit of blood

Charge, large, scars, heart—these words echo each other within the lines, and the echo emphasizes key words.

Repetition of Lines.   Plath's poem also shows this kind of repetition, both word for word ("there is a charge . . .") and grammatically similar ("the eyeing of my scars . . . the hearing of my heart"). Paul Simon's *Richard Cory* (page 178) repeats a line to build emphasis—"Oh, I wish that I could be . . . Richard Cory"—and the emphasis underlines the irony of the last line, in which we find Richard Cory dead.

Rhythm.   Most poems have rhythmic patterns of rising and falling movement. Both Robinson's and Simon's versions of "Richard Cory" have regular rhythm. Simon's version adds to the shock of the last lines by breaking the expected rhythm. Rhythm supports and reflects emotion in a poem. The lilting rhythm of Wordsworth's "I Wandered Lonely as a Cloud" is lighthearted:

I wandered lonely as a cloud
    That floats on high o'er vales and hills,
When all at once I saw a crowd,
    A host, of golden daffodils,
Beside the lake, beneath the trees,
    Fluttering and dancing in the breeze.

The jazzy syncopation of Gwendolyn Brooks's "We Real Cool" reflects the cockiness of the characters who are speaking:

We real cool. We
Left school. We

Lurk late. We
Strike straight.

And the choppiness of Bob Dylan's "Subterranean Homesick Blues" mocks the mindless routine of conventional life:

Ah, get born, keep warm,
Short pants, romance, learn to dance
Get dressed, get blessed
Try to be a success
Please her, please him, buy gifts,
Don't steal, don't lift.

Line and Stanza Division.   "We Real Cool" shows the importance of line division. Placing "We" at the end of each line, Brooks creates her syncopated rhythm and emphasizes the pronoun, stressing the egotism of the characters. Note e. e. cummings' all-important line division here:

1 (a
le
af
fa
11
s)
one
l
iness

The typographical isolation (especially *1* and *one*) illustrates the idea of loneliness.

There is logic to the way lines are grouped together into stanzas, too. Each stanza has a certain coherence with itself and contributes as a unit to the total effect of the poem. Some stanzaic forms are set by tradition (like sonnet, villanelle, terza rima) and the functions of the stanzas follow conventional principles. The reference books listed at the end of this chapter explain these special patterns. Many poems follow no conventional form: the writer divides the stanzas and lines according to the internal reason of the poem.

In your analysis, you must attempt to uncover the principles the writer followed in building patterns of sound, rhythm, and structure.

The following excerpt from a student paper shows how Theodore Roethke's versification in the poem "I Knew a Woman" is related to its meaning.

> The smoothly flowing meter, iambic pentameter, and the unobtrusive but definite rhyme pattern complement the perfection, the wholeness of the woman. When read out loud, the poem sounds quite natural and very complete. One does not feel as though Roethke had to struggle to make it perfect, but rather that it came very easily to him. It sounds almost as though he is just speaking in prose, calmly and naturally, and that his words just happen to come out in iambic pentameter, rhyming subtly and sounding whole. For example, the lines, "She played it quick, she played it light and loose;/ My eyes, they dazzled at her flowing knees," sound like the words of someone intently speaking as his thoughts occur to him. However, the meter in this poem is complex, and the fact that the rhymes are so unobtrusive indicates the skill with which Roethke writes. The woman, being described by his words, seems to possess the same qualities of complexity yet is enveloped by easy, natural wholeness and beauty. The first line—"I knew a woman, lovely in her bones"—emphasizes that this woman was beautiful all the way through, not just superficially but inherently. And her oneness with nature, her serenity are shown in the next line: "When small birds sighed, she would sigh back at them."
>
> —Sue Loellbach.

Explore the Theme

Every work probably brings up more than one idea—even the little Blake poem on page 237 brings up at least two which will be discussed in the sample student paper in this section (the woman's socialized urge to please, and the bitter results of acting on that urge too well.) It is unwise to say that just one of those ideas is *the theme* of the work: usually a theme involves a fairly complicated network of related ideas. Reducing the theme to a single sentence is quite difficult and often unsatisfactory.

Also, some works defy thematic analysis: some poems, H. D.'s "Heat," for instance, are attempts at perfect sensory description of an event, place, or person. These works do not contain themes as we usually define them: religious, political, psychological, or social observations. Such literature lends itself better to essays about imagery or structure or versification.

Most literature does contain themes that you can identify and write about. Begin by jotting down a list of all the ideas that a specific work brings to mind. Probably two or three closely related ideas on the list will seem more weighty than the others. A concise statement of these ideas in two or three sentences, suggesting how the ideas are related to each other, will do nicely for an introduction to your essay.

To organize the body, you may break down the basic theme into several component ideas, giving examples from the work. Here is an outline of such an essay about Kate Chopin's *The Awakening*:

   I. Introduction—*The Awakening* is a feminist novel.

  II. The traditional role of wife is presented as restrictive.

 III. The traditional role of mother is presented as unsatisfying.

 IV. Women's sexuality is dealt with openly—devastating the Victorian concept of woman as asexual.

  V. Conclusion—Chopin shows her heroine rejecting society as she discovers her sexuality and her selfhood.

Another possible organization classifies the different ways the theme is supported and developed in the novel. Here is such an outline of another essay on *The Awakening*:

   I. Introduction—*The Awakening* is a feminist novel.

  II. The imagery of the novel reflects desire for freedom and hatred of restriction.

 III. The main character is unsatisfied with traditional women's roles.

 IV. The final scene of the novel lends itself to feminist interpretation.

  V. Conclusion—Chopin's heroine rejects husband, children, and home as she awakens to her potential as a human being.

This outline uses imagery, character, and incident to show how the main idea is conveyed. Other idea-carriers may be setting, organization, or action.

No matter what organization you choose, remember to state clearly the idea you are dealing with in the first sentence of every paragraph, and support each idea with specific references to the work. In your conclusion, you can tell how the ideas presented in the work affected you personally—whether they were convincing or unconvincing, old or new to you, relevant or irrelevant to your life or the lives of others today.

The following student paper does an excellent job of exploring the ideas in Blake's poem.

According to *Webster's New Collegiate Dictionary,* an epigram is "a concise poem dealing pointedly and often satirically with a single thought or event and often ending with an ingenious turn of thought." William Blake, an eighteenth century poet, adopted this epigrammatic form to express his evaluation of females in the short piece "Her Whole Life Is an Epigram." Because of the nature of the epigram itself, Blake's final equivocal line can lead to two interpretations of the poem. "Her Whole Life Is an Epigram," can, therefore, be read not only as a statement about the female's sexual role but also as a comment upon the confining life faced by many women.

If Blake's poem is first read keeping in mind the time period and the poet's male voice, then definite physical and sexual connotations can be derived from the poet's words. The "smack smooth" and "neatly penned" qualities of this female's life reflect a flawless beauty, contrived to appeal to men. Later, Blake observes that this female's life is also "plaited quite neat to catch applause." The word "plaited" introduces the image of carefully groomed hair for the reader, an image with sexual overtones suggesting that the applause is expected in tribute to her artfully created allure.

If one accepts Blake's view of females as contriving to make themselves sexually enticing, then the final line of this epigram has an equally sexual twist. The picture of females presented in the opening line shows creatures that not merely attract men but actually ensnare them. The final line, "With a sliding noose at the end," implies that the artfully smooth woman uses her attractiveness to trap the unsuspecting male. The noose can be viewed as a yonic symbol which binds tightly to capture men through their sexuality.

Even though Blake probably had sexual commentary foremost in mind when he wrote "Her Whole Life is an Epigram," the poem can also convey quite a different message. If viewed from a feminist standpoint, this epigram shows not the physically applaudable woman, but the socially applaudable one. The "smack smooth" quality would refer not to the woman's physical beauty but to her domestic efficiency and unruffled temper. Furthermore, "neatly penned" can suggest that she is literally penned—i.e., confined—by her female role. It is not surprising, then, to expect this woman's life to be "plaited quite neat" instead of being loose and free. Assigned to the limited role that society has structured for her, the woman can do little more than follow prescribed behavior patterns which restrict her life in the same way that the pattern of interweaving used in plaiting confines long hair. Therefore, the applause she receives is nothing more than society's approval of her living within her fixed role.

If the first part of this poem does describe the proper role of women, then the final line of the piece is fittingly ironic. The female life that society judges to be perfectly interwoven proves to be a strangling existence. This time, however, instead of ensnaring a man, the woman is being trapped within a role because of her own sexuality. Even though William Blake probably intended "Her Whole Life Is an Epigram" to be a witty satire on the female as man-trap, the reader today may note more serious implications in the piece because of the final biting line.

—Rhonda Johnson.

Evaluate the Whole

What do you mean when you tell a friend that a certain poem is good, or the latest best-seller is really poor? When you write a paper evaluating a work, you must try to get to the roots of your positive, negative, or neutral response. Investigating your response, you are likely to find that you evaluate a work according to traditional standards such as the ones Roberts identifies in *Writing Themes About Literature*. Here are some of those standards which may provide you with paragraph topics:

Truth. People often like literature that strikes them as being true to life: the characters are believable, the plot is plausible, the emotions or ideas expressed seem to echo the reader's own experience. Some literary subjects—like aging, growing up, having crises of faith—reflect human experiences so common that works focusing on these subjects are believed to possess *universality*. Perhaps it's a feeling of truth that makes Twain's *Huckleberry Finn* and J. D. Salinger's *The Catcher in the Rye* such popular classics.

A student explains her positive response to *Rebecca* by analyzing the truth of a character:

> At the outset of the story, Du Maurier does not allow her youthful major character any heroic attributes, yet we are in immediate rapport with the naive, sensitive girl approaching the adult world. The girl is neither beautiful nor striking in any way, and the reader suffers for her in her shyness, the acute embarrassment we all know so well, of a young adolescent trying to discover who she is.
>
> —Laura Hurst.

Forcefulness. You have probably read books that will affect you for the rest of your life because of the powerful emotions and thoughts they sparked as you read. This permanent involvement with a work, in contrast to a temporary response, is one standard of excellence. Forceful works usually possess vitality—that is, repeated readings of them will be more enlightening than your first reading, rather than more boring. Dalton Trumbo's *Johnny Got His Gun* is a compelling example of a forceful and memorable novel.

Beauty. Literature is often admired for its beauty—of style, structure, characterization, imagery, or other elements. For instance, a novel has beauty of structure if you can look back on it and see that every incident, every flashback, every authorial comment, contributed to the total effect of the book. The removal or displacement of any part would disturb your final impression. Most readers would agree that

Dylan Thomas's "Do Not Go Gentle Into That Good Night" is a poem beautiful in structure, sound, and imagery.

Personal Taste. Of course, you know there is fierce disagreement about what literature is good, bad, and fair. Your personal taste is like no one else's: you may find a dark, gloomy character beautifully portrayed while your friend would call the same portrayal unrealistic. Or you may find a story touching when it leaves others cold. Your taste depends on your own experiences, and in an evaluative paper, you may relate a work to your own life as a defense of the work's value. Be careful, though, not to condemn a work solely because it fails to support—or perhaps contradicts—your personal prejudices.

Speculate about Style

If you have read stories by Joyce Carol Oates and by Ernest Hemingway, you could easily identify which writer wrote which of two unfamiliar passages set side by side. The difference lies in the writers' styles: Oates's style and Hemingway's are distinct. When writing a paper about style, you try to put your finger on those distinctive elements of a writer's syntax, diction, rhythm, and sound which contribute to the total effect of the work.

Analyzing style requires detailed examination, so you should choose a short representative passage to focus upon. You may find it helpful to copy out the passage by hand: such an exercise makes you more closely aware of each word and phrase. Then note your observations about the following three components of style.

Sentences. Are they long or short? (An average sentence is about twenty words long.) What grammatical types occur (simple, compound, complex, compound-complex, fragment)? What functional types appear (statement, question, command, exclamation)? Is the word order usual or unusual? (Note the contrast between, "The clock struck nine, and we all trembled," and "Nine the clock struck, and trembled we all.") Is there deliberate repetition of grammatical patterns in phrases, clauses, or sentences?

Diction. Diction means word choice; here you will consider characteristics of individual words. What parts of speech predominate? Are the words general or specific? Abstract (love, freedom, honesty) or concrete (toenail, ice-cream cone, radiator cap)? Formal or informal? Denotative or connotative? Common or unusual? Long or short?

Rhythm and Sound. Both prose and poetry make use of these elements. Look for alliteration (repetition of similar consonant sounds) and assonance (repetition of similar vowel sounds). Read the passage aloud and listen for the dominance of either hard sounds (like *k, t, ch*) or soft sounds (like *s, oo, l*). Listen, too, for regular rhythms and for length or shortness of cadence groups (that is, word groups that a speaker would fit together without pausing).

After you have made notes on all these characteristics of sentences, diction, rhythm, and sound, you must choose only the ones that are significant to write about. Some of the features you have noted are probably just incidental, like the way we often accidentally alliterate when we speak. But other stylistic features can be related to the writer's purpose. You could say, for instance, that Holden Caulfield's unusually long, rambling sentences in *Catcher in the Rye* reflect the character's confused and burdened state of mind. Or that soft sounds produce a soothing, pleasant effect and hard sounds a harsh or severe effect in a poem. Or that a predominance of verbs over other parts of speech conveys a high level of activity.

The following introduction shows that the writer intends to identify stylistic elements in one passage and to relate them to character in the novel *Player Piano*.

> The passage to be discussed is a short telephone conversation between Paul Proteus and his wife Anita. A brief description of Anita's attitude and actions concludes the section. The purpose of this passage is to show that the people who are successful in the executive world of Ilium must themselves be mechanical in their behavior and feelings or be pushed by someone equally mechanical. The style used helps to achieve this.
>
> The repetition of the closing of the telephone conversation (lines seven and eight) gives the reader the impression of pure habit—of mechanical statement and reply—instead of the impression of real love and mutual affection between husband and wife.
>
> —Erin McCarthy Trnka.

The elements of style, combined with elements of imagery and versification, produce an identifiable *tone* or *mood* in a passage of literature. A passage with a playful tone is likely to have informal diction, colorful images, and lilting rhythm; a passage with a somber tone is likely to have formal diction, gloomy images, and a slow beat; a passage with an ironic tone is likely to express a playful, humorous message while using formal diction, dark imagery, and mournful rhythm.

In your conclusion, attempt to show relationships among the stylistic features you have discussed. See if you can apply some general terms to describe the style as a whole and tell whether the style in other parts of the work deviates from the style you have described. Be sure also to mention how the style contributes to or complements the meaning of the text.

Scrutinize a Section

As you read literature, you should note chapters, scenes, speeches, or stanzas that seem particularly significant to you. One of these passages may be a good subject for a paper of close reading. In such a paper, you concentrate all your critical skills on one section of a work, attempting to give a complete analysis of that segment. The selection should not be too long. From Sylvia Plath's *The Bell Jar,* for example, you might choose to do a close reading of just the two or three pages in which the heroine ends up tossing her fashionable, expensive clothes, piece by piece, off the roof of a New York hotel.

Make a copy of the passage you select. Then begin to analyze *what it does*. It may give you new or fuller insight into a character. It may reveal a central conflict. It may add to your understanding of the work's theme. It may build an atmosphere. It may heighten the readers' emotional involvement. It may be a key part of plot development.

The passage probably does several of these things. For instance, Hamlet's often-analyzed "To be or not to be" speech reveals character, pinpoints a conflict within the character, explores the theme of death, and involves the reader emotionally in Hamlet's dilemma.

As you analyze *what* the passage does, consider *how* it does it too. The passage may set tone and mood through the use of imagery; for instance, a hopeful, expectant atmosphere could be conveyed through the images of sunrise, birds twittering, the smell of flowers. Or a passage may convey character through sentence patterns, as we mentioned in our earlier example of Holden Caulfield's rambling sentences. Scrutiny of the style and imagery of the passage will help you discover how it achieves its effects.

One student wrote this passage after closely reading a section of Chapter 25 of *The Grapes of Wrath*.

> Probably most obviously, this passage contributes to the reader's emotional involvement in the story, and it does so in several ways. First of all, a pitiful situation is described to us. We are told of the burning of the corn, the children dying of pellagra, the people kept from retrieving the potatoes from the river by guards. Because of our sense of right and wrong and our capabilities for compassion, we can feel the frustration and anger of the workers. As this happens we respond with feelings of outrage and anger growing within ourselves.
>
> As we read the words and grasp their meanings, we are subtly being influenced by the writer's style. Early in the passage his sentences are

short, and key phrases are often repeated, producing a type of delivery similar to that used by a speaker at a rally to get the people excited and fired up about something—here, the plight of the migrant workers. The parallel structure of the first three sentences in the third paragraph creates a powerful expression of the hopelessness of the oppressive situation. Toward the end of the passage, in the fourth paragraph, the sentences grow in length and take on a more calm but even more sorrowful cadence. In the longer sentences, the fiery anger of the beginning settles into a deeper bitterness.

—Laura Arnold.

Systematically inspecting a passage from many different approaches can help you untangle the meaning of a particularly tough segment. It can also show the complexity of an apparently simple part. In the conclusion of your paper, be sure to make a general statement about the revelations concerning theme that your close reading yielded.

WRITING A BOOK REPORT

In order to prove that you have done some outside reading, you may be asked to write a book report. This common assignment can be utterly defeating unless you take the situation firmly in hand from the beginning. Any book report can include three items: summary of the ideas or plot, analysis of the book in the light of your other knowledge about its subject, and your subjective response to the work. Ask your instructor to give you an idea about which of these items to emphasize in your book report. If that fails to help, follow this three-part organization:

1. Show that you understand the theme of the book. This task may require summarizing, but keep it to a minimum: it will be unimpressive to anyone who has read the book and boring to anyone who has not. Concentrate on summing up the main ideas that the writer conveys. Any good book has at least one controlling idea: Ross MacDonald's detective novels, for instance, usually support the idea that genetic makeup and childhood environment influence a person's life more than individual human will does.

2. Show how the writer conveys the theme or produces the effects in the book. For suggestions, look over the nine kinds of literary papers we have outlined here. For internal evidence, you can point to the writer's style, characterization, plot structure, imagery, or other elements. Ideally, all these elements should support the idea of the work. Choose one or more elements to review, depending on the projected length of your paper.

3. Give your personal response. This response could be your evaluation of the book, whether the ideas are valid and well-supported, whether the plot is

believable, whether the characters are sufficiently motivated, and so on. Such a discussion could also lead to your emotional response to the book: how fully involved you were, whether you found it depressing or exhilarating, boring or humorous, valuable or a waste of time.

GETTING EXTRA HELP: USEFUL REFERENCE BOOKS

Cirlot, J. E. *A Dictionary of Symbols,* trans. Jack Sage. New York: New York Philosophical Library, 1976.

Cohen, B. Bernard. *Writing About Literature,* rev. ed. Glenview, Ill.: Scott, Foresman, and Co., 1973.

Frazer, Sir James G. *The Golden Bough: A Study in Magic and Religion,* abridged ed. New York: Macmillan, 1922, 1958.

Guerin, Wilfred, L., Earle G. Labor, Lee Morgan, and John R. Willingham. *A Handbook of Critical Approaches to Literature.* New York: Harper & Row, 1966.

Irmscher, William F. *The Nature of Literature: Writing on Literary Topics.* New York: Holt, Rinehart, and Winston, 1975.

Roberts, Edgar V. *Writing Themes About Literature,* 3rd ed. Englewood Cliffs, N.J.: Prentice-Hall, Inc., 1973.

Thrall, William Flint, Addison Hibbard, and C. Hugh Holman. *A Handbook to Literature,* 3d ed. New York: Odyssey, 1972.

chapter Ten
Researched
Writing

At some time you may be asked to write a paper that does not spring entirely from your own mind. You may be expected to do research—to read fairly widely on a certain subject, to synthesize (to combine a number of different ideas into a new whole) and organize this accumulated information, and then to get your new knowledge down on paper in clear and coherent prose. The whole process may seem like busywork when assigned by your English instructor, but be assured: you will be learning a valuable skill, one that will be essential in your advanced college classes and that will prove useful in compiling on-the-job reports after graduation.

Traditionally, research papers involve argument. You may be expected to choose a topic which is somewhat controversial, investigate the issues thoroughly on both sides, and take a stand. The writing process for a research paper is essentially the same as for any other, except that you begin with a thesis question which you later turn into a thesis statement. You still need to narrow the subject to a topic you can handle in the number of pages assigned. And the bulk of the writing in the paper should be yours, stating your evaluation of what you have learned from your sources. You will quote from and give credit to the authors you have read, but a cut-and-paste job (in which you merely string together ideas and quotations from your sources) will not do.

SCHEDULING YOUR RESEARCH PAPER

Writing a research paper is a time-consuming job. This is one paper that you simply cannot put off until the last minute. If you divide the project into units, you can keep the work under control.

Set Deadlines for Yourself

If your completed paper is due in, say six weeks, you could put yourself on a schedule something like this:

1st week: Complete preliminary bibliography cards locating all of your sources.
Try to narrow your topic down to a workable thesis question to investigate.

2d week: Read and take notes.
Settle on a preliminary thesis question.
Try to come up with a preliminary outline.

3d week: Continue reading and taking notes.

4th week: Complete reading and note-taking.
Turn your thesis question into a statement.
Wrestle the outline into shape.

5th week: Write the first draft.
Let it cool—rest yourself.
Begin revising and editing.
Get someone reliable to read your second draft and tell you whether every sentence is clear, every quotation properly introduced, and every paragraph nicely coherent.

6th week: Polish the paper.
Type the final draft.
Let it rest at least overnight.
Proofread it carefully.

That is a fairly leisurely schedule. You can, of course, do the work in a shorter time if required to. You will just have to be more industrious about the reading. Some instructors deliberately ask students to complete the project within a month in order to allow no chance for procrastination. Whatever your time limit, devise a schedule for yourself and stick to it.

Narrowing Your Topic

If you have an area of interest but no ideas about any way to limit that topic, your first step might be to consult a good encyclopedia. Perhaps your father recently underwent abdominal surgery; as a result of spending many hours with him, you have become interested in hospitals. An encyclopedia article on hospitals will briefly discuss their history, some specialized kinds, services provided, intern training, difficulties with sanitation, and cost of care, among other things. Remembering that your dad contracted a staph infection while recovering from his operation, you might decide to investigate the problem of infections in hospitals. Why have they become prevalent? What is being done about them? Or, as you read the article, you might encounter a new term and become interested in *hospices*—specialized hospitals that attempt to provide comfort and dignity for the dying. Are these proving successful? Should we have more of them in this country? Something in an encyclopedia article on your subject is likely to provide the spark needed to fire your curiosity and give you a focus for your research.

Expanding Your Associations

Once you have narrowed your topic, you may need momentarily to expand it again in order to locate all the relevant information in the library. As indexes and other reference tools do not necessarily classify information the way you do in your head, you need to think of other headings under which your subject might be indexed. Before going to the library, you should make a list of topics related to your research subject. If you are planning to investigate hospices, your list might go like this:

Hospice
Dying
Death
Aging
Geriatrics
Health care
Old people

EXERCISE   **10-1**

For each of the following subjects, list at least three related topics that you could look under in reference books.

1. No-fault divorce
2. High school students' legal rights
3. Fad diets
4. Detective fiction by women
5. Use of the word *ain't*
6. Tax shelters
7. Horror movies

TOPICS FOR RESEARCHED WRITING

If your mind remains a blank and your instructor will allow you to borrow a topic from us, here are some ideas that we think might be interesting to research.

For Writing an Informative Paper

1. Research the history of a familiar product or object, such as Coca-Cola, Mickey Mouse, the dictionary, the typewriter, the nectarine, the Afro hairstyle, black mass, black magic, vampire movies.
2. Research and analyze a fad, craze, or custom: telephone booth stuffing, streaking, the platform shoe, the twist, fraternity initiation, pierced ears, "smile" buttons, troll dolls, any fad diet.
3. How can autistic children be helped?
4. How can alcoholics be helped?
5. How can rape victims be helped?
6. Why do people become alcoholics?
7. What is *anorexia nervosa* and can it be prevented?
8. What is *agoraphobia* and what can be done about it?
9. How can battered women be helped?
10. Why do women allow themselves to be beaten by their husbands?

For Writing about Literature

1. How effective is the ending of *Huckleberry Finn?*
2. Is the governess sane or insane in James's "The Turn of the Screw"?
3. What are the characteristics of the "Hemingway hero"?
4. What are the mythological implications of Welty's "Moon Lake"?
5. What was Zola's contribution to literary naturalism?

For Persuasion or Argumentation

After doing the appropriate research, defend either side of one of the following issues.

1. Is nuclear waste disposal safe? or suicidal?
2. The use of animals in research should (should not) be allowed.
3. Clear cutting of forests should (should not) be stopped.
4. It is (is not) better for children if their incompatible parents get a divorce.
5. The children's toys now on the market often encourage (discourage) destructiveness and discourage (encourage) creativity.
6. The federal government does (does not) have the right to monitor activities of United States citizens whom it regards as dangerous to national security.

7. The fashion industry does (does not) exploit consumers. Or substitute any area of business that interests you: the cosmetics industry, the funeral business, the car manufacturers, the oil industry, etc.
8. Having a working mother does (does not) harm a child's development.
9. Automation has (has not) hindered our culture more than it has helped.
10. Violence on children's TV shows is (is not) harmful to children.
11. Newspaper reporters should (should not) have the right to protect their sources.
12. Compulsory education until the age of sixteen should (should not) be abolished.
13. Parents should (should not) have the right to censor the textbooks and literature taught in their children's schools.
14. Internment of Japanese-American families after the United States entered World War II was a grave injustice (was necessary for the national security).
15. Is sexual harassment in the workplace a serious problem—or a myth?

SOME CLUES ON USING THE LIBRARY

Once you have your deadlines set and your topic chosen, you need to get acquainted with your library. Most college libraries offer orientation courses to show students how to find things. If the course is not required, take it anyway. An orientation course is your surest bet for learning your way around a library. If no such course is offered, your library will at least have available a handbook explaining what's where. A few minutes spent studying these instructions may save you many hours of aimless wandering. After reading the handbook carefully, if you search and still fail to find what you need, ask for help. Librarians are seldom snarly about answering questions and will often take you in tow, lead you to the material you want, and give you valuable advice.

Locating the Major Resources

We can offer here some general instructions to help you find your way around your library.

The Card Catalog.   Somewhere near the entrance to the library you will see imposing rows of polished wood cabinets with small drawers in which are alphabetically filed cards listing all of the books, periodicals, microfilm, and pamphlets available on the premises. These cards (listed by author, title, and subject) provide the *call number* that you need in order to track down the material.

Be advised that in some libraries separate cabinets are used to house the subject cards. If you want to find a biography of Mark Twain, for instance, and look him up in the author/title section, you will be directed to try again under "Samuel Langhorne Clemens," his real name. When you locate the box with the Clemens cards, you may find only books *by* Mark Twain. If so, you must locate the cabinets containing subject headings. Here, under "Clemens," you will discover numerous books *about* Twain, i.e., books with Twain (or his work) as their subject matter.

Your library may have a computer which will save you the trouble of leafing through the cards. If so, you will be able to call up the information needed to locate your material by the touch of a keyboard.

The Stacks. Those seemingly endless numbered shelves on which books are stored are called the stacks (computer abbreviation: *stx*). In many libraries the stacks are open, and you are free to wander along the aisles, examine the books, and decide which ones you want to check out. If the stacks are closed, the library provides someone to do the finding for you.

The Circulation Desk. In a closed-stack library, you present your call slips at the circulation desk and wait for a clerk to bring your books to you. (A *call slip* is a form provided by the library on which you write the call number, author, title, and possibly volume number of the item you want.) If the library has open stacks, you take your call slips, find the books yourself using the call numbers, and return to the circulation desk to check out the ones you want. Someone at the circulation desk can tell you if a book you could not locate is checked out or—worse luck—lost. If the book is simply out, you may put a "hold" on it, and when it is returned, you will be notified. If the book is lost, you can request a search. Should the librarians be able to find the book, you will receive notice. But if the book is genuinely lost—or, more likely, stolen—you are out of luck. Eventually the library will reorder the item, but probably not in time for you to use now.

The Reserve Desk. Books (and sometimes copies of articles) being intensively used in courses may be put "on reserve" by faculty members and will be held at the reserve desk (or in the reserve room) where they are easily available to students. Materials on reserve are usually restricted for library use only—often by the hour. The card catalog will identify any item placed on reserve so that you need not exhaust yourself searching futilely in the stacks.

Reference Materials and Periodicals. Libraries arranged according to types of material will have a separate *periodicals room* in which you may read recent copies of popular magazines and journals for all disciplines. A separate *reference room* will include bibliographical indexes, reference volumes, encyclopedias, and dictionaries for every area of research. These materials must be used where they are. You should not move them, and you are never allowed to check them out (i.e., they are *noncirculating*).

In many new libraries the materials are arranged by subject, divided floor-by-floor. All the resources—including reference tools and periodicals—for the social sciences, for instance, are collected on a single floor. Separate floors may be devoted to education, to the humanities, to the hard sciences, and to government documents. These *subject divisional libraries*, as they are called, also include on the main floor an easily accessible array of nonspecialized reference books and bibliographies, as well as a collection of the most often-used books from every academic discipline. (This area is called the "General College Library," or GCL.)

HOW TO FIND WHAT YOU NEED IF YOU DON'T KNOW WHAT IT IS

When you begin compiling your preliminary bibliography—your list of books, articles, and chapters in books on your topic—you will not know what these are or where to find them. Do not despair. What sounds like a difficult task is actually fairly simple.

Begin with the Card Catalog

You will find the books available on your topic by looking it up by subject in the card catalog (or by using the handy computer). The cards you will find there will look like those in Figure 10-1. Remember to also look under related subjects if you fail to find enough material on your first try.

Consult Indexes and Bibliographies

The task gets a bit tricky when you move on to the next step, which involves finding out what articles and essays are available on your topic. The chief tools you need are mammoth sets of books which index, year by year, all of the articles in a multitude of magazines.

You need to know first which indexes cover what type of magazines, or you could waste a lot of time scanning titles that have no

Author   Title   Translator

Call
number

Book has a 14-
page preface,
is 306 pages
long, has
illustrations,
and measures
22 centimeters

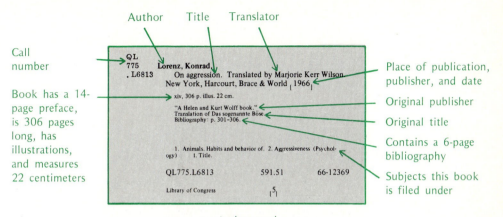

Place of publication,
publisher, and date

Original publisher

Original title

Contains a 6-page
bibliography

Subjects this book
is filed under

a Author card

Filed under
"On" in card
catalog (under
"Aggression" in
the computer)

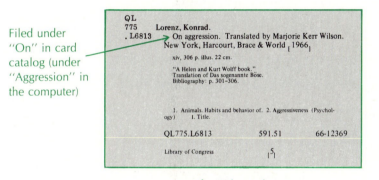

b Title card

This card is
filed under
both
"Animals" and
"Aggressiveness"

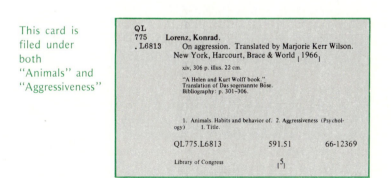

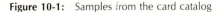

c Subject card

Figure 10-1: Samples from the card catalog

The symbols mean vol. 115, pages 106 through 107 and continued (+) in the back of the February 1982 issue.

Cross reference to an item listed under the name of a joint author.

This article includes a portrait (por).

This entry lists a short story, not an article.

The asterisk means this article is available as a talking book for the blind.

These articles are all illustrated (il).

Dubin, Susan Schraub
    Falling for the wrong man: when to call it quits.
        Harpers Bazaar 115:106-7+ F '82
Dubinsky, Robert
    (jt auth) See Morgenstern. Richard D. and Du-
        binsky. Robert
Dubovay, Diane
    I want another kind of life. por McCalls 109:8+
        Mr '82
Dubus, Andre
    The new boy [story] Harpers 264:50-6+ Jn '82
Duck. Robert
    Duck's ducks were just ducky in the duck
        races, and that's no quackery. R. L. Drinon.
        il Sports Illus 56:64+ Mr 1 '82 •
Duck cooking. See Cooking—Poultry
Duck shooting
    The club. J. Samson. il Field Stream 86:60-1+ F
        '82
    I'll never hunt ducks again. J. D. Nunnally.
        il Outdoor Life 169:50-1+ Mr '82
    Toward season's end. T. Trueblood. il Field
        Stream 86:28+ Ja '82

Another cross reference.

Figure 10-2: An entry from the *Readers' Guide to Periodical Literature*

potential usefulness. (Figure 10-3 provides a list of reference tools arranged by specialized areas.) The *Readers' Guide to Periodical Literature* (familiarly known as the *Readers' Guide*) will be of little value if your paper is on Edgar Allan Poe, for instance, because it indexes popular magazines, not scholarly ones. How often does *Mechanics Illustrated* come out with a big spread on Poe? But if you are investigating possibilities for cutting down pollution from automobile exhaust, *Mechanics Illustrated* may have just the article you want. Or if you are writing on some aspect of current events, the *Readers' Guide* will lead you to articles in *Newsweek, Time, U.S. News and World Report,* as well as to magazines which analyze current events, like *Harper's,* the *Atlantic,* and the *National Review.* A typical entry from the *Readers' Guide* is shown in Figure 10-2. Another useful index for any research involving current events is the *Public Affairs Information Service Bulletin* (PAIS). Here you will find indexed articles dealing with various topics of public interest.

For that Poe article, you would be better off consulting the *Humanities Index* (formerly part of the *International Index*), or, if you want the really scholarly articles, the *MLA Bibliography* (which works just like the other indexes, but you may have to troop off to the humanities area to find it). If you would like to find out what Poe's contemporaries thought of his writing, look him up in *Poole's Index to Periodical Literature*, which covers the major nineteenth-century magazines.

There are several other reference works of general interest. One of the most valuable is the *Essay and General Literature Index*. This treasure allows you to locate essays buried in books and to find chapters of books that may pertain to your topic, even though the title might give no clue. Then there is the *Book Review Digest*, which tells you briefly what various reviewers thought of a book when it came out (if it came out since 1905) and gives you informed guidance concerning the potential usefulness or possible partiality of a source you may be considering. All you need is the approximate year of publication in order to know which volume to consult. *The New York Times Index* will furnish you with the date of any noteworthy event since 1851, allowing you to look it up in the files of your local newspaper—or in the *Times* itself on microfilm. The *Social Sciences Index* (formerly part of the *International Index* and, until very recently, combined with the *Humanities Index*) should prove useful if you are looking for articles related to sociology, psychology, anthropology, political science, or economics. Articles pertaining to history or literature are listed in the *Humanities Index*.

One more tip: just because some periodical index lists a magazine does not mean that your library will necessarily *have* that magazine. Before you tire yourself searching the stacks, spend a minute checking the list of periodical holdings for your library to find out whether the magazine will be there.

Figure 10-3:   Specialized indexes and bibliographies (bold type) and reference volumes

Applied science, technology, and agriculture
> **Applied Science and Technology Index**
> **Bibliography of Agriculture**
> *McGraw-Hill Encyclopedia of Science and*
>   *Technology*

Art
> **Art Index**
> **Guide to Art Reference Books**
> *Encyclopedia of World Art*
> *McGraw-Hill Dictionary of Art*

Biography

Biographical Dictionaries Master Index
Biography Index
Dictionary of American Biography
Dictionary of National Biography (British) ⎱ Dead notables
Notable American Women, 1607–1950 ⎰

Who's Who Among Black Americans
Who's Who of American Women ⎱ Living notables
Who's Who in America
Who's Who (primarily British) ⎰

Twentieth Century Authors
Webster's Biographical Dictionary
World Authors, 1950–1970 (with supplements)

Business and economics

Business Periodicals Index
Index of Economic Articles
International Bibliography of Economics
Journal of Economic Literature (abstracts)
Public Affairs Information Service Bulletin
Wall Street Journal Index
Business Information Sources
*Poor's Register of Corporations, Directors, and
    Executives of the U.S. and Canada*

Drama

Play Index
Theatre and Allied Arts: A Guide to Books
The Oxford Companion to the Theatre

Education

**Complete Guide and Index to ERIC
    Reports** (1964 to 1969) ⎫ Guide to ERIC
Current Index to Journals in Education ⎬ (Educational Re-
Resources in Education ⎭ sources Informa-
                                            tion Center)

Education Index
Encyclopedia of Educational Research
Encyclopedia of Education

Government documents
Congressional Information Services
Index to U.S. Government Periodicals
Monthly Catalog of United States Government Publications

History
America: History and Life
Harvard Guide to American History
Historical Abstracts
Humanities Index
An Encyclopedia of World History
Encyclopedia of American History

Literature
Book Review Digest
Cambridge Bibliography of English Literature
New Cambridge Bibliography of English Literature
Essay and General Literature Index
An Index to Black Poetry
MLA International Bibliography
Short Story Index
Cambridge History of English Literature
Encyclopedia of Poetry and Poetics
Literary History of the United States (includes bibliographies)

Music
Music Index
Dictionary of Music and Musicians
International Cyclopedia of Music and Musicians
The New Oxford History of Music

Mathematics
Mathematical Reviews
Universal Encyclopedia of Mathematics

Philosophy and religion
Humanities Index
Religion Index One: Periodicals
Dictionary of the Bible
The Encyclopedia of Philosophy
Encyclopaedia of Religion and Ethics
*Nelson's Complete Concordance of the Revised Standard
    Version Bible*

Social sciences
Public Affairs Information Service Bulletin
Social Sciences Index
International Encyclopedia of the Social Sciences
Political Science
International Bibliography of Political Science
Psychology
Harvard List of Books on Psychology
Psychological Abstracts
Encyclopedia of Psychology
Sociology and Anthropology
International Bibliography of Social and Cultural Anthropology
International Bibliography of Sociology

Sciences
Bibliography of North American Geology
Biological and Agricultural Index
Biological Abstracts
Chemical Abstracts
General Science Index
Physics Literature: A Reference Manual
Van Nostrand's Scientific Encyclopedia

Assorted useful reference books
Bartlett's Familiar Quotations
Dictionary of Black Culture
Dictionary of Slang and Unconventional English
Facts on File
Information Please Almanac
New Larousse Encyclopedia of Mythology
Oxford English Dictionary
World Almanac and Book of Facts

Specialized reference tools
Bibliography of Bibliographies
Sheehy's (formerly Winchell's) **Guide to Reference Books**

Also, just because a magazine or book is supposed to be in the library does not, in fact, guarantee that the item *will* be there. Theft is a major problem in libraries these days. You should report lost or ripped-out materials to someone at the circulation desk so that the missing items can be replaced.

Ask about the Others.   If you plan to do some really high-powered research, you may need more specialized indexes than the ones discussed here. There are countless more covering every conceivable field, some of which are listed in Figure 10-3. The indexes and bibliographies come first in bold type. In order to use these reference books, you may need to go to the section of the library where the books and magazines in the special field are located.

> *Remember:*   **The *Readers' Guide* index might well appear in almost every category.**

Get It All Down

Every time you consult a new source, *copy all the information necessary for documentation* (that is, for indicating the source to your readers). If you fail to record all the essential data, you may find yourself tracking down a book or article weeks later in order to look up an essential publication date or volume number that you neglected to record initially. The book may by this time be checked out, lost, or stolen, so get it all down the first time.

Use three- by five-inch or four- by six-inch note cards to keep track of the information. They should come out looking something like the examples in Figure 10-4 (see p. 272). Note the pertinent data and get it *all* down.

For books:

1. Author or editor
2. Title (underlined)
3. Place of publication
4. Publisher
5. Date of publication (plus date of edition, if the book had more than one)
6. Library call number

For articles:

1. Author (or "Anonymous")
2. Title (in quotation marks)
3. Name of magazine or newspaper (underlined)
4. Volume number (if a scholarly journal)
5. Date of issue
6. Pages the article covers

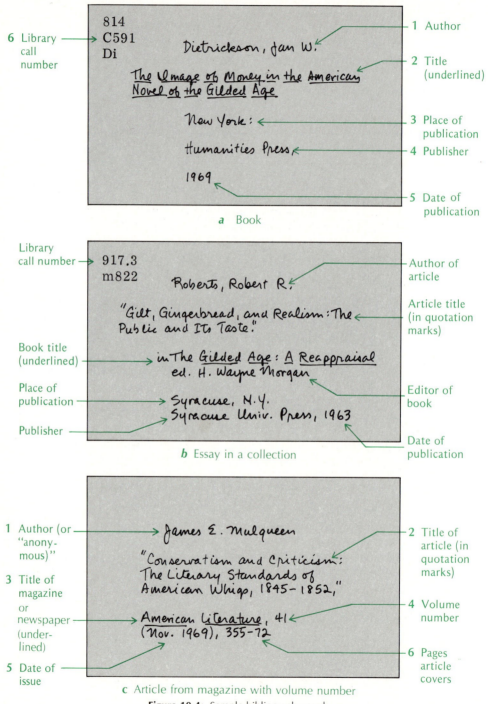

6 Library call number

814
C591
Di

Dietrickson, Jan W.

1 Author

The Image of Money in the American Novel of the Gilded Age

2 Title (underlined)

New York:

3 Place of publication

Humanities Press,

4 Publisher

1969

5 Date of publication

a Book

Library call number

917.3
m822

Roberts, Robert R.

Author of article

"Gilt, Gingerbread, and Realism: The Public and Its Taste."

Article title (in quotation marks)

Book title (underlined)

in The Gilded Age: A Reappraisal ed. H. Wayne Morgan

Editor of book

Place of publication

Syracuse, N.Y.
Syracuse Univ. Press, 1963

Publisher

Date of publication

b Essay in a collection

1 Author (or "anonymous)"

James E. Mulqueen

2 Title of article (in quotation marks)

"Conservatism and Criticism: The Literary Standards of American Whigs, 1845-1852,"

3 Title of magazine or newspaper (underlined)

American Literature, 41 (Nov. 1969), 355-72

4 Volume number

5 Date of issue

6 Pages article covers

c Article from magazine with volume number

Figure 10-4: Sample bibliography cards

List the library references you would use to find the answers to the following questions:

1. What is the address of the TV station in Peoria, Illinois?
2. Is there an alternative to root-canal work?
3. Did Ernest Hemingway have any brothers and sisters?
4. How long did it take to film *The Wizard of Oz?*
5. What was the major cause of death in the United States in 1970?
6. What are the recent discoveries about subatomic particles?
7. Is there a bibliography of articles and books about Spenser's *Faerie Queen?*
8. Did Joseph Heller's *Catch-22* get good reviews when it first came out?
9. Who is Artemis?
10. Are there articles that define what a *free school* is?
11. What do you call the architectural style of your county courthouse?
12. What effect does left-handedness have on learning to read?
13. Who was Machiavelli?
14. What are the roots of the Jewish religious laws of eating only kosher food?
15. What is the history of the word *boycott?*

ON TO THE READING

Using your bibliography cards, you next need to locate all the materials that look promising and try to decide which ones will be genuinely useful. As you are pondering what articles and books to study thoroughly and what ones to eliminate at this stage, you should give some thought to their reliability as well as their relevance to your thesis question.

Consider Your Sources

You could be reasonably sure, even before reading it, that you would not get an unbiased comment from Theodore Roosevelt concerning the Spanish-American War. This does not mean, however, that you should ignore Roosevelt's statements if you are writing an appraisal of the reasons the United States entered that war. But you should be constantly wary when the sources you are reading could hardly be considered impartial.

You might expect an unprejudiced analysis of an event from journalists who were present, but again you must stay alert because not all publications achieve—or even *try* to achieve—objective reporting.

You may be certain that the conservative *National Review* will offer an appreciably different appraisal from that of the ultraliberal *Mother Jones.* And the *Congressional Record,* which sounds like an unimpeachable source, is actually one of the least reliable, since anyone in Congress can have any nonsense whatsoever read into the *Record.* You must sample several authorities so that you are able to weigh the matter and discount the prejudices. This is one reason that research papers require extensive bibliographies. You could probably scare up most of the facts from reading one *unbiased* source, but the problem is to discover a source that is unbiased—if one exists.

Do not make the mistake of embracing what you consider a reliable source and then placing your trust in it till death do you part. Too many of us do just this: we put our faith in the Bible, the *National Lampoon,* the *Wall Street Journal,* or *Time* magazine, and never bother to think again. You will discover writers and publications whose viewpoint is similar to yours. These will naturally strike you as the most intelligent, perceptive, reliable sources to consult. But be careful that you do not fall into the comfortable habit of reading these publications exclusively. And remember that book reviews can provide the most reliable help if you are trying to evaluate a book-length source.

The date of a publication often makes a difference in its value or reliability. If you are doing a paper analyzing the relative safety of legal and illegal abortions, you will find an article written in 1936 of little use. If, on the other hand, you are writing a paper on the *history* of the long struggle to legalize abortion, a 1936 article could be quite important. In general, we place the highest value on recent articles simply because the latest scholar or scientist has the advantage of building on all that has gone before.

Making the Outline Easier

Keeping your thesis in mind, you can get started on the reading. Have your note cards handy. At the same time you are doing research, you will be working out an outline. The note cards, each containing information related to a single idea, can be shuffled around later and slipped into appropriate sections of your outline. Taking notes consecutively on sheets of paper makes this handy sorting of ideas difficult.

Use Subject Headings.   Chances are that your outline may not really take shape until you are well along with your reading—possibly not until you have finished it. As you take notes, put subject headings indicating in a word or two what each note is about in the upper right-hand corner of your note cards. Eventually these subject headings probably will correspond to sections of your outline. As you collect more and more cards, leaf through them occasionally to see if they can be arranged into three or four main categories to form the major headings of an outline. The sooner you can get the organization worked out, the more efficient your research becomes. You know exactly what you are looking for and avoid taking notes that would eventually prove off the point and have to be discarded.

If an idea sounds potentially useful, copy it down whether it fits exactly or not. If the idea recurs in your reading and gathers significance, you may decide to add a section to your outline or to expand one of the existing sections. Later, at the organizing stage, if you have cards with ideas that just do not seem to fit in anywhere, let them go. Let them go cheerfully. Do not ruin the focus and unity of your paper by trying to wedge in every single note you have taken. Unless you are an uncommonly cautious note-taker, you will have a number of cards that you cannot use.

Tips on Note-Taking

Of necessity you will do a considerable amount of reading for your research paper. If you remember that most published articles are put together according to the same advice we have given you in this book, you can summarize more efficiently. Read the introductory paragraphs of an essay quickly to discover the writer's thesis. If that main idea is relevant to your own thesis, continue reading carefully and jot down any useful ideas on note cards. Pay special attention to beginning and ending sentences of paragraphs; these will likely be topic sentences conveying or summarizing major ideas.

If you are examining a book, the author's thesis will appear in the preface. You can thus get a quick clue concerning the usefulness of the volume. Usually a book will have a broader scope than your paper. You can tell from the table of contents which chapters may be pertinent to your investigation, and you need only consult those sections. If the book has an index, try to locate your topic there. You will then be directed to precisely the relevant pages and can treat yourself to a coffee break in the time saved.

Again, do not forget to record *on each card:*

1. Author's last name
2. Abbreviated title
3. Page number or numbers

If you get in the habit of writing down these essentials before you take notes, there is less chance of forgetting an item.

Summarize the ideas in your own words, except when you think you might want to quote directly (verbatim). Then copy the author's exact words and *enclose them in quotation marks.* If you carelessly forget the quotation marks and use those words in your paper, you will have committed a serious literary offense, *plagiarism* (see page 278). Do not simply omit the specific examples when you summarize, because you are going to need some yourself. Remember that you must give credit for these examples, as well as for the ideas they illustrate, even if you put them in your own words when you incorporate them into your paper. Otherwise you will lapse into plagiarism. Your note cards should look something like the one shown in Figure 10-5.

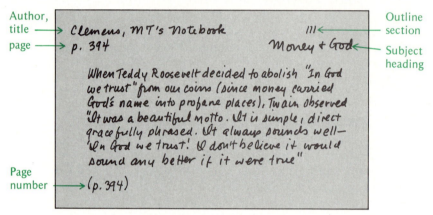

Author,
title
page

Outline
section

Subject
heading

Clemens, MT's Notebook   111

p. 394   Money + God

When Teddy Roosevelt decided to abolish "In God we trust" from our coins (since money carried God's name into profane places), Twain observed "It was a beautiful motto. It is simple, direct gracefully phrased. It always sounds well— 'In God we trust! I don't believe it would sound any better if it were true"

Page
number   (p. 394)

Figure 10-5: Sample note card

The Photocopying Option.   If the time you can spend in the library is limited and your finances are not, you might want to photocopy articles or pertinent portions of books in order to have these materials available to study at your convenience. You can then underline and make marginal notes without defacing the library's copy. And if later you want to check the accuracy of a quotation in your rough draft, you will be spared making yet another trip to the library to do so. But do not fail to note the source of the material directly on the photocopy.

How to Write a Quality Summary

Another kind of summary—much more exacting—is called a *précis* (pronounced *pray-see*). Précis writing is a valuable and challenging craft, highly useful in business and government work. Busy executives and top-level officials need precise summaries of the endless piles of papers that daily cross their desks. You would not take the trouble to write a bona fide précis when taking notes for a documented paper, but learning how to write a précis will sharpen your skills for summarizing in general. After mastering the art of the précis, you will be able to take ordinary notes more carefully and accurately. You cannot skim a passage and hope to produce a good précis, because you are expected to include all the important ideas from the original passage in your shortened version. Furthermore, you are expected to mention these ideas in the same *order* and in the same *tone,* using your own words. You may quote an impressive phrase or two, but *do not forget the quotation marks.*

While you must write clear, coherent sentences in your précis, nobody expects the summary to be as stylistically pleasing as the original: the point is to make it considerably shorter. You need to eliminate all nonessential information by reading each paragraph carefully and setting down in your own words the main ideas that you remember. If you have not had much practice in summarizing, you should begin by working on a sentence at a time. Consider this one from Pete Axthelm's "A Really Super Bowl" (*Newsweek,* Jan. 22, 1979):

> In an effort to keep everyone buying tickets and watching television as far as possible into this elongated sixteen-game season, the NFL juggled its schedule so that strong teams faced the toughest tests and weaker members were able to kindle local hopes while playing fellow stragglers. [46 words]

Now ask yourself: What did he say? You might jot down something like this:

> To keep fans interested through the long season, the NFL scheduled teams against others of equal strength. [18 words]

Now, reread the sentences to see if you left out any important ideas. There is the bit at the beginning about buying tickets that is not included in the summary. Since finances no doubt provided the motivation for the unusually long season, the idea *is* important. You would do well to substitute *buying tickets* for the single word *interested.* Accuracy is more important than brevity.

After you have finished summarizing all the sentences in the passage, go back over your first draft and prune it down even more by combining sentences and dropping any unnecessary words. (See pages 71–79 for further help.) How much you can shorten a passage depends upon the style and substance of the original. Naturally you can condense the information in a paragraph by Ralph Waldo Emerson in fewer words than you can a passage of the same length by Ernest Hemingway. Most expository prose can be greatly reduced—

usually by half, at least. You must, of course, resist the temptation to add comments of your own. Remember, you are *summarizing, not analyzing,* in a précis.

Here is a paragraph from Christopher Hitchens' article about the peculiarities of the Nobel Prize awards ("The Faded Laurel Crown," *Harper's,* Nov. 1977), followed by a précis of the passage.

> There are further ironies in the way the Peace Prize is awarded. On several occasions it has gone to institutions rather than to individuals, but more often than not these recipients only serve to emphasize the element of futility in the donor. The International Red Cross, which won the prize in 1917, 1944, and 1963, is, after all, an organization which accepts war as inevitable and tries to palliate its effects. The same can be said of the Office of the United Nations High Commissioner for Refugees (1954). And it comes as a surprise to see some laureates, such as Theodore Roosevelt or Austen Chamberlain, on a list of peace crusaders. (111 words)

> Ironically, the Peace Prize has been given to institutions whose function underlines the futility of the award. The International Red Cross (winner in 1917, 1944, and 1963), and the United Nations High Commissioner for Refugees (1954), rather than working to prevent war, merely try to relieve the suffering. And some winners, like Theodore Roosevelt and Austen Chamberlain, appear strange choices as peacemakers. (61 words)

TIPS ON AVOIDING PLAGIARISM

Plagiarism, as you know, means using somebody else's writing without giving proper credit. Most teachers consider plagiarism close to a criminal offense. In some schools students may be expelled for plagiarism. The most lenient penalty is an F in the course. Deliberate plagiarism is, after all, a form of cheating. You can avoid accidental plagiarism by using a moderate amount of care in taking notes. Put quotation marks around any material—however brief—that you copy verbatim. As you leaf through the note cards trying to sort them into categories, circle the quotation marks with a red pencil so you cannot miss them. There remains the problem of avoiding the author's phrasing if you decide not to quote directly but to paraphrase. This dilemma is not so easily solved. You naturally tend to write the idea down using the same phrasing, changing or omitting a few words. *This close paraphrasing is still plagiarism.* To escape it you must not even look at your source as you take notes that are not direct quotations. We suggest that you use both methods—verbatim notes and summarizing notes—and let the summaries condense several pages of reading onto a single card. You will scarcely be able to fall into the author's phrasing that way. Or if your writer uses an eye-catching phrase—something like Thorstein Veblen's *code of pecuniary honor*—get that down in quotation marks in the middle of your summary. A summarizing note card will look something like the card in Figure 10-6.

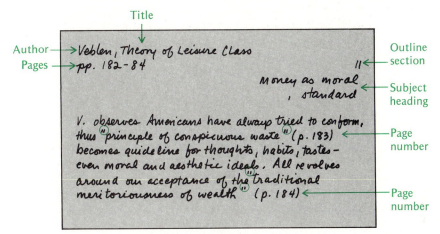

Title

Author

Pages

Outline
section

Subject
heading

Page
number

Page
number

Veblen, Theory of Leisure Class
pp. 182-84   11

Money as moral
, standard

V. observes Americans have always tried to conform,
thus "principle of conspicuous waste" (p. 183)
becomes guideline for thoughts, habits, tastes—
even moral and aesthetic ideals. All revolves
around our acceptance of the traditional
meritoriousness of wealth" (p. 184)

Figure 10-6: Sample summary note card

Paraphrase carefully

Sometimes, of course, you must do fairly close paraphrasing of important ideas. Since plagiarism is often accidental, we will give you a couple of examples to show you exactly what plagiarism is. Here is a passage from Marvin Harris's *Cows, Pigs, Wars, and Witches: The Riddles of Culture* (1978), which, we will assume, you need to use in making a point in your paper:

> No one understood better than Ghandi that cow love had different implications for rich and poor. For him the cow was the central focus of the struggle to rouse India to authentic nationhood.

If you incorporate that material into your paper this way, you have plagiarized:

> Ghandi understood the different implications of cow love for rich and poor. He saw the struggle to rouse India to authentic nationhood focused on the cow.[5]

[5] Marvin Harris, *Cows, Pigs, Wars, and Witches* (New York: Vintage Books, 1978), p. 21.

The fact that the source is cited suggests that this plagiarism might have resulted from ignorance rather than deception, but it is plagiarism nonetheless. Changing a few words or rearranging the phrases is not enough. Here is another version, somewhat less blatant but still plagiarism:

> Ghandi well knew that rich and poor were affected differently by cow love, which he saw as a means of inspiring his people to authentic nationhood.[5]

There are still two phrases there that are distinctly Harris's: *cow love* and *authentic nationhood*. It is quite all right to use those phrases but *only if you put them in quotation marks*. We also think you should acknowledge your source in the text of your paper—as well as in your note—whenever possible, like this:

> According to Harris, Ghandi well knew that rich and poor were affected differently by "cow love," which he saw as a means of inspiring his people "to authentic nationhood."[5]

Notice, by the way, that the phrase *rich and poor* in the original does not appear in quotation marks in this acceptable version. The phrase is so simple, so commonly used—and so nearly impossible to replace without using many more words—that quotation marks are unnecessary. Here is another acceptable version in which none of the original phrasing is used:

> Harris suggests that Ghandi well knew that rich and poor were affected differently by reverence for the sacred cow but saw this symbol as a means of uniting his people.[5]

> *Remember:* **If you are paraphrasing, put the passage into your own words; if you are quoting directly, put the passage in quotation marks.**

WRITING THE FIRST DRAFT

After you have read all the material you feel is necessary to cover your topic thoroughly, gather up your note cards and shuffle them to fit the sections of your outline. If your outline is still a flabby hulk, now is the time to whip it into shape and turn your thesis question into a thesis statement. The actual writing of the paper is the same as writing any other paper, except that you incorporate the material from the note cards into your text (either in your own words or through direct quotations) and give credit in endnotes to the original authors both for ideas borrowed and actual passages quoted. Quickly review chapters 5, 6, and 7 if you are having difficulty at this stage.

To Quote or Not to Quote

Never quote directly unless (1) the material is authoritative and convincing evidence in support of your thesis or (2) the statement is extremely well phrased or (3) the idea is controversial and you need to assure your readers that you are not slanting or misinterpreting the source. You would want, for instance, to quote,directly an observation as well-put as this one:

> Bernard Rosenberg defines pragmatism as "a distinctly American philosophy whose only failing is that it does not work."
> —"A Dictionary for the Disenchanted," *Harper's*, Nov. 1970.

There is no need, however, for the direct quotation in the following sentence:

> The ICC, in an effort to aid the rail industry, has asked for a "federal study of the need and means for preserving a national passenger service."

You could phrase that just as well yourself. But remember, even after you put the statement into your own words, you still need a note to show where you got the information.

Quoting Quotations

Sometimes in your reading you will come across a quotation that says exactly what you have been hoping to find. If the quotation is complete enough to serve your purpose, and if you honestly do not think you would benefit from tracking down the original, then don't bother. Instead, include that quotation in the usual way. But notice that your note should include "Quoted by" or "Quoted from":

> George Cukor once told Scott Fitzgerald, "I've only known two people who eat faster than you and I, and they are both dead now."[1]
>
> [1] Quoted by John Aaron Latham in "A Day at the Studio: Scott Fitzgerald in Hollywood," *Harper's*, Nov. 1970, p. 39.

> Mark Twain relates that he once knew a Miss Sexton, who pronounced her name "Saxton to make it finer, the nice, kindhearted, smirky, smily dear Christian creature."[2]
>
> [2] Quoted from Mark Twain's unpublished papers by Dixon Wecter in *Sam Clemens of Hannibal* (Boston: Houghton Mifflin, 1952), p. 103.

Indenting Long Quotations

If you are writing a paper on some topic in the humanities, you are expected to set off quotations longer than four typewritten lines by indenting them ten spaces. You triple-space, indent, omit the quotation marks (since the spacing indicates that the material is quoted), and single-space the quotation, like this:

```
In his satirical sketch, "Disgraceful Persecution of a

Boy," Mark Twain illustrates that any child growing up

in San Francisco in the 1850's would naturally have

learned racial prejudice:
```

```
        A Chinaman had no rights that any man was
    bound to respect. . . . Everybody, individuals,
    communities, the majesty of the State itself,
    joined in hating, abusing, and persecuting
    these humble strangers.
        And, therefore, what could have been more
    natural than for this sunny-hearted boy,
    tripping along to Sunday-school, with his mind
    teeming with freshly-learned incentives to high
    and virtuous actions, than to say to himself:
        "Ah, there goes a Chinaman!  God will not
    love me if I do not stone him!"9
```

Unless you are quoting two or more paragraphs, as we did in our example, you would not use any paragraph indention. If you are quoting two or more paragraphs, indent each one three spaces. Notice that if you want to quote conversation, indenting the whole passage is a handy way of avoiding an untidy clutter of quotation marks within quotation marks.

Working Quotations in Smoothly

If you want your research paper to read smoothly, you must take care in incorporating quotations into your own writing. You must have ready a supply of introductory phrases with which to slide them in gracefully—phrases like "As Quagmire discovered," "Mr. Clyde Crashcup notes," and "According to Dr. Dimwit." If you run through the examples in this section on quoting, you will find a generous assortment of these phrases. Borrow them with our blessing.

Notice, please, that the more famous the person, the less likely we are to use Mr., Miss, Mrs., or Ms. in front of the name. "Mr. Milton" sounds quite droll. If the person has a title, you can use it or not, as you think appropriate: Dr. Pasteur or Pasteur, Sir Winston Churchill or Churchill, President Lincoln or Lincoln.

Introduce Your Quotations.   Most of the time you will introduce a quotation before beginning it, like this:

> As Mark Twain observed, "Heaven for climate, hell for society."*

But you may want to break one up in the middle every so often for variety, this way:

> "But if thought corrupts language," cautions George Orwell, "language can also corrupt thought."

Or you can make most of the sentence yours and quote only the telling phrases or key ideas of your authority, like this:

> Lily B. Campbell considers King Henry's inability to fight "a saintly weakness."

Or this:

> The play's effectiveness lies, as E. M. W. Tillyard points out, in "the utter artlessness of the langauge."

But do introduce your quotations, please. Some people just slip them in without comment, forcing readers to check the notes to discover who said what. The note is necessary either way, but a note should be optional for readers. They may glance at it if they want further information; they should not be forced to read it because insufficient information appears in the text.

If you have difficulty introducing your authorities gracefully in the text of your paper, perhaps you are using too many direct quotations.

Make the Grammar Match.   When you integrate a quotation into your own sentence, you are responsible for making sure that the entire sentence makes sense. You must adjust the way your sentence is worded so that the grammar comes out right. Read your quotations over carefully to be sure they do not end up like this one:

---

* We have omitted many citations in this book to save space. But remember, you do not have this option in a documented paper. Whenever you quote directly, you *must* cite the source.

> When children are born, their first reactions are "those stimuli which constitute their environment."

"Reactions" are not "stimuli." The sentence should read this way:

> When children are born, their first reactions are to "those stimuli which constitute their environment."

What a difference a word makes—the difference here between sense and nonsense. Take particular care when you are adding someone else's words to your own; you get the blame if the words in the quotation do not make sense, because they *did* make sense before you lifted them out of context.

Use Special Punctuation.   When you write a documented paper, you probably will need to use some rather specialized marks of punctuation: *ellipsis dots* (to show that you have omitted something from a quotation) and *brackets* (to make an editorial comment within a quotation). You will find both of these useful devices discussed fully in our alphabetized "Revising Index," Chapter 13.

To Note or Not to Note

The main purpose of notes—either footnotes or endnotes—is to give credit for ideas, information, and actual phrasing that you borrow from other writers. You cite sources in order to be honest and to lend authority to your own writing. You also include notes to enable your readers to find more extensive information than your paper furnishes, in case they become engrossed in your subject and want to read some of your sources in full.

We are all troubled occasionally about when a note is necessary. We can say with authority that you must include a note for

1. All direct quotations
2. All indirect quotations
3. All major ideas that are not your own
4. All essential facts, information, and statistics that are not general knowledge—especially anything controversial

The last category is the one that causes confusion. In general, the sort of information available in an encyclopedia does not need a citation. But statements interpreting, analyzing, or speculating on such information should be documented. If you say that President Warren G. Harding died in office, you do not need a note because that is a widely known and undisputed fact. If you say that Harding's administration was one of the most corrupt in our history, most people would not feel the need for a note because authorities agree that the Harding scandals were flagrant and enormous. But if you say that Harding was sexually intimate with a young woman in the White House cloakroom while President of the United States, we strongly suggest a note. Because such information is not widely known and is also debatable, you need to cite your source so that your readers can judge the reliability of your evidence. Then, too, they might want further enlightenment on the matter, and your note will lead them to a more complete discussion. Probably it is better to bother your readers with too many notes than to have them question your integrity by having too few.

PRACTICAL ADVICE ON NOTE FORMS

Since your readers may want to consult the sources that you quote in your paper, you must give them all the information necessary to allow them to look up the articles and locate the books that you used. Most teachers these days will allow you to insert the note numbers in the appropriate places in the text, then list the actual notes together at the end of your paper just before the bibliography. Remember to title the page *Endnotes* instead of *Footnotes* for the sake of accuracy. Or just *Notes* will do nicely.

Consolidation of References

As W. C. Fields once observed, though, "Reading footnotes is like going down to answer the doorbell on your wedding night." So try to keep your documentation from intruding any more than necessary. If you mention in the text of your paper the person (or source) whose words (or ideas) you are borrowing, you can save yourself a clutter of note numbers by crediting several sources in a single citation at the end of the paragraph:

> At a federal hearing on discrimination against women, Dr. Pauli Murray, lawyer, teacher, and candidate for ordination to the priesthood, called ridicule of women "the psychic counterpart of violence against blacks." Speaking to fellow journalists, Ellen Cohn reiterated a point that others have also made: sexism is the only form of bigotry still treated as good clean fun by the American press. Women are beginning to look at what lies behind the ridicule, the mocking bigotry, the endless derisive stereotypes. As Stephanie Harrington observes, "Women have been made to look ridiculous. Women humorists ought to start focusing on what is ridiculous about those reasons."[42]
>
> —Casey Miller and Kate Swift, *Words and Women: New Language for New Times* (1976).

The endnote, with sources separated by semicolons, reads like this:

[42] Pauli Murray, testimony before Rep. Edith Green's special sub-committee on Education in Support of Section 805 of H.R. 16098, June 19, 1970, U.S. Government Printing Office, 1970, p. 330; Ellen Cohn, speaking May 12, 1974, at the MORE Convention in New York; Stephanie Harrington, "Women Get the Short End of the Stick," *New York Times,* November 18, 1973, "Arts and Leisure" section, p. 21.

The above method is recommended in the *MLA Handbook.* Writers in the social sciences commonly condense information from several sources and give credit in a single note at the end of the paragraph without even mentioning the sources in the text. Before you adopt this simplified method, be sure that your instructor has no objections.

Citing Literary Sources. If you are writing about literature (whether using library materials or not), you should eliminate excessive notes by citing the information necessary to identify the edition of the novel, the play, the short story or poetry collection you are using in the first reference only. After that, the page numbers belong in parentheses in the paper itself. The first note should go like this:

[1] Joyce Carol Oates, "Accomplished Desires," in *Wheel of Love and Other Stories* (Greenwich, Conn.: Fawcett, 1970), p. 127. All further references to this work appear in parentheses in the text.

Your subsequent acknowledgments in the text will be done this way:

Dorie was not consoled, although Mark "slid his big beefy arms around her and breathed his liquory love into her face, calling her his darling, his beauty" (p. 129).

Note the placement of the quotation marks—before the parentheses, which are followed by the period. *But* if the quotation is a long one that you need to indent without quotation marks, the period comes *before* the parentheses.

Informational Notes. You know from reading this text that notes can be used to include material that is not essential but might be interesting or helpful to the readers anyway. Rather than wedge these asides into the text, it is better to let your readers decide whether they want to stop and read them or not. There is a small problem involved with using informational notes in a paper having all the notes typed at the end: you run the risk that your readers may not bother with notes until they *come* to them, at which time these choice bits will be out of context. Careful readers, however, will slide your notes out and keep them beside the paper so that they can glance at them when necessary.* For this reason you should never staple a term paper together or bind it in one of those perpetual-care folders unless asked to. A paper clip will serve nicely to keep it together.

Accuracy Is the Aim

After years of being told to be original, to be creative, to think for yourself, you are now going to be told—on this one matter, at least—to fall into line and slavishly follow the authorities. What you might consider a blessed bit of variety will not be appreciated in the slightest. If you put a period after the first note, put a period after every note. Get the form correct every time, right down to the last comma, colon, and parenthesis.

The information (date, publisher, place of publication) necessary for notes and for bibliographical entries is located on the title page and on the back of the title page of each book. For magazines you usually can find it all on the cover.

When in Doubt, Use Common Sense

Keep in mind that the purpose of notes and bibliographies is dual:

1. To give credit to your sources
2. To allow your readers to find your sources in case they want further information on the subject

If you are ever in doubt about note form (if you are citing something so unusual that you cannot find a similar entry in the samples here), use your common sense and give credit the way you think it logically should be done. Be as consistent as possible with other notes.

You will find instruction on documentation styles for all academic disciplines at the end of this chapter, beginning on page 300.

REVISING THE PAPER

Since a research paper requires the incorporation of other people's ideas and the acknowledgement of these sources, you need to take special care in revising.

---

* If you are using the social science system discussed on page 314, you must use asterisks for informational notes (and place the note at the bottom of the page), since the numbers are being utilized for another purpose. This, by the way, is an informational note.

Check the Usual Things

1. Be sure the introduction states your thesis.
2. Be sure each paragraph is unified, coherent, and directly related to your thesis.
3. Be sure the transitions between paragraphs are smooth.
4. Be sure your conclusion evaluates the results of your research; if the paper is argumentative, be sure the last sentence is emphatic.

Check the Special Things

1. Be sure that you have introduced direct quotations gracefully, using the name and, if possible, the occupation of the person quoted.
2. Be sure each note is accurate.
3. Be sure that paraphrases are in your own words and that the sources are clearly acknowledged—both in the paper and in the notes.
4. Be sure to underline the titles of books and magazines; put quotation marks around the titles of articles and chapters in books.
5. Be sure to avoid excessive noting by consolidating references.
6. Be sure that you have written most of the paper yourself; you need to examine, analyze, or explain the material, not just splice together a bunch of quotations and paraphrases.
7. Be sure always to separate quotations with some comment of your own.
8. Be sure to use ellipsis dots if you omit any words from a quotation that your readers would not otherwise know were missing; never leave out anything that alters the meaning of a sentence.
9. Be sure to use square brackets, not parentheses, if you add words or change verb tenses in a quotation.
10. Be sure that you have not relied too heavily on a single source.
11. Be sure to indent and single-space long quotations—without quotation marks.

Before you work on your final draft, give your entire attention to the following instructions on form.

Preparing the Final Draft

1. Provide margins of at least one inch at the top, bottom, and sides.
2. Double-space—except for long quotations (of more than four lines), which should be indented ten spaces and single-spaced. Only if you are writing a thesis or planning to publish your paper do you need to double-space long quotations.
3. Do not put the title of your paper in quotation marks.
4. Insert corrections neatly in ink *above the line* (if allowed by your instructor).
5. Do not use fancy, perpetual-care folders or staples since your endnotes should slide out for easy reference. Use a paper clip.

6. Put page numbers in the upper-right hand corner. But do not number the title page or the first page of the paper. After the title page and the outline, count all pages in the total as you number. Note correct page numbering on the sample student paper, which follows.

7. Single-space your bibliography and endnotes, double-spacing between entries. Some instructors may prefer that you double-space the notes, triple-spacing between entries. Graduate papers are usually double-spaced throughout, including long quotations.

8. Proofread. You may well be close to exhaustion by the time you finish copying your paper, and the last thing you will feel like doing is rereading the blasted thing. But force yourself. Or force somebody else. But do not skip the proofreading. It would be a shame to allow careless errors to mar an otherwise excellent paper.

SAMPLE RESEARCH PAPER

A well done research paper written by a freshman, Jan Stewart, appears on the following pages. The assignment required the students to investigate an issue thoroughly and argue for one side or the other after deciding which side to support. Before writing your paper, be sure to find out whether your instructor wants you to write an argumentative paper or to present an objective synthesis of available information, keeping your opinions to yourself.

We have added comments in the margin of Jan's paper pointing out pertinent particulars about style (in regular type) and content (in italics).

SEXISM IN CHILDREN'S TEXTBOOKS

by

Jan C. Stewart

Center each line. Space information attractively. If no title page is required, put your name and section number in upper right-hand corner of first page; skip four lines before title.

English 101

Section 27

Outline

Thesis: Sexism in textbooks has a negative effect on
children.

I. Evidence of sexism in texts is abundant.

    A. Texts give unequal attention to females
and males.

    B. Books present negative stereotyping of girls.

    C. Math and science texts are especially biased.

II. Sexism in textbooks is unfair to children.

    A. Children learn traditional sex roles in school.

    B. Both sexes are conditioned to accept inequality.

    C. Children should be allowed to determine their
own lives as much as possible.

Center title; triple-space to first line; indent paragraphs five spaces.

Raise note numbers without punctuation—no parentheses, periods, squiggles, or stars. No space between period and number; space twice to next sentence.

Writer begins with broad generalization about function of textbooks, then narrows statement to direct attention to subtle way textbooks often reinforce sexist attitudes ingrained in our culture. Last sentence of paragraph focuses directly on thesis.

Notice smooth "echo" transition picking up the word sexism from last sentence of paragraph 1 to use at beginning paragraph 2.

Sexism in Children's Textbooks

Textbooks, which are very important in a child's edu-   [1]
cation, have the main function of providing specific information on a variety of subjects. Indirectly, though,
textbooks teach children the ethical and moral values of
their society and provide children with standards of how
women, men, boys, and girls should behave.[1] These standards
that are portrayed in textbooks pattern a student's way of
thinking and help explain the existence of the sexist attitudes that our culture holds. The controversial subject of
what effect, if any, sexism in textbooks has on children has
recently gained attention along with the rise of the Women's
Liberation Movement. There is no doubt that sexism has been
widespread in textbooks and has had, I think, a negative
effect on children.

Sexism has appeared in children's textbooks in various   [2]
ways. One subtle way was through the amount of attention
given to males as compared to females. Recently a group
from the National Organization for Women (NOW) read and
evaluated 2,760 children's stories for sexist content. The
study concludes that there were five boy-centered stories
for every two girl-centered stories, six male biographies
for every one female biography, and six occupations for
males portrayed for every one occupation for females.[2]

Credit sources in the text whenever possible. Mention occupations (if you can) to show that people quoted are authorities.

2

Lenore Weitzman and Diane Rizzo, sociology professors at the University of California at Davis, conclude that since fifty-one percent of the population are women, it is only fair to expect women to comprise half of the illustrations in texts. They found, though, that in 8,000 pictures they analyzed, sixty-nine percent showed males while females made up only thirty-one percent of the total.[3] Celeste Brody, an education professor at San Jose State College, observes that this disproportionate inclusion of males to females has led to the complete omission of females from many texts. This invisibility usually happened in textbooks beginning in the sixth grade, where images of female roles almost completely disappeared.[4]

Sexism has also been evident in the images textbooks provide of children. Girls often have been shown as depending on boys for help, as in this example from an elementary school reader: "'My Sally has fallen into the water,' the little girl tells Dick. 'Can't you save her?'"[5] The writers of Dick and Jane as Victims report that in most elementary readers girls have been portrayed simply looking on (often with their hands clasped behind their backs) while the boys accomplished things. Females in the readers have been "almost without exception . . . subordinate to males."[6]

Weitzman and Rizzo conclude that in textbooks boys have been presented as active, skillful, adventurous,

Use single quotation marks (the apostrophe on your typewriter) inside double quotation marks for material quoted within a quotation.

Use three periods (ellipsis dots) to show something is omitted within a quotation.

[3]

[4]

3

intelligent youngsters while girls were pictured as affectionate, emotional, or passive youngsters.[7] In many elementary readers, girls were made to look stupid and clumsy.
Even when a girl was presented as a heroine in a story,
she was usually shown in a traditional female role, as in
this example:

> . . . Kirsten, the heroine of a third
> grade story, wins over the girls who have
> rejected her by making Danish cookies and
> having the most popular booth at the
> school fair. The moral in this story is
> that girls can succeed by cooking and
> serving. But Kirsten slights herself at
> the very skill that earned her favor when
> she says, "It's easy; even I can do it,
> and you know how stupid I am." Thus even
> when girls succeed, they tend to deprecate
> themselves. In contrast, boys show a
> great deal of confidence and pride.[8]

The amount of sexism in textbooks has varied in dif- [5]
ferent academic subjects. For example, in science books
seventy-four percent of the pictures were of males. Boys
were shown involved in science experiments, while girls
were shown as observers of the experiments. Only males
were pictured as astronauts and only boys were told to
imagine themselves as astronauts.[9] Linda Harrison and
Richard Passero, of Western Michigan University, report
that one elementary school science textbook they examined
showed women in only four illustrations and in two of these
pictured them "scouring pots and pouring water from one pot
into another."[10] In mathematics texts sexism has been
especially pronounced. The research done by the NOW

When quotations run four lines or more (typed), set them off by identing ten spaces and single-spacing. Omit quotation marks since indention shows that material is quoted. If quotation marks are used *within* the passage, retain double marks, as illustrated.

Summary note card used for note 8

Source (always include page number)

Weitzman & Rizzo,
p. 49

Section of Outline

I-B
Stereotyping
(boys and girls)

Heading

Boys made to look active, skillful, adventurous, intelligent,
accomplishing work-related skills. Never shows boys
crying — or showing any emotion.

Girls shown doing domestic things — shopping for clothes,
cooking. Usually seen as affectionate, emotional, passive.

(p. 49)

Repeat page number

4

Notice the major transition. The writer has been documenting sexism in children's textbooks; remainder of paper will establish its negative influence. The phrase "this sexism" refers back to previous passages as rest of sentence introduces next main argument.

collective led to the conclusion that "Math books have boys solving problems in astronomy and chemistry or buying stock or life insurance; girls are usually measuring curtains for a window or flour for a cake."[11]

I believe that this sexism in children's textbooks [6] has had a definite influence on children. One of the effects pointed out by Celeste Brody is that females tend to center their interests on males, while males focus their attention on the goals they hope to achieve.[12] Children learn from reading these texts that there are expected roles for both men and women. These roles portray men as the providers for the family, women as homemakers and mothers. If females are never shown as having careers, then girls are subtly encouraged to pattern their lives around the home. Males are then left with the responsibility of being the sole breadwinners--sometimes a burden too heavy to handle without help. According to Newsweek magazine, forty percent of the jobs in this country are now held by women.[13] Thus the domestic picture of women presented in textbooks no longer reflects the reality of many children's lives. Yet, as Barbara Grizzuti Harrison points out, ". . . one of the few textbooks /ā first-grade reader/ that showed a woman working placed her in her daughter's school cafeteria--cooking."[14] These stereotyped portrayals help explain why career goals for girls are not as common as for boys, who are constantly encouraged to seek

Three periods beginning direct quotation are ellipsis dots and show that a phrase or clause was omitted from beginning of the quotation. Without the dots, no one could tell anything was left out. If you quote only part of a sentence, don't use ellipsis dots:

> Harrison points out that although not many textbooks showed women working outside the home, one of the few that did pictured a mother working "in her daughter's school cafeteria—cooking."

Summary (plus direct quotation) note card used for note 11

Source (unsigned article) →

"Changing Textbooks,"
p. 28

I-C ← Section of Outline Heading
Stereotyping
(math & science)

"Math books have boys solving problems in astronomy and chemistry or buying stocks and life insurance; girls are usually measuring curtains for a window or flour for a cake."

Science books show more of the same patterns — except that even fewer females are included.

(p. 28) ← Page number

5

challenging jobs.

Some people think that sexism--these different roles [7]
for females and males--should be maintained. They view
such roles as appropriate and beneficial to society. I
believe these people are being unjust in thus advocating
inequality of the sexes. Sexism in textbooks has, in fact,
been found to have negative effects on children. For
example, Celeste Brody shows that in textbooks boys learn
that female role behavior is distasteful, while girls learn
that masculinity is the highest valued role attainable--yet
something they are not supposed to attain.[15] This condi-
tioning has a negative effect because boys will not see
girls as equals and in turn will be likely to discriminate
against females. Also, the insignificance or absence of
females in junior high and high school texts subtly conveys
to the female student the notion that women are less
important in the world of adults than men are.[16] This
assumption makes equality between the sexes extremely difficult to achieve.

Those people who advocate sex discrimination and see [8]
no harm in its existence are basing their arguments entirely
on values and attitudes that they themselves have learned.
They are comfortable people who are thus unconcerned about
the obvious lack of equality which may cause discomfort to
others. I see sexism in textbooks as unneeded and harmful
to children who might prefer to make up their own minds

Writer acknowledges argument of the opposition—that some believe sex roles beneficial to society—then counters that argument.

In concluding paragraph writer once more mentions viewpoint of opposition to show they are self-serving in clinging to basically unfair values.

Writer uses good quotation to support final argument and concludes with strong sentence stating own position.

6

about how they wish to live their lives, rather than being programmed to follow society's present unfair pattern. As Celeste Brody observes, ". . . there are no masculine and feminine virtues. There are only human virtues, and these are desirable for both sexes."[17] Both females and males should be portrayed as active, intelligent, strong, compatible individuals if the movement for equality is going to accomplish its goal.

Signed article in scholarly journal using volume number. Omit "p." for "page" when citing volume number. Do the same for books using volume numbers.

Unsigned article in scholarly journal using volume number.

Abbreviated form referring to signed article or book already cited in full. (If you have used another source by the same person, add shortened title:

Weitzman and Rizzo, "Sex Bias," p. 49.

Omit writer's first name since it was mentioned in the paper.

Booklet written by a collective with no publisher given; a revised edition. "Quoted by" means material quoted in this paper was quoted in the booklet from yet another source.

Second reference to unsigned article already cited. (If title is long, abbreviate.)

Article in popular magazine not needing volume number, written by more than three people. Use name listed first, then *et. al.*, abbreviation for Latin *et allus* ("and others").

7

NOTES

¹Lenore J. Weitzman and Diane Rizzo, "Sex Bias in Textbooks," Today's Education, 64 (Jan.-Feb. 1975), 49.

²"Changing the Textbooks," American Education, 9 (June 1973), 26.

³Weitzman and Rizzo, p. 49.

⁴Brody, "Do Instructional Materials Reinforce Sex Stereotyping?" Educational Leadership, 31 (Nov. 1973), 121.

⁵Quoted by Women on Words & Images, Dick and Jane as Victims, rev. ed. (Princeton, N.J., 1975), p. 55.

⁶Dick and Jane, p. 24.

⁷Weitzman and Rizzo, p. 49.

⁸Weitzman and Rizzo, p. 52.

⁹Weitzman and Rizzo, p. 50.

¹⁰Harrison and Passero, "Sexism in the Language of Elementary School Textbooks," Science and Children, 12 (Jan. 1975), 25.

¹¹"Changing the Textbooks," p. 27.

¹²Brody, p. 121.

¹³Merrill Sheils, et al., "A Woman's Agenda," Newsweek, 28 Nov. 1977, p. 60.

¹⁴Harrison, Unlearning the Lie: Sexism in School (New York: Liveright, 1973), p. 38.

¹⁵Brody, p. 121.

¹⁶This notion of women's unimportance is reflected in the second-rate wages paid to women. Newsweek reports that "On the average, a woman's salary is 62 percent of a man's—the same gap that existed ten years ago—and roughly that of Biblical times, when the Lord told Moses that a man is worth 50 shekels of silver, a woman only 30. In many cases, a janitor or a handyman earns more than a secretary with a college education" (Merrill Sheils, et al., p. 60).

¹⁷Brody, p. 122.

Standard form for book with writer's name cited in text.

Informational note. Statistics cited here pertain only indirectly to writer's thesis. Source given in parentheses at end—second reference to previously cited article.

"Sources Consulted" means you've included references studied but not cited in the paper.

Alphabetize entries using *hanging indentation*. Alphabetize unsigned articles and pamphlets according to first important word in title (ignore *A, An, The*).

Include page numbers for articles to indicate length. Do not include pages for books, unless citing an article in a book.

For pamphlets and booklets use whatever publication information there is. Booklet in last entry did not give publisher's name.

8

SOURCES CONSULTED

Brody, Celeste M. "Do Instructional Materials Reinforce Sex Stereotyping?" Educational Leadership, 31 (Nov. 1973), 119-122.

"Changing the Textbooks." American Education, 9 (June 1973), 26-28.

Guidelines for Equal Treatment of the Sexes in McGraw-Hill Book Company Publications. New York: McGraw-Hill, 1975.

Harrison, Barbara Grizutti. Unlearning the Lie: Sexism in School. New York: Liveright, 1973.

Harrison, Linda, and Richard N. Passero. "Sexism in the Language of Elementary School Textbooks." Science and Children, 12 (Jan. 1975), 22-25.

Sheils, Merrill, et al. "A Woman's Agenda," Newsweek, 28 Nov. 1977, pp. 57-63.

Weitzman, Lenore J., and Diane Rizzo. "Sex Bias in Text-books." Today's Education, 64 (Jan.-Feb. 1975), 49-52.

Women on Words & Images. Dick and Jane as Victims: Sex Stereotyping in Children's Readers. Rev. ed. Princeton, N.J., 1975.

CHOOSE THE APPROPRIATE NOTE FORM

Just to complicate matters, different disciplines use different systems of documentation. We have grouped these marvelously varied systems into four categories: (1) the humanities, (2) business and economics, (3) education, and (4) the natural and social sciences. Choose the style you need according to the subject of your paper or the instructions of your teacher.

For the Humanities

If you are doing a brief, informal paper using limited research, you can simply acknowledge your sources *within the text* of your essay and be done with the matter like this:

> Josephine Hendrin (*The World of Flannery O'Connor,* Bloomington, Ind.: Indiana Univ. Press, 1970, p. 19) observes that baptism "becomes the supreme act of property. . . . "

Or, if you prefer:

> Josephine Hendrin—*The World of Flannery O'Connor* (Bloomington, Ind.: Indiana Univ. Press, 1970), pp. 27–32—agrees that . . .

or:

> In *The World of Flannery O'Connor* (Bloomington, Ind.: Indiana Univ. Press, 1970), p. 27, Josephine Hendrin concludes . . .

But in longer, more formal papers you are expected to follow a system (detailed in the *MLA Handbook for Writers of Research Papers, Theses, and Dissertations,* New York: Modern Language Association, 1977), which involves inserting consecutive numbers after borrowed material and then identifying the source of this material in correspondingly numbered notes. This system would be fairly simple if we never used the same source twice. But, of course, we often do refer to a good source several times in different parts of a paper. Sometimes we quote a couple of ideas in a row from the same author. In order to avoid writing out the complete information each time, the system gives you abbreviated forms which you are expected to use. It works like this:

First reference to a work:

> [1] Susan Miller, "How Writers Evaluate Their Own Writing," College Composition and Communication, 33 (May 1982), 176.

Another reference to the same work: If you have only one author by this name in your bibliography, you simply write the last name, plus the abbreviation *p.* (for *page*) and the page number. Use this form whether or not other notes have intervened:

> [4] Miller, p. 179.

If you have acquired more than one Miller, or if you are using a couple of books by this particular Miller, you need only distinguish them by giving a brief title and the page number after the last name for repeat entries:

> [6] Miller, "How Writers Evaluate," p. 178.

If you are quoting an unsigned article or pamphlet, you will have no author's name for repeat entries. Instead, abbreviate the title and cite the page number, as shown in footnote 2 below:

> [1] "New Places to Look for Presidents," Time, Dec. 15, 1975,
> p. 19.

> [2] "New Places . . . ," p. 20.

The old faithful *ibid.*, which used to be standard form for entries like the one above, is now out of fashion. So is *op. cit.*

A Minor Complication. If you are quoting from an introduction, preface, foreword, or afterword written by someone other than the author of the main text, cite this writer's name first in the note (but not in the bibliography). Omit quotation marks around Introd., Pref., Foreword, or Afterword, like this:

> [1] Hershel Parker, Foreword, The Confidence Man by
> Herman Melville (New York: Norton, 1971), p. ix.

Remember also that brevity in documentation is a virtue. You are expected to use abbreviated forms and to shorten dates and publisher's names.

That's about all there is to it, except that different kinds of materials (books, essays in books, encyclopedias) require different kinds of citations. The sample entries which follow should cover all but the most esoteric sources.

Sample Notes

1. A book with one author:

> [1] Lois Gould, <u>A Sea Change</u> (New York: Avon, 1976), p. 75.

[If the author's full name is given in the text, you may use only the last name in the note. Repeat the title even if you mentioned it in the text.]

2. A paperback reprint of an earlier publication:

> [2] Frederick Lewis Allen, <u>Only Yesterday</u> (1931, rpt. New York: Perennial-Harper, 1964), p. 28.

[The abbreviation *rpt.* stands for *reprinted.*]

3. A revised edition:

> [3] Edward Wagenknecht, <u>Mark Twain: The Man and His Work,</u> 3rd ed. (1935, 1961; rpt. Norman: Univ. of Oklahoma, 1967), p. 278.

4. A book with two or more authors or editors:

> [4] K. L. Knickerbocker and H. Willard Reninger, eds., <u>Interpreting Literature</u>, 3rd ed. (New York: Holt, 1965), pp. 78–79.

[The abbreviation *pp.* stands for "pages." If a work has more than three authors or editors, use the name of only the first one, followed by *et al.,* meaning "and others."]

5. A work in several volumes:

> [5] Albert Bigelow Paine, <u>Mark Twain: A Biography</u> (New York: Harper, 1912), II, 673.

[Note that the abbreviation for page (or pages) is omitted when you use a volume number. This holds true for periodical entries with volume numbers also.]

6. An essay in a collection, casebook, or critical edition:

> [6] William York Tindall, "The Form of <u>Billy Budd</u>," rpt. in <u>Melville's</u> Billy Budd <u>and the Critics</u>, ed. William T. Stafford (Belmont, Calif.: Wadsworth, 1961), p. 126.

[According to the *MLA Handbook,* "When a normally underlined title appears within another underlined title, the shorter title appears neither underlined nor in quotation marks" (Section 13c).]

7. A work in translation:

> [7] Eugene Ionesco, <u>Rhinoceros and Other Plays</u>, trans. Derek Prouse (New York: Grove, 1960), p. 107.

8. An anonymous article (magazine):

> [8] "A Beatle Roundup," <u>Newsweek</u>, Sept. 7, 1970, p. 85.

9. An anonymous article (newspaper):

> [9] "Smog Group to Consider Tougher Rules," <u>Eugene</u> (Ore.) <u>Register-Guard</u>, Sept. 13, 1970, Sec. 1, p. 2, col. 3.

10. A signed article in a periodical not requiring a volume number (i.e., in a *popular* magazine, one indexed by *The Readers' Guide to Periodical Literature*):

> [10] Tom Wicker, "Nixon's the One—But What?" <u>Playboy</u>, Oct. 1970, p. 105.

[Notice, no comma after the question mark ending the title. Do not stack up punctuation.]

11. An article in a scholarly periodical requiring a volume number (i.e., a periodical indexed by a specialized bibliography):

> [11] Marcus Smith, "The Wall of Blackness: A Psychological Approach to <u>1984</u>," <u>Modern Fiction Studies</u>, 14 (Winter 1968–69), 425.

12. An unsigned encyclopedia article:

> [12] "Abolitionists," <u>Encyclopedia Americana</u>, 1974 ed.

13. A signed encyclopedia article:

> [13] T[homas]P[ar]k, "Ecology," <u>Encyclopaedia Britannica</u>, 1968 ed.

[Articles in encyclopedias are sometimes signed with initials. The authors are identified somewhere, though—in the front or the back of the volume, or in the index volume for the whole set. You should look up and include the author's name if initials follow the article. The brackets in the above entry indicate that you have added the full name to the signed initials, which were *T. Pk.,* in this case.]

14. An article from the *Dictionary of American Biography:*

> [14] A[llan] N[evins], "Warren Gamaliel Harding," <u>DAB</u> (1932).

[The entry for an article from the *DNB,* the British *Dictionary of National Biography,* would be done the same way.]

15. An anonymous pamphlet:

¹⁵ <u>Preparing Your Dissertation for Microfilming</u> (Ann Arbor, Mich.: University Microfilms, n.d.), p. 3.

[The abbreviation *n.d.* means no date was given. Be sure to include this notation; otherwise your readers may think you carelessly omitted the date. If there are no page numbers in your pamphlet, just put a period after the parenthesis.]

16. A reference to the Bible:

¹⁶ Amos II, 6–7.   or ¹⁶ Amos 2:6–7.

[Notice you identify only the book (Amos), the chapter (2), and the verses (6–7). Your readers are expected to recognize the source as the Bible.]

17. A reference to a letter:

In a *published* collection:

¹⁷ Twain to James Redpath, <u>Mark Twain's Letters</u>, ed. A.B. Paine (New York: Harper, 1917), I, 190–91.

An *unpublished* letter:

¹⁷ Letter from Wharton to William Brownell, 6 Nov. 1907, Wharton Archives, Amherst College, Mass.

A *personal letter:*

¹⁷ Letter received from Gore Vidal, 2 June 1976.

18. A personal or telephone interview:

¹⁸ Personal interview with Ken Kesey, 28 May 1977.

¹⁸ Telephone interview with Joan Didion, 10 April 1977.

19. A review, signed or unsigned:

¹⁹ John Updike, "Who Wants to Know?" rev. of <u>The Dragons of Eden</u>, by Carl Sagan, <u>The New Yorker</u>, 22 Aug. 1977, p. 87.

¹⁹ Rev. of <u>Ring</u> by Jonathan Yardley, <u>The New Yorker</u>, 12 Sept. 1977, p. 159.

20. A lecture:

²⁰ Rise Axelrod, "Who Did What with Whom," MLA Convention, Chicago, 30 Dec. 1977.

21. A document from ERIC:

> [21] Joseph Lucas, <u>Background for Builders</u>, Curriculum Lab
> (New Brunswick, N.J.: Rutgers, The State Univ., 1975), p. 6
> (ERIC ED 127 459).

Bibliographical Form. Be advised that bibliographical form is not the same as footnote form. It has several discernible differences that you can see in this example.

> Kaufman, Sue. <u>Diary of a Mad Housewife</u>. New York:
> Random House, 1967.

1. The item is indented backwards: *hanging* instead of regular indention.
2. The last name is listed first for ease in alphabetizing.
3. The author's name is followed by a period, instead of a comma.
4. The title is followed by a period instead of a parenthesis or a comma.
5. No parentheses are used, except to enclose dates for articles in periodicals using volume numbers.
6. No page numbers are listed for books.
7. Page numbers for an article or for an essay in a book indicate the length of the selection (i.e., the page on which the piece begins, followed by the page on which it ends: pp. 376–84. With popular magazines in which articles begin at the front and are continued in the back, the only realistic solution is to give the beginning page numbers and use a plus sign (+) to indicate that there's more at the back).

A Couple of Clues Concerning Complications. When a work lists several copyright dates, use the latest one or perhaps the first and last. Often books list a couple of places of publication, like New York and London. Just pick New York, unless you have reason to do otherwise.

If you should use two or more books by the same author, do not repeat the author's name. Instead, use a line, followed by a period. Then give the title and the rest of the information as usual:

> Hemingway, Ernest. <u>A Farewell to Arms</u>. New York:
> Scribner's, 1929.

> —————. <u>For Whom the Bell Tolls</u>. New York: Scribner's, 1940.

The following bibliographical samples are not alphabetized but are given the same order as the footnote models on the previous pages for easier reference. *You must alphabetize your bibliography.*

Sample Bibliographical Entries

1. A book with one author:

Gould, Lois. <u>A Sea Change</u>. New York: Avon, 1976.

2. A paperback reprint of an earlier publication:

Allen, Frederick Lewis. <u>Only Yesterday: An Informal History of</u>
<u>the Nineteen-Twenties</u>. 1931; rpt. New York: Perennial-
Harper, 1964.

[Note that bibliographical form includes the full title. In notes you omit
subtitles.]

3. A revised edition:

Wagenknecht, Edward. <u>Mark Twain: The Man and His Work</u>. 3rd
ed. 1935, 1961; rpt. Norman: Univ. of Oklahoma, 1967.

4. A book with two or more authors:

Knickerbocker, K. L., and H. Willard Reninger, eds. <u>Interpreting</u>
<u>Literature</u>, 3rd ed. New York: Holt, 1965.

[The first author's name is reversed for alphabetizing but additional authors' names go in regular order.]

5. A work in several volumes:

Paine, Albert Bigelow. <u>Mark Twain: A Biography</u>. 3 vols. New
York: Harper, 1912.

6. An essay in a collection, casebook, or critical edition:

Tyndall, William York. "The Form of <u>Billy Budd</u>." Rpt. in
<u>Melville's Billy Budd and the Critics</u>. Ed. William T. Stafford.
Belmont, Calif.: Wadsworth, 1961, pp. 125–31.

7. A work in translation:

Ionesco, Eugene. <u>Rhinoceros and Other Plays</u>. Trans.
Derek Prouse. New York: Grove, 1960.

8. An anonymous article (magazine):

"A Beatle Roundup." <u>Newsweek</u>, Sept. 7, 1970, pp. 85–86.

[Alphabetize this entry under "B," not "A."]

9. An anonymous article (newspaper):

"Smog Group to Consider Tougher Rules." Eugene (Ore.) Regis-
ter-Guard, Sept. 13, 1970, Sec. 1, p. 2, col. 3.

10. A signed article in a periodical not requiring a volume number:

Wicker, Tom. "Nixon's the One—But What?" Playboy, Oct. 1970,
p. 105.

11. An article in a scholarly periodical requiring a volume number:

Smith, Marcus. "The Wall of Blackness: A Psychological Approach to 1984." Modern Fiction Studies, 14 (Winter
1968–69), 423–33.

12. An unsigned encyclopedia article:

"Abolitionists," Encyclopedia Americana. 1974 ed.

13. A signed encyclopedia article:

P[ar]k, T[homas]. "Ecology." Encyclopaedia Britannica. 1968 ed.

14. An article from the *Dictionary of American Biography:*

N[evins], A[llan]. "Warren Gamaliel Harding." DAB (1932).

15. An anonymous pamphlet:

Preparing Your Dissertation for Microfilming. Ann Arbor, Mich:
University Microfilms, n.d.

16. A reference to the Bible:

The Bible. Trans. J. M. P. Smith, Edgar J. Goodspeed, et al.
Chicago: Univ. of Chicago Press, 1939.

[You need not list the Bible in your bibliography, unless you want your
readers to know, for some reason, that you have referred to one of the new
translations, rather than to the familiar King James Version. If so, you
would alphabetize the entry under "B."]

17. A reference to a letter:

In a *published* collection:

Paine, A. B., ed. <u>Mark Twain's Letters</u>. 2 vols. New York: Harper, 1917

An *unpublished* letter:

Wharton, Edith. Letter to William Brownell, 6 Nov. 1907. Wharton Archives. Amherst College, Amherst, Mass.

A *personal letter:*

Vidal, Gore.   Letter to author.   2 June 1976.

18. A personal or telephone interview:

Kesey, Ken.   Personal interview.   28 May 1977.

Didion, Joan.   Telephone interview.   10 April 1978.

19. A review, signed or unsigned:

Updike, John. "Who Wants to Know?" Rev. of <u>The Dragons of Eden</u>, by Carl Sagan. <u>The New Yorker</u>, 22 Aug. 1977, pp. 87–90.

Rev. of <u>Ring</u>, by Jonathan Yardley. <u>The New Yorker</u>, 12 Sept. 1977, pp. 159–60.

20. A lecture:

Axelrod, Rise. "Who Did What with Whom." MLA Convention, Chicago. 30 Dec. 1977.

21. A document from ERIC:

Lucas, Joseph. <u>Background for Builders: Related Science and Trade Information for the Building Trades</u>. Curriculum Lab. New Brunswick, N.J.: Rutgers, The State Univ., 1975. ERIC ED 127 459.

For Business and Economics

If your paper is for a business or economics class, the system is quite similar to the one used for the humanities, but your notes can be even shorter, citing only the author's last name, the title of the work, and the page number. You need not anguish over the endless complications (such as omitting the abbreviation for *page* in using a volume number) that make the humanities system such a headache. Just read our explanation of how the system operates; then follow the samples.

You have your choice of four types of documentation:

1. Endnotes (or footnotes) plus a bibliography
2. Endnotes containing complete information without a bibliography—for fewer than five sources
3. Numbers referring to a list of references at the end (the system used in many scientific papers; see pages 310–313)
4. Citations within the text (like the ones on page 300)

Endnotes are probably the most commonly used form. Be sure, though, to ask your instructor what type of documentation is preferred and use that kind. Your endnote and bibliographical entries will look like the following samples (borrowed with permission from H. A. Murphy and C. E. Peck, *Effective Business Communications* [New York: McGraw-Hill, 1976], p. 614).

Sample Notes

1. An article:

    [1] Rogers and Toethlisberger, "Barriers and Gateways to Communication," p. 29.

2. A book:

    [2] Shore, Operations Management, p. 242.

3. A newspaper article:

    [3] "Restaurant Employees Adopt New Rules," Seattle Times.

4. An interview:

    [4] Statement by Helen Smith, President, City Restaurant Managers.

Sample Bibliographical Entries.   Note that here you use hanging (backward) indention to emphasize the last names of the authors. Divide your sources into the four categories listed below, and *alphabetize* the entries within each category.

1. An article:

    Rogers, Carl R., and S. J. Roethlisberger, "Barriers and Gateways to Communication," Harvard Business Review, July–August 1968, pages 29–36.

2. A book:

> Shore, Barry. <u>Operations Management</u>, McGraw-Hill Book
> Company, New York, 1973, 544 pages.

3. A newspaper article:

> "Restaurant Employees Adopt New Rules," <u>The Seattle Times</u>,
> December 3, 1975, page C-4.

4. An interview:

> Smith, Helen, President of City Restaurant Managers, December
> 10, 1975.

For Education

If you are doing your paper for an education class, you have considerable leeway. There is no set style for the field that we can discover. Your best bet is probably to adopt the style of documentation used by one of the leading journals. Or you can ask whether your instructor has a preference.

The periodical *Science and Children* uses a handy system of consecutive numbers in parentheses inserted in the text which refer to a list entitled "References" at the end. If a reference is repeated, the entry is repeated in full in the list. The entries look like this.

For an article:

1. Rosenfelt, Deborah, and Florence Howe. "Language and Sexism: A Note." <u>MLA Newsletter</u>: 5–6, December 1973.

For a book:

2. Oxenhorn, Joseph M., and Michael N. Idelson. <u>The Earth We
   Live On</u>. Globe Book Company, New York. 1968. P. 42.

For the Natural and Social Sciences

If you are writing a paper for one of the natural sciences, social sciences, or mathematics, you are in luck because the systems of documentation are much more efficient than those used in the humanities. Because scientific research builds on earlier research, dates are emphasized. Frequently, entire works are referred to, rather than specific pages. The documentation systems are simplified, but unfortunately not all disciplines use the same system. We will explain the variations (following Kate Turabian's *A Manual for Writers,* 4th ed., Chicago Univ. Press, 1973).

Citing References.   Instead of using notes plus a bibliography, scientific papers conclude with a "List of References" or a "Literature Cited" section (either numbered or alphabetized) which lists all the sources mentioned in the paper. Individual citations referring to this list are *inserted in the text* of the paper.

If the reference list is alphabetized, insert (either in parentheses or in brackets) the author's last name and the date of publication, like this:

> This long-accepted theory has recently been questioned (White, 1977).

> White (1977) has now questioned this long-accepted theory.

If the list is numbered, you cite the appropriate entry number (plus the page number, if you want to be specific):

> Funk (5:32) discovered that many subjects reacted negatively to the stimulus.

You may cite several sources at once, this way:

> Recent research (3-7-8) has now shown that the negative response is to be expected.

If you want to make a specific reference to something (like a chart or diagram) in your sources, do so in the text of your paper, like this:

> Fox (1969, p. 7, Table 3) shows a marked increase since 1960. Examination of the most recent evidence (Jiminez, 1977, Fig. 2) suggests that these changes may be crucial.

Documentation in the Sciences.

Since few disciplines in the sciences use precisely the same style for recording sources, we will illustrate some of the methods most commonly used.

Biology.   Use numbers in the text to refer to numbered references at the end listed in the order mentioned in the paper (as explained above). Use capital letters for authors' names. Abbreviate journal titles and underline volume numbers with a wavy line to indicate boldface type. Use sentence capitalization with no quotation marks for article titles. Do not underline book titles.

For an article:

38. OUTHRED, R. K., and E. D. GEORGE. 1973. Water and ions in muscles and model systems. Biophys. J. **13**:97.

For a book:

10. LING, G. N. 1962. A Physical Theory of the Living State. Blaisdell, New York.

For further information, consult the Council of Biology Editors' *CBE Style Manual*, 3d ed., 1972.

Chemistry. Do not include a reference list. Use numbers in the text to refer to endnotes, as explained on pages 310–311. Omit titles of articles. Abbreviate journal titles and underline the volume number with a wavy line to indicate boldface type. Note: enclose book titles in quotation marks.

For an article:

(2) T. T. Paukert and H. S. Johnson, J. Chem. Phys., **56**, 2824 (1972).

For a book:

(13) Pauling, L., "The Nature of the Chemical Bond," Cornell U.P., Ithaca, 1960, p. 234.

For complete information, consult the American Chemical Society's *Handbook for Authors of Papers in the Journals of the American Chemical Society,* 1967.

Geology. Make citations in the text by author and year, referring to an alphabetized list of references at the end (as explained on page 311). Capitalize all letters in names of authors; use standard title capitalization for books but sentence capitalization for articles; use a colon to separate titles from place of publication. Note the abbreviations *p.* for pages and *v.* for volume, as well as the shortened journal title.

For an article:

GATES, W. L., 1979, The effect of the ocean on the atmospheric general circulation: Dyn. Atmos. Oceans, v. 3, p. 95–109.

For a book:

DOTT, R. H., and BATTEN, R. L., 1979, Evolution of the Earth: New York, McGraw-Hill, 649 p.

Mathematics.   Put the list of references at the end, numbered and alphabetized. Refer to these entries by number in the text, as shown on pages 310–311. Use capital letters for authors' names, but sentence capitalization for titles of articles. Put book titles in quotation marks. Use wavy lines to underline volume numbers of journals to indicate bold type. Note abbreviations in journal title.

For an article:

1. R. ARENS and I. KAPLANSKY, Topological representations of algebra, Trans. Amer. Math. Soc. **63** (1948), 457–481.

For a book:

5. A. T. BHARUCHA-REID, "Random Integral Equations," Academic Press, New York, 1972.

For further information, consult the American Mathematical Society's *Manual for Authors of Mathematical Papers*, 4th ed., 1971.

Physics.   Do not include a reference list. Use raised numbers in the text to refer to endnotes, as explained on pages 310–311. Omit titles of articles. Abbreviate journal titles but do not underline. Instead, underline the volume number with a wavy line to indicate boldface type. Endnote numbers are raised also.

For an article:

7. J. J. Degnan, App. Opt., **12,** 1026 (1973).

For a book:

10. M. A. Heald and C. B. Wharton, Plasma Diagnostic with Microwaves (Wiley, New York, 1965), Chap. 6.

For further information, consult the revised *Style Manual* issued by the Publications Board of the American Institute of Physics, 1973.

Physiology.   Alphabetize your list of references using sentence capitalization and no underlining. Citations referring to this list should be inserted in the text of the paper, as explained on pages 310–311. Note abbreviation of journal titles.

For an article:

Rosenberg, C. D. 1974. Some uses of biomedical computer programs. Ant. Review 42:583.

For a book:

Hildebrand, M. 1976. Anatomical preparations. Univer. of California Press, Berkeley.

Documentation in the Social Sciences.

Social scientists also use relatively uncomplicated systems of documentation. The styles described here are the most common.

Anthropology.   Most anthropologists cite the author's last name in the text, followed by year of publication and page number, like this: (Sherman 1976:18). Entries in the alphabetized reference list at the end look like this. Note sentence capitalization of titles without quotation marks or underlining.

For an article:

Sherman, B.
    1976   Studies in the stratification of an American Indian
              village. American Anthropologist 34:147–63.

For a book:

Harris, M.
    1977   Cannibals and kings. New York: Random House.

Political Science.   Make citations in the text by author and year of publication. Alphabetize your list of references using sentence capitalization; underline titles of books and journals.

For an article:

Hart, H. L. A. 1955. Are there any natural rights? The Philo-
    sophical Review 65: 175–91.

For a book:

Chalidze, Valery. 1974. To defend these rights: human rights
    and the Soviet Union. New York: Random House.

Consult a current issue of the *American Political Science Review* for further information.

Psychology.   Make citations in the text of your paper by author and year of publication or by using a numbered list of references, as explained on pages 310–311. If citing by author, alphabetize your list of references using sentence capitalization; underline titles of journals and their volume numbers.

For an article:

Lee, D. J. Visual perceptions in nonverbal communications.
Australian Journal of Psychology, 1972, **83**, 246–59.

For a book:

Smith, K. Behavior and conscious experience: A conceptual analysis. Athens, Ohio: Ohio Univ. Press, 1969.

The American Psychological Association's *Publication Manual of the
American Psychological Association,* 2nd ed., 1974, provides complete information.

Sociology. Citations in the paper usually give author and year of
publication, as shown on pages 310–311. Make an alphabetized list of
references. Use sentence capitalization for titles of articles. Note abbreviation of journal titles.

For an article:

Caplan, N.
   1970   The new ghetto man: A review of recent empiri-
          cal studies. J. Soc. Issues 26:59–74.

For a book:

Buckley, Walter
   1964   Sociology and Modern Systems Theory. Englewood
          Cliffs, New Jersey: Prentice-Hall, Inc.

Some journals use quotation marks around article titles, others do not.
Some underline book titles, others do not. You should seek your instructor's preference in the matter. Consult a current issue of *American Sociological Review* for further information.

chapter Eleven
Practical Career Writing

Almost everything we have said about theme writing applies to writing in general. You should always say clearly what's on your mind in the most effective way. The difference between the writing you do in college and the writing you will do on the job is mainly a difference in form. Instead of writing essay examinations, you will write memos to people you work with. Instead of writing a term paper on the life cycle of platypuses, you will write case studies, lesson plans, law briefs, or drilling reports. Instead of just writing letters to your Aunt Helen, you will also write letters to people in industry—often people who are strangers to you.

Professional success often depends on successful communication. Letters, memos, and reports must be written clearly and concisely so that the people who receive them can quickly understand exactly what the writer had in mind. Writing that is not clear or leaves out essential information invariably leads to extra work, extra memos, extra letters—hence extra cost—to straighten out the confusion caused by the original unclear message.

People who do the hiring understand these hard facts. They are second in line—right after English teachers—to point out the value of writing skills. Howard W. Blauvelt, chief executive officer of the Continental Oil Company, attests that "Business needs skilled communicators. . . . The ability to listen, digest, distill, and further communicate information is fundamental."[1] Most professional people, whether employed in private industry or a government agency, spend much of their working time writing. By learning to write well, you have gone a long way toward preparing yourself for a promising career.

[1] Quoted by Elizabeth M. Fowler, "Careers: Practical Skills for Graduates," *New York Times*, Sec. D, p. 17, col. 3.

WRITING EFFECTIVE LETTERS

Letter writing is the most useful writing skill that people practice after finishing school. More of us convey information, ideas, suggestions, thanks, complaints, and requests in letters than in any other productive way. Everyone needs to be able to write them well. For those taking jobs in business, industry, or in the governmental bureaucracy, effective letter writing is essential for a successful career.

Cultivate the "You" Attitude

The best way to write a really persuasive letter is to show *you*, the reader, what the writer can do for *you*—how *you* will profit and why. As Robert L. Shurter observes, "Nothing related to business correspondence is more important than this point of view, known for years as the *you attitude:* we can most readily persuade others to do what we want them to do by demonstrating that it is to their advantage to do it."[2] You have to be honest about it, of course. If you dream up some phony reason or resort to shameless flattery, your reader will reject your letter at once. Observe the *you attitude* in operation in the following examples, which we have borrowed from Shurter. The first one (Figure 11-1) illustrates the *wrong* way to make a request:

```
Dear Sir:

I need a lot of information on the way in which
business people react to the current crises in
our colleges, and I selected you and some
others to send this questionnaire to because
your names were mentioned in the newspapers.

I have to have this information in two weeks,
because my paper is due then, and I hope you will
help me by returning the questionnaire promptly.

                              Sincerely yours,
```

Figure 11-1 Typical request letter that exhibits the *I attitude.*

Figure 11-2 shows the same request, improved by incorporating the you attitude. Notice how the first letter focuses on the needs of the writer: *I* need, *I* selected, *I* have to, *I* hope. In the second letter the

[2] Donald J. Leonard, *Shurter's Communication in Business,* 4th ed. (New York: McGraw-Hill, 1979), p. 84.

Dear Mr. Jones:

You and several other prominent business people were recently quoted in <u>The Record</u> concerning the present crises in our colleges--and your comments so interested me that I decided to write my term paper on "Business's View of Today's Colleges."

Your answers to the enclosed questionnaire--all you need to do is check yes or no--will be kept completely confidential. If you wish, I will send you a summary of the results based on my survey of 50 prominent business people in this area.

You will recognize that I am attempting, in a small way, to open communication between education and business by means of a realistic survey. You can help by checking the answers and returning the questionnaire in the enclosed, self-addressed envelope.

Sincerely yours,

Figure 11-2 Request letter that incorporates the *you attitude*.

focus shifts to *you* and *your*. No one would doubt that the second letter is more effective.

The *you attitude* is easier to adopt with some types of letters than with others. It's difficult, for instance, when requesting a letter of recommendation, but easier—and more essential—when writing a letter applying for a job. Try to incorporate the *you attitude* into your thinking when you plan what to write. Use it when it works. When it will not, settle for a graceful compliment.

Organize Before You Write

A good letter is lean; it sticks to the point. In order to write a lean letter, you must organize your thoughts. Jot down the things you must say (just as you would in outlining an essay) and consider how the ideas are logically related. Put the points in order, then write one short, clear paragraph for each main item, making sure that you include all necessary information. Wind up politely, perhaps with a word of thanks.

Organization is important in all writing. It is especially important in the writing you do on the job, because time is money: clarity is essential. If you write a long, rambling letter that fails to focus on your purpose, the reader may just toss your letter in the nearest wastebasket. At the very least, you are not likely to get the response you want if you tax your readers' minds with vagueness and tire their eyes with excess words.

Consider Tone and Level of Usage

Just as you must adopt a tone appropriate to your purpose in writing essays, so should you match tone to purpose in a letter. Try to strike a balance between being formal and being friendly. Since you are usually trying to get your reader to do something (whether it's buying from your company or granting you a job interview), do not be sarcastic or too aggressive. Be confident, not slavish: "I beg you to consider me for this job" is too servile. Be courteous but not stuffy. Using the impersonal *one* often sounds stilted: "One hopes that the Magnum Oil Corporation will consider one's credentials." You can use *I* and *you* and sound natural without becoming too chummy. Try to adopt the tone that you would find most appealing in a stranger's letter to you.

While most letter writers do not use strictly formal language, neither do they use colloquial or slangy language. In most cases, try to be temperate and use informal language. (You can review usage levels on pages 457–458.) Instead of high-sounding phrases like *due to the fact that*, use the plainer *since* or *because*. Avoid old-fashioned business phrases like *pursuant to, be advised that, enclosed herewith*, and *in receipt of*. Avoid clichés like "I'll give it the old college try" and "We'll give them a run for their money." Arranging plain English words in concise sentences that say clearly what you mean will leave a favorable impression.

One last piece of advice: give bad news gently. If you should decide to turn down a prospective job, say "I was pleased to receive your offer, but . . ." instead of "Fortunately, I got a better offer." Your meaning will be the same, but you will not offend someone you may need to contact later in your new job. A callous attitude might get you to the top quickly, but it's more likely to land you among the unemployed even faster.

Follow the Standard Format Faithfully

When you write to your Aunt Helen you probably pick up any handy piece of paper and jot down a message. You never give a thought to format because you are writing a personal note. Auntie loves you and is unlikely to be offended by the casual appearance of your letter.

Such casualness will seldom be appropriate for business letters for a couple of reasons. First, the person you are writing to is likely to be a stranger or someone you know only slightly. Generally, correspondence between strangers is fairly formal. Then too, the person you are writing is likely to respond on the basis of the way your letter looks, as well as to what you say in it. If your letter is sloppy, your reader might justifiably decide you are a slob and ignore you.

Since most business correspondence follows a standard format (as shown in Figure 11-3), you will do well to follow it. Letters are usually typed in one of two standard formats. In the *full block* format all lines begin at the left margin. In the *modified block* format, which is the most popular, the longest lines of both the heading and the closing end at the right margin. Although your margins will vary so that the letter is centered, all letters should have margins of at least 1¼ inches on all sides.

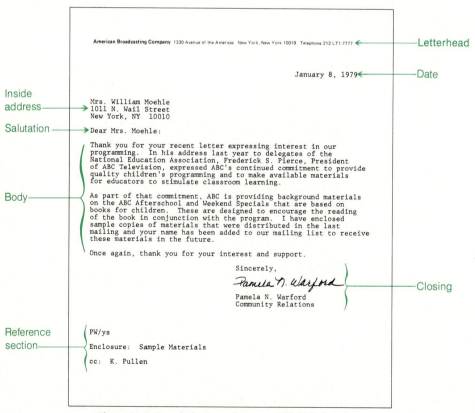

Figure 11-3 Sample business letter, modified block format.

Aside from appearance, the main reason for using a standard format is that it always places important information in the same easy-to-find places. As you read the following explanation of each part, refer to Figure 11-3 to see how it should be typed.

1. The *heading* supplies the name and address of the sender, which is you. Naturally, letterhead stationery includes all this information. All you need to add is the date, with the month spelled out first, then the day and the year. If you do not use letterhead stationery, type the heading, single-spaced, with your own address this way in the upper right-hand corner:

   > 3818 18th Street
   > San Francisco, CA 94114
   > July 12, 1982

2. The *inside address* contains the full name, business title, company name, and address of the person to whom you are writing. Notice that before the person's name you use a courtesy title, like Ms., Mr., or Dr. The inside address is used in case the envelope is separated from the letter in a company's mail room.

3. The *salutation* is a polite greeting. Usually it is followed by a colon. If possible, *try to address an individual by name:*

   > *Dear Ms. (or Mr. or Dr.) Wakoski:*

   If you do not know the person's name, find it. On page 327, we explain how. If you are unable to locate the person's name, you can open this way:

   > *Dear Personnel Manager:*
   > *Dear People in the Credit Department:*

   Dear Sir and *To Whom It May Concern* are now considered too impersonal to be effective. You may, however, use simply *Ladies* or *Gentlemen,* if you are sure that the people you are addressing are all of one sex. *Dear Joan* (or *John*) is appropriate if you are on friendly terms with the person you are addressing.

4. The *body* is the heart of a letter. The message must be clearly written and well organized. Note that the paragraphs are single-spaced and begin at the left margin. A double space separates paragraphs. You may indent the first line of each paragraph, but many people do not.

5. The *closing* is a polite way of ending a letter. The first line, or complimentary close, is followed by a comma. You can use one of the old standbys:

Formal	Informal
Yours truly,	Warmly,
Very truly yours,	Cordially yours,
Sincerely yours,	Best regards,
Yours sincerely,	With best wishes,

Avoid being too offbeat or too cute. Your signature and typed name complete the closing. If you are representing a firm, your title appears directly under your name.

6. The *reference section,* which is used as needed, may include enclosure or copy notations. The reference notation lists the writer's initials and, if you are lucky enough to have one, the typist's initials. The enclosure notation simply calls the reader's (or the mail room's) attention to the inclusion of other items with the letter (and tells how many inclusions there are) like this:

> Enclosure
>
> Enc. 3
>
> Enclosure: one set of blueprints

The copy notation indicates that copies were sent to other people.

> cc: Ms. Wakoski

As you probably guessed, *cc* means carbon copy; *pc* means photocopy.

TYPES OF CORRESPONDENCE

The majority of letters ask the reader to *do* something, to supply information or support some worthy cause. But different purposes require different approaches. Three common types are letters of request, letters of persuasion, and letters of complaint.

Letters of Request

Organize requests like this: (1) explain exactly what you want and give any specific information that is necessary; (2) explain why you want what you want; and (3) thank your reader for the expected help. See the sample in Figure 11-4. Notice that the message states the request clearly and politely, and that it gives the exact title of the catalog, all in one paragraph. Virtually every item of merchandise has a number (with other numbers for every part) for easy identification. So always include the necessary numbers. If your letter requests several separate things, like three or four booklets, consider numbering them and listing them on separate lines to make it easier for your readers to fill your requests. Address your request to a specific person or department if possible.

Requesting a Reference.   A particular kind of request letter that you are likely to write sooner or later is a request for a reference. The same rules apply in this case, but you should also take care to identify

```
                          1228 Spruce Street
                          Bloomington, IL  61701
                          July 10, 1983



High Blood Pressure Information Center
120/80 National Institutes of Health
Bethesda, MD   20014

Dear Friends:

     Would you please send me your Public Affairs
Pamphlet No. 483A, entitled "Watch Your Blood
Pressure!" by Theodore Irwin?

     You are performing a valuable public service
by distributing this free information.  Thanks
for the good work.

                          Yours sincerely,

                          Mary Beth Marlow

                          Mary Beth Marlow
```

Figure 11-4 Sample letter requesting information.

yourself and to supply some extra information that will help the reader compose a useful reference letter for you (see Figure 11-5).

Besides the self-addressed postcard, you may want to include other personal information, such as your grade point average, honors and scholarships, and activities, memberships, or offices. Be sure to give specific guidelines for writing the recommendation, if there are any. Many college placement services provide special, easily duplicated forms for letters, which you should be sure to include.

Letters of Persuasion

Certainly job application letters must be persuasive since you are, in effect, selling yourself, but we discuss these important letters in a separate section (see pages 329–333). The kind of persuasive letters

```
                                310 Darby Drive
                                Colfax, IL  61728
                                June 17, 1983


Dr. Lucia Getsi
Department of English
Illinois State University
Normal, IL  61761

Dear Professor Getsi:

I am applying for a proofreading job at The Daily Deluge
in Colfax, Illinois (my hometown), and I would be grate-
ful if you would write a letter of recommendation for me.

In the fall semester of 1981 I took your course in "The
American Short Story, 1860-1920," and wrote my term paper
on "Mythological Implications in Eudora Welty's 'Moon
Lake.'"  I received an A in the course, which I found
informative and enjoyable.

If you are willing to write a letter for me, please
address it to

                        Ms. Patricia Gilbey
                        Managing Editor
                        The Daily Deluge
                        110 South Main Street
                        Colfax, IL  61728

It should arrive before July 1.  If you feel unable to
recommend me, would you please return the enclosed post-
card to let me know?

Thank you for doing me this favor.

With warm regards,

Margie Sanford
Margaret Sanford
```

Figure 11-5 Letter requesting a reference.

that we are talking about here are the ones you may want to write to editors, members of Congress, cabinet members, or even the President, in order to express your viewpoint on matters of public policy that affect your life.

When you write such a letter, you really are writing a brief persuasive essay. Choose your tone carefully. Keep your audience (that

```
                                       418 Fairview Avenue
                                       Bloomington, IL   61761
                                       March 14, 1983


Editor, The Daily Pantagraph
201 West Washington Street
Bloomington, IL   61701

To the Editor:

I am alarmed by the Agriculture Department's plan to use
the pesticide mirex--which kills birds and marine life--
in a new attempt to eliminate the fire ant.  Mirex also
has been shown to cause cancer in mice and birth defects
in rats.

Mirex is one of the chlorinated pesticides, like DDT and
dieldrin, which spread through the environment and remain
active for many years.  DDT, for instance, is found in
Antarctic seals, although it was never used in Antarctica.

Dieldrin is in the milk of Illinois mothers at a concen-
tration 5.6 times that considered safe for infants by the
Food and Drug Administration.  Once these chemicals enter
a human body, they tend to stay there.

Spraying pesticides over wide areas is expensive, ineffec-
tive, and alarmingly dangerous.  The money used to spread
mirex could be more judiciously spent.  Other insects
have been controlled by using hormones to lure them into
traps and by introducing relatively harmless natural
enemies into infested areas.  These and other possibili-
ties should be fully explored before the Agriculture
Department again spreads a damaging and long-lived pesti-
cide over millions of acres of farmland where it almost
certainly will enter our food and water.

                                       Sincerely yours,
```

```
                                       Dan LeSeure
```

Figure 11-6 Example of a persuasive letter.

is, your reader or readers) constantly in mind. Present your arguments clearly, concisely, and logically. At the end, offer your solutions to the problems discussed, if possible. Your persuasive letter might come out something like the one shown in Figure 11-6. You can increase the effectiveness of your letter by sending copies to the Secretary of Agriculture, your senators, and the President.

Letters of Complaint

Just as you want to avoid being sarcastic when you write a letter of persuasion, you want to remain reasonable when you write a letter of complaint. Calling your reader names is not the way to solve your problem, whether it is a new car that refuses to start or a computer that likes to add other people's bills to your account. Unless your goal is

---

216 West Boyd St.
Gilman, IL   60938
September 7, 1983

Mr. Leon White
Consumer Affairs
Persis Products, Inc.
312 State Street
Chicago, IL   60637

Dear Mr. White:

I have been having trouble with my new Hot'N'Heavenly hair dryer (model 1040c, no. 6737). It no longer heats properly.

I bought the dryer at Meyer and Frank's in Eugene, Oregon (see enclosed copy of receipt), and was quite satisfied with it at first. Now that it is not working, I can not find a store in Gilman, Illinois, that carries your dryers.

Since it is only two months old, I am sure you will want to replace or repair my hair dryer, but I do not know where to send it.

I will appreciate hearing from you concerning this problem at your earliest convenience.

Yours sincerely,

Russ Finley

Russell Finley

Figure 11-7 Sample letter of complaint.

simply to let off steam, try something like the letter shown in Figure 11-7 when you write to a consumer relations manager. This letter is reasonable, despite the writer's annoyance at the hair dryer's frailty. Notice also how the letter expresses confidence in the manufacturer's fairness (third paragraph) instead of speculating on whose fault the failure was.

Find a Person's Name

If possible, direct your letter of complaint to a specific person: it's the best way to get speedy results. If you are having trouble with a local business, call and get the owner's or the manager's name first. If you are dealing with a large business, you may want the name of the person who has responsibility for consumer complaints or the person in charge of a specific department, like the service manager, customer relations manager, or credit manager. If you are dealing with a large corporation, write to the president, the vice-president in charge of public relations, or a specific division manager. You can get the names of corporate officials at your library from *Thomas' Register of American Manufacturers* or *Poor's Register of Corporations, Directors, and Executives*. Chambers of commerce and better business bureaus may also provide names or assistance.

Once you have the name, get busy. But remember these four things:

1. Be reasonable.
2. Give exact details about your problem.
3. Give all information (like model or serial numbers, amount paid) that may be needed.
4. Thank your reader in advance for the assistance.

It matters not what your complaint is—poor service in a store, on a plane or train; gadgets that refuse to work; promises that are not kept; pollution that stifles you and your dog; or food that is inedible—you will get more action for your effort by following these four rules than you would with pages of obscenity or sarcasm.

A Word about Envelopes

The envelope should include your return address, typed in the upper left corner, and the mailing address, typed as shown in Figure 11-8*a*. Since the Postal Service uses clever machines to read the mailing address from the bottom up, make sure that city, state, and zip code (in that order) are on the last line and the street address (or box number) is on the line above that. If there is an apartment number or room number, it should go directly after and on the same line as the street address. Names, titles, and any other information must appear on lines *above* these last two. The Postal Service has also supplied convenient two-letter abbreviations for the states. Use them without periods. (See Figure 11-8*b*.)

POSTAL POINTERS

Return address →

Sue LeSeure
500 W. Main St.
Normal, IL 61761

Ms. Maria Valdez
Personnel Manager
Great Western Publishing Corp.   ← Mailing address
7777 State St., Room 456
Chicago, IL 60606

a

Alabama AL	Kentucky KY	Ohio OH
Alaska AK	Louisiana LA	Oklahoma OK
Arizona AZ	Maine ME	Oregon OR
Arkansas AR	Maryland MD	Pennsylvania PA
California CA	Massachusetts MA	Puerto Rico PR
Colorado CO	Michigan MI	Rhode Island RI
Connecticut CT	Minnesota MN	South Carolina SC
Delaware DE	Mississippi MS	South Dakota SD
District of Columbia DC	Missouri MO	Tennessee TN
Florida FL	Montana MT	Texas TX
Georgia GA	Nebraska NB	Utah UT
Guam GU	Nevada NV	Vermont VT
Hawaii HI	New Hampshire NH	Virginia VA
Idaho ID	New Jersey NJ	Virgin Islands VI
Illinois IL	New Mexico NM	Washington WA
Indiana IN	New York NY	West Virginia WV
Iowa IA	North Carolina NC	Wisconsin WI
Kansas KS	North Dakota ND	Wyoming WY

b

Figure 11-8 Postal pointers: (a) sample envelope, (b) postal service abbreviations.

In each of the following exercises, use a standard business-letter format (block or modified block) and remember to be clear, concise, and polite.

1. Write a letter requesting:
   a. A reference from one of your professors or employers
   b. An instruction manual and repair booklet for an electric toaster
   c. Information on how your favorite beer is brewed
   d. Information from your local agricultural extension office on how to have your garden soil analyzed
2. Write a persuasive letter to your local newspaper or to the politician you like the least about:
   a. Conflicts of interest in Congress (or state legislatures)
   b. Preserving our wilderness areas (wildlife, clean air or water, Victorian architecture, or whatever)
   c. The high cost of housing (or apartments)
   d. The social responsibility of corporations
   e. Improvement of the mass transit system in your town
3. Write a reasonable letter of complaint about:
   a. An electric can opener that snarls at you but refuses to open cans
   b. A new leather coat that split at the shoulder seam and that the store refuses to take back
   c. A telephone bill that lists eleven calls to Perth, Australia
   d. A new stereo speaker that has been "repaired" twice but still has a surly growl
   e. Police officers who were rude and overbearing when they came to ask you to keep the noise down at a party

WRITING APPEALING JOB APPLICATIONS AND RÉSUMÉS

Now that you have mastered the general techniques of letter writing, it is time to move on to the type of letter that will probably be crucial to you soon: the job application letter. Your letter could make the difference between getting a job and remaining unemployed. It also could mean the difference between spending half your waking hours doing something relatively satisfying and spending those endless hours doing something you actively dislike.

Practical Advice about Application Letters

We have badgered you again and again about keeping your reader in mind when you write. In your job application letter, you must studiously cultivate the *you attitude* discussed on pages 317–318. Your letter must say more than "I need a job." It must say instead: "This is what I can do for your organization if you hire me." Even the advantage of a college or post-graduate education is not going to let you escape the realities of a job market that has a surplus of qualified employees.

There are three other things you should keep in mind while writing your letters of application. *First, your tone should be polite and confident.* You want to present your best qualifications—your education and experience—in the most favorable light. But if you appear too aggressive, too confident, employers may fear that you will be unable to get along with the mere mortals they already employ. Nor should you go to the other extreme and beg for a job because you have a family or an aging parent to support. Such appeals simply do not work. *Second, you should always use a standard business-letter format,* like the one in Figure 11-9. Many people in business judge job applicants as much on the way their letters look as on what they say. *Finally, your letter should be brief and to the point*—no longer than one typewritten page, possibly three or four short paragraphs.

                                                    500 West Main Street
                                                    Normal, IL   61761
                                                    March 15, 1978

Ms. Maria Valdez
Personnel Manager
Great Western Publishing Corp.
7777 State Street, Room 456
Chicago, IL   60606

Dear Ms. Valdez:

Effective opening →

Do you need a good, experienced proofreader or copy editor?

Presenting qualifications {

For two summers I worked as a proofreader at The Daily Deluge in Colfax, Illinois, and for three years as a part-time advertising copywriter for radio station WXYZ in Normal. As the enclosed resume indicates, I majored in English and minored in journalism at Illinois State University.

Summarizing experience {

My experience with various writing and proofreading assignments could prove useful to your firm. I know a position with your nationally known firm would be satisfying to me, as it would further my ambition to become a professional editor.

Setting up interview →

May I come in for an interview at your convenience? Thank you for your consideration.

                                    Sincerely,

                                    Sue LeSeure

                                    Sue LeSeure

Enclosure: Resume

Figure 11-9 Sample job application letter.

Since you must accomplish a great deal in a brief space, we have broken the body of a basic job application letter into three parts: *effective opening, presentation of qualifications,* and *setting up an interview.* The following sections will show you what to concentrate on in each of the parts.

Write an Effective Opening.   Often the best way to begin your letter is the most direct way, like this:

> My training and experience as a proofreader and copy editor should be useful to your firm.

This opening makes clear *what* kind of job you want, *why* you are qualified for it, and *how* your skills can be valuable to a particular business (the *you attitude*). Naturally, if you are applying for a job that was advertised, you will say so. If you know someone in the organization who will agree to speak well of you, by all means mention that person's name. When you apply for your first full-time job after college, however, you may have to write to a number of large companies that employ people with your skills. In that case, you will be fishing for an opening and will have to generalize your qualifications and incorporate the *you attitude* as imaginatively as possible. You may prefer a copy-editing job, but mention proofreading also to increase your chances of getting some job—one that could lead to the job you really want.

Another way of opening your application letter is to ask a question: "Do you need a good, experienced copy editor?" That catches the reader's attention and gets right to the point. You must be sure, however, that you back up your claim in the next paragraph.

Present Your Qualifications.   The heart of your application letter is the proof that you can do for a prospective employer what you say you can do. Creating a good impression is important, but proof that you are qualified is the clincher. You need not be long-winded about it because you will include a résumé supplying the details. Your letter should mention only those things that *best* qualify you for the job. These days that usually means experience, like this:

> For two summers I worked as a proofreader on the *Daily Deluge* in Colfax, Illinois, and for three years as a part-time advertising copywriter for radio station WXYZ in Normal. As the enclosed résumé indicates, I majored in English and minored in journalism at Illinois State University.

If you do not have much work experience, you can emphasize your training (and your grades, if they are good). Or ransack your past for other useful experience. Many jobs require you to deal with the public. If you sold tickets at the college theater or were a member of a club that raised money for charity, mention those volunteer jobs to show you have had experience in dealing with people. Another common skill that business needs is organizational ability. If you planned activities at a summer camp or organized church socials, you can list those things as examples of your ability to organize. Be as resourceful as you can when considering your skills, but do not exaggerate them.

If you know what your long-range career goal is, you might mention it as an indication of your commitment.

> My experience with various writing and proofreading assignments could prove useful to your firm. I know that a position with your nationally known firm would be satisfying to me, as it would further my ambition to become a professional editor.

Employers like employees who are devoted to their work. They also prefer employees who have a high opinion of the company they work for, so in keeping with the *you attitude*, try to work in an indirect compliment ("your nationally known firm"). Just be careful not to overdo it. You might also want to refer to your present status.

> When I finish school in June . . .

or

> A position in your accounting department would offer me more opportunity for advancement than I have with my present excellent, though smaller, firm.

Notice that you should explain your desire to change jobs in a positive way. Employers take a dim view of employees who change jobs because of personal disagreements or disputes over how to run the place. Salary is a subject that should not be dealt with in application letters. If an advertisement asks for your requirement, suggest that the matter be discussed in your interview.

Set Up an Interview.   The real object of your application letter is to obtain an interview, since few good jobs are handed out without one. Conclude your letter by offering to be interviewed at the company's convenience, and add a polite word of thanks.

> May I come in for an interview at your convenience? Thank you for your consideration.

In today's tight job market, you may possibly be expected to pay your own expenses if the job you seek is out of town. Try to go, because without the interview, you have little chance of getting the job. If you are applying to a large company, you might ask to be interviewed at a regional office near your home. But certainly you should make every effort to appear for an interview if offered one.

Other Things to Consider.   You must try to direct your letter to a specific person, usually the head of the department you are interested in or perhaps the company's personnel manager. This personal touch shows you are serious, knowledgeable, and sufficiently energetic to locate the name. (Try *Thomas' Register of American Manufacturers* or *Poor's Register of Corporations, Directors, and Executives.*) If you absolutely cannot find a name, "Director of Personnel" will do in a pinch. You should type each letter of application individually. Form letters with blanks filled in may be faster, but they are not likely to be considered seriously. (Your résumé may be commercially duplicated, however.)

Make Your Letter Perfect.   Finally, take the time to prune your letter down to the essentials. Ask a loved one to read it and make suggestions. Use correct spelling, grammar, and punctuation. Proofread the final typed version at least twice. Call on your loved ones again. Typos and spelling mistakes will kill your chances.

Write a Follow-up.   After you have had your interview, you should write a brief follow-up letter to the interviewer. In this letter you could comment on some feature of the company which impressed you, but primarily you should thank your interviewers for their time and consideration. Since your purpose is merely to keep your name in the interviewer's mind, a few *brief*, friendly lines will do. If, however, the interview ended on a "Don't call us, we'll call you" note, no follow-up letter will help.

Tips for Creating an Effective Résumé

A résumé (or *vita*) is a listing, in easy-to-read form, of everything about you that might be useful to an employer: your work experience, your education and technical training, personal details, and a list of references—at least three people who will testify to your sterling character and considerable capabilities.

When and How to Use a Résumé.   Always include a résumé with your application letter. Your résumé is your representative—a personal record of your accomplishments. It should be as attractive and informative as you can make it. Since your résumé need not be written in full sentences and since there is no standard form for headings, you have a lot of leeway to present your best points effectively. *Try to fit everything on one typed page.* Brevity is just as important as an attractive format. Limiting yourself to one page forces you to stick to the essentials. Be sure it looks appealing. Once it is perfect, you may want to have your résumé duplicated commercially. The sample résumé in Figure 11-10 shows one way to organize and type all the information. Remember, though, that you can make up your own form to emphasize your own strong points.

```
Sue LeSeure
500 W. Main St.
Normal, IL  61761
Telephone:  309/452-9999

                              Experience

Oct. 1976 to present    Station WXYZ, Normal IL
(during school term)    Part-time, 20 hours per week.  Wrote advertising copy
                        and solicited ads.

June-August 1979/       The Daily Deluge, Colfax IL
June-August 1978        Full-time proofreader (substituted for head proofreader,
                        1979)

June-August 1977        Gilbey's Variety Store, Colfax IL
                        Sales clerk (with stocking and pricing duties).  Also
                        made deliveries and called in supply orders.

June-August 1976        Unemployed

Jan. 1974-Aug. 1975     Alice's Restaurant, Colfax IL
                        Waitress and cashier

                              Education

Sept. 1977-June 1980    Illinois State University
                        Will receive B.A. in English, June 1980.
Sept. 1976-June 1977    Baskerville Community College
Sept. 1972-June 1976    Octavia High School

Scholastic honors:      Earned a 3.46 grade point average (on a 4.0 scale).
                        George Canning Scholarship in English Literature, 1979-80.
                        Illinois State Scholarship, 1976-80.

Technical training:     Attended a two-week seminar on "Advertising in Today's
                        Marketplace," sponsored by College of Business and
                        McLean County Association of Commerce and Industry.

                           Personal Data

Age:        24                      Married, no children
Health:     Excellent               Willing to relocate
Memberships: Student Association for Women; Journalism Club (President, 1979-80)
Hobbies:    photography, swimming

                            References

Ms. Mary Gilbey, Owner    Dr. Charles Harris        Mr. Waldo Withersnorp
Gilbey's Variety Store    Assoc. Prof. of English   Advertising Manager
555 S. Fifth Street       Illinois State University Radio Station WXYZ
Colfax IL   61763         Normal  IL   61761        112 Beaufort Avenue
Phone:  309/723-9999      Phone: 309/436-9999       Normal IL    61761
```

Figure 11-10 Sample résumé.

What to Say: Developing the Form.   Begin with your name, address, and telephone number. Make each of the four parts—education, experience, personal data, and references—a separate heading. List either experience or education first, depending on which is stronger in your case. Refer to Figure 11-10 while reading this explanation of the four parts:

Experience.   List your jobs in reverse order: the present one first, then the job before that, and so on, since employers are most interested in what you have been up to lately. If you have not had much work experience, be sure to list all jobs, no matter how unimportant they seem. Explain briefly what you did instead of merely listing a job title that may not convey the full scope of your duties. It's best not to leave any gaps, so you may have a listing like "June–August 1982: Unemployed." The experience section is the best place to list on-the-job awards and major promotions, especially if they merit a separate "Awards and Promotions" section.

Education.   List all your formal education and degrees, at least back through high school. Again, start with the most recent. You can use separate subheadings for scholastic honors or scholarships and for technical or management training that you received with a private company or in the armed services.

Personal Data.   This category includes information like age, height, weight, health, and marital status. Since federal and some state laws prohibit discrimination on the basis of race, religion, and sex, you may omit that information if you wish. You may want to mention your military service record, membership in clubs, and offices held.

References.   List at least three people who have agreed to write reference letters for you. Give their complete business addresses (and telephone numbers, if they do not object). Never list anyone who has not agreed to give you a reference or anyone you think may not give you a wholehearted recommendation. If you are using your college placement service, you need only list the names (with titles) and add "References available upon request from the University of Illinois Placement Service," plus the address.

EXERCISE   **11-2**

Go through the help-wanted advertisements of your local newspaper and choose a job that sounds like one you might like. Write a letter of application and a résumé. Do not mail them unless you want the job, but do not throw them away either. You can use the letter as a model when you write the real thing. If you keep your résumé, you will only need to update it.

PART THREE
Handbook

chapter Twelve
Background in Grammar

The ideal grammar of English would explain how human beings produce and understand the millions of utterances that they actually do produce and understand daily. That is a tall order, involving study of language history, physiology, brain functions, gesture, tone, emphasis—and even silence—as well as words and sentences.

WHAT YOU NEED TO KNOW

But you do not need a complete and thorough theory of grammar in order to write well. You do need a basic vocabulary, shared by you and your teachers and other writers, in which you can talk about sentences. Learning the terminology of traditional grammar can help you identify and correct sentence fragments, comma splices, and run-on sentences. It can help you decide where to put commas and semicolons. It can help you untangle sentences that are blighted by dangling modifiers, misplaced modifiers, or pile-ups of prepositional phrases. It can help you perk up your style as you cultivate sentence variety and weed out ineffective use of the passive voice.

In this chapter, we avoid the right-and-wrong rules that many people mistakenly associate with the study of grammar. We are more interested in describing how English sentences do work than in how persons of refinement should speak: that is a much more slippery subject, called *usage,* which we take on in the glossary at the end of this book. We have used the traditional aid of the sentence diagram so you can see the system we describe. Like many teachers of English, we have developed an eye for the beauty of this system. Maybe you will too. At least you will benefit from the order it shows underlying a seemingly unruly subject.

IN THE BEGINNING WAS THE WORD: PARTS OF SPEECH

You have probably grappled before with sorting words into parts of speech or word classes. This time, remember that you can classify a word dependably only if it is in a sentence, since many words in English act as more than one part of speech.

       verb
A. He will *line* his denim jacket with the blue plaid fake fur.

       noun
B. Clarissa told the team to stand with their noses on the white *line*.

       adjective
C. Ed did a clever *line* drawing of Sue's feet.

A group of words—a phrase or clause—can act as a single part of speech in a sentence too.

       preposition   adj.   n.
D. Claude said that he required fresh orange juice *in the morning.*
       adverb

The phrase *in the morning* modifies *required,* and thus acts like an adverb even though none of the words in the phrase is an adverb.

       pronoun vb.   infinitive
E. Rita replied that he had better find a girlfriend *who likes to squeeze*
       adjective
  n.
oranges.

The clause modifies *girlfriend,* and thus plays the part of an adjective.
    If you feel lost—if everything you ever knew about phrases and clauses seems to have fallen out of a hole in your head—stay with us. We will explain phrases and clauses right after we explain the eight parts of speech. As you read about them, try to think of parts of speech as roles words can play within sentences. You can see relationships among words in sentence diagrams, which we will offer throughout this chapter. You can also use tests to find out what part a word is playing, just as you test to find out what chemicals are in a solution. We will show you how. Nouns, verbs, and adjectives are the easiest parts of speech to pin down, so let's start with those.
    For each part of speech, we will give you (1) a definition, (2) examples of the roles it plays in sentences, (3) categories within that part of speech, and (4) diagrams.

Nouns

n

A noun names a person, place, thing, quality, idea, condition, or activity. Yes, the list got longer since you were in the fourth grade; but the definition still lacks precision.

To find out whether a word is acting as a noun in a sentence, try either (or both) of these tests.

Test 1. Can you substitute a personal pronoun for the word in a sentence? (Personal pronouns are *he, she, it, I, me, you, him, her, we, us, they, them.*)

A. *Sue* nailed up *lath* so *Andrea* could plaster the *walls.*

  she   it   she   them

By no stretch of the imagination could you reasonably substitute a personal pronoun for *nailed, up, so, could plaster,* so you know they are not acting as nouns.

Test 2. Can the word be used after one or more determiners within or outside a particular sentence? (*Determiners* are adjectives that classify: *a, an, the, this, these, that, those, some, any, no, his, her, its,* and other possessives, *seven, four,* and other numbers.)

B. *Tests* are a good *way* to sort *parts* of *speech.*

> the tests, those tests
> some way, no way, one way
> seven parts, these parts
> a speech, her four speeches

These four words sound natural with determiners, so you know they are nouns.

Roles Nouns Play. The most familiar role a noun plays in a sentence is that of *subject.*

subject of sentence
C. The *submarine* leaked.

subject of clause
D. The captain, whose *knees* shook violently, installed screen doors.

A prepositional phrase has a noun as its object.

subj.   *object of prep.*
E. The *sea* flowed through the *screen.*

Nouns also act as *complements* (see Figure 12-1 on page 363).

> *subj.*   *direct object of verb*
> **F.** The *submarine* followed *sharks.*

> *indirect*
> *subj.*   *object d. obj.*
> **G.** The *leaks* gave the *crew trouble.*

> *subj.*   *d. obj.*   *obj. of prep.*
> **H.** The *crew* threw the *captain* to the *sharks.*

> *subj.*   *predicate nominative (refers to subj.)*
> **I.** The *submarine* was a *hazard.*

> *objective complement (refers to d. obj.)*
> **J.** We thought Claudius a *bore.*

An *appositive*, which renames a noun preceding it, contains a noun.

> **K.** Mr. Bly, the *captain,* was nervous.

Nouns act as terms of *direct address.*

> **L.** *Ishmael,* please don't slam that screen door.

Noun Categories.   Sometimes justifiably and sometimes as a result of a neurotic need for order, we classify nouns into different groups like the following:

Abstract nouns: justice, flippancy, Darwinism, boredom, reality, habit
Concrete nouns (in contrast to abstract nouns): heliotrope, hammer, aardvark, elbow, hangnail
Collective nouns: audience, crowd, committee, group, collective
Proper nouns: Ishmael, Idaho, Lucy, Mr. Bill, Vegematic, Yellowstone Park, English
Common nouns (in contrast to proper nouns): violet, moss, stone, shoelace, mathematics
Mass nouns: water, lasagna, rice, population, salt
Count nouns (in contrast to mass nouns): person, helicopter, egg, bullet

Another important category is the *nominal,* which substitutes for a noun in a sentence by filling one of its roles. A nominal can be one word or a group of words.

Nominals include two kinds of verbals. *Verbals* are words that come from verbs, but act like other parts of speech. One verbal noun is the *gerund,* the *-ing* form of a verb, which passes the tests for a noun in these sentences:

> M. *Dancing* is a form of self-expression.
>   ↓
>   It

(Test 1; role: subject of the sentence.)

> N. After his conviction, he had to wait a month for *sentencing.*
>   *his* sentencing, *a* sentencing, *the* sentencing

(Test 2; role: object of a preposition.)

An *infinitive,* which is another kind of verbal, sometimes acts as a noun in a sentence. An infinitive is the simple form of a verb beginning with *to:* to walk, to jump, to levitate.

> O. His first idea was *to disappear.*

In this sentence, *to disappear* is the name of an idea. Role: predicate nominative.

> P. *To stay* out of trouble was not his main goal.

In this sentence, *to stay* is the name of an activity. Role: subject of the sentence. Phrases and clauses are nominals sometimes, too, as you will see in the discussion at the end of this chapter, pages 362–367.

Verbs

$$vb$$

A verb describes the action, existence, or occurrence of a subject. Here are two tests to help you identify verbs in sentences.

Test 1. Can you put it in the past tense?

> A. Anyone who *goes* to that saloon *is looking* for disaster.
>   ↓   ↓
>   went   was looking

You are not likely to mistakenly identify *salooned, fored,* or *disastered* as natural English words.

Test 2.   Can you conjugate it in first, second, and third person?

B. Whenever I *walk* in there, I *see* a fight.

I walk, you walk, he walks   I see, you see, she sees

Although *fight* can be conjugated, it is easy to see that it acts as a noun in the sentence above: it has an article before it, and thus clearly passes noun test 2.

Roles Verbs Play.   The verb in a sentence tells what a subject is or does. A complete sentence always has a main verb.

main vb.

C. Charmaine *decorates* her apartment beautifully.

A sentence is likely to include verbs in dependent clauses as well.

vb. in dependent clause   main vb.

D. Even if she *is staying* only a month, Charmaine *decorates* her apartment beautifully.

Besides showing action and being, the verb in a sentence expresses the time of the action. You can express twelve different time relations with these different verb forms:

Present:	He delays
Past:	He delayed
Future:	He will delay
Present perfect:	He has delayed
Past perfect:	He had delayed
Future perfect:	He will have delayed
Present progressive:	He is delaying
Past progressive:	He was delaying
Future progressive:	He will be delaying
Present perfect progressive:	He has been delaying
Past perfect progressive:	He had been delaying
Future perfect progressive:	He will have been delaying

The verb also shows whether the subject is acting or being acted upon because it can be in *active* or *passive* voice.

E. She shot. (*active*)   She was shot. (*passive*)

Passive voice adds twelve more possible verb forms to our list, although some of them sound unlikely.

Present:	He is delayed
Past:	He was delayed
Future:	He will be delayed
Present perfect:	He has been delayed
Past perfect:	He had been delayed
Future perfect:	He will have been delayed
Present progressive:	He is being delayed
Past progressive:	He was being delayed
Future progressive:	He will be being delayed
Present perfect progressive:	He has been being delayed
Past perfect progressive:	He had been being delayed
Future perfect progressive:	He will have been being delayed

Finally, the verb indicates the manner of expression: the *mood.* Three moods exist:
Indicative, for ordinary statements or questions about facts:

F. I'll eat at four. When will you eat lunch?

Imperative, for making requests:

G. Eat your zucchini.

Subjunctive, for expressing wishes or statements contrary to fact:

H. If I were rich, I would eat pizza every night.

The subjunctive mood has all but vanished from informal usage: look up *Subjunctive Mood* in Chapter 13 to get the full story.

Verb Categories. Every verb has an *infinitive* and three *principal parts,* which are used alone or combined with auxiliary verbs to form the various tenses. An infinitive can act as a noun, as we explained earlier, and also can fill the role of an adjective or adverb, as we will explain later. The three principal parts are *present, past,* and *past participle.*

Infinitive	Present	Past	Past Participle
to jump	jump	jumped	jumped
to fight	fight	fought	fought
to lose	lose	lost	lost
to see	see	saw	seen
to be	am	was	been

Verbs that form the past and past participle simply by adding a suffix of *-d, -ed,* or *-t* are *regular verbs,* like *jump* and *lose* above. *Fight, be* and *see* are *irregular verbs* because they form the past and past participle in an odd way. In Chapter 13, under *Tense,* we list some common irregular verbs.

Verbs also have present participles, which are formed by adding *-ing* to the present. Present participles are verbals, sometimes used as gerunds (see *Nouns,* page 341); sometimes used as adjectives, as in "She felt she had reached a *turning* point in life"; and sometimes used in progressive tenses to show future time ("I am *going* to Denver in March") or continuing action ("I've been *asking* too many questions for my own good.")

Auxiliary verbs are used in combination with other verbs to signal the tense of or add meaning to the other verbs. Two kinds of auxiliaries exist: The plain auxiliaries are *be, do,* and *have:*

I. I *am* trying to keep Lenin the cat out of the philodendron.   (be)
I *do* want a few leaves left this spring.   (do)
She *has* nibbled the edges of every one.   (have)
I *have been* politely advising her to stop this destructive habit.   (have, be)

When plain auxiliaries are used as main verbs, they have definite meanings of their own:

J. I *am* a writer.
I *have* three philodendrons.
I *do* yoga exercises every morning.

The modal auxiliaries are *can, may, might, must, should:*

K. You *can* learn yoga too.   (are able to)
You *should* practice every day.   (ought to)
I *may* teach you some exercises.   (possibly will)

Modal auxiliaries affect the meaning of the main verb when they are used as auxiliaries, but they are never used by themselves as main verbs. Short answers are exceptions: Do you have any brick cheese left? We *should.* Does Sheila intend to make dinner tonight? She *may.*

Linking verbs show the relationship between the subject of the sentence and a nominal or adjective in the predicate. They connect the subject to a word that renames or describes it.

subj. linking vb. pred. adj.
L. His *costume looked outrageous.*

subj. linking vb. pred. nom.
M. The *hat was* a watering *can* covered with blue glitter.

Common linking verbs are *appear, be, become, seem, taste, smell, feel, look,* and *sound.*

   Transitive verbs have objects which complete their meaning.

   vb. i. obj.   d. obj.
N. We *gave him* first *prize* in the costume contest.

   Intransitive verbs make sense without objects.

   intransitive vb.
O. His eyes *sparkled* with joy.

Most verbs work both ways.

   transitive
   vb.   d. obj.
P. I *ate* pistachio *cheesecake* for breakfast.

   intransitive
   vb.
Q. I *ate* unconventionally this morning.

   How It Looks. Sentence diagrams show the relationships among words in a sentence. The diagram is a visual representation of what words fill what roles in the sentence. Nouns and the verbs that describe them are diagrammed as follows (we will ignore other parts of speech for now):

   subj.   vb.
R. Charla runs.

```
   Charla  |  runs
 _____|_____
           |
```

   subj.   vb.   d. obj.
S. Charla runs a drill press.

```
   Charla  |  runs  |  press
 _____|_____|_____
           |
```

   subj.   vb. i. obj.   d. obj.
T. The company gave Charla a raise.

```
   company  |   gave   |  raise
 _____|_____|_____
            |    \
            |     \  Charla
```

subj. vlk.*   *pred. nom.*
U. Charla is a dependable worker.

| Charla | is | \\ worker |

Adjectives

Adjectives describe or limit nouns or noun substitutes. Here are two tests for identifying adjectives:

Test 1.   Can it be used between a determiner and a noun?

A. Sonia's *lazy* boss lives in a *prestigious* suburb

       ↓   ↓

      the lazy boss   *that prestigious suburb*

and drives a *flashy* Mercedes.

        ✓

      one flashy Mercedes

B. Sonia is not *envious,* because her boss is *unhappy.*

      ↓   ✓

    the envious clerk   *seven unhappy dwarves*

Test 2.   Can degrees of the word (changes in form to show comparative quality or quantity—like "good, better, best") be shown?

C. The *unhappy* boss gets no pleasure from his *big* house,

      ✓   ✓

  unhappier, unhappiest   *bigger, biggest*

his *plush* furniture, or his *selfish* children.

   ↓   ↘

  more plush, most plush   *more selfish, most selfish*

Roles Adjectives Play.   The most easily identified role of an adjective is to describe a noun or pronoun.

      adj.   *n.*   *adj.*   *n.*   *adj.*   *n.*
D. That *sensational* headline is a *perfect* example of *shoddy* journalism.

---

* *vlk.* is the abbreviation for *linking verb.*

In the sentence above, the words *that* and *a* are also adjectives. Their role is to *limit;* that is, they point out which one or how many or whose. Adjectives sometimes show degrees of comparison.

                adj.   *n.*
  E. I'll take the *cheapest* harmonica you have.

You usually think of adjectives as coming before the words they modify, but sometimes they spring up later in the sentence. A *predicate adjective* comes after a linking verb and describes the subject of the sentence:

         n.   *pred. adj.* *pred. adj.*
  F. Dan's hair is *thick* and *beautiful.*

An *objective complement* comes after an object and modifies it.

                                      obj. comp.
  G. This harmonica costs only $10, but I think I can find one *cheaper.*

    Adjective Categories.   Other than the basic descriptive adjectives, two kinds of adjectives occur often. *Determiners* limit nouns, and are usually thrown in with adjectives even though they do not always pass the adjective tests. The determiners are:

Articles:	*a, an, the*
Demonstratives:	*this, that, these, those*
Possessive adjectives:	*his, her, its, their, our, my*
Question words:	*which, what, whose*
Numbers:	*one, seven, five,* etc.
Others:	*no, whichever, whatever, all, some*

Remember that these words are determiners only when they modify nouns, not when they stand by themselves in a sentence.

    determiner
  H. *Which* child has the measles?

                          pron.
  I. The measles are contagious, *which* means all three children will get them.

    det.
  J. *That* illness should only last four or five days.

    pron.
  K. *That* is no great comfort to me.

Verbals are sometimes adjectives, too. Here is an infinitive used as an adjective:

inf.
L. I want a good book *to read.*
↘
(modifies *book*)

And present and past participles can act as adjectives:

participle
M. *Tired* of his meaningless existence, the boss
↘
modifies *boss*

part.
stared into his *swimming* pool.
↘
modifies *pool*

How It Looks.   In sentence diagrams, adjectives usually hang down on slanted lines from the nouns they modify. Predicate adjectives go on the main line of the diagram after the verb and are separated from it by a slanted line, like predicate nominatives.

adj. subj. vb. d. obj.
N. Lazy bosses make trouble.

bosses | make | trouble
Lazy

adj.   adj.   subj.   vb.
O. Many impatient employees quit.

employees | quit
Many

vlk.
adj. subj.   pred. adj.
P. My boss is lazy.

boss | is \ lazy
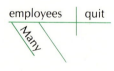
My

Adverbs

adv

Adverbs modify verbs, adjectives, other adverbs, or whole clauses. You can identify an adverb by its function in the sentence because all adverbs answer one of these questions:

How?
To what degree?
When?
Where?
Why?
True or False?

A. Dierdre had *completely* forgotten about the test.
↓
To what degree?

B. Her mind was *soon* confused as she wandered the *almost* deserted hall-
ways. ↓ ↓
When? *To what degree?*

C. When she *successfully* found the classroom, everyone inside turned
↓
How?

slowly and stared *balefully* at her.
↓ ↓
How? *How?*

D. She was *not* wearing shoes or a coat in midwinter; *consequently,* she
↓ ↓
True or false? *Why?*
looked strange.

E. As she *slowly* walked *inside,* she realized that she was *surely* dreaming.
↓ ↓ ↓
How? *Where?* *True or false?*

Roles Adverbs Play. Adverbs have so much power that if you cannot for the life of you figure out what part of speech a word in a sentence is, you are probably safest calling it an adverb. In fact, an adverb modifies any word or group other than a noun or pronoun.
Adverbs modify verbs:

adv. *vb.*
F. Leta *quickly* chased the villain.

Notice that the adverb can move to several places in the sentence and still make sense: *Quickly,* Leta chased the villain. Leta chased the villain *quickly.*

Adverbs modify adjectives.

adv.   adj.

G. The villain's mustache looked *especially* sinister.

Adverbs modify other adverbs.

vb.   adv.   adv.

H. When he saw Leta approaching, the villain retreated *very cautiously*.

Adverbs modify whole clauses.

adv.

I. *Finally,* he admitted his folly.

Adverbs modify verbals.

participle adv.

J. Sinking *slowly* to the ground, he wept.

In any of these roles, adverbs can show degree.

adv.   adv.

K. Leta forgave him *more quickly* than he expected. *Most thoughtfully,* she even provided a handkerchief.

Adverb Categories. One group of adverbs does not modify verbs—just adjectives or adverbs. This group of *intensifiers* makes the words that follow (or sometimes precede) stronger or weaker.

much more confused
very strange
no one *at all*
too deserted
quite uplifting

Adverbials are other parts of speech or word groups that fulfill the role of adverbs in sentences. Sometimes an *infinitive* is an adverbial.

L. I went to Virginia *to collect samples of American dialect.*

The infinitive answers the question *Why?*

Some sentences use *prepositional phrases* (see *Prepositions,* page 356) as adverbials.

    M. *At this point,* I feel *like giving up.*

At this point answers the question *When?* and *like giving up* answers the question *How?*

    Nouns can be adverbials when they express time, place, degree, or manner.

    N. Clyde left *Sunday.*
    O. Sylvia worked a *year* as a bartender.

    An *adverb clause* includes a noun and verb and answers questions about the main clause of the sentence.

    P. *Before Ann became a farmworker,* she was a veterinarian's assistant.

The clause answers the question *When?*

    Q. She acts *as if she likes her new job.*

The clause answers the question *How?*

    How It Looks.   Adverbs, like adjectives, hang down on slanted lines from whatever they modify.

        subj.   vb.   adv.
    R. They stared balefully.

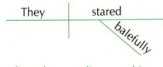

    adj. adv.   adj.   subj.   vb.   adv.
    S. The almost deserted hallways echoed eerily.

FUNCTION WORDS

The next three parts of speech—pronouns, prepositions, and conjunctions—are different from nouns, verbs, adjectives, and adverbs, and are sometimes called *function words.* This term signifies that their meaning is not as concrete and visual as the meanings of nouns, verbs, adjectives, and adverbs (*form words*). Just try to visualize—or even define—the meanings of *of* and *that* (in contrast with, say, *sinister* and *chocolate cream pie*).

Function words serve to show the relationships among the other words in a sentence. They are basically there for their grammatical function, not for their inherent lexical (vocabulary) meaning. And since the basic grammar of English sentences does not change much, new function words do not appear in the language. In contrast, new nouns are invented and added to our language all the time—monorail, leisure suit, disco, quark.

Pronouns

`pron`

A pronoun takes the place of a noun. Therefore, a pronoun is a nominal (see *Nouns*, page 341). Sometimes the group of words including nouns and pronouns is called *substantives*.

Roles Pronouns Play. Pronouns substitute for nouns when nouns would be too awkward or repetitious in a sentence. The noun that a pronoun substitutes for is its *antecedent*.

A₁. *With pronouns:*	Ann offered to lend Mark her socket set after *she* finished using *it*.
A₂. *Without pronouns:*	Ann offered to lend Mark her socket set after Ann finished using the socket set.
B₁. *With pronouns:*	*He* had fallen into a deep depression *which* got worse with every step *he* took.
B₂. *Without pronouns:*	Arthur had fallen into a deep depression. Arthur's depression got worse with every step Arthur took.

Pronoun Categories.   There are six important kinds of pronouns.

Personal pronouns substitute for the names of animate and inanimate things and indicate their number and sex: *he, she, it, I, me, you, him, her, we, us, they, them.*

C. Did *we* hear *you* say that *he* told *her* to give *it* to *them*?

Demonstrative pronouns take the place of things being pointed out: *this, these, that, those.*

D. *Those* are my favorite blue jeans.

Reflexive pronouns occur in sentences in which the doer and receiver of the action are the same: *myself, herself, himself, yourself, themselves, itself, oneself, ourselves.*

    E. Marcella caught *herself* grinding her teeth again.

Possessive pronouns refer to a belonging: *his, hers, mine, yours, ours, theirs.* (But *her, my, your,* which go before nouns, are adjectives.)

    F. *Mine* is funkier than *hers.*
    G. Your Chevy runs, but *ours* flies.

Indefinite pronouns refer to nouns that you cannot quite pin down: *anybody, someone, everyone, many, neither, no one, others, several, all, another, little.*

    H. *Others* may say I'm insane.
    I. *Everyone* agreed that we must choose, but *many* felt that the choices were too limited.

Relative pronouns refer to people and objects. When a relative pronoun is the subject of a clause, the entire clause acts like an adjective (see *Dependent Clauses,* page 365). *Who, that, which, whose, whom* are relative pronouns.

    J. The woman ⌐*who* wants to be a homemaker⌐ must have many inner resources.
    K. The kitten ⌐*that I want*⌐ is unusually friendly.

How It Looks. In a sentence diagram, a pronoun is placed where the noun it substitutes for would be.

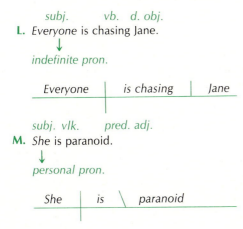

       subj.   *vb.*   *d. obj.*
  L. *Everyone* is chasing Jane.

indefinite pron.

| Everyone | is chasing | Jane |

      subj. vlk.   *pred. adj.*
  M. *She* is paranoid.

personal pron.

| She | is \ paranoid |

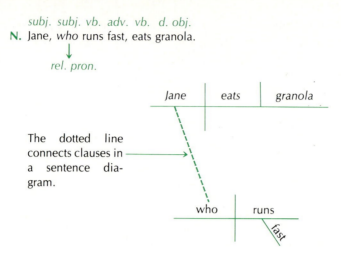

    subj. subj. vb. adv. vb. d. obj.
N. Jane, *who* runs fast, eats granola.

rel. pron.

The dotted line connects clauses in a sentence diagram.

Prepositions

Prepositions are function words that act as *connectors:* they show relationships between certain parts of a sentence.

Roles Prepositions Play.   Prepositions are followed by nominals (see *Nouns*, page 341), and these nominals are called the *objects* of the prepositions. A preposition, its object, and the object's modifiers make up a *prepositional phrase.* The preposition connects the object to another word or to the whole sentence.

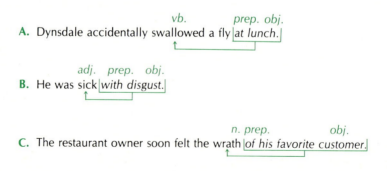

                     vb.   *prep. obj.*
A. Dynsdale accidentally swallowed a fly |at lunch.|

        adj. *prep.* *obj.*
B. He was sick |with disgust.|

                               n. prep.   *obj.*
C. The restaurant owner soon felt the wrath |of his favorite customer.|

In A, the prepositional phrase relates to a verb, and therefore acts as an adverb. In B, the prepositional phrase relates to an adjective, also acting as an adverb. In C, the prepositional phrase relates to a noun, and therefore acts as an adjective.

Prepositions most commonly show relationships of *space* (a fly *in* his potato soup), *time* (an incident *during* lunch), or *possession* (the anger *of* the customer).

Preposition Categories.   Some of the most common single-word prepositions are *about, above, across, after, against, at, before, below, between, by, down, during, except, from, in, into, like, of, off, on, outside, since, through, till, to, until, up, upon, with.*
Some prepositions are made up of more than one word, and are therefore called *compound prepositions.* Some familiar ones are: *according to, because of, except for, in back of, in front of, in spite of, instead of, out of.*

How It Looks.   In a sentence diagram, prepositions hang off whatever they modify on slanted lines. The objects go on flat lines, with modifying words hanging down.

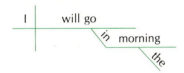

D. I will go in the morning.

Conjunctions

conj

Conjunctions, like prepositions, are *connectors.* A preposition, however, can only relate a nominal to another word in a sentence. A conjunction, on the other hand, can join many different sentence elements.

Roles Conjunctions Play.   A conjunction can link single words within a sentence.

A. I brought food *and* nails.

Or it can link phrases.

B. I figure we'll need the food *either* during our project *or* after it.

A conjunction can also connect clauses. (A *clause* is a string of words with both a noun and a verb, plus the related modifiers. See pages 364–369.)

    C. *Unless* we're done early, my husband will make us sandwiches *while* we work.

    D. Claudia likes avocado and walnut sandwiches; *however,* I would prefer avocado and sprouts.

Conjunction Categories.   Four kinds of conjunctions exist.
The **coordinating conjunctions** are *and, but, or, for, nor, yet,* and *so.* They often join two sentences.

    E. Clovis knows how to mix plaster, *but* I know how to put up drywall.

    F. He has the right tools, *and* I have plenty of patience.

We put commas before the coordinating conjunctions when they separate two sentences: He has the right tools. I have plenty of patience. Coordinating conjunctions also link pairs or groups of nouns, verbs, phrases, and dependent clauses.

                             n.   *n.*
    G. Hand me the hammer *and* nails.

              vb.   *vb.*
    H. Clovis stepped on the edge of the drywall panel *and* ruined it.

                ┌——*prep. phrase*——┐   ┌——*prep. ph.*——┐
    I. We put drywall tape between the panels *and* along the inside corners of the room.

                            ┌*dependent clause*┐ ┌——*dep. cl.*——┐
    J. Let's try to keep our minds on what we're doing *and* how we're doing it.

    Subordinating conjunctions also relate two clauses, but they make one clause *depend* on the other clause to complete its meaning.
    They define relationships of time, manner, cause, or result between the clauses. Thus, a dependent clause introduced by a subordinating conjunction is often an *adverb clause* (see *Adverbs,* page 351).

Some common subordinating conjunctions are

after	only	till
although	since	unless
as, as if	so as	until
because	so far as	when, whenever
before	so that	whereas
if	though	while

   K. *If* you want a smooth joint between pieces of drywall, you must use a six-inch taping knife.
   L. Don't try to get by with your little putty knife *because* the goop will ooze out from under it and make ugly ridges.
   M. *As* you try to smooth out one ugly ridge, the putty knife makes a bump in another place.

Notice that when the subordinating conjunction and its clause come first in the sentence, we separate the clauses with a comma (K and M). Also, notice that putting a subordinating conjunction before a clause makes it sound incomplete as a sentence by itself:

   As you try to smooth out one ugly ridge.

   If you want a smooth joint between pieces of drywall.

   Conjunctive adverbs are adverbs used as conjunctions.
   The most common ones are *however, thus, therefore, consequently, indeed, furthermore.* Conjunctive adverbs do *not* make the clauses that follow them dependent as subordinating conjunctions do.

A conjunctive adverb is often preceded by a semicolon, although a period would be fine too.

   N. He used the wrong nails to put up the drywall; *thus,* the nails popped right out when spring came.
   O. His daughter had told him to use special nails; *however,* he hated to follow her advice.

Sometimes a conjunctive adverb simply interrupts one independent clause. In such a case, do not put a semicolon before it.

   P. *Wrong:* The nails; therefore, popped out of the wall.
      Right: The nails, therefore, popped out of the wall.

   Correlative conjunctions are coordinating conjunctions that are used in pairs to relate two parallel sentence elements (two phrases, two adjectives, two nouns, and so on).

Common correlative conjunctions are *either . . . or, neither . . . nor, not only . . . but also, both . . . and.*

> **Q.** Clovis should *either* hold up the drywall *or* get out of the way.
> **R.** *Not only* does he constantly complain, *but* he *also* continually loses our tools.

How It Looks.   In diagrams, conjunctions appear on dotted lines between the sentence elements they connect.

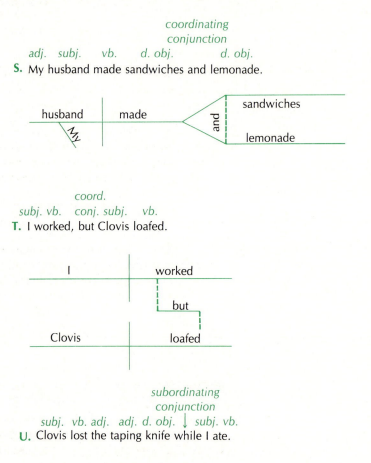

coordinating
conjunction
adj.   subj.   vb.   d. obj.   d. obj.
S. My husband made sandwiches and lemonade.

coord.
subj. vb.   conj. subj.   vb.
T. I worked, but Clovis loafed.

subordinating
conjunction
subj.   vb. adj.   adj. d. obj. ↓ subj. vb.
U. Clovis lost the taping knife while I ate.

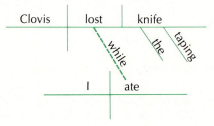

Interjections

Interjections are not strictly classifiable as either form or function words. They are grammatically independent of sentence structure. They can be sounds (*oh, ah*), profanity, or other parts of speech used to express a strong emotion (*fiddlesticks!*). Interjections attract the attention of the listener, express a general strong emotion on the speaker's part, or inject themselves into speech as a habit.

    A. *Wow,* what a great concert!
    B. *Oh,* I didn't think it was that great.
    C. *Well,* wasn't it terrific when the band smashed up all their equipment and threw it out the window?
    D. *Hey,* I think that was pretty decadent.

How It Looks.   Because interjections are not related to sentence structure, they are placed on a line separate from the rest of the sentence diagram.

       int. subj. adv. vb. adv.
  E. Hey, you finally got here!

PUTTING THE WORDS TOGETHER

Isolated words, as we have pointed out, often mean very little. What does someone mean, for example, by the word *set?* Bridge players, tennis buffs, china collectors, and math teachers no doubt have certain concepts in mind when they use the word—concepts that are superficially unrelated to each other. Only through considering the words around it and the social situation in which it's used can anyone decide with certainty what the word means.

Because words depend on context for meaning, we have already had to bring up the terms *phrase* and *clause,* even though we tried not to. We found that we could not discuss prepositions outside of prepositional phrases, and we could not write about conjunctions without mentioning the clauses they connect. Now we will look more closely at phrases and clauses and how they work.

Phrases

A phrase is a string of related words that does *not* include a subject and verb combination. As a unit, a phrase acts as a part of speech in a sentence. First we will quickly list the seven kinds of phrases and then show how they act as nouns, adjectives, and adverbs within sentences.

Kinds of Phrases

1. **Noun phrase:** a noun plus its modifiers

   the six-foot submarine sandwich

2. **Prepositional phrase:** a preposition, its object, and the object's modifiers

   with dill pickles

3. **Infinitive phrase:** a plain verb with *to* before it plus its modifiers and complements (See Figure 12-1.)

   to eat the six-foot submarine sandwich

4. **Gerund phrase:** an *-ing* word derived from a verb plus its modifiers and complements (called a gerund phrase only when used as a noun)

   eating the six-foot submarine sandwich

5. **Participial phrase:** an *-ing* or *-ed* word derived from a verb plus its modifiers and complements (called participial only when used as an adjective)

   having studied grammar
   bored with life

6. **Verb phrase:** an action or being verb plus the related auxiliary verbs

   have been
   should be willing
   will dance

7. **Absolute phrase:** a word group that modifies another part of the sentence or all of it, but is not related to it with a conjunction or relative pronoun. An absolute phrase usually consists of a nominal and a participle.

   All told, the situation is grim.
   His life ruined, Jake smiled bravely.

Subject	Verb	Complement
		d. obj.
A. Raythel	made	a cherry cheesecake.
		i. obj. *d. obj.*
B. He	fed	George a slice.
		pred. adj.
C. The cheesecake	was	creamy.
		pred. nom.
D. Raythel's cooking	was	a success.
		adv.
E. Unfortunately, I	was	here.
		Where? (*adverb of place*)

Figure 12-1 The Flattering Complement. A *complement* is the last part of a garden variety English sentence (and is included in the term *predicate*). It is an adjective, nominal, or adverb of place that completes the meaning of a verb or verbal.

Roles Phrases Play. Every phrase, short or long, acts like a single part of speech within a sentence.

1. Phrases used as nouns:

    A. The best place to spend Sunday afternoon is in bed.

In bed is a prepositional phrase acting like a noun, in this case the predicate nominative.

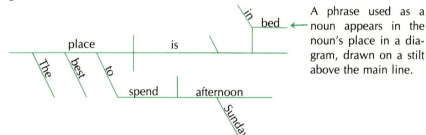

A phrase used as a noun appears in the noun's place in a diagram, drawn on a stilt above the main line.

    B. To read anything complicated is unwise.

To read anything complicated is an infinitive phrase acting as a noun, the subject of the sentence.

    C. I enjoy drowsing off in midpage.

Drowsing off in midpage is a gerund phrase used as the direct object of *enjoy*.

2. Phrases used as adjectives:

    D. Most of the newspaper is too grim to read for fun.

Of the newspaper is a prepositional phrase used as an adjective modifying *most*.

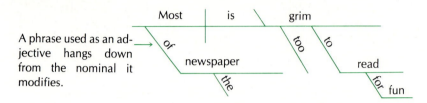

A phrase used as an adjective hangs down from the nominal it modifies.

E. The best thing to read in bed is a Sherlock Holmes story.

To read in bed is an infinitive phrase used as an adjective modifying *thing*.

F. Tired of reading, I can depend on Holmes to solve the murder without me.

Tired of reading is a participial phrase used as an adjective modifying *I*.

3. **Phrases used as adverbs:**

G. I slumber peacefully until suppertime.

Until suppertime is a prepositional phrase used as an adverb modifying the verb *slumber*.

A phrase used as an adverb hangs down from the verb, adjective, adverb, or verbal it modifies.

H. I am lucky to have Sundays free.

To have Sundays free is an infinitive phrase used as an adverb modifying the adjective *lucky*.

Clauses

cl

Clauses contain both subjects and verbs plus all their related modifiers and complements (see Figure 12–1). The two kinds of clauses are *independent* (sometimes called *main*) and *dependent* (sometimes called *subordinate*).

Independent Clauses.   Independent clauses are complete sentences. Their usual pattern is

Subject + verb

or

Subject + verb + complement
↓
d. obj.
d. obj. plus i. obj.
pred. nom.
pred. adj.
adv. of place

Here are some labeled independent clauses.

subj.   *vb.*
A. Her tires squealed.

complement
subj. vb. | d. obj.
B. Flying gravel hit the sidewalk.

comp.
subj.   vb. | i. obj.   d. obj.
C. Shana's driving gave her father the creeps.

comp.
subj. vb. | pred. nom.
D. He was her driving teacher.

comp.
subj. vb. | pred. adj.
E. He was usually terrified.

comp.
subj. vb.   adv. | adv.
F. Shana was rarely here.

Dependent Clauses.   Dependent clauses do not sound like complete sentences when they are spoken or written by themselves. They *depend* on an independent clause to complete their meaning. The word that makes all the difference is the subordinating conjunction or relative pronoun that introduces the clause. For instance, suppose a stranger walked up to you and said

> I eat blue bananas.

You would understand those words as a complete, though odd, utterance. In contrast, suppose the stranger said

> Since I eat blue bananas,

or

> That I eat blue bananas,

or

> After I eat blue bananas.

You would think this even more unusual: you would want the stranger to finish the sentence. The words *since, that,* and *after* make the clauses dependent.

Like phrases, dependent clauses act as single parts of speech within a sentence. They can function as nouns, adjectives, or adverbs.

Noun Clauses. You can tell when a dependent clause is functioning as a noun by making up another sentence in which you substitute a single noun or pronoun for the clause.

A. |*What you told me*|will remain locked in my heart.

Your *secret* will remain locked in my heart.

The italicized parts act as the subject of each sentence.

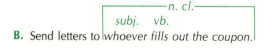

B. Send letters to|*whoever fills out the coupon.*|

Send letters to *everyone.*

The italicized parts are both objects of the preposition *to.*

Besides acting as subjects and as objects of prepositions, noun clauses can be direct objects and predicate nominatives. Here are some sentences with noun clauses diagrammed on two-legged stilts above the main line.

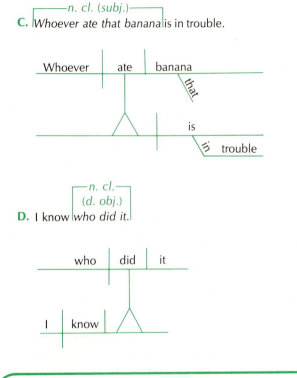

C. Whoever ate that banana is in trouble.

D. I know who did it.

EXERCISE   **12-1**

Find the noun clauses in the following sentences. Underline each one and label it *subject, direct object, predicate nominative,* or *object of the preposition.*

1. I remember what you told me.
2. Which way he turned was their major disagreement.
3. Sheila asked when she could go.
4. What you see is what you get.
5. The question about why housewives leave home was never considered.

Adjective Clauses.   An adjective clause is introduced by a relative pronoun (who, which, that, whose, whom) and usually follows the noun or pronoun it modifies. In the following diagrams, we connect the adjective clause to the rest of the sentence by drawing a dotted line between the relative pronoun and the word it relates to.

———adj. cl.———

E. The price, which was outrageous, included state tax.

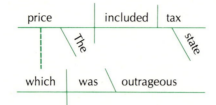

——— adj. cl.———

F. The lawyer whose donut you ate is famous.

EXERCISE   **12-2**

Identify the adjective clauses and the nouns or pronouns they modify in the following sentences.

1. She was the only student whose favorite subject was philosophy.
2. Her teachers liked having a student who was so enthusiastic.
3. These were memories that gave her pleasure.
4. She disliked Nietzsche, whom she considered depressing.
5. R. D. Laing's views were the ones that seemed realistic to her.

Adverb Clauses.   Like an adverb, an adverb clause answers the following questions: How? When? Where? Why? To what degree? True or false? It modifies a verb, an adjective, or another adverb. Here are some examples.

———adv. cl.———

G. After Clothilde ate the banana, her stomach felt funny.

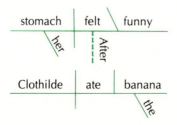

‎ ‎—*adv. cl.*—

H. The banana was blue *because it was a mutation.*

‎ ‎—*adv. cl.*—

I. It was so bright *that we carried it in a cardboard box.*

‎ ‎—*adv. cl.*—

J. Everyone was surprised *that Clothilde ate all of it.*

EXERCISE   **12-3**

Identify the adverb clauses in the following sentences.

1. If you learned grammar in seventh grade, this exercise should be easy.
2. When you study a foreign language, you will find your knowledge of English grammar useful.
3. Transformational grammar is so unfamiliar that many students are frustrated by it.
4. Transformational grammar, however, is fascinating to some people because it challenges them.
5. Grammarians are welcome at parties because they are lively and eccentric.

COMPREHENSIVE EXERCISE   **12-4**

Label parts of speech, independent and dependent clauses, and phrases.

1. Many cures for insomnia exist.
2. Drinking warm milk is a common home remedy for sleeplessness.
3. Milk contains calcium, which is a natural tranquilizer.
4. When you heat the milk, you make the calcium in it easier for your body to absorb.
5. The warm milk cure does not work for everyone.
6. Some people believe in counting sheep.
7. This boring activity quickly makes them drowsy.
8. Others claim that long nineteenth-century novels will produce sleep efficiently.
9. Alarmed at such barbarism, nineteenth-century fiction scholars are frantically trying to find alternative sedatives.
10. Their most recent work, which is now in experimental stages, involves Wordsworth's "Prelude."

chapter
Thirteen
Revising Index

We do not expect you to sit down and read this chapter straight through. But before you begin writing, it may help you to read the sections that pertain to the writing process: Unity, Coherence, Transitions, Logic, and Thesis Statement, for example. After that, use this alphabetized index to get quick advice during your revising process. For the convenience of both you and your instructor, the entries are keyed to common theme correction symbols. Table 13-1 presents a punctuation guide as a quick reference for determining correct punctuation.

Our advice covers current standard English, the language used by educated people in our society. While standard English is not necessarily any better than the language you may hear at the grocery store or in your local tavern (it may, in fact, be less vigorous and colorful), standard English is the language required of college students and in the business world.

We have also included exercises so you can get some practice on especially knotty problems. If you want to identify some of your difficulties before you begin to write papers, try the comprehensive exercise on pages 455–456. Your instructor has the answers and can direct you to entries in this index which will help you correct your mistakes.

Abbreviation

ab

1. **Abbreviate only the following terms in formal writing.**

A. **Personal titles:** Mr., Ms., Mrs., Dr.
   Abbreviate doctor only before the person's name: Dr. Dustbin—but never "The dr. removed my appendix."
   By the same token: St. Joan—*but:* "My mother has the patience of a saint."

Table 13-1 **Quick Punctuation Guide***

Between two whole sentences	Between a phrase or dependent clause and a whole sentence	In a whole sentence interrupted by a phrase or dependent clause	In a list or series
(.) usually (,) if followed by *and, but, or, nor, yet, so, for* (see p. 396) (;) if they are closely related in meaning (see p. 438) (:) if the second one restates the first (see p. 393) (;) if followed by a conjunctive adverb (like *however, thus, nevertheless*) (see p. 438)	(,) if the phrase or dependent clause comes first and is long (see p. 395) ( ) no punctuation if the whole sentence comes first followed by a phrase or clause	(○~○) no punctuation if the interrupter limits the meaning of the word before it (see p. 395) (,)~(,) if the interrupter simply adds information or detail (see p. 395) (~~~~) to play down interrupter (see p. 426) (⊖~⊖) to stress interrupter (see p. 406)	(,) between each parallel item (see p. 397) (;) between all items when one of the items already has a comma in it (see p. 440)

* A glance at this table will solve most (but not all) of your punctuation quandaries. Decide which one of the four situations (given in the column headings has you baffled and find the appropriate solution in the table.

B. **Academic degrees:** Ph.D., M.D., D.V.M., R.N.
C. **Dates or time:** 1000 B.C. or AD 150 (periods are optional here)
   10:00 a.m., 3 p.m., or 10 A.M., 3:00 P.M.
   (*but not:* "Sylvester succumbed to exhaustion in the early a.m.")
D. **Places:** Washington, D.C. or DC, the U.S. economy (*but not:* "Ringo flew to the U.S. on a jumbo jet.")
E. **Organizations:** IRS, FBI, ITT, UNICEF, YWCA.
   Many organizations are commonly known by their abbreviations (usually written in capital letters without periods). If you are not certain whether your readers will recognize the abbreviation, write the name out the first time you use it, put the initials in parentheses following it, and use the initials only thereafter.
F. **Latin expressions:** e.g. (for example); i.e. (that is); etc. (and so forth)—but do not use *etc.* if you can possibly avoid it.

2. In endnotes (or footnotes) for research papers abbreviate the following.

    A. The month (except for March, April, May, June, and July)
    B. The word *University* (Yale Univ. Press)
    C. The names of states, if cited (Boston, MA *or* Boston, Mass.)
    D. The words *page* (p.) and *pages* (pp.)
    E. The words *editor* (ed., eds.) and volume (v.)

Sample note:

[1] William T. Stafford, ed., *Melville's* Billy Budd *and the Critics* (Belmont, Calif.: Wadsworth, 1961), p. ix.

3. Avoid using symbols (%, #, &).
    In scientific papers, however, you are expected to use both numerals and symbols.
    See also *Numbers.*

4. The abbreviations for states mandated by the U.S. Postal Service are listed on p. 328.

---

adv

Active Voice   See *Passive Voice.*

adj

Adverb/Adjective Confusion

1. Adverbs usually end in *-ly*.

Adjective	Adverb
beautiful	beautifully
rapid	rapidly
mangy	mangily

Naturally there are exceptions—adjectives that end in *-ly* like *sickly, earthly, homely, ghostly, holy, lively, friendly, manly*—but these seldom cause difficulty. Also, there are adverbs that do not end in *-ly*— *now, then, later, there, near, far, very, perhaps, only*—but hardly anybody messes these up either.

2. Adverbs modify verbs, adjectives, and other adverbs.

                subj.   *vb.*   *adv.*
  A. *Standard:*   The car was vibrating badly.

                subj.   *vb.*   *adj.*
    Faulty: The car was vibrating bad.

<pre>
                    subj.   vb.   adv.   adv.
  B. Standard: The car was moving really rapidly.
                    subj.   vb.   adj.   adv.
     Faulty: The car was moving real rapidly.
                    subj. vb. adv.   adj.
  C. Standard: The car was badly damaged.
                    subj. vb. adj.   adj.
     Faulty: The car was damaged bad.
</pre>

3. Adjectives modify *nouns* or *pronouns*.

<pre>
        n. vb.   adj.   n.
  A. Fido is a frisky pup.
      pron. vb.   adj.
  B. She looks frisky.
</pre>

4. *Adjectives* also follow *linking verbs (to be, to feel, to appear, to seem, to look, to become, to smell, to sound, to taste)* and refer back to the noun or pronoun subject.

<pre>
      subj. vlk. adj.
  A. Fido feels bad.
      subj. vlk. adj.
  B. Fido smells bad.
</pre>

Notice that a verb expressing action requires an adverb in what appears to be the same construction, but the adverb here modifies the verb:

<pre>
      subj. vb.   adv.
  C. Fido eats messily.
      subj.   vb.   adv.
  D. Fido scratches frequently.
</pre>

5. Some short adverbs do not need the *-ly* ending in informal writing.

Drive slowly!   Drive slow!
Yell loudly.   Yell loud.

Now you can quit worrying about whether to say

I feel bad   or   I feel badly.

Or you can just say, "I feel wretched" and be done with it.

6. **The distinction between** *good* **and** *well.*

Good is an adjective: it can be compared (*good, better, best*). *Well* can be an adverb (as in "Kevin writes well.") or an adjective (as in "Carla is well now.") What you want to avoid, then, is using *good* as an adverb.

    A. *Wrong:* Kevin writes *good.*
         Right: Kevin writes *well.*

    B. *Wrong:* Carla's job pays *good.*
         Right: Carla's job pays *well.*

Remember, though, that the linking verbs take predicate adjectives, so you are right to say:

            linking *pred.*
      subj. *vb.* *adj.*
    C. Kevin looks good.

              linking *pred.*
        subj. *vb.* *adj.*
    D. Carla's attitude is good.

If in doubt, find a more precise expression.

    Kevin looks healthy (or happy or handsome).
    Carla's attitude is positive (or cooperative or hopeful).

EXERCISE   **13-1**

In the following sentences choose the correct form to use in writing standard English.

    1. Tony certainly dances (good, well).
    2. The candidate talked too (loud, loudly).
    3. Larry responds to requests (lazy, lazily).
    4. Onion soup tastes (yummy, yummily).
    5. Sodium nitrite reacts (dangerous, dangerously) in your stomach.
    6. Joseph had been arguing (extreme, extremely) (loud, loudly).
    7. Be (careful, carefully)!
    8. Martha appears to be (good, well).
    9. Rhinoceroses seldom move very (quick, quickly).
    10. (Rippling, ripplingly), the stream flowed through the park.

Agreement (Pronoun and Antecedent)

1. Pronouns should agree in number with their antecedents (the words they stand in for).

> **A.** Charlene shucked *her* sweater.
> **B.** Charlene and Susie shucked *their* sweaters.
> **C.** Neither Charlene nor Susie shucked *her* sweater.

Some indefinite pronouns can be singular or plural, depending on the construction.

> **D.** All of my money is gone.
> **E.** All of my pennies are spent.
> **F.** Some of this toast is burned.
> **G.** Some of these peas are tasteless.

2. The *indefinite* pronouns *sound* plural but have been decreed grammatically singular.

anybody	none	someone	neither
anyone	no one	everyone	either

Consider, for instance, the logic of these grammatically correct sentences:

> Because everyone at the rally spoke Spanish, I addressed him in that language.

> Everyone applauded, and I was glad he did.

> After everybody folded his paper, the instructor passed among him and collected it.

Robert C. Pooley points out in *The Teaching of English Usage* that grammarians since the eighteenth century have been trying to coerce writers into observing this arbitrary, often illogical, distinction. Professor Pooley, in summarizing his findings on current usage, reports:

> It may be concluded, then, that the indefinite pronouns *everyone, everybody, either, neither,* and so forth, when singular in meaning are referred to by a singular pronoun and when plural in meaning are referred to by a plural pronoun. When the gender is mixed [includes both females and males] or indeterminate [possibly includes both sexes] the plural forms *they, them, their* are frequently used as common gender singulars.[1]

---

[1] Pooley, *The Teaching of English Usage*, 2d ed. (Urbana, IL: National Council of Teachers of English, 1946, 1974), pp. 83–87.

Thus, we may now write in standard English,

    A. *Everyone* should wear *their* crash helmets.
    B. *Neither* of the puppies has *their* eyes open yet.
    C. *None* of those arrested will admit *they* were involved.

That takes care of what used to be a really troublesome problem with pronoun agreement. But you should realize that there are still plenty of people around who will look askance at this usage. Many people who learned standard English, say, twenty years ago will declare you wrong if you write *everyone* followed by *their.* If you prefer to avoid ruffling such readers, you can easily observe the old rule and consider these pronouns as always singular: *anybody, anyone, someone, everyone, none, neither, either.* Unless you are discussing a group that's entirely female, you will write

    D. *Everyone* should wear *his* crash helmet.
    E. *Neither* of the informers escaped with *his* life.
    F. *None* of those arrested will admit *he* was involved.

There remains, too, the sticky problem of what pronoun to use if your indefinite pronoun is strictly singular in meaning. This dilemma occurs frequently because we are programmed to write in the singular. Many people would write

    G. *Each* student must show *his* permit to register.

Just as effectively, you can write

    Students must show *their* permits to register.

or, try this:

    Each student must show *a* permit to register.

The meaning remains the same and you have included both sexes.
    Occasionally you may need to write a sentence in which you emphasize the singular:

    H. *Each* individual must speak *his* own mind.

But the sentence will be just as emphatic if you write it in this way:

    Each one of us must speak *our* own minds.

Try to break the singular habit and cultivate the plural. You can thus solve countless agreement problems automatically.

In the following sentences, select one or more words suitable for filling the blank in a nonsexist way. If you cannot think of such a word, revise the sentence.

1. Everyone on the plane should fasten _____ seat belts.
2. Anyone living outside of town should leave _____ job early to avoid getting _____ car stuck in a snow drift.
3. A good student does _____ homework.
4. Someone has left _____ car lights on.
5. Our dog has lost _____ collar.
6. The writer must consider _____ audience.
7. Everyone must present _____ ID at the door.
8. Anyone wishing to improve _____ tennis game should work on _____ backhand.
9. After listening to the patient's heartbeat, the doctor removed _____ stethoscope.
10. Each person must cast _____ own vote.

Agreement (Subject and Verb)

1. **Subjects and verbs should agree in *number* (singular or plural).**

   plural plural
   subj.   vb.
   A. Artichokes are a struggle to eat.

   singular singular
   subj.   vb.
   B. An artichoke is a struggle to eat.

   Note. **The *to be* verb (*am, was, were, being, been,* etc.) agrees with the subject (a noun before the verb), not the predicate nominative (a noun following the *to be* verb).**

   subj. pred. nom.
   C. My favorite fruit is peaches.

   subj.   pred. nom.
   D. Peaches are my favorite fruit.

2. **Most nouns add -*s* to form the plural.**

   snips and snails and puppydogs' tails

But with most verbs, the singular form ends in *-s* and you drop it to form the plural.

> one squirrel gnaws, several squirrels gnaw

3. **Do not let intervening modifiers confuse you.**

Sometimes a modifier gets sandwiched in between subject and verb to trip the unwary, like this:

> subj.   vb.
> A. *Wrong:*   The full <u>extent</u> of his crimes <u>have</u> now <u>been</u> <u>discovered</u>.

"Crimes have now been discovered" sounds fine, but *crimes* is *not* the subject of that sentence. The actual subject is the singular noun *extent*, with *crimes* serving as object of the preposition *of*. The sentence should read:

> subj.   vb.
> *Right:*   The full <u>extent</u> of his crimes <u>has</u> now <u>been</u> <u>discovered</u>.

Here are more correct examples of sentences with intervening modifiers.

> subj.
> B. The <u>bother</u> of packing clothes, finding motels, and searching for restaurants
> vb.
> <u>takes</u> the joy out of vacation.

> subj.   vb.
> C. <u>Pictures</u> showing nude women and men having sexual contact <u>are</u>
> shocking.

> subj.   vb.
> D. <u>Books</u> full of adventure <u>are</u> what Lucy likes.

4. **Singular subjects connected by *and* require a plural verb.**

> *1*   +   *1*   = *plural*
> A. The <u>pitcher</u> and the <u>catcher</u> <u>are</u> both great players.

But sometimes we complicate matters by connecting singular subjects with *correlative conjunctions* (*not . . . but, not only . . . but also, neither . . . nor, either . . . or*) instead of *and*. Then the verb should be singular, although the idea may still come out plural:

> B. Not only the pitcher but the catcher also is getting tired.
> C. Neither the pitcher nor the catcher is still frisky.
> D. Either the pitcher or the catcher is slowing down.

5. Compound *plural* subjects connected by *or* require a plural verb.

> Fleas or ticks are unwelcome.

6. If one subject is plural and the other singular, the verb agrees with the subject closest to it.

> A. Leather or hubcaps remind me of you.
>
> B. Hubcaps or leather reminds me of you.

> *Warning:* Some constructions appear compound but really are not. Singular subjects followed by words like *with, like, along with, as well as, no less than, including, besides* are still singular because these words are prepositions, not coordinating conjunctions. The idea in the sentence may be distinctly plural, but be advised that the subject and verb remain singular.

> C. My cat, as well as my parakeet, is lost.
>
> D. Seymour, together with his St. Bernard, his pet alligator, and his piranha fish, is moving in with us.
>
> E. Claudia, no less than Carlyle, is responsible for this outrage.

7. **Always find the grammatical subject, and make the verb agree.**
We do not always follow the usual subject-followed-by-verb sentence pattern:

> *vb.*   *subj.*   *vb.*
> A. Where have all the flowers gone?

If the sentence is longer, you may have trouble:

> B. *Wrong:* Where has all the hope, gaiety, yearning, and excitement gone?

> *Note.* The adverb *where* can never be the subject of a sentence, so you must look further. The actual subject is compound: "hope, gaiety, yearning, and excitement," which means the verb should be *plural.*

> *Right:* Where have all the hope, gaiety, yearning, and excitement gone?

We often invert subject and verb for stylistic reasons.

                                                                      vb.   *subj.*

C. *Right:*   In poverty, injustice, and discrimination <u>lies</u> the <u>cause</u> of Juan's bitterness.

                        vb.   *subj.*   *subj.*

D. *Right:*   Here <u>are</u> my friend <u>Seymour</u> and his cousin <u>Selma</u>.

Like the adverbs *here* and *where*, the word *there* often poses alluringly at the beginning of a sentence, looking for all the world like the subject. Do not be deceived. *There* can never be the subject; it is either an adverb or an *expletive* (a "filler" word that allows variety in sentence patterns). So before you automatically slide in a singular verb after *there*, find out what the subject really is.

                       vb.   *subj.*

E. *Right:*   There <u>is</u> great <u>hope</u> for peace today.

                       vb.   *subj.*

F. *Right:*   There <u>are</u> two great <u>hopes</u> for peace today.

The pronoun *it* can also be an expletive, but unlike *there*, it can be the subject of a sentence and always takes a singular verb, even when functioning as an expletive.

G. *Right:*   <u>It</u> <u>is</u> a mile to the nearest phone.

H. *Right:*   <u>It</u> <u>is</u> miles to the nearest phone.

8. Collective nouns can be singular or plural.

Some words in the language (like *group, staff, family, committee, company, jury*) can be either singular or plural, depending upon the context. To suggest that the members are functioning together as a single unit, you can write

A. The office <u>staff</u> <u>is</u> <u>working</u> on the problem.

B. The <u>jury</u> <u>has</u> <u>agreed</u> on a verdict.

Or to suggest that individual members are functioning separately within the group, you can write

C. The office <u>staff</u> <u>are</u> <u>debating</u> that proposal.

D. The <u>jury</u> <u>have</u> not yet <u>agreed</u> on a verdict.

EXERCISE 13-3

In the following sentences choose the correct word.

1. There (is/are) my cousin Ralph and his friend Rudolph, jogging in the rain.
2. Where (has/have) the toothpaste and the hairbrush gone?
3. Not only adults but children also (has/have) problems.
4. Bananas and peanut butter (make/makes) a tasty sandwich.
5. Caffein or cigarettes, in quantity, (cause/causes) damage to the body.
6. Cigarettes or caffein, in quantity, (cause/causes) damage to the body.
7. The impact of these statistics (has/have) not yet been fully analyzed.
8. Movies packed with violence (is/are) still a favorite with the public.
9. In great poetry (lie/lies) many great truths.
10. Our family (is/are) in disagreement about where to spend our vacation.

Analogy

An *analogy* **is a form of comparison, either brief or extended.**

A brief analogy will be a metaphor or simile. (See *Figures of Speech.*) An extended analogy provides a more thorough comparison and can be a means of organizing a paragraph, perhaps even a whole essay. You use something familiar to explain something unfamiliar. Geologists, for instance, often describe the structure of the earth's crust by comparing the strata to the layers of an onion. Sometimes writers use analogy in an attempt to persuade, as advocates of legalizing marijuana are likely to argue that the present laws are as ineffective and unnecessary as prohibition laws in the twenties. Although analogy is not purely logical, you can certainly use analogy persuasively—as long as your analogy is indeed persuasive.

Antecedent See *Agreement (Pronoun and Antecedent).*

Appositive See *Case of Pronouns,* number 3.

Apostrophe

apos

1. **The apostrophe signals possession** (except for the possessive pronouns, which do not need apostrophes: *ours, yours, its, theirs*).

Clarence's car
the Joneses' junk
Yeats's yearnings or Yeats' yearnings

2. An apostrophe signals that some letters (or numbers) have been left out.

we've (for *we have*)

something's (for *something has* or *something is*)

mustn't (for *must not*)

class of '75 (for *class of 1975*)

o'clock (for *of the clock*)

3. The *its/it's* confusion.

Use the apostrophe only for the contraction. *It's* = it is. If you use the apostrophe to form the possessive of *it* and write

That dumb dog chomped it's own tail.

you have really said

That dumb dog chomped it is own tail.

And your readers may wonder about you as well as the dog. Make a mental note to check every *its* and *it's* when you proofread if you tend to be careless about apostrophes.

> *Remember:* **its** = "of it"—possessive (The dog chomped its tail.)
> **it's** = "it is"—contraction (It's not an intelligent dog.)

4. Apostrophes are optional in forming the plural of numbers, titles, letters, and words used as words.

The 1970's [or 1970s] proved quieter than the 60's [or 60s].

We hired two new Ph.D.'s. [or Ph.D.s]

Seymour makes straight A's. [or As]

Those two *and's* [or *ands*] are ineffective.

You are learning the *dos* and *don'ts* of English usage.

Horace rolled three consecutive 7's [or 7s].

But no apostrophe in

Horace rolled three consecutive sevens.

13-4

Choose the correct word in the following sentences.

1. The (Cox's, Coxes) will be gone for two weeks.
2. That donkey is not known for (it's, its) docility.
3. The (begonia's, begonias) finished blooming.
4. Some lucky (dogs', dogs) houses are as warm as toast.
5. Mind your (ps and qs, p's and q's).
6. We want to be home before (its, it's) dark.
7. Steve smashed up Bill (Smiths', Smith's) car.
8. Melvin is learning the (ins and outs, in's and out's) of computer programming.
9. Marcia's children are already in their (teens, teens').
10. Harold has gone to see the (Harrises', Harris's, Harris') new house.

Article

Articles are words used to limit or identify nouns: *a, an, the*.

Auxiliary verb   See *Verbs*, page 346.

Bafflegab   See *Diction*, number 4.

Balanced Sentence

1. **A sentence that has balanced (or *parallel*) structure includes a series or pair of elements that are grammatically similar:**

A. **Series of prepositional phrases**

The juggler tosses ninepins over his head, behind his back, and under his knee.

B. **Series of three adjectives**

Ignorant, sullen, and mean-spirited, the young man did not seem to be a promising father.

C. **Pair of clauses**

She hoped that she argued the case well and that she achieved justice quickly.

2. **Make items in series parallel.**

Most of the time, similar grammatical constructions pair up naturally, but sometimes they get jumbled. You must then decide what grammatical construction you want and make the items in the series or pair fit that construction.

> A. *Jumbled:*   She never got used to the drudgery, depression, and being so ill-paid for her work at the nursing home.

That example has two nouns and a gerund phrase.

> *Improved:*   She never got used to the drudgery, depression, and low pay of her work at the nursing home.

Now all are nouns.

> B. *Jumbled:*   This new kind of therapy promises to make you happy, to improve your love life, and that it will make your hair shiny.

This one has two infinitive phrases and an adjective clause.

> *Improved:*   This new kind of therapy promises to make you happy, to improve your love life, and even to make your hair shiny.

Now all three items are infinitive phrases.

> C. *Jumbled:*   The bell was about to ring, the students closed their books, and watched the clock anxiously.

The third item is not a clause.

> *Improved:*   The bell was about to ring, the students closed their books, and everyone watched the clock anxiously.

Now all the items are independent clauses.

3. **Balance sentences for effect and emphasis.**

Practice writing parallel constructions for their beauty and impact. These qualities shine in the conclusion of a review of Dee Brown's *Bury My Heart at Wounded Knee,* a book detailing the deplorable treatment of American Indians by white Americans who desired their land. The paragraph is effective for several reasons, but mainly because of the balanced structure:

> The books I review, week upon week, report the destruction of the land or the air; they detail the perversion of justice; they reveal national stupidi-

ties. None of them—not one—has saddened me and shamed me as this book has. Because the experience of reading it has made me realize for once and all that we really don't know who we are, or where we came from, or what we have done, or why.

—Geoffrey Wolff, *Newsweek*, Feb. 1, 1971.

4. All items in a formal outline should be parallel (or balanced).

All should be complete sentences or all should be meaningful fragments (or topics).

EXERCISE   **13-5**

Put items in the following sentences into parallel constructions. Revise as much as you like.

1. The first part of the Bus Stop, a disco dance, consists of three steps backwards, a touch step, and then stepping forward three times.
2. The dancer should remember to act unruffled, self-composed, and as though the steps came naturally.
3. After the dancer repeats the first part, a sideways two-step is executed, and the dancer two-steps back into the starting position.
4. Experienced dancers say that the hops and touches in the third part of the Bus Stop are the most exciting and also hard to teach to others.
5. The final step is executing a ninety-degree kick-turn and to start the pattern over from the beginning.
6. Patti knows all about how to pack a suitcase and finding clothes that wash easily.
7. Roommates are told everything from grades to who went out with whom the night before.
8. Fred's designs are simple in pattern and bold colors.
9. Mainly poor people, retired people, and those who have lost their jobs are protesting.
10. Horace leaps to his feet, runs upstairs, grabs his tennis racquet, and then is unable to find a partner.

Brackets

[ ]

Use brackets as a signal for readers in the following cases.

1. To change verb tenses in a quotation.

Usually you can adjust your phrasing to suit a quotation, but if the quotation is past tense and you are writing in present tense (or vice versa), it is considerably easier to change the verb in the quotation than to rewrite your paper. If you want to make a past tense quotation about H. L. Mencken fit your present tense essay, do it like this:

Original in past tense:

"He defended prostitution, vivisection, Sunday sports, alcohol, and war."[2]

Changed to present tense:

"He defend[s] prostitution, vivisection, Sunday sports, alcohol, and war."[2]

2. To clarify any word in a quotation.

"In those days [the early 1940s] until the post-war repression set in, the [Communist] Party was a strange mixture of openness and secrecy."[3]

3. To enclose sic.

When you quote a passage that contains an error, you must copy the error. The word *sic* ("thus" in Latin) means, "Honest, it really was written that way."

"The correspondent, as he rowed, looked down as [sic] the two men sleeping underfoot."[4]

4. To enclose parenthetical material that is already within parentheses.

Use brackets this way only if you cannot avoid it, as in a scholarly note, like this one:

(For an informed appraisal of her relationship with the Rev. Mr. Wadsworth, see Richard B. Sewall, *The Life of Emily Dickinson* [New York: Farrar, Straus, and Giroux, 1974], II, 444–462.)

You may not have keys for brackets on your typewriter. Do *not* substitute parentheses. If you use parentheses, your readers will assume that the material appeared in the original quotation and may become either hopelessly confused or endlessly annoyed. All you need to do is skip two spaces as you type; then neatly write in the brackets later with a pen. Or you can make brackets with the slash and underscore keys, like this:

$$\underline{} \qquad \underline{}$$

---

[2] William Manchester, *H. L. Mencken: Disturber of the Peace* (New York: Collier, 1962), p. 79.
[3] Jessica Mitford, *A Fine Old Conflict* (New York: Knopf, 1977), p. 67.
[4] Stephen Crane, *The Red Badge of Courage and Selected Prose and Poetry*, ed. William M. Gibson, 3rd ed. (New York: Holt, Rinehart, and Winston, 1950), p. 285.

Capitalization

1. **Begin each sentence with a capital letter, including sentences you quote.**

> Ambrose Bierce says that "Diplomacy is the patriotic art of lying for one's country."

2. **Begin each line of poetry with a capital letter only if the poet has used capitals.**

> Candy
> Is dandy
> But liquor
> Is quicker.
>
> —Ogden Nash.

> God has a brown voice,
> as soft and full as beer.
>
> —Anne Sexton.

3. **Always capitalize the pronoun *I*.**

4. **Use caution in capitalizing words to express emphasis or personification** (Truth, Justice, Beauty), unless you are writing poetry.

5. **Capitalize proper nouns**—the names of specific persons, places, historical events and periods, organizations, races, languages, teams, and deities.

Lowercase	Capitalized
the town square	Washington Square
go to the city	go to Boston
our club secretary	the Secretary of State
travelling east	visiting the Far East
a historical document	the Monroe Doctrine
reading medieval history	studying the Middle Ages
taking Latin, chemistry, and math	Latin 100, Chemistry 60, Math 240
an industrial town	the Industrial Revolution
a political organization	Common Cause
an ethnic group	an American Indian
our favorite team	the Galveston Gophers
buttered toast	French toast
the Greek gods	Buddha, Allah, Zeus

6. Most people capitalize pronouns referring to the Christian God or Jesus.

> Our Father, Who art in heaven, hallowed be Thy name . . .
> In His name, Amen.

7. When in doubt, consult your dictionary.

If the word is capitalized in the dictionary entry, you should always capitalize it. If you find a usage label, like "often cap." or "usually cap.," use your own judgment. Occasionally a word will acquire a different meaning if capitalized:

> Abraham Lincoln was a great democrat.
> Lyndon Johnson was a life-long Democrat.
> The Pope is Catholic.
> Carla's taste is catholic (all-encompassing).

8. Capitalize the *first* and *last* words of titles; omit capitals on articles, conjunctions, and prepositions of fewer than five letters.

If you are unable to tell an article from an artichoke or a preposition from a pronoun, see our Chapter 11, "Background in Grammar."

> *Pride and Prejudice*
> *Gone with the Wind*
> *Shakespeare Without Tears*
> *Been Down So Long It Looks like Up to Me*
> *One Flew Over the Cuckoo's Nest*

9. Capitalize after colons.

Always capitalize the first word following the colon in a title.

> *Problems of Urban Renewal: A Reconsideration*

A capital letter on the first word after a colon in a sentence is optional—unless a question or quotation follows; then capitalize.

Case of Pronouns

case

1. Pronouns change form with function.

Although nouns do not change form to show case when they move from being subjects to objects, pronouns do. We can write

> A. Martha resembles my sister.
> B. My sister resembles Martha.

But with pronouns, alas, we must use a different form for subjects and objects.

    C. *She* resembles my sister. **D.** My sister resembles *her.*

The case forms are easy:

Subjective	Objective	Possessive
I	me	mine
he	him	his
she	her	hers
you	you	yours
it	it	its
we	us	ours
they	them	theirs
who	whom	whose
whoever	whomever	whosever

Most of the time the possessives give no trouble at all, except for the confusion of the possessive *its* with the contraction *it's* (see *Apostrophe*, section 2). But problems do come up like the following:

2. When the subject or object is compound, drop the noun momentarily to decide which case to use.

    A. *Faulty:*   Sylvester and *me* went to a lecture.
        Preferred: Sylvester and *I* went to a lecture.
    B. *Faulty:*   Martha sat with Sylvester and *I.*
        Preferred: Martha sat with Sylvester and *me.*

If in doubt about which pronoun to choose, drop the noun momentarily and see how the pronoun sounds alone:

    I went?   or   *me* went?

    Martha sat with *me?*   or   Martha sat with *I?*

Your ear will tell you that "me went" and "sat with I" are not standard constructions.

Remember that although prepositions are usually short words (like *in, on, at, by, for*), a few are deceptively long (like *through, beside, among, underneath, between*). Long or short, prepositions always take the objective pronoun:

    between Homer and *me*
    among Homer, Martha, and *me*
    beside Martha and *me.*

3. **When pronouns are used with appositives, drop the noun momentarily to decide.**

    A. *Faulty:*   *Us* cat lovers are slaves to our pets.
       Preferred: *We* cat lovers are slaves to our pets.
    B. *Faulty:*   Spring is a delight for *we* hedonists.
       Preferred: Spring is a delight for *us* hedonists.

Once more, if in doubt about which pronoun to choose, drop the noun and your ear will guide you: "*We* are slaves to our pets," not "*Us* are slaves to our pets"; "Spring is a delight for *us*," not "Spring is a delight for *we*."

4. **When pronouns are used in comparisons, finish the comparison in your mind.**

    Faulty: Demon rum is stronger than me.
    Preferred: Demon rum is stronger than I.

These comparisons are incomplete (or *elliptical*). If you finish the statement—at least in your mind—you will eliminate any problem. You would not be likely to write, "Demon rum is stronger than *me* am." Naturally, "stronger than *I* am" is standard English. How about "Henrietta's husband is ten years younger than her"? Younger than *her* is? No, younger than *she* is.

5. **When the choice is between *who* and *whom*, substitute *he* or *she* to decide the proper usage.**

    Colloquial usage now allows *who* in all constructions because when we begin a sentence in conversation, we scarcely know how it's going to come out.

    But in writing you can always see how your sentence comes out, so you need to know whether to use *who* or *whom*. When the choice occurs in midsentence you can fall back on substitution. Replace the prospective *who* or *whom* with *she* or *her* in the following sentence, and your ear will tell you whether to choose the subjective or objective form.

    Kate Chopin was a superb writer (who/whom) literary critics have neglected until recently.

Ask yourself

    Critics have neglected *she*?

or

    Critics have neglected *her*?

We would all choose *her*, naturally. Since *her* is objective, the sentence needs the objective *whom:*

> Kate Chopin was a superb writer whom literary critics have neglected until recently.

There is also a sneaky way to avoid the choice. If you are writing an exam and have no time to think, try using *that:*

> Kate Chopin was a superb writer *that* literary critics have neglected until recently.

Although many people still find this usage distasteful, it is now standard English. But do not ever substitute *which* for *who* or *whom*. Standard usage still does not allow *which* to refer to people.

> *Preferred:*   the woman *whom* I adore
> *Acceptable:*   the woman *that* I adore
> *Faulty:*   the woman *which* I adore

EXERCISE   13-6

Choose the correct pronoun in each sentence.

1. You can't win if you run against (she/her) and Coreen.
2. At the next meeting Sherman and (I/me) are going to present a modern morality play.
3. For too long (we/us) taxpayers have been at the mercy of Congress.
4. Monty Python's Flying Circus is the group on (whom/who/which) I base all hope for humor on television.
5. (Who/Whom) is going to deliver the keynote address?
6. You will never persuade the people (who/whom/that) you need the most to go along with your proposal.
7. The very person (who/whom/that) you are trying to help is the least likely to accept your plan.
8. If you will agree to see us tomorrow, Sedgewick and (I/me) will go home now.
9. Stanley and (I/me) are planning to become transcendentalists.
10. The public should be spared commercials (who/whom/that/which) are an insult to our intelligence.

Clause   See pages 364–369.

Cliché   See *Triteness.*

coh

Coherence

Good writing must have *coherence*—a logical relationship among the parts. In short, it must *hang together*.

1. **Organize your ideas before you begin.**
   Each point should clearly follow the one before it. Make sure that all points pertain to the idea contained in your *thesis* or main idea. (See also *Unity*.)

2. **Keep your audience in mind.**
   In order not to lose your readers when you move from one example to the next (between sentences) or from one main idea to the next (between paragraphs), you must provide *transitions*—words like *for example, for instance, namely, next, besides, finally, otherwise, but, since, thus, therefore*. (See also our lists of subordinating conjunctions and conjunctive adverbs, page 359.)

3. **Use plenty of specific, concrete examples.**
   You cannot expect your readers to read your mind. Whenever you make a *generalization* (a general statement, a main point), be sure to follow it with specific examples or precise explanations to make sure that your readers can follow your thinking.

Collective Noun   See *Agreement* (*Subject and Verb*), number 8.

Colloquial   See pages 12–13.

colon

Colon

:

For quick advice, see our handy punctuation chart (Table 13-1) at the beginning of this chapter.

1. **Use a colon to introduce lists of things: single words, phrases, or subordinate clauses.**

   A. A hawk sometimes catches small animals: chickens, rabbits, moles, and mice.
   B. "It is by the goodness of God that in our country we have those three unspeakably good things: freedom of speech, freedom of conscience, and the prudence never to practice either of them."

   —Mark Twain.

2. Use a colon to connect two independent clauses when the second enlarges on or explains the first.

    A. The students had an inspired idea: they would publish a course guide.

    B. Only later did the truth come out: Bumper had gambled away his inheritance, embezzled the company funds, and skipped town with the manager's daughter.

If the second clause poses a question, begin with a capital letter.

    The main question is this: What are we going to do about the nuclear arms race?

3. A colon should be used only after a complete sentence.

    A. My favorite animals are the following: lions, tigers, aardvarks, and hippopotamuses.

Many people, though, will stick in a colon without completing the first independent clause

    B. *Faulty:* My favorite animals are: lions, tigers, aardvarks, and hippopotamuses.

Careful writers would eliminate the colon in that sentence.

    Right: My favorite animals are lions, tigers, aardvarks, and hippopotamuses.

4. Use a colon (or a comma) to introduce a direct quotation.

    As Emerson observes: "Travel is a fool's paradise."

    Camus puts the matter strongly: "Without work all life goes rotten—but when work is soulless, life stifles and dies."

5. Use a colon to separate numerical elements.

    Time: 9:35

    Biblical chapter and verses: Revelations 3:7–16 *or*
                                          Revelations III:7–16

    Act and scene: II:2

    Act, scene, and verse: IV: iii: 23–27 *or*
                                   IV, iii, 23–27

6. **Use a colon after the salutation of business letters.**

> Dear Mr. Shuttlecock:
> Dear Credit Manager:

7. **Use a colon between the title and subtitle of a book or article.**

> *American Humor: A Study in the National Character*
> "The Money Motif: Economic Implications in *Huckleberry Finn*"

> *Note.* **When typing, leave one space after colons, except in biblical references, between hours and minutes, and between volume and page numbers in some endnote styles (5:47–49).**

Combine Sentences for Fluency

If your sentences tend to be fairly simple and monotonous in structure, combine one or two of them.
Say you are writing too many repetitive sentences like these:

> Cucumber beetles begin their life cycle as white larvae. These larvae are hatched from yellowish eggs. The eggs are deposited in the soil around the cucumber plants.

What you need to do is combine the three ideas there into a single sentence, like this:

> Cucumber beetles, which begin their life cycle as white larvae, are hatched from yellowish eggs deposited in the soil around the plants.

Or, if you want to emphasize instead the larval stage, you could combine the material this way:

> Cucumber beetles, which are hatched from yellowish eggs deposited in the soil around the plants, begin their life cycle as white larvae.

For other material about combining ideas, see *Subordination and Coordination, Emphasis,* and *Overburdened Sentences.* And for a more thorough discussion of sentence combining, see pages 71–75.

Comma

↗   *comma*

See also *Comma Splice.*

Tear here before mailing

Magazine	Term	Mag. Code	Reg. Price	USS Price
Alfred Hitchcock	9 iss.	AK	$19.50	$11.97
American Film	1 year	AF	$20.00	$12.97
Am. Photographer	8 iss.	AP	$13.27	$6.65
Analog Sci. Fiction	8 iss.	AS	$19.50	$11.97
Atlantic	12 iss.	AT	$15.00	$9.95
Audio	12 iss.	AU	$17.94	$8.97
Baseball Digest	10 iss.	BS	$9.96	$7.97
Basketball Digest	8 iss.	BK	$9.95	$6.97
Bicycling	9 iss.	BI	$14.97	$9.97
Boardroom Reports	12 iss.	BR	$24.50	$14.97
Bottom Line/Pers'l	12 iss.	BP	$19.50	$9.99
Bowling Digest	6 iss.	SD	$12.00	$9.97
Boy's Life	13 iss.	BL	$11.70	$9.96
Car Craft	1 year	CF	$12.94	$7.97
Car & Driver	1 year	CA	$14.98	$8.99
Changing Times	1 year	CH	$11.25	$8.00
Child Life (ages 7-9)	1 year	CL	$11.95	$9.97
Children's Digest	1 year	CT	$11.95	$9.97
Children's Playmate	1 year	CM	$11.95	$9.97
Christian Herald	1 year	XH	$15.97	$12.97
Columbia Jnl. Review	1 year	CJ	$16.00	$9.95
Common Cause	6 iss.	CC	$12.00	$9.97
Computers & Elect.	1 year	PE	$15.97	$12.97
Consumer's Digest●	1 year	CD	$13.97	$10.97
Cycle Guide	1 year	CG	$13.97	$6.99
Cycle World	12 iss.	CW	$13.94	$6.97
Ebony*	1 year	EN	$16.00	$12.00
Ellery Queen	9 iss.	EM	$19.50	$11.97
Essence**	1 year	ES	$10.00	$8.00
Fantasy & Sci. Fctn.	10 iss.	FF	$14.60	$11.20
Field & Stream	1 year	FS	$13.94	$7.94
Football Digest	10 iss.	FD	$12.95	$7.97
Forbes●*	1 year	FO	$40.00	$28.00
Fortune	26 iss.	FT	$39.00	$19.50
Freebies	6 iss.	FE	$15.97	$6.97
Games	1 year	GA	$15.97	$15.97
Golf	1 year	GO	$13.94	$8.97
Golf Digest	1 year	GD	$19.94	$9.97
Health	1 year	FH	$18.00	$9.00
High Fidelity	1 year	HF	$13.95	$6.98
Hockey Digest	8 iss.	HD	$9.95	$6.97
House & Garden	12 iss.	HG	$24.00	$18.00
Humpty Dumpty	1 year	HU	$11.95	$9.97
Income Op'tunities	10 iss.	IO	$7.95	$5.98
Inside Sports	10 iss.	IS	$15.00	$9.97
Instructor	9 iss.	IR	$20.00	$18.00
Jack & Jill	1 year	JJ	$11.95	$9.97
Learning	1 year	LE	$18.00	$12.96
Life	10 mos.	LI	$22.50	$22.50
Mechanix Illust.	1 year	MI	$11.94	$6.94

Magazine	Term	Mag. Code	Reg. Price	USS Price
Modern Photography	1 year	MP	$13.98	$6.99
Money Maker●	1 year	MM	$19.95	$9.98
Mother Jones	1 year	MJ	$18.00	$12.00
Motor Cyclist	1 year	MR	$11.94	$5.97
Motor Trend	12 iss.	MT	$13.94	$6.97
National Lampoon*	1 year	NL	$11.95	$6.95
New Republic*	1 year	NR	$48.00	$28.00
New Shelter	9 iss.	NS	$10.97	$9.97
New York	1 year	NK	$33.00	$19.98
1001 Home Ideas	1 year	DI	$18.00	$9.00
Omni	12 iss.	OM	$24.00	$18.00
Organic Gardening	1 year	OG	$12.97	$9.97
Outdoor Life	1 year	OT	$13.94	$7.97
Outside	1 year	OT	$16.00	$12.00
Parents	1 year	PA	$18.00	$9.00
Penthouse*	1 year	PH	$30.00	$30.00
Personal Computing	1 year	PC	$18.00	$11.97
Photographic	1 year	PH	$13.94	$6.97
Playboy*	1 year	PL	$22.00	$18.50
Popular Photography	9 iss.	PP	$8.98	$4.49
Prevention	1 year	PP	$8.98	$4.99
Radio Electronics	1 year	RA	$15.97	$12.97
Record	12 iss.	RC	$12.00	$9.00
Road & Track	1 year	RO	$17.94	$12.97
Savvy	9 iss.	SY	$9.00	$4.50
Sea Magazine	1 year	SE	$15.97	$4.97
Ski	8 iss.	SK	$11.94	$6.97
Skiing	7 iss.	SN	$9.98	$4.99
Skin Diver	1 year	SD	$9.00	$4.50
Soccer Digest	6 iss.	SD	$7.95	$4.97
Sport	1 year	SP	$12.00	$8.97
Stereo Review	1 year	ST	$9.98	$4.99
Success	1 year	SU	$14.00	$8.97
Tax Hotline	6 iss.	TH	$19.50	$9.99
Teen	12 iss.	TE	$12.95	$7.95
Tennis	1 year	TT	$13.95	$6.98
The Progressive	1 year	TP	$20.00	$15.00
Theatre Crafts	1 year	TC	$19.95	$9.99
The Runner	8 iss.	TR	$11.31	$7.80
True Story	1 year	TS	$14.95	$8.65
Turtle (ages 2-5)	1 year	TU	$11.95	$8.97
US	17 iss.	UM	$15.65	$9.97
Vanity Fair	12 iss.	VF	$12.00	$7.50
Video	1 year	VD	$15.00	$9.97
Weight Watchers	12 iss.	WW	$12.00	$7.80
Women's Sports	12 iss.	WO		
Working Woman	1 year	WN	$18.00	$15.00
World Press Review	1 year	AW	$17.95	$11.98
Writer's Digest	1 year	WD	$15.75	$11.97
Young Miss	10 iss.	YM	$14.00	$10.95

Please allow 6-8 weeks for weeklies and 8-12 weeks for others to start. Special rates are subject to publisher's change and good in U.S.A.   *Payment with order only.   ●Only for new subscription.

For quick advice, see the handy punctuation chart (Table 13-1) located at the beginning of this chapter.

1. Use commas to set off interrupters (nonessential modifiers).

A word, phrase, or clause that interrupts the normal flow of the sentence *without changing the meaning* is nonessential or *nonrestrictive*. You need a comma both *before* and *after* the interrupter.

c1

> **A.** Magnum Oil Company, our best client, cancelled their account.
> **B.** Our instructor, who usually dresses conservatively, wore jeans and a headband today.
> **C.** "Being merciful, it seems to me, is the only good idea we have received so far."
>
> —Kurt Vonnegut.

If in doubt about whether something actually interrupts or not, read the sentence aloud. If you pause, you need commas.

2. Do not use commas around essential (or *restrictive*) modifiers.

c2

> **A.** *Restrictive:* All students who can't swim must wear life jackets on the canoe outing.
> **B.** *Nonrestrictive:* Melvin, who can't swim, must wear a life jacket on the canoe outing.

Notice that "who can't swim" is essential to the meaning of the first example (it *restricts* the subject) but can easily be left out in the second without changing the basic meaning. Thus in sentence B the modifier "who can't swim" is nonessential and is set off by commas. But commas around "who can't swim" in sentence A would mislead readers. The difference in meaning between restrictive and nonrestrictive modifiers should be clear in these two sentences:

> **C.** Any students who are lazy should be flogged.
> **D.** Students, who are lazy, should be flogged.

3. Use a comma for clarity.

After any longish introductory element (like a dependent clause or a long phrase), a comma makes the sentence easier to read.

c3

> **A.** Since we've run out of lemons, we'll have to make do with limes.
> **B.** After all the trouble of sneaking into the movie, Arnold didn't like the film.

Once in a while you may write a sentence that needs a comma simply to make it easier to read, like this one:

The main thing to remember is, do not light a match.

Smoking permitted, the passengers all lit up.

Do not write unclear sentences, though, and depend upon a comma to make them intelligible. If in doubt, rewrite the sentence.

c4	**4. A comma precedes a coordinating conjunction (*and, but, or, for, nor, yet, so*) that connects two complete sentences (*independent clauses*).**

A. Myrtle splashed and swam in the pool, but Marvin only sunned himself and looked bored.

Notice, there are three coordinating conjunctions in that example, but a comma precedes only one of them. The *ands* connect compound verbs (splashed *and* swam, sunned *and* looked), not whole sentences the way the *but* does. Thus, a comma before a coordinating conjunction signals your readers that another complete sentence is coming up, not just a compound subject or object. Here are two more examples:

B. Curtis adores coconut cream pie, yet three times he has suffered ptomaine poisoning from eating it.
C. Harvey went to the library, so he may well be lost in the stacks.

c5	**5. Use a comma to separate independent clauses if they are *short* and *parallel in structure*.**

A. "We shall fight on the beaches, we shall fight on the landing grounds, we shall fight in the fields and in the streets, we shall fight in the hills; we shall never surrender."

—Sir Winston Churchill

B. "It was the best of times, it was the worst of times. . . ."

—Charles Dickens.

c6	**6. Use a comma before a phrase or clause tacked on at the end of a sentence.**

A. "The universal brotherhood of man is our most precious possession, what there is of it."

—Mark Twain.

B. I just failed another math exam, thanks to Rob's help at the local tavern.

Note. **You can use a dash instead of a comma for greater emphasis.**

C. I just failed another math exam—thanks to Rob's help at the local tavern.

7. Use a comma to separate a direct quotation from your own words introducing it—if you quote a complete sentence.

c7

A. F. L. Lucas observes, "Most style is not honest enough."

Omit the comma if you introduce the quotation with *that* or if you quote only a part of a sentence.

B. F. L. Lucas observes that "Most style is not honest enough."
C. F. L. Lucas observes that in writing we are often "not honest enough."

If your introduction interrupts the quotation (as sometimes it should, for variety), you need to set off your own words with commas as you would any other interrupter:

D. "Most style," observes F. L. Lucas, "is not honest enough."

8. Use commas to set off nouns of direct address and other purely introductory or transitional expressions.

c8

A. Direct address

Dr. Strangelove, your proposal boggles the mind.
Your proposal, Dr. Strangelove, boggles the mind.
Your proposal boggles the mind, Dr. Strangelove.

B. Introductory and transitional words

Well, anywhere you go, there you are.
Yes, we are now hopelessly lost.
My, how the child has grown.
In the first place, we must clean up the environment.
We must, however, consider one thing first.
We must first consider one thing, however.

9. Use commas to separate elements in series.

c9

A. Gertie ordered tomato juice, bacon and eggs, pancakes, and coffee with cream.

B. Some of the old moral values need to be revived: love, pity, compassion, honesty.

Note: **For variety you can omit the *and*, as we did in sentence B. In sentence A the comma before *and* is now optional.**

Another option: For emphasis, replace the commas with *ands*.

C. Some of the old moral values need to be revived: love and pity and compassion and honesty.

10. Use a comma to separate adjectives in series before a noun if you can insert *and* between them.
Suppose you want to write,

Tigers have thick short orange and black striped fur.

Can you say *thick and short?* You can. Can you say, *short and orange?* Yes. What about *orange and and?* No way. *And and black?* Surely not. *Black and striped?* Sure. *Striped and fur?* No. So you need only three commas:

Tigers have thick, short, orange and black, striped fur.

11. Use commas to separate numerals and place names and to set off names of people from titles.

A. Eudora, who was born November 15, 1950, in Denver, Colorado, moved to Dallas, Texas, before she was old enough to ski.
B. You may write to Laverne at 375 Fairview Avenue, Arlington, TX 20036.
C. My friend Laverne lives in Arlington, Texas.
D. Arthur Schlesinger, Jr. writes intelligently and persuasively.
   Or: Arthur Schlesinger, Jr., writes intelligently and persuasively.
E. The committee chose Lola Lopez, attorney-at-law, to present their case.

See also *No Punctuation Necessary* for advice about where *not* to use a comma.

EXERCISE   13-7

Try your hand at putting commas in the following sentences, if needed.

1. Your new hairstyle is stunning Selma.
2. Oh I'll finish the job all right but it won't be because you inspired me.
3. My point however must not be misunderstood.

4. In the first place Heathcliff should never have taken the job.
5. Heathcliff should never have taken the job in the first place.
6. Although Irving takes his studies seriously he still flunks math regularly.
7. I said you made a slight miscalculation not a mistake.
8. The tall willowy red-haired girl with the short squinty-eyed longhaired dog is Jocasta.
9. Before getting all excited let's find out if the money is real.
10. He intends to help you not hinder you.
11. The principal without a shred of evidence accused Leonard of inciting the riot.
12. If you go out please get me some cheese crackers pickles and a quart of ice cream.
13. "Whatever you do" begged Florence "don't tell Fred."
14. Percy had a fearful time talking his way out of that scrape yet two days later he was back in trouble again.
15. Barbara's new address is 1802 Country Club Place Los Angeles CA 90029.

Comma Splice

cf

cs

A comma splice (or *comma fault* or *comma blunder*) occurs when a comma is used to join ("splice") two independent clauses together, instead of the necessary semicolon or colon.

1. Use a semicolon or possibly a colon—*not a comma*—to separate closely related independent clauses.

These sentences are correctly punctuated:

A. Morris has been listless all day; he appears to have a cold.
B. It's tough to tell when Morris is sick: he just lies around all day anyway.
C. Tonight he skipped dinner; Morris must be sick if he misses a meal.

If you end up with comma splices, you are probably not paying attention to the structure of your sentences. You are writing complete sentences (independent clauses) without realizing it. Study the section on independent clauses in our "Background in Grammar" chapter to be sure you know what constitutes a simple sentence.

2. Conjunctive adverbs cannot connect sentences.

There's another devilish complication that can produce comma splices. Conjunctive adverbs—transitional words like *indeed, therefore, nevertheless, however*—sound for all the world like coordinating conjunctions, *but they are not.* They cannot connect two independent clauses with only a comma the way coordinating conjunctions can. The solution to this seemingly baffling difficulty is to memorize the coordinating conjunctions: *and, but, or, for, nor, yet, so.* Then all you have to do is remember that all those other words that *sound* like pure conjunctions really are not; hence you need a semicolon.

> **A.** It's tough to tell when Morris is sick; indeed, he just lies around all day like a rug.

One final word of warning: try not to confuse the conjunctive adverbs (listed on page 439) with subordinating conjunctions (listed on page 359). A subordinating conjunction at the beginning of a clause produces a *dependent,* not an independent, clause. Thus, you do not need a semicolon in the following sentence because there is only one independent clause.

> **B.** It's tough to tell when Morris is sick because he just lies around all day anyway.

If you know you have difficulty with comma splices, slip a bookmark into your text to mark the list at page 439, and another at page 359. Get into the habit of checking your punctuation when you revise.

3. Independent clauses (except short, balanced ones) must be separated by something stronger than a comma.
You have all these options:

A. Use a semicolon.

> Morris feels better today; he's outside practicing chip shots.

B. Use a period.

> Morris feels better today. He's outside practicing chip shots.

C. Use subordination to eliminate one independent clause.

> Morris apparently feels better today since he's outside practicing chip shots.

D. Use a comma plus a coordinating conjunction.

> Morris feels better today, so he's outside practicing chip shots.

E. Use a semicolon plus a conjunctive adverb.

> Morris feels better today; indeed, he's outside practicing chip shots.

EXERCISE   13-8

Correct any comma splices in the following sentences. Just to increase the challenge, we have included a couple that are already correct.

1. We just passed Clark Kent, he was changing his clothes in a telephone booth.
2. Doris says she doesn't want to live on a cannibal isle, she'd be bored.
3. Once a week I go out into the country and fill my lungs with clean air, this outing gives me a chance to remember what breathing used to be like.
4. Henrietta spent a grim half-hour shampooing Bowser to get rid of fleas, Bowser probably preferred to keep them.
5. Hunched over her typewriter, Flossie doggedly pecks out her term paper, it isn't even due until Monday.
6. Monroe complains that his history class offers little intellectual challenge, yet he never even reads the textbook.
7. This paper is due at nine o'clock in the morning, thus you'll have to go swimming without me.
8. You can't control your temper, Throckmorton, you shouldn't be teaching a Carnegie course.
9. Seymour's a polite young man, as far as I know, he never swears.
10. My opinion of Orville is not high, because he has a closed mind, I doubt that he'll be a good teacher.

Common Noun   See *Proper Noun.*

Comparison, Degrees of   See *Adjectives* and *Adverbs.*

Comparisons, Incomplete or Illogical

1. **Comparisons must involve at least two things being compared.**

A. *Incomplete:*   Calculus is the hardest course.
   Improved: Calculus is the hardest course I've ever taken.
B. *Incomplete:*   Eloise has fewer inhibitions.
   Improved: Eloise has fewer inhibitions now that she's Maybelle's roommate.

While the comparison in "improved" sentence B is still only implied, the meaning is easy to understand. But if you want to avoid all possibility of confusion, state the comparison flat out, like this:

Better: Eloise has fewer inhibitions than she did before becoming Maybelle's roommate.

2. The second element of any comparison must not be ambiguous, vague, or illogical.

> *Illogical:*   A passionate kiss is Scarlett O'Hara and Rhett Butler in *Gone with the Wind*.
>
> *Improved:*   A passionate kiss is one like Rhett Butler gives Scarlett O'Hara in *Gone with the Wind*.

3. Do not compare words that denote absolutes, like *unique, omnipotent, infinite*.

> *Illogical:*   Clovis came up with a very unique design.
>
> *Improved:*   Clovis came up with a unique design.

Complement   See page 363.

Complex Sentence   See *Sentence Types*.

Compound Sentence   See *Sentence Types*.

Compound-Complex Sentence   See *Sentence Types*.

Conciseness   See *Wordiness*.

Concrete Examples   See *Coherence*, number 3.

mng?

Confused Sentence

Take care that every sentence you write makes sense.

Be careful not to begin a sentence one way, lose track in the middle, and finish another way.

> **A.** *Confused:*   The first planned crime will tell how well a boy has learned whether or not he is caught to become a juvenile delinquent.
>
> *Improved:*   Whether or not a boy is caught in his first planned crime may determine whether he will become a juvenile delinquent.
>
> **B.** *Confused:*   When frequently opening and closing the oven door, it can cause a soufflé to fall.
>
> *Improved:*   Frequently opening and closing the oven door can cause a soufflé to fall.

Usually such sentences result from sheer, unpardonable carelessness. You should catch them when you revise. *Do not forget to proofread.*

EXERCISE 13-9

Try to straighten out the following confused sentences. Some of them are not easy to patch up. You will need to back off and begin again in a different way.

1. The second qualification for my ideal roommate would have to be easy going.
2. Prison, bringing deprivation and degradation, is many hardships.
3. By driving too fast on the freeway, it can lower your gasoline mileage.
4. A political tone is dominant through reference to economic hardship.
5. People who are continually placed in a certain category, especially a dehumanizing one, in order to achieve an appropriate self-image.
6. We often treat strangers better than how we relate to those in our own families.
7. The difficulty in achieving goals can be determined early in an individual's development of a problem personality.
8. The flooding gets really serious and will be difficult to keep emergency vehicles running.
9. Whether a person makes the choice to go to college or not has both its problems and rewards.
10. The judge ruled that the plaintiff, even though failing to appear since ill, she could not challenge the decision.

Conjunctions, Coordinating   See *Comma Splice*, number 2.

Conjunctions, Correlative   See *Agreement (Subject and Verb)*, number 4.

Conjunctions, Subordinating
See *Comma Splice*, number 2.
See *Comma*, number 3.
For a list of subordinating conjunctions, see *Fragment*, number 2.

Conjunctive Adverb
See *Comma Splice*, number 2.
For a list of conjunctive adverbs, see *Semicolon*, number 2.

Connotation and Denotation

Words are symbols that often carry two meanings:

1. **Denotative meaning**—the actual person, thing, or abstract quality referred to; the term *mother*, for instance, denotes a woman who gives birth to and cares for a child.

2. **Connotative meaning**—those feelings usually associated with the word; the term *mother* suggests to most of us warmth, love, security, comfort, apple pie.

Whether you choose to refer to the President as a *statesman* or as a *politician* may well reveal your political sympathies. Consider, for example, Frederick Lewis Allen's description of Woodrow Wilson as a "Puritan Schoolmaster . . . cool in a time of great emotions, calmly setting the lesson for the day; the moral idealist. . . , the dogmatic prophet of democracy. . . ." The word *Puritan* suggests a moralist with no human warmth. Allen could have said *high-minded* and lessened the chill factor. And what does the word *schoolmaster* suggest that the neutral word *teacher* does not? Again, a strict, no-nonsense, unsmiling disciplinarian. The word *cool* reinforces this same feeling, as does *calmly*. The term *moral idealist* sounds at first totally complimentary—but is it? We associate idealists with good intentions, but a tinge of daydreaming unpracticality clings to the word. *Dogmatic* denotes closed-mindedness. And *prophet* suggests an aura of fanaticism, since the biblical prophets were always exhorting the fun-loving Old Testament sinners to repent of their evil ways or face the wrath of Jehovah. Allen has told us perhaps more through connotation in the sentence than he did through denotation. He uses connotative words to convey a picture of Wilson that he feels is accurate—the image of a cold, determined, perhaps misguided man with the best intentions.

Without the use of emotion-laden words, writing becomes lifeless. But you must be *aware* of connotations as you choose lively words or you run the risk of producing unfortunate effects. Ignoring connotations can produce regrettable sentences, like this one:

Sandor moped around for a week before he killed himself.

The connotations of the phrase "moped around" are too frivolous for that statement (unless the writer has no sympathy whatsoever for Sandor). This sentence might be better:

Sandor was deeply depressed for a week before he killed himself.

For more advice on connotations and tone, see pages 51–52 and 15–17.

Contraction   See *Apostrophe*, number 2.

Coordinating Conjunction   See *Comma Splice*, number 2.

Coordination   See *Subordination and Coordination.*

Correlative Conjunction   See *Agreement (Subject and Verb),* number 4.

Dangling Modifier

$$\boxed{dm}$$

A *modifier* is a word, a phrase, or a clause that describes, qualifies, or in some way limits another word in the sentence.

1. Every modifier in a sentence needs a word to modify.

A. *Dangling:*   Staring in disbelief, the car jumped the curb and crashed into a telephone booth.

   Improved: While I stared in disbelief, the car jumped the curb and crashed into a telephone booth.

B. *Dangling:*   When a girl of sixteen, we courted each other.

   Improved: When I was sixteen, we courted each other.

   Improved: When she was sixteen, we courted each other.

C. *Dangling:*   When only seven years old, her father ran off with another woman.

   Improved: When Marcella was only seven years old, her father ran off with another woman.

2. Be sure introductory elements have something to modify.

Unwise use of the passive voice often causes dangling modifiers. (In the last example here, *you* is understood as the subject of both *pin* and *cut.*)

Dangling: After carefully pinning on the pattern, the material may then be cut.

Improved: After carefully pinning on the pattern, you may then cut out the material.

Improved: First pin on the pattern; then cut the material.

In order to avoid dangling modifiers, think carefully about what you are writing. You can eliminate many of your modifier problems by writing consistently in the active voice: "I made a mistake," rather than "A mistake was made."

Identify any dangling modifiers in the sentences below, and then revise to eliminate the problem.

1. After removing the reporters, the meeting resumed.
2. Driving through the lush, pine-scented forest, the air was suddenly fouled by the sulfurous belchings of a paper mill.
3. After bolting down lunch and racing madly to the station, the train left without us.
4. Looking back in history, Americans have often professed individualism while rewarding conformity.
5. The drive up there was quite scenic with its rolling hills and beautiful lakes.
6. I think love is when you get married and have children for the rest of your life.
7. Skiers like the wind blowing through their hair seeking adventure and excitement.
8. The poor child's face turned pure white and starts throwing up all over the place.
9. When writing on a formal level, dangling modifiers must be avoided.
10. After graduation, farming with a bank loan is my goal.

Dash

For quick advice, see the punctuation chart in Table 13-1.

The dash—which requires your readers to pause—is more forceful than a comma. You can use dashes to gain emphasis, as long as you use them sparingly.

1. Use a dash to add emphasis to an idea at the end of a sentence.

Emphatic: Maybelle had only one chance—and a slim one at that.
Less emphatic: Maybelle had only one chance, and a slim one at that.

2. Use dashes, instead of commas, around an interrupter to emphasize the interrupting material.

To take away emphasis from an interrupter, use parentheses.

Emphatic: My cousin Caroline—the crazy one from Kankakee—is running for the legislature.
Less emphatic: My cousin Caroline, the crazy one from Kankakee, is running for the legislature.
Not emphatic: My cousin Caroline (the crazy one from Kankakee) is running for the legislature.

3. Use dashes around an interrupter if commas appear in the interrupting material.

> All the dogs—Spot, Bowser, Fido, and even Old Blue—have gone camping with Cullen.

4. Use a dash following a series at the beginning of a sentence.

> Patience, sympathy, endurance, selflessness—these are what good mothers are made of.

If you want to be more formal, use a colon instead of the dash.

> *Note.* **Do not confuse the dash with the hyphen. On your typewriter, strike *two* hyphens to make a dash. To use a hyphen when you need a dash is a serious mistake: hyphens connect, dashes separate.**

Denotation See *Connotation.*

Determiner See page 341.

Diction

mng?

d

Diction (meaning which words we choose and how we put them together) is vitally important since it affects the clarity, accuracy, and forcefulness of everything we write and say. (See also *Connotation, Triteness, Wordiness.*)

1. Select exactly the right word.

> *Inaccurate:* I was *disgusted* because rain spoiled our picnic.
> *Accurate:* I was *disappointed* because rain spoiled our picnic.
> *Accurate:* I was *disgusted* by the mindless violence in the movie.

Use your dictionary to be sure the word you choose really means what you want it to mean. If you cannot think of the perfect word, consult your thesaurus for suggestions; then check the dictionary meaning of the term you select to be certain you have the right one. Even synonyms have different shades of meaning: you must keep thinking and looking until you find the precise word.

2. Do not—we repeat, *do not*—confuse words because they sound alike or are similar in meaning.

Wrong word: Today's society has been *pilfered* with a barrage of legalized drugs.

Improved: A barrage of legalized drugs has *proliferated* in today's society.

Wrong word: The Russians have not been sufficiently *forthcoming* about the treaty.

Improved: The Russians have not been sufficiently *forthright* about the treaty.

3. Use lively, concrete, specific terms.

Limp: We got into the car.

Improved: All four of us piled into Herman's Honda.

Limp: This dog came up, all excited.

Precise: "[A dog] came bounding among us with a loud volley of barks and leapt round us wagging its whole body, wild with glee at finding so many human beings together."

—George Orwell, "A Hanging."

See also pages 45–47.

4. Avoid bafflegab.

Bafflegab (or gobbledygook) is inflated, pretentious language that sounds impressive but obscures meaning.

Bafflegab: The production of toxic and noxious residue by hydrochloric acid obviates its efficacious application since it may prove incompatible with metallic permanence.

Translation: Don't use hydrochloric acid: it eats hell out of the pipes.

See also page 55.

5. Avoid doublespeak.

Doublespeak is language that deliberately obscures the meaning with intent to deceive:

"protection reaction strike" (meaning *bombing*)

"to terminate with extreme prejudice" (to *assassinate*)

"that statement is inoperative" (it is *untrue*)

See also page 54.

6. **Be selective with euphemisms.**
   Euphemisms obscure meaning but in a benign way:

   powder room (meaning *women's toilet*)
   unmentionables (*underwear*)
   passed away (*died*)
   sanitation engineer (*garbage collector*)

Consider your audience. If you think they would be shocked by blunt language, then use a harmless euphemism. (See also page 54.)

7. **Be careful with jargon and slang.**
   Jargon can mean the same thing as gobbledygook. But *jargon* also means the technical language used in a trade, profession, or special interest group: *printer's jargon, medical jargon, sports jargon.* If you are certain your readers will understand such specialized language, go ahead and use it. Otherwise, stick to plain English and define any technical terms that you cannot avoid.
   Slang can contribute a lively tone to *informal* writing, but you need to be sure your readers will understand current slang. Remember also that today's slang is tomorrow's cliché. Do not write vague expressions, like these:

   Maybelle is simply far out.
   Clyde's a real cool cat.
   That movie just blew me away.

If you decide to use slang, do not apologize for it by putting it in quotation marks. Use it boldly. (See also page 55.)

8. **Do not mix formal and colloquial language—unless you do so deliberately for effect.**
   You will give your readers a considerable jolt if you write a basically formal sentence and drop in a slang term:

   One anticipates that the Boston Symphony will deliver its customary *dynamite* performance.

See also pages 10–13.

EXERCISE 13-11

All of the sentences below misuse words in various ways. Point out what is wrong with each sentence and then revise it using more effective diction.

1. *The Pawnbroker* is a heavy movie.
2. Time was when the past wasn't nearly so nostalgic.
3. This disturbed sibling does not observe sociologically compatible behavioral parameters.
4. "We will continue to fight in Vietnam until the violence stops."
   —President Lyndon B. Johnson
5. The government apparently doesn't dig the potential disaster inherent in the problems of nuclear waste disposal.
6. The doctor asked to be appraised of any changes that might occur in the patient's condition, irregardless of the hour.
7. My dearly beloved Fido has departed this vale of tears.
8. We need to rethink this scenario in order to maximize resource utilization.
9. Several meanings can be implied from this poem.
10. Consumer elements are continuing to stress the fundamental necessity of a stabilization of the price structure at a lower level than exists at this point in time.

Digression   See *Unity.*

Doublespeak   See *Diction*, number 5.

Ellipsis Dots

. . .

1. **Use three dots to show that you have omitted words from a direct quotation.**

A. **Something left out at the beginning.**

About advice, Lord Chesterfield wrote ". . . those who want it the most always like it the least."
   —Letter to his son, 1748.

B. **Something left out in the middle.**

"The time has come . . . for us to examine ourselves," warns James Baldwin, "but we can only do this if we are willing to free ourselves from the myth of America and try to find out what is really happening here."
   —*Nobody Knows My Name.*

C. **Something left out at the end.**

> Thoreau declared that he received only one or two letters in his life "that were worth the postage" and observed summarily that "to a philosopher all *news,* as it is called, is gossip. . . ."
> —*Walden,* Chapter 2.

Note.   **The extra dot is the period.**

2. If you are quoting only a snatch of something—and your readers can *tell*—do not use ellipsis dots.

> Occasionally, like Eliot's Prufrock, we long to be "scuttling across the floors of silent seas."
> Cady notes that the consular service provided needy writers "a subsidized term of foreign residence."

3. Use either ellipsis dots or a dash to indicate an unfinished statement, especially in recording conversation.

> "But, I don't know whether . . . ," Bernice began.
> "How could you . . . ?" Ferdinand faltered.

Elliptical Construction   See *Case of Pronouns,* number 3.

Emphasis

Work especially hard on the beginnings and ends of things—of sentences, of paragraphs, of essays—because those are the positions which require the most emphasis.

Anytime you vary the normal pattern of your writing, you gain emphasis. Try the following variations:

1. Periodic sentences.
Save the main idea until the end (just before the period):

> One thing they assuredly do not run at Bob Jones University is a democracy.
> —Larry L. King.

See also page 62.

2. Balanced sentences.
Make all grammatical elements balance precisely:

> Wherever you go, I will go; and wherever you lodge, I will lodge; your people shall be my people, and your god my god; wherever you die, I will die, and there will I be buried.
>
> —Ruth, I:16–17.

See also pages 63–66.

3. *Ands* to separate a series.
Instead of commas, use *ands* to emphasize items in series:

> It is his privilege to help man endure by lifting his heart, by reminding him of the courage and honor and hope and pride and compassion and pity and sacrifice which have been the glory of his past.
>
> —William Faulkner.

See also pages 68–69.

4. Dashes.
Set off with dashes elements you want to emphasize.

A. At the beginning:

> Cardinals, blue jays, finches, doves—all come to frisk in the fountain.

B. In the middle:

> The trial allowed—indeed, required—a jury to pick between numerous flatly incompatible theories spun by credentialed experts.
>
> —George F. Will.

C. At the end:

> Dandy ideas these—or so it seemed at the beginning.
>
> —John Hurt Fischer.

See also pages 69–70.

5. Deliberate repetition.
Repeat key words deliberately for emphasis:

> Her working-class, middle-aged life was buffeted by an abusive husband, an abusive son, and a series of abusive supervisors at a succession of low-level jobs.
>
> —Hugh Drummond, M.D.

See also page 67.

6. **Short sentences.**

A short-short sentence following sentences of normal length will get attention:

> If there is to be a new etiquette, it ought to be based on honest mutual respect, and responsiveness to each other's needs. Regardless of sex.
>
> —Lois Gould.

See also pages 67–68.

7. **A one-sentence paragraph.**

Punctuate a single sentence as a paragraph to make it extremely emphatic. (See pages 109–110.)

Euphemism See *Diction*, number 6.

Exclamation Point

!

1. **Do not use exclamation points merely to give punch to ordinary sentences. Write a good, emphatic sentence instead.**

> *Ineffective:* LeRoy's room was a terrible mess!
> *Improved:* We declared LeRoy's room a disaster area.

2. **Use exclamation points following genuine exclamations:**

> O kind missionary, O compassionate missionary, leave China! Come home and convert these Christians!
>
> —Mark Twain, "The United States of Lyncherdom."

> I'm mad as hell, and I'm not going to take it anymore!
>
> —Paddy Chayefsky, *Network*.

> *Note.* **Never stack up punctuation. Do not put a comma after an exclamation point or after a question mark.**

See also *Quotation Marks*, number 8.

Expletive

1. **An *expletive* can be an oath or exclamation, often profane.**

You will have no trouble thinking of the four-letter ones, so we will mention some socially acceptable ones: Thunderation! Tarnation! Drat! Oh, fudge! Use only when reproducing conversation.

2. **The words** *it* **and** *there,* **also expletives, serve as "filler" words to allow for variety in sentence patterns.**

> *It* is raining.
> *There* are two ways to solve the problem.

See also *Agreement* (*Subject and Verb*), number 7.

Figures of Speech

Figures of speech involve the imaginative use of language and can give your writing greater vividness and clarity, if used effectively.

1. Metaphors and similes.

These devices are imaginative comparisons characteristic of poetry but used frequently in prose.

> **A.** *A metaphor* is an *implied* comparison.
> Clarence was a lion in the fight.
> **B.** *A simile* is a *stated* comparison (with *like* or *as*).
> Clarence was like a lion in the fight.

The term *metaphor* now serves to describe both figures of speech. Here are some examples used in prose by professional writers:

> New York is a sucked orange.
>
> —R. W. Emerson.

> Like soft, watery lightning went the wandering snake at the crowd.
>
> —D. H. Lawrence.

> His voice was as intimate as the rustle of sheets.
>
> —Dorothy Parker.

> The [courtroom] was as dismal and breathless as a tenement fire escape in August.
>
> —Katherine Anne Porter.

See also *Analogy.*

2. Extended metaphors.

Skillful writers sometimes write imaginative comparisons that go on for several sentences, perhaps for a full paragraph, like this one describing the trials of editing bad prose:

And so, anticipating no literary treat, I plunged into the forest of words of my first manuscript. My weapons were a sturdy eraser and several batteries of sharpened pencils. My armor was a thesaurus. And if I should become lost, a near-by public library was a landmark, and the Encyclopedia of Social Sciences on its reference shelves was an ever-ready guide.

—Samuel T. Williamson.

3. Mixed metaphors.

Be careful of metaphors that do not compare accurately—that start off one way and end another way:

A. Our quarterback plowed through their defense and skyrocketed across the goal lines.
B. The FTC does nothing but sit on its hands and fiddle while Rome burns.

Remember: Figures of speech should clarify the meaning through comparisons that increase understanding. Ambiguity fascinates the mind in poetry but tries the patience in expository prose. So, be creative; but when you revise, be sure that your metaphors clarify rather than confuse.

4. Personification.

Personification means giving human characteristics to nonhuman things (objects or animals). Use with restraint.

The missiles lurk in their silos, grimly waiting for the inevitable day when at last they will perform their duty.

5. Avoid *trite* figures of speech. See *Triteness.*

Formal Usage See the discussion of levels of usage in Chapter 14, the "Glossary of Usage" (page 457).

Fragment

frag

1. A sentence fragment is only part of a sentence punctuated as a whole.

Many professional writers use fragments for emphasis, or simply for convenience, as in the portions we have italicized in the following examples:

Man is the only animal that blushes. *Or needs to.*

—Mark Twain.

I did not whisper excitedly about my Boyfriends. *For the best of reasons.* I did not have any.

—Gwendolyn Brooks.

This leaves me with only the dog and the wood duck and my own short-sighted blundering into other people's apartments and tulip beds, to deal with. *Which is just as well.*

—James Thurber.

Easy to say, but hard to practice.

—F. L. Lucas.

We shall no doubt learn of a suitor for [Chrysler's] hand in a take-over move. *Maybe Volkswagen, even though such a deal has been denied. Maybe one of a half-dozen cash-laden oil companies.*

—Paul Samuelson.

So Shelly asked her what was "real" and the student responded instantly, "Television." *Because you could see it.*

—Harlan Ellison.

2. Avoid fragments in formal writing (term papers, business reports, scholarly essays).

Fragment: Pollution poses a serious problem. *Which we had better solve.*
Complete: Pollution poses a serious problem—which we had better solve.
Complete: Pollution poses a serious problem, which we had better solve.

Note.   **If you write fragments accidentally, remember that a simple sentence beginning with one of the following subordinating words will come out a fragment:**

after	since	unless
although	so as	until
as, as if	as far as	when
because	so that	whenever
before	still	whereas
if	though	which
only	till	while

Fragment: Although I warned him time after time.
Complete: I warned him time after time.
Complete: Although I warned him time after time, Clyde continued to curse and swear.

Note. **Words ending in *-ing* and *-ed* can cause fragments also. Although such words sound like verbs, sometimes they're *verbals*—actually nouns or adjectives. Every complete sentence requires an honest-to-goodness verb.**

Fragment:	Singing and skipping along the beach.
Complete:	Juan went singing and skipping along the beach.
Fragment:	Abandoned by friends and family alike.
Complete:	Alice was abandoned by friends and family alike.
Complete:	Abandoned by friends and family alike, Alice at last recognized the evils of alcohol.

3. Use fragments in asking and answering questions, even in formal writing:

When should the reform begin? At once.

How? By throwing self-serving politicians out of office.

4. Use fragments for recording conversation, since people do not always speak in complete sentences:

"I suppose that during all [my sickly childhood] you were uneasy about me?"

   "Yes, the whole time."

   "Afraid I wouldn't live?"

   After a reflective pause, ostensibly to think out the facts, "No—afraid you would."

—Mark Twain, *Autobiography.*

5. Be sure that two constructions connected with a semicolon are complete sentences.

Questionable:	He looked a lot like Quasimodo; although I couldn't see him too well.
Improved:	He looked a lot like Quasimodo, although I couldn't see him too well.
Improved:	He looked a lot like Quasimodo; I couldn't see him too well, though.

EXERCISE 13-12

Some of the following constructions are not complete sentences. Correct the ones that you consider faulty. Defend the ones that you find effective.

1. Marion was late to his own wedding. To his eternal sorrow.
2. Broadcasting moment-by-moment, hour-by-hour, day-by-day reports.

3. What is the best policy? To do nothing— diplomatically.
4. Wealth, a taking advantage of another's resources by materialistic means.
5. A slow taking over, a slow control of the economy leading eventually into a usurpation of political principles.
6. The executive, who at the end of the day, can return to the comforts of home.
7. As an explorer with an intellectual curiosity, the scientific undoer of a riddle by empirical means.
8. One in which she was dictator, and because she was dictator, she held the reins.
9. A society's ignorance of a condition of human wants and needs.
10. Our highways, bridges, and water systems must be repaired. Regardless of the cost.

Function Words   See pages 353–360.

Fused Sentence   See *Run-on Sentence.*

Generalizations   See *Coherence,* number 3.

Hyphen   *div*

Unlike exclamation points, hyphens are much in fashion today as a stylistic device.

1. Hyphenate clichés to revitalize them.

Emily Dickinson challenges the time-heals-all-wounds adage.

2. Hyphenate descriptive phrases used as a whole to modify a noun.

George needs to get rid of his holier-than-thou attitude.

3. Hyphenate compound adjectives when they come before the noun.

child-care centers   heavy-hearted losers
high-speed railroads   lighter-than-air balloon

4. Omit the hyphen if the descriptive phrase comes after the noun.

centers for child care   losers who were heavy hearted
railroads running at high speed   a balloon lighter than air

5. **Hyphenate most compound words beginning with *self-* and *ex-*.**

self-employed	ex-wife
self-deluded	ex-slave
self-abuse	ex-President

6. **Never use a hyphen in the following words.**

yourself	himself	itself
themselves	herself	selfless
ourselves	myself	selfish
oneself (or one's self)		

7. **Consult your dictionary about other compound words.**
   Some words change function depending on whether written as one word or two:

Verb: Where did I *slip up?*
Noun: I made a *slipup* somewhere.

8. **Use a hyphen to divide words at the end of a line.**
   Divide only between syllables. Consult your dictionary if in doubt. Never put a hyphen at the beginning of a line.

Infinitive   See *Split Infinitive* and also page 345.

Informal Usage   See the discussion of *Levels of Usage* on page 12.

Interjection   See *Exclamation Point* and also page 361.

Intransitive Verb   See page 347.

Irregular Verb   See *Tense*, number 4.

Italics   See *Underlining.*

Jargon   See *Diction*, number 7.

Levels of Usage   See pages 10–13.

Linking Verb

Linking verbs connect the subject of the sentence with the comple-ment.

vlk

The most common linking (or copulative, as they used to be bluntly called) verbs are these: *to be, to feel, to appear, to seem, to look, to become, to smell, to sound, to taste.* See also *Adverb/Adjective Confusion,* number 4.

Logic

logic

Your purpose in writing is to convey your thoughts into the heads of your readers, but in order to be convincing, your thoughts must be logical. You should be aware of the most common pitfalls of slippery logic so that you can avoid them in your own thinking and writing, as well as detect them in the arguments of others.

1. Avoid oversimplifying.

Most of us have a tendency to like things reduced to orderly, easily grasped *either-or* answers. The only problem is that things are seldom that simple. Be wary of arguments that offer no middle way— the "either we continue to build nuclear weapons or the Russians will wipe us out" sort of reasoning.

2. Avoid stereotyping.

Stereotypes involve set notions about the way different types of people behave. Homosexuals, according to the stereotype, are all neurotic, promiscuous, immoral people bent only on sex and seduction. Such stereotypes seldom give a truthful picture of anyone in the group and could never be accurate to describe all the members.

3. Avoid faulty (sweeping or hasty) generalizations.

You will do well to question easy solutions to complex problems. A faulty generalization (broad statement) can result from stating opinion as fact:

> Rock music causes grave social problems by creating an attitude of irresponsibility in the listener.

The statement needs evidence to prove its claim, and such proof would be nearly impossible to find. Since you cannot avoid making general statements, be careful to avoid making them without sufficient evidence. At least, *qualify* your assertions.

> *Sweeping:*   *All* Siamese cats are nervous.
> *Better:*   *Many* Siamese cats are nervous.

Statements involving *all, none, everything, nobody,* and *always* are tough to prove. Instead, try *some, many, sometimes,* and *often.*

4. **Watch for hidden premises.**

Another sort of generalization that is likely to deceive involves a *hidden premise* (a basic idea underlying the main statement). This observation, upon first reading, may sound entirely plausible:

> If those anti-nuke demonstrators had left when the police told them to, there would have been no trouble, and no one would have been injured.

The hidden premise here assumes that all laws are just and fairly administered; that all actions of the government are honorable and in the best interest of all citizens. The statement presumes, in short, that the demonstrators had no right or reason to be there and hence were wrong not to leave when told to do so. Such a presumption overlooks the possibility that in a free country the demonstrators might legitimately protest the right of the police to silence their original protests.

5. **Do not dodge the issue.**

People use a number of handy fallacies in order to sidestep a problem while appearing to pursue the point. One of the most effective—and most underhanded—involves playing on the emotional reactions, prejudices, fears, and ignorance of your readers instead of directly addressing the issue.

> If we allow sex education in the public schools, the moral fiber of the nation will be endangered, human beings will become like animals, and the Communists will just walk right in and take over.

That sentence, which contains no evidence whatever to prove that sex education is either good or bad, merely attempts to make it sound scary.

In a variation of this technique (called *ad hominem*), people sometimes attack the person they are arguing with, rather than the issue being argued. They call their opponents "effete, effeminate snobs" and hope nobody notices that they have not actually said anything to the point.

Another favorite dodge is called *begging the question* or *circular argument*. You offer as evidence arguments which assume as true the very thing you are trying to prove. You say that pornography is evil because pornography is evil, but you have to say it fancy, like this:

> If we want a society of people who devote their time to base and sensuous things, then pornography may be harmless. But if we want a society in which the noble side is encouraged and mankind itself is elevated, then I submit that pornography is surely harmful.

—John Mitchell

6. Keep an open mind.

Thinking is your best defense against logical fallacies. Think while you are reading or listening and think some more before you write. Be prepared to change your mind. Instead of hunting for facts to shore up your present opinions, let the facts you gather lead you to a conclusion. And do not insist on a nice, tidy, clear-cut conclusion. Sometimes there isn't one. Your conclusion may well be that both sides for various reasons have a point. Simply work to discover what you honestly believe to be the truth of the matter, and set that down, as clearly and convincingly as you can.

See also *Analogy, Coherence, Connotation and Denotation,* and *Unity.*

Misplaced Modifier

mm

Keep modifiers close to what they modify (describe, limit or qualify).

Faulty:	Once married, the church considers that a couple has signed up for a lifetime contract.
Improved:	The church considers that a couple, once married, has signed up for a lifetime contract.
Faulty:	I had been driving for forty years when I fell asleep at the wheel and had an accident.
Improved:	Although I had driven safely for forty years, last night I fell asleep at the wheel and had an accident.

EXERCISE   13-13

In the following sentences move any misplaced modifiers so that the statements make better sense.

1. Also soft and cuddly, the main appeal of a kitten is its playfulness.
2. Registration assignments will not be accepted from students until the door attendant has punched them.
3. Although similar in detail, my purpose is to show how these two sea urchins differ.
4. Clem was robbed at gunpoint in the elevator where he lives.
5. At college I hope to start singing with a scholarship.
6. A crutch is a device to take the weight off an injured leg or foot by sticking it under the arm and leaning on it.
7. When I got there, I saw two men putting on ghost costumes just like the ones that robbed my house.
8. I found a marble that looked like candy walking home from church.
9. I do not see my Aunt Frieda much in Colorado.
10. Maribelle told her first falsehood in a panic by telephone.

Modifiers
>See *Dangling Modifiers.*
>See *Misplaced Modifiers.*
>See *Squinting Modifiers.*

Mood   See *Verbs,* page 345, and *Subjunctive Mood.*

Nominal   See *Nouns,* page 341.

Nonrestrictive Clause   See *Comma,* number 2.

No Punctuation Necessary

no punc

William Blake wrote that "The road of excess leads to the palace of wisdom," but all of us English teachers are sure that he was not referring to commas. If you are a comma fiend, you may be the victim of the ill-conceived and misleading rule that says commas belong wherever you would pause in speaking. That rule simply does not work: we pause far too often in speech, and different speakers pause in different places. Here are some situations that seem particularly tempting to comma abusers.

1. **When main sentence parts are long.**
   Some writers mistakenly separate the subject from the verb or the verb from the complement, like this:

   A. *Wrong:*   Tall people with large feet, are particularly good autoharp players.
   B. *Wrong:*   By the end of the year we all understood, that using too many commas would make us grow hair on our palms.

Neither of those sentences should have a comma in it. In sentence B, the clause is restrictive (see *Comma,* number 2), and thus should not be set off with a comma.

2. **When a restrictive clause occurs in the sentence.**
   Putting a comma on one end of an adjective clause and no punctuation at all on the other end is never correct. Nonrestrictive clauses always need punctuation on both ends (see *Comma,* section 2), and restrictive ones need no punctuation. Avoid errors like this one:

   Wrong: Ruthie's poem that compared a school to a prison, was the most moving one she read.

No comma is necessary in that sentence.

3. **When the word *and* appears in the sentence.**

Some people always put a comma before the word *and,* and they are probably right more than half the time. It's correct to put a comma before *and* when it joins a series or when it joins independent clauses. But when *and* does not do either of those things, a comma before it is usually inappropriate. This sentence, for instance, should have no comma:

> *Wrong:* Mark called the telephone company to complain about his bill, and got put on "hold" for an hour.

Noun See page 341.

Numbers

1. **Spell out numbers one hundred and under.**

2. **In general, write numbers over one hundred in figures.**

3. **Spell out round numbers requiring only a couple of words (two hundred tons, five thousand dollars).**

If a series of numbers occurs in a passage, and some of them are over one hundred, use figures for all of them.

4. **Always use figures for addresses (27 White's Place), for times 1:05 P.M.), for dates (October 12, 1950), and for decimals, code and serial numbers, percentages, measurements, and source references.**

> *Exception:* **Never begin a sentence with a numeral; spell it out or rewrite the sentence.**

Object See *Prepositions,* page 356, *Complement,* page 342, and Figure 12-1.

Overburdened Sentence

Do not try to cram more into one sentence than it can conveniently hold.

> The plot concerns a small boy, somewhat neglected by his mother, a recently divorced working woman who is evidently having a difficult time keeping her family, her emotions, and her household together, who discovers by mysterious means and befriends a small adorable extraterrestrial creature.

That's just too much. It should be divided into two more graceful sentences.

> Two of the story's characters are a small boy and his somewhat negligent mother, a recently divorced working woman who is evidently having a difficult time keeping her family, her emotions, and her household together. By mysterious means, the boy discovers and befriends a small adorable extraterrestrial creature.

Paragraph

¶

The proofreader's mark ¶ means that your instructor thinks you should indent to begin a new paragraph at that point. When all your sentences are closely related, sometimes you forget to give your readers a break by dividing paragraphs.

Remember to indent when you shift topics or shift aspects of a topic. For instance, look at the break between the preceding paragraph and this one. Both of these paragraphs are on the same subject (paragraphing), but the topic shifts from *why* to begin a new paragraph to *when* to begin a new paragraph. Because of this shift, we indented.

When you notice that you have written a paragraph over eight sentences long, it's time to look for places to break it into two separate paragraphs.

Parallel Structure See *Balanced Sentences*, page 383.

paral

Parentheses

( )

For quick advice, see the punctuation chart in Table 13-1 at the beginning of this chapter.

1. Use parentheses around parts of a sentence or paragraph that you would speak aloud as an aside.

A slight digression or some incidental information that you do not particularly want to emphasize belongs in parentheses. The downplaying function of parentheses may be straightforward:

> **A.** John Stuart Mill (1806–1873) promoted the idea of woman's equality with men.

or tongue-in-cheek:

> **B.** He insisted on ordering another tequila sunrise (he'd only had five so far), although we warned him that we would not carry him out of the bar later.

2. **Sometimes you will choose parentheses to separate a part of a sentence that could be enclosed in commas.**

Commas separate material that is directly relevant to the main passage, and parentheses separate material that is indirectly related or less crucial. When you use dashes around a part of a sentence, they strongly stress that part, as neither commas nor parentheses do.

3. **Use parentheses around numerals when you number a list.**

> Her professor did three things that bothered her: (1) he called her "honey," even though he didn't know her; (2) he graded the class on a curve, even though there were only ten students; (3) he complained that male students no longer wore suitcoats and ties to class.

4. **Punctuation goes inside the parentheses if it punctuates just the words inside.**

> Consumers can use their power by boycotting a product. (The word *boycott* is from Captain Charles C. Boycott, whose neighbors in Ireland ostracized him in 1880 for refusing to reduce the high rents he charged.)

5. **Punctuation goes outside the parentheses if it punctuates more than just the enclosed material.**

The comma does this in example 1B above. A numbered list, like that in number 3, is the *only* case in which you may put a comma, semicolon, colon, or dash before an opening parenthesis.

EXERCISE 13-14

Choose the best punctuation (parentheses, dashes, commas, or brackets) to put in place of the carats in the sentence below. Remember, dashes *stress*, parentheses *play down*, and commas *separate* for clarity.

1. The 1960 *World Book* encyclopedia claims that smoking marijuana ˄ *cannabis sativa* ˄ causes fits of violence.
2. I tasted his omelette and found ˄ how disgusting! ˄ that it was runny inside.
3. Stewart Alsop ˄ who my mother claims as a distant relation of ours ˄ was a well-known conservative journalist.
4. People often mistakenly think that Lenin ˄ our black and white cat ˄ was named after John Lennon of the Beatles.
5. Bateson includes in his reading list the "elongated biographical pieties ˄ about Carlyle ˄ of D. A. Wilson." (Bateson is reviewing D. A. Wilson's book, and you added the phrase "about Carlyle" to Bateson's words.)
6. Maria ran the entire obstacle course in record time ˄ three minutes!
7. Hubert ˄ the coordinator of our newsletter ˄ says he will crack up unless we get more typists.

8. If you are going to get married ˏ and most people eventually do ˏ you must not develop rigid daily habits.
9. Edgar Allen Poe ˏ 1809–1849 ˏ believed that beauty was the goal of poetry.
10. He thought ˏ in fact, he knew ˏ that if he continued his life of crime he would one day find himself at the bottom of the river.

Participle

See *Verbs,* page 343.
See *Adjectives,* page 348.
See *Tense.*

Participle Endings

Do not omit the *-ed* from the ends of participles.
An adjective formed from a verb is called a participle. Examples are

a tired writer (from *tire*)
an embarrassing moment (from *embarrass*)
a delayed reaction (from *delay*)

Many of the participles ending in *-ed* are said aloud without the *-ed* sound; thus, sometimes you forget to put the ending on in writing. Some examples of this error we have seen are

old fashion ice cream
air condition theater
vine ripen tomatoes
prejudice attitudes

Those phrases should read:

old-fashioned ice cream
air-conditioned theater
vine-ripened tomatoes
prejudiced attitudes

Passive Voice

pass

Passive voice contrasts with active voice as you can see in the following examples:

A. *Active:* My daughter solved the problem.
B. *Passive:* The problem was solved by my daughter.
C. *Passive:* The problem was solved.

In active voice, the agent of the action (the person who does the solving, in this case) is also the subject of the sentence. In passive voice, the agent of the action is not the subject of the sentence. In both example B and example C, even though the daughter did the solving, *problem* is the subject of the sentence, and in example C, the daughter is left out altogether and gets no credit for her ingenuity.

For further discussion—and an exercise—see pages 80–82 in Chapter 3.

Period

Use a period at the end of a complete declarative sentence and after most abbreviations (see *Abbreviations*).

If a sentence ends with an abbreviation, let its period serve as the final period of the sentence, too: do not double up.

Personification   See *Figures of Speech.*

Phrase

A phrase is a string of words that does not include a subject and verb combination. See *Phrases,* page 362.

Point of View   See *Shifts in Tense and Person.*

Possessives
See *Apostrophe.*
See *Case of Pronouns.*

Possessives with Gerunds

1. **A gerund is a verb with an *-ing* on it that acts like a noun in a sentence.**

A. Squishing cake between your toes is a sensual pleasure.

Squishing is the subject of the sentence, and thus acts like a noun.

B. He got back at the telephone company by folding his computer billing card each month.

Folding is the object of a preposition, and thus acts like a noun.

2. Use possessive nouns and pronouns before gerunds because gerunds act as nouns.

You probably would not forget to use a possessive before a regular noun in a sentence like this:

A. I was embarrassed by John's insensitivity.

But you may forget to use the possessive before a gerund. The preferred usage is as follows:

B. I was embarrassed by John's popping out his glass eye to attract the waitress's attention.

Not "*John* popping out his glass eye."

C. I disapproved of his acting so indelicately.

Not "*him* acting so indelicately."

If you have other problems with possessives, see *Apostrophe*.

Predicate

The predicate of a sentence is the verb plus the complement (if there is one).

Predicate Adjective   See *Adjectives*, page 348.

Predicate Nominative

A predicate nominative is a noun or a nominal that follows the *to be* verb and renames the subject of the sentence.

Predication, Faulty

faulty pred

1. This error comes from not rereading your sentences closely enough. A sentence with faulty predication is one whose predicate

adjective or predicate noun does not match the subject in meaning.

   A. *Faulty:* Your first big city is an event that changes your whole outlook if you grew up in a small town.
   B. *Faulty:* The importance of graceful hip movement is essential when doing the Bump.
   C. *Faulty:* Smoothness and precision are among the basic problems encountered by beginning dancers.

In sentence A, a city is not really an event; in B, the writer probably did not want to say something as banal as "importance is essential"; and in C, smoothness and precision are not problems.

To correct such errors, you can revise the subject, the predicate, or both to make them match up better. Here are possible revisions of our problem sentences:

   A. *Improved:* Your first visit to a big city is an experience that changes your whole outlook if you grew up in a small town.
   B. *Improved:* Graceful hip movement is essential when doing the Bump.
   C. *Improved:* Roughness and imprecision are among the weaknesses of beginning dancers.

2. Your predication can be merely weak instead of utterly illogical. Important words should appear as the subject and predicate.

   A. *Weak:* One important point of his speech was the part in which he stressed self-reliance.

In A, the key subject and predicate words are *point . . . was . . . part,* which do not carry much meaning in the sentence. Here's an improvement:

   A. *Improved:* At one important point, his speech emphasized self-reliance.

Now the key subject and predicate words are *speech . . . emphasized . . . self-reliance,* which are more meaningful.

Preposition See page 356.

Pronoun
    See page 354.
    See *Agreement (Pronoun and Antecedent).*
    See *Case of Pronouns.*
    See *Reference of Pronouns.*

Proper Noun

A common noun names a class (like *dog, city*); a proper noun names a specific person, place, or thing (like *Rover, Chicago*).

Qualification   See *Logic*, number 3.

Quotation Marks

quot

Quotation marks are among the most confusing marks of punctuation, perhaps because they serve so many different functions. We hope to clear up any confusion in your mind by first showing you the uses of quotation marks and then showing how to use other punctuation in combination with them. Here are the uses:

1. Put quotation marks around words that you copy just as they were written or spoken, whether they are complete or partial sentences.

    A. "Gloria, please don't practice your quacky duck imitation while I'm trying to do my income tax," she said.

    B. She said that Gloria's barnyard imitation made her "feel like moving to New York for some peace and quiet."

2. A quotation within a quotation should have single quotation marks around it.

    I remarked, "I've disliked him ever since he said I was 'a typical product of the Midwest,' whatever that means."

Do not panic if you read a book or article that reverses double and single quotation marks (that is, uses single around quotations and double around quotations within quotations). The British do it the opposite of the American way, so that book or article is probably British.

3. If you paraphrase (i.e., change words from the way they were written or spoken), you are using indirect quotation and you need not use quotation marks.

    A. She said that Gloria's pig grunt was particularly disgusting.

Her actual words were, "Gloria's pig grunt is the worst of all."

    B. He told me that he loathed levity.

He actually said, "I despise levity."

4. When you write dialogue (conversation between two or more people), give each new speaker a new paragraph. But still put related nondialogue sentences in the same paragraph.

> After our visitor finally left, I was able to ask my question. "What did he mean by 'a typical product of the Midwest'?" I said.
> "Maybe he meant you were sweet and innocent," Mark suggested.
> "Fat chance," I replied. "He probably meant I was corny." I doubt that he was that clever, though.

5. Put quotation marks around titles of works that you think of as *part* of a book or magazine rather than a whole by itself: articles, stories, chapters, essays, short poems. Do not, however, put quotation marks around titles of your own essays.

Examples:

"Petrified Man," a short story by Eudora Welty

"We Real Cool," a poem by Gwendolyn Brooks

"My View of History," an essay by Arnold Toynbee

6. Underline the titles of works you think of as a *whole:* books, magazines, journals, newspapers, plays, and movies (*Walden, The New York Times, Casablanca*). Also underline the names of works of visual art (Dali's painting, *Civil War*).

Italics in print mean the same thing as underlining by hand or on a typewriter.

7. Do not use underlining or quotation marks around the titles of series (Masterpiece Theatre) **or parts of books** (Preface, Appendix, Index).

8. Underline or put quotation marks around words used as words.

A. You used <u>but</u> and <u>and</u> too often in that sentence.

B. He thought "sophisticated" only referred to stylishness.

9. In general, do not put quotation marks around words that you suspect are too slangy.
It's tempting to do this:

A. *Weak:* Phys ed was really a "drag."

B. *Weak:* On the first day of class, my philosophy instructor showed that he was really "hot" on the subject.

But you should take the time to decide whether the informality suits your style or not. If it does, there's no need to set it off with quotation marks. If it does not, you should find a more fitting expression. In sentence A, since the writer used the slangy, abbreviated form of physical education, the informal word *drag* is suitable without any quotation marks. In B, the writer should probably substitute *enthusiastic about* for *"hot" on.*

Do not use quotation marks as a written sneer, either. Learn to express your feelings in a more exact way.

10. Periods and commas always go inside quotation marks.

> **A.** "Never eat at a restaurant named *Mom's,*" my brother always said.
> **B.** In James Joyce's story "Eveline," the main character is at once frightened and attracted by freedom.

Notice in examples 1A, and 4A that we substitute a comma for the period at the end of a quoted sentence when the sentence is followed by tag words (like *he whined, she said, Gloria grunted*). When tag words interrupt a quoted sentence, the first part of the quotation needs a comma after it:

> **C.** "I must admit," Seymour said, "that Gloria sounds more like a rooster than anyone else I know."

11. Colons, semicolons, and dashes always go outside the quotation marks.

> "If at first you don't succeed, try, try again"; "It takes all kinds"; "You can't get something for nothing": these shallow mottos were his entire philosophy of life.

12. Exclamation points and question marks go inside the quotation marks if they are part of the quotation and outside if they are not.

> **A.** "That man called me 'Babycakes'!" Sandra screeched.
> **B.** He said, "Hey there, Babycakes, whatcha doin' tonight?"
> **C.** Isn't that what my father calls "an ungentlemanly advance"?

EXERCISE   13-15

Add single or double quotation marks or underlining to these items if needed.

> **1.** Did you see the article Dietmania in *Newsweek?* she asked.
> **2.** He called Gloria's performance an embarrassment to man and beast.
> **3.** Until I heard Gloria, I thought that oink was the basic pig sound.

4. At first, Gloria said, I just did easy ones like ducks and lambs.
5. In March she mourned, I will never get the emu call right; however, by May she had learned it perfectly.
6. Deedee calls everything cute or nice.
7. Did you say a good life or a good wife? she asked.
8. After I read the story Death in the Woods, I reexamined my life.
9. The grass is always greener on the other side of the fence: I surely found this saying true.
10. Look! There's Patty! the bank customers yelped.

Redundance

If you are not considering your word choice carefully, you can accidentally pile up two or more words that say the same thing, like these:

emotional feelings
round in shape
earthtone shades of color
fatally murdered

To avoid this redundance, just *emotions, round, earthtones,* and *murdered* would serve.

Redundant Prepositions

Avoid using a preposition at the end of any sentence involving *where.*

Colloquial: Can you tell me where the action's at?
Standard: Can you tell me where the action is?
Colloquial: Where is our money going to?
Standard: Where is our money going?

Reference of Pronouns

1. Make sure pronouns have clear antecedents.

Pronouns are useful words that stand in for nouns so that we don't have to be forever repeating the same word (see page 354). Occasionally pronouns cause trouble, though, when readers cannot tell for sure *what* noun the pronoun stands for (or refers to). Say you write

A. Seymour gave Selma her pet parrot.

There's no problem: *her* clearly means Selma. But suppose you write instead

    B. Seymour gave Clyde his pet parrot.

Instant ambiguity: *his* could mean either Seymour's or Clyde's. In order to avoid baffling your readers in this fashion, you must rephrase such constructions in a way that makes the pronoun reference clear.

    C. Seymour gave his pet parrot to Clyde.

or

    D. Clyde got his pet parrot from Seymour.

If you have difficulty with vague pronoun reference, start checking pronouns when you proofread. Be sure each pronoun refers clearly to only *one* noun. And be sure that noun is fairly close, preferably in the same sentence. You cannot expect your readers to track back two or three sentences to find the antecedent for a pronoun.

2. Use *this* and *which* with care.

Whenever you use the word *this*, try to follow it with a noun telling what *this* refers to. We're naturally lazy and take advantage of such a handy word which can be a pronoun and stand there all by itself meaning nothing in particular. Naturally, *this* will mean something to you when you write it, but you must be sure that the idea also gets onto the page. Too often *this* refers to an abstract idea or to a whole cluster of ideas in a paragraph, and your readers would require divine guidance to figure out exactly what you had in mind. So, if you write

    A. The importance of this becomes clear when we understand the alternatives.

at least give your reader a clue: "this *principle*," "this *qualification*," "this *stalemate*" or even "this *problem*," if you cannot pinpoint the meaning any better than that. It takes extra time and energy, even though you may know exactly what you mean. But searching for a single word to express the idea sharpens your thinking and helps your readers understand you. If every *this* is followed by a noun, you are probably being clear.

Which causes similar problems. Often this handy pronoun refers to the entire clause preceding it. Sometimes the meaning is clear, sometimes not. Suppose you write

    B. Jocasta has received only one job offer, which depresses her.

That sentence can be interpreted in two different ways:

C. Jocasta is depressed about receiving only one job offer, even though it's a fairly good job.

or

D. Jocasta has received only one job offer—a depressing one, at that.

Remember that such ambiguity is undesirable in expository prose. Check every *this* and *which* to be sure your readers will understand these words to mean exactly what you intended.

Look up *Agreement (Pronoun and Antecedent)* for a discussion of more pronoun problems.

EXERCISE   13-16

Revise the following sentences to eliminate unclear pronoun reference.

1. He prepared a delicious meal for Al and then criticized his cooking throughout dinner, which irritated him immensely.
2. Juan told Al that his soufflés never rose as high as his.
3. Al asked if Juan allowed a speck of egg yolk or a particle of grease to pollute the egg whites. This might keep the whites from fluffing up as much as they should.
4. Al also suggested making a foil collar for the soufflé pan, which encourages the soufflé to puff higher.
5. Juan told Al that he might as well just give up and try quiche instead.
6. The problems with elaborate cooking projects are so serious that Sherri dreads them.
7. Eating a simple meal in an outdoor setting, which I prefer, relaxes both host and guests.
8. This makes the evening enjoyable and free from anxiety.
9. She told her that her husband simply refused to eat casserole dishes.
10. The chefs were eager to discuss their problems with white sauce, but they were not very serious.

Regular Verb

See *Verbs*, page 343.
See *Tense*.

Repetition

rep

Carefully designed repetition of terms can add emphasis and coherence to a passage, like this one by Hugh Drummond:

> I watched a woman slip into madness recently. Her working-class, middle-aged life was buffeted by an abusive husband, an abusive son, and a series of abusive supervisors at a succession of low-level jobs. She would come home day after day, year after year from her file-clerk tedium, exhausted by the subway commute and the stained city's air, only to begin caring for her indulged, soured men; with their impatient appetites and their bottom-rung entitlements, they waited for her like beasts in a lair.
>
> —Power, Madness, and Poverty,'' *Mother Jones,* Jan. 1980, p. 23.

The repetition reflects the tedious repetitiousness of the woman's life.

Careless repetition, though, lends emphasis to a word or phrase awkwardly and unnecessarily:

> **A.** After the performance, we went to Karl's house to discuss whether it was an effective performance.
> **B.** The length of his hair adds to the wild appearance of his hair.

Those sentences need revision because the repeated words have no reason to be emphasized.

> **A.** After the performance, we went to Karl's house to discuss whether our production was effective.
> **B.** The length of his hair adds to its wild appearance.

Restrictive Clauses   See *Comma,* number 2.

Run-On Sentence (Fused Sentence)

run-on

Do not run two sentences together without a period between them.

fs

> **A.** Horace has a mangy dog without a brain in his head his name is Bowser.

Such a lapse is guaranteed to drive even the most patient readers to distraction. When you proofread, make sure that each sentence really *is* an acceptable sentence.

> **B.** Horace has a mangy dog without a brain in his head. His name is Bowser.

Those sentences are standard English, but a good writer would revise further to avoid wordiness.

> **C.** Horace has a mangy, brainless dog named Bowser.

EXERCISE 13-17

Put end punctuation where it belongs in the following items, and revise to avoid wordiness where necessary.

1. Playing blackjack is an absorbing hobby it might even absorb your bank account if you're not careful.
2. Blackjack is the only Las Vegas game in which the house does not have an overwhelming advantage in fact the players have an advantage if they use a system.
3. The best blackjack system involves remembering every card that has turned up the player keeps a running count of what cards are left in the deck and makes high or low bets accordingly.
4. The system is based on statistical tables compiled by computer expert Julian Braun of the IBM Corporation Braun does not play blackjack himself.
5. System players must be dedicated learning the system well takes 200 hours of memorization and practice.
6. Slot machines, on the other hand, are quite simple they do not require any practice.
7. However, the house has a stupendous advantage over the slot machine player the slot machine addicts cannot quite believe this.
8. Slot machine addicts are always hoping for the big jackpot these hopes are encouraged by the design of the machines.
9. Each machine boasts of its jackpot prize in large letters and pictures each one also makes loud noises whenever any payoff, however small, is won.
10. In spite of my wisdom I did start to play slots more often after January 1979 that is when I saw a man win a Cadillac on a machine at the El Cortez.

Semicolon

;

semi

For quick advice see the punctuation chart in Table 13-1.

1. The semicolon, which is similar to a period, means stop briefly; then go ahead.

Complete sentences connected by semicolons should be closely related.

A. The story has three narrators; one of them is insane.
B. When angry, count four; when very angry, swear.

—Mark Twain

2. Use a semicolon (instead of only a comma) when sentences are joined with a conjunctive adverb rather than with a coordinating conjunction: *and, but, or, for, nor, yet, so.*

Here is a list of the most commonly used conjunctive adverbs:

accordingly	indeed	nonetheless
besides	instead	otherwise
consequently	likewise	then
furthermore	meanwhile	therefore
hence	moreover	thus
however	nevertheless	too

3. The type of connective you choose need not change the meaning, but it will change the punctuation.

The following sentences appear to require identical punctuation, but in standard usage the first requires a semicolon, the second only a comma.

A. The demonstrators have a valid point; however, I can't condone their violence.
B. The demonstrators have a valid point, but I can't condone their violence.

This rule may seem senseless, but there *is* a reason for the distinction. The conjunctive adverb is not a pure connective in the way the coordinating conjunction is. *However* in the first example can be picked up and moved to several other spots in the sentence as it suits your fancy. You could write:

C. The demonstrators have a valid point; I can't, however, condone their violence.

or

I can't condone their violence, however.

or even

I, however, can't condone their violence.

You cannot take such liberties with the coordinating conjunctions without producing nonsentences like these:

I can't, but, condone their violence.
I can't condone their violence, but.
I, but, can't condone their violence.

It's easy to tell the difference between the pure conjunctions and the conjunctive adverbs if you have memorized the seven coordinating conjunctions: *and, but, or, for, nor, yet, so.* Other words likely to deceive you into thinking they are coordinating conjunctions are actually conjunctive adverbs.

4. Do not use a semicolon to connect an independent clause with a dependent clause (a fragment).

> *Faulty:*   He looked a lot like Robert Redford; although I couldn't see him too well.
>
> *Improved:*   He looked a lot like Robert Redford, although I couldn't see him too well.

5. The semicolon substitutes for the comma in separating items in series when any of the items listed *already contains commas*.
For example:

> **A.** Ann went to college and dropped out; lived with her parents for a year; worked as a veterinarian's assistant, a teacher's aide, and a clerk; and finally found her niche as an organic farmer.

Sometimes the series may follow a colon.

> **B.** Henry made several New Year's resolutions: to eat sensible, well-balanced meals; to study harder, sleep longer, and swear less; and to drink no more rum, tequila, or gin.

EXERCISE   13-18

Add semicolons to the following items where appropriate.

1. He believed that spicy foods were good for the heart, therefore, he ate jalapeña peppers for breakfast each morning.
2. He was tall, handsome, and rich, everyone loved him.
3. She divided her life into four distinct eras: blissful childhood, 1940–1954, carefree student life, 1954–1964, motherhood, 1964–1974, and finally, liberation, 1974 to the present.
4. He forgot to add oil, thus finding himself the victim of thrown rods and other incomprehensible malfunctions.
5. Seymour asked me to bring wine, preferably a rosé, baby Swiss cheese, and rolls, ideally fresh-baked whole wheat ones, little did he know I'd already packed peanut butter sandwiches, strawberry Koolaid, and cheese curls.
6. The picnic, however, was a smashing success.
7. We had to coax Seymour out of the fountain in front of City Hall, he was about to get arrested.
8. Our high spirits were due to good food, weather, and company, a city-wide air of celebration, fun, and song, and a holiday from work.
9. Although Seymour made a fool of himself, no one cared.
10. We ended the day with a swim at the gravel pit, then everyone went home.

Sentence Types

Every time you write a complete sentence, it falls into one of four categories: simple, compound, complex, and compound-complex. You may wonder what earthly good it does you to become acquainted with the four sentence types. For one thing, it gives you a pleasant sense of order to think of all those billions of sentences falling neatly into four groups. And more practically, the knowledge may help your style. Unless you are consciously striving for parallel sentences, you do not want a whole string of the same type: you want some variety in each paragraph.

1. A simple sentence consists of one independent clause and as many modifying words or phrases as you like.

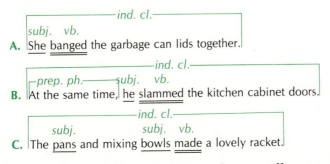

Example C has a compound subject, but is still a simple sentence. Simple sentences may also have compound predicates.

2. A compound sentence consists of two or more independent clauses joined by a coordinating conjunction (*and, but, or, for, nor, yet, so*)

A compound sentence may have any number of modifying words and phrases too.

3. A complex sentence has one independent clause, one or more dependent clauses, and perhaps some modifying words or phrases.

A. After the neighbors began to complain, the couple started both their motorcycles and roared off.

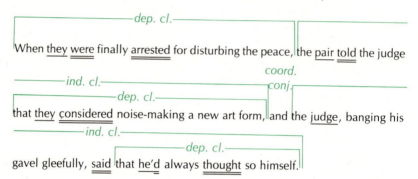

ind. cl.

subj. *vb.*

B. They went in search of an authentic air raid siren, a prize that they

dep. cl.

vb.

considered the ultimate in noisiness.

4. A compound-complex sentence, as you may have guessed, has two or more independent clauses, and can be plain or fancy.

dep. cl.

When they were finally arrested for disturbing the peace, the pair told the judge

coord.

ind. cl.

dep. cl.

conj.

that they considered noise-making a new art form, and the judge, banging his

ind. cl.

dep. cl.

gavel gleefully, said that he'd always thought so himself.

One more sentence type may have sprung to your alert mind by now: the sentence fragment. We have not forgotten it. Look up *Fragment*. Also see *Balanced Sentences* to learn about parallel structure.

shift

Shifts in Tense and Person

Sometimes your prose gets rolling along, and you shift into the wrong gear while you are moving, which results in an unpleasant grinding noise in your readers' heads. These shifts occur in tense and person.

1. You may write in either present or past tense, depending upon how you approach your material.
This sentence, for instance, is written in present tense:

A. Laurie cleans the dining room and stairway.

Past tense would be

B. Laurie cleaned the dining room and stairway.
C. Laurie was cleaning the dining room and stairway.

There is a good bit of variety within the two tenses, which we discuss under *Verbs* in Chapter 12 and under *Tense* in this chapter.

2. Choose either present or past tense and stay with it unless you have a reason to change.

Here's an example of faulty tense switch:

> **D.** Laurie was quietly cleaning the dining room when in comes Sue with a bunch of her loud friends and puts on her B-52s record at full volume. Laurie had to go upstairs and sulk.

There's no call for the change from past to present tense. If Laurie *was cleaning*, then Sue *came* in and *put* on the B-52s. You can, of course, switch tenses to indicate a change occurring in time:

> **E.** Laurie was cleaning the dining room, but now she is sulking.

Just be sure that you do not mix tenses without meaning to.

3. When you are writing about literature, be especially careful about mixing past and present tense in your discussion of what happens in the book.

It's traditional to describe literary happenings in the present tense (called the *historical present*):

> Kingsley Amis's hero, Lucky Jim, *has* an imaginative humor that constantly *gets* him in trouble.

4. Shifting *person* in a passage is a similar error.

Here's an example of a triple whammy:

> **A.** *Faulty:* As students we learn the ghastly effects of procrastination. You find out that you just can't appreciate reading ten chapters of geography the night before a test. Most students know the grim thud in the gut that they feel when they stare at an exam and don't even understand the questions.

In that example the writer refers to the students in three different ways: *we* (first person plural), *you* (second person), and *they* (third person plural). To revise the passage, stick to one pronoun.

> **B.** *Revised:* As students, we learn the ghastly effects of procrastination. We find out that we just can't appreciate reading ten chapters of geography the night before a test. We become familiar with the grim thud in the gut that we feel when we stare at an exam and don't even understand the questions.

EXERCISE   **13-19**

Correct the tense and person shifts in the following passages.

1. At the end of *Jane Eyre*, Jane is rewarded for her courage and virtue. She found happiness in an egalitarian marriage.
2. People often forget to file a change-of-address card at the post office when you move.
3. I saw that he was growing angry, so I jump up and leave the room.
4. My sister couldn't stand it when I wear her favorite jeans, but what can you do when all of yours are dirty?
5. Everyone who reads knows that government is corrupt. You can never be sure, though, that we know just how corrupt it is.
6. Sheila's new haircut is badly mangled, but I don't know what you can do about it.
7. Steve arrives, obnoxious as usual, and insulted the people at Lynn's party.
8. Richard wants to go see the play but claims that he didn't have time.
9. The philosophy students had a potluck last Friday, but then they ruin it by arguing about whether the food exists or not.
10. Dan's truck needed alignment, but he complains constantly about the cost.

Simile   See *Figures of Speech.*

Simple Sentence   See *Sentence Types.*

Slang   See *Diction,* number 7.

Spelling

sp

See *Spelling Appendix,* page 487.

If you get certain pairs of words confused, like *accept* and *except* or *affect* and *effect,* the "Glossary of Usage" beginning on page 457 will help you.

Split Infinitive

To many people, a split infinitive reads like a fingernail on the blackboard sounds. Such people would prefer that you keep the *to* and the verb (as in *to appreciate, to understand, to walk*) smack up against each other—not stick an adverb between them. But current usage finds most split infinitives perfectly acceptable, like:

adv.
A. He tried *to* secretly *cause* fights between Chris and Ann.
inf.

Really is a common infinitive-splitter, and it can usually be left out of the sentence entirely.

adv.
B. *Split:*   I began *to* really *appreciate* jug band music.
inf.

Improved: I began to appreciate jug band music.

Delete the infinitive-splitting adverb if it does not add appreciably to the meaning of the sentence.
A widely split infinitive can be awkward.

C. *Widely split:*   He tried *to* purposely, secretly, and with malicious intent *cause* fights between Ann and Chris.
Improved: Purposely, secretly, and with malicious intent, he tried *to cause* fights between Chris and Ann.

Squinting Modifier

sm

A squinting modifier is an ambiguous one; it's placed between two words (or phrases), and could conceivably refer to either one of them.

Squinting: Marla thought *secretly* James ate too much.

Move the squinting modifier to a less confusing place in the sentence.

Clear: Marla *secretly* thought James ate too much.
Marla thought James *secretly* ate too much.

Subject
See *Nouns*, page 341.
See *Agreement (Subject and Verb)*.

Subjunctive Mood

mood

See *Verbs*, page 343, for a discussion of *mood*.
The verb forms you are most familiar with and use most often are

in the *indicative* mood: I *cook*, you *eat*, he *washes* dishes, they *sweep* the floor. Indicative mood is used for statements of fact. For statements and wishes contrary to fact (or highly unlikely) or for suppositions, some people use *subjunctive* mood.

Indicative		Subjunctive		Indicative	Subjunctive
I am	I was	I be	I were	I take	I take
he is	he was	he be	he were	he takes	he take
you are	you were	you be	you were	you take	you take
they are	they were	they be	they were	they take	they take

Remember Patrick Henry's "If this *be* treason"? And the phrase "if need be"? Those are examples of subjunctive mood. It used to be commonplace to use the subjunctive mood of all verbs, like, "If he *take* to his bed, he will surely expire." But now the subjunctive mood of the *to be* verb is practically the only one anyone worries about.

Many people believe in polishing up the old subjunctive mood and restoring it to everyday use. They want you to say, "If I *were* . . ." instead of "If I *was*. . . ." These folks can get quite nervous about your mood, so perhaps you should figure out whether they are in your reading audience. If they are, follow these rules:

1. **Use subjunctive mood to express something contrary to fact, highly unlikely, doubtful, or speculative.**

   A. If I were more refined, subjunctive mood would sound natural to me.
   B. Suppose he were confronted with an audience of subjunctive mood fanatics: he'd be in trouble if he were to use it incorrectly.
   C. He acts as though he were the smartest graduate of Podunk High, but he certainly doesn't know subjunctive mood.

2. **Use subjunctive mood to express a strong necessity or a motion in a meeting.**

   A. It's crucial that you be present at this week's meeting.
   B. I'm going to move that all whale hunting be immediately banned.
   C. "To write well and worthily of American things one need even more than elsewhere to be a master."

   —Henry James.

Subordination and Coordination

sub

1. **You can enrich a sentence or series of sentences by subordinating some of the clauses—that is, by changing independent clauses to dependent ones or phrases.**

Plain simple and compound sentences may be the easiest ones to write, but they do not always get across the relationships between your ideas in the clearest way possible. And if you use simple sentences too often, you will have a third-grade writing style. Here are a couple of plain simple sentences:

Lucy forgot how to spell *exaggerated.* She used the word *magnified* instead.

The idea in one of those sentences could be subordinated in these ways:

A. By using subordinating conjunctions and adverbs (*after, when, because, if, while, until, unless,* etc.)
Since Lucy forgot how to spell exaggerated, she used the word *magnified* instead.

B. By using an adjective clause
Lucy *who forgot how to spell* exaggerated, used the word *magnified* instead.

C. By using a participial phrase or an adjective
Having forgotten how to spell exaggerated, Lucy used the word *magnified* instead.

2. Avoid stringing together simple sentences with coordinating conjunctions.

Subordinate some of the ideas, using parallel structure (see also *Balanced Sentences*).

Ineffective: Phoebe got a hot tip on the phone, and she grabbed her tape recorder and hurried to the corner and an angry mob was gathered there, and she ran to a phone booth and called the paper's photographer and said, "Dave, get down here quick!"

Improved: After getting a hot tip on the phone, Phoebe grabbed her tape recorder and hurried to the corner where an angry mob was gathered. She ran to a phone booth, dialed the paper's photographer, and said, "Dave, get down here quick!"

3. Choose the subordinating element that best shows how the ideas are connected, and be sure the main idea ends up in the *independent* clause, unless you are writing satire.

Faulty: Anna met Alexis in the lobby of the casino, while he complimented her on her gown.

Improved: Alexis complimented Anna on her gown when they met in the lobby of the casino.

EXERCISE 13-20

The following sentences are examples of excessive coordination. Revise each sentence, using subordination.

1. Moose is my cat, and he has stripy fur and is inordinately lazy, but he is busy now and is washing himself.
2. Clarence has a new motorcycle, and it's a huge Harley-Davidson, and he went to a wild party on it and drank six beers, and then crashed into a tree at sixty miles per hour.
3. Jocasta was lonely, so she joined the YWCA, signed up for disco dancing lessons and has been practicing her bored expression and has got her hip movement perfect and is now the life of the party.
4. Our fire fighters went on strike and are now in jail because they want a written contract and better working conditions and also they want their lieutenants in the union, but the town council opposes the fire fighters' demands, so the situation is at a stalemate.
5. Joyce Carol Oates writes superb short stories and is interested in women and in their fear of loneliness and she shows that women perpetually fear rape and violence and abandonment and she seems to suggest that women feel this way because they have few options and thus seek connections with men to give meaning to their lives.
6. Our trip to Bloomington was perfect and we had dark beer and spinach salads and stayed up late but we felt great the next day anyway.
7. Mark is out running errands and he plans to go to the bank and then he will stop and talk to his boss and then he needs to pick up some papers from my office.
8. I always remember my mother's birthday but I have a hard time figuring out what to get her and sometimes I'm afraid I got her the same thing I got her last year.
9. Laurie plays lead guitar in a rock and roll band and all the band members are female and they choose old songs that are from the male point of view and rewrite the lyrics to reflect the female point of view.
10. Marsha has a job at a gift shop and it is much more demanding than it sounds and she has to take inventory and arrange displays and do the bookwork and work as a cashier also.

Tense

t

Tense indicates time relationships. When you start trying to explain how it all works, you realize how amazing it is that most people do it right. Here are the basic tenses of English:

Present:	I walk
Past:	I walked
Future:	I will walk

Present perfect: I have walked
Past perfect: I had walked
Future perfect: I will have walked

1. **When you are writing about an event in present tense, it is natural to use past tense for past events and future for future events.**

> I think that Hornsby wanted Clara to quit her job yesterday because he will not need as many clerks after the Christmas rush is over.

2. **When you are writing about an event in past tense, you must use past perfect for events earlier in the past.**

> Hornsby regretted that he had hired Clara for a permanent, full-time job.

3. **The three perfect tenses (present perfect, past perfect, and future perfect) always show completed action.**

> A. I have ridden the bus to campus for the past month.
> B. I had expected my Subaru to be fixed by last Monday.
> C. By the time I get my car back, I will have paid $215.39 just to get that windshield wiper fixed.

4. **Sometimes the tense of a statement gets tricky when the surroundings of the statement are in past or future tense, but the statement itself is presently true or applicable.**

> A. Clara realized last week that Hornsby is a greedy, manipulative phony.

Hornsby is still a greedy, manipulative phony, so the present tense is appropriate even though Clara figured him out a week ago.

> B. Jacob said that reading fiction is so pleasant it feels sinful.

Jacob said this in the past, but his statement about fiction still applies today, so the present tense is fine.

5. **Every English verb has three principal parts that you need to know in order to form the tenses.**
   Usually, the principal parts are just the present infinitive plus *-d*, *-ed*, or *-t:*

Present	Past	Past participle
walk	walked	(have, had) walked
dance	danced	(have, had) danced
spend	spent	(have, had) spent

6. **Some verbs are *irregular*; that is, they form their past tense or past participle in odd ways.**

You just have to memorize the principal parts of these verbs. Here are twenty of the most common irregular verbs:

Present	Past	Past participle
begin	began	begun
break	broke	broken
burst	burst	burst (*not* busted)
choose	chose	chosen
come	came	come
do	did	done
drag	dragged	dragged (*not* drug)
drink	drank	drunk
forget	forgot	forgotten (*or* forgot)
get	got	got (*or* gotten)
lay	laid	laid (meaning "placed")
lead	led	led
lie	lay	lain (meaning "reclined")
ride	rode	ridden
rise	rose	risen
run	ran	run
see	saw	seen
swim	swam	swum
take	took	taken
wake	waked (*or* woke)	waked (*or* woke)

Also see *Verbs*, page 343.

Thesis Statement

A successful essay needs a *thesis*, or controlling idea, either expressed in a single sentence in the introduction or implied, as in narrative or descriptive writing.

1. **Narrow the topic.**

If you're assigned a 500-word paper on "Solving the Energy Shortage," you need to find a suitable thesis idea that you can handle within the word limit. You might, for instance, focus on the need to develop alternative energy sources. But that's still too broad a topic to cover in 500 words. You could then narrow your idea to one neglected source, like solar energy. But you still need an approach—a *focus*—for your paper.

2. **Give the direction of your thinking.**

Your thesis should state more than just your general topic. Don't settle for just "solar energy" or even "the need for solar energy."

Write a complete sentence—with a *verb* as well as a subject—to indicate what you're going to say about the subject. You might propose the need for solar energy like this: "Our economy needs to convert to solar power because it remains our only nonpolluting source of energy."

3. **Make all ideas relate to your thesis.**

   Once you've decided on a clear, concise thesis statement, make sure that every major and minor point in the paper relates directly to that controlling idea so that your essay will be unified.

This and Which

These words are often used too loosely. See *Reference of Pronouns*, number 2.

Titles

Your title should tell the readers, as far as possible, what the paper is about.

1. **Do not use a complete sentence but give more than a hint about your topic.**

   Useless: The Teacher and Research
   Better: The Teacher and Research in Education
   Good: Practical Research Ideas for High School Teachers

2. **Experiment with a colon.**
   Sometimes a colon can make an uninspired title more impressive.

   Grass Roots Organization: A Key to Political Success
   Legal Liability: What Everyone Needs to Know about Mercy Killing

3. **Do not put quotation marks around your own title.**
   See also *Quotation Marks*, number 3, for advice on punctuating other people's titles.

Topic Sentence

The topic sentence expresses the central idea of a paragraph. Most of your paragraphs should have one. See pages 87–95.

Transitions

1. **Transitional words are verbal signals that help your readers follow your thought.**

Some of the most useful ones function this way:

A. **To move to the next point:** also, besides, too, furthermore, moreover, next, in the first place, second, third, again, in addition, further, likewise, finally.

B. **To add an example:** for instance, for example, in the same manner, such as, that is, in the following manner, namely, in this case, as an illustration.

C. **To emphasize a point:** in fact, without question, especially, without doubt, primarily, chiefly, actually, otherwise, after all, as a matter of fact.

D. **To contrast a point:** yet, although, after all, but, still, on the other hand, on the contrary, nevertheless, contrary to, however, nonetheless, conversely, granted that.

E. **To conclude a point:** thus, therefore, in short, consequently, so, accordingly, then, as a result, hence, in sum, in conclusion, in other words.

2. **Use special transitional techniques when moving from one point to the next.**

A. Occasionally you can pose a question for yourself and answer it, like this:

How does vitamin E work to repair body tissues? Nobody knows for sure, but . . .

B. A more useful method is the *echo transition* in which you touch on the idea from the previous paragraph as you introduce the idea for your next one, like this:

He also *gave up coffee, cigarettes, and alcohol.*

Despite *this stringent health program,* Sylvester continued to be depressed until . . .

3. **Within paragraphs provide transitions by repeating nouns and using pronouns to refer back to them, thus linking your sentences together.**

Dan loves remodeling projects, especially if they are big and complex. In fact, the bigger and more complex they are, the better he likes them.

Transitive Verb

See *Verbs,* pages 343–348.

Triteness

trite

A *cliché* is a worn-out series of words which usually expresses a simple-minded or trite idea: "It takes all kinds to make a world." But you can express superficial ideas without using clichés too. Here's an example of a sentence your reader might think trite:

> Motherhood is a joyful experience that no woman should miss.

The writer of that sentence has not thought very deeply about the idea. Is motherhood joyful for a poor woman with nine children? Are women's personalities so alike that such a generalization could be true?

We all find ourselves mindlessly writing down unexamined ideas once in a while. A thoughtful rereading of whatever you write can help you avoid making this weakness public.

Underlining

und

ital

Underlining by hand or by using a typewriter is the same as italics in print. It is used three ways:

1. **To indicate titles of long or self-contained works.**
   See *Quotation Marks* for a list of what titles to underline and what titles to enclose in quotation marks.

2. **To point out words used as words.**

   A. <u>Manipulative behavior</u> is my probation officer's favorite phrase.
   B. You have used twelve <u>in other words's</u> in this paragraph.

3. **To indicate foreign words.**
   In informal writing, you do not have to underline foreign words that are widely used, like et cetera or tortilla or tango.
   But underline foreign words when they are less familiar or when you are writing formally.

> After graduation, Jocasta seemed to lose her <u>joie de vivre</u>.

Underdeveloped Paragraphs

¶ *dev*

A friend of ours says that throughout college she got her papers back marked with "Underdeveloped ¶" in the margins. To correct this problem, she would carefully restate the topic four or five different ways in each paragraph, and she would still get "Underdeveloped ¶" marked in her margins.

Our friend finally realized, too late, what *underdevelopment* meant. She resents the fact that her teachers never wrote in her margins, "Add an example or illustration here," or, "Give some specific details," or, "Describe your reasoning step-by-step." She would have understood *that.*

When you find one of your skimpy paragraphs marked *undernourished* or *lacks development,* you will know what it means: add examples, provide specific details, describe your reasoning, or do all three.

Unity

un

Unity is something we never require of casual conversation: it's fine if you wander a little off the track and tell about the Bluebird Saloon in Denver in the middle of a discussion about Humphrey Bogart films.

But in an expository essay, unity is important: you must not go on about the Bluebird in the middle of an essay about Bogart films, even though you had a beer there after seeing *The Maltese Falcon* at a nearby theatre. Such a departure from the main subject is called a *digression.* A paragraph or essay has unity if it sticks to the main point. It lacks unity if it wanders across the street for a drink.

See also *Coherence.*

Usage

See *Levels of Usage*, p. 457.
See *Diction*, number 6.

Variety   See *Sentence Types.*

Verb

See *Verbs*, pages 343–348.
See *Agreement (Subject and Verb).*
See *Linking Verb.*
See *Tense.*

Verbal   See *Nouns*, pages 341–343.

Word Division   See *Hyphen.*

Wordiness

A *wordy* sentence has words and phrases which add nothing to its meaning; in fact, extra verbiage can actually blur the meaning and spoil the style of a sentence. Here, for instance, is a wordy rewriting of the last sentence:

> A sentence that is wordy usually consists in part of words and phrases which do not add anything in the area of meaning; in fact, the meaning of a sentence, in addition to its style, can be blurred or otherwise spoiled due to the fact that it is wordy.

To cure your writing of wordiness, practice sentence-by-sentence revision, hacking and slashing zealously. Passive voice makes a sentence wordy (see *Passive Voice.*) So does using canned phrases like *due to the fact that* instead of *because* and *in addition to* instead of *and.*

For further discussion and an exercise to practice on, see pages 78–79 in Chapter 3.

COMPREHENSIVE EXERCISE   **13-21**

Correct or improve each of the following sentences.

1. Care should be taken by new students not to alienate their roommates.
2. Every semester, Sandra makes two resolutions, first, not to spend all her money on tropical fish, and second, not to put off schoolwork until the last minute.
3. Hubert went to school five days early, and found himself alone on campus.
4. Luckily, he had remembered to actually bring his copy of *Paradise Lost* in case he had leisure reading time.
5. Hubert did feel badly because his roommate was not there to share the fun.
6. Sandra on the other hand did not arrive until a week after registration began.
7. She had only 3 paperback books with her.
8. She surprised her teachers by acting as though she was right on time.
9. Each of the books Sandra brought were special to her.
10. The books were Libra: Your Horoscope, Adventures of Huckleberry Finn, and Webster's New World Dictionary.
11. Although she didn't really believe in astrology Sandra found that reading over the list of Libra's good qualities cheered her up in times of depression.
12. *Huckleberry Finn* also cheered her up, supported her philosophy of life, and she never got bored no matter how many times she read it.
13. These characteristics of the novel were important to Sandra, for it meant that she never lacked a good book to read.

14. She sometimes forgot how to spell long words, therefore the dictionary was essential.
15. The dictionary was frequently used when she wrote papers.
16. It also helped her become drowsy when she'd drank too much coffee.
17. Huberts ability to spell was much better than most peoples.
18. His ability to dance, though, was lower than an elephant.
19. Sandra admired Hubert coming up with the correct spelling of *embarrass* every single time.
20. In her opinion, she had to admit that in the field of dancing, Hubert's Hustle was hopeless.
21. Sandra learned the Hustle at the New Age discotheque.
22. The surprising thing about some of Hubert's dance attempts, that include stumbles, jerks, and sometimes falls, do look quite fashionable sometimes.
23. Spelling, Hubert explained to Sandra, is a problem that can be cured only through memorization.
24. Dancing, Sandra explained to Hubert, becomes easy as pie with practice.
25. Hubert was eager to improve his dancing. Sandra wanted to become a better speller. They agreed to give each other lessons.
26. Hubert suggested, We could create a dance called the disco dictionary.
27. It's already created replied Sandra. I read about it in an article called Discomania in the New York Review of Books.
28. Walking into Sandra's room, Hubert's eye was caught by all the empty bookshelves.
29. He thought her lack of books was very strange he decided not to mention it, though.
30. She might still have her books packed up, he thought. Although it was the fifteenth week of the semester.
31. Sandra wasn't embarrassed by her empty bookshelves, in fact, she thought people often filled their shelves up just to impress others.
32. After supper on Tuesday, Sandra asked Hubert if he'd like to go to a lecture on how the *Oxford English Dictionary* was compiled in two hours.
33. She said that if students went to all the lectures that came up, you'd be busy every night of the week.
34. Hubert believed that people whose interests changed with every passing breeze were building on a foundation of jelly.
35. Sandra decided to go to the lecture while Hubert practices his Bump in front of the mirror.

chapter
Fourteen

Glossary of Usage

In this section we distinguish between a number of words that people often confuse, like <u>sit</u> and <u>set</u>, <u>effect</u> and <u>affect</u>. We also describe the current usage of some terms that are questionable as standard English, like the word <u>irregardless</u> and the use of <u>quotes</u> as a noun. In making decisions on usage, we have been guided by Robert C. Pooley, <u>The Teaching of English Usage</u>; Roy H. Copperud, <u>American Usage: The Consensus</u>; Theodore Bernstein, <u>Dos and Don'ts and Maybes of English Usage</u>; several current collegiate dictionaries; a stack of widely used composition handbooks; and sometimes our own generous hearts.

LEVELS OF USAGE

Usage simply means the way the language is used. But different people use the language in different ways. And even the same people use the language differently on different occasions. You probably speak more carefully in the classroom or on the job than you do when relaxing among friends. Good usage, then, is a matter of using language *appropriate* to the purpose and the occasion. In this chapter we give you clues about which expressions are appropriate for various occasions. Although we have already discussed *levels of usage* in some detail in Chapter 1, we will review them again here briefly:

Standard:	Safe for any level of usage—formal, informal or colloquial. Be sure *all* terms are standard if you are writing on the formal level.
Formal:	Much of your college writing and considerable business writing must be done on a formal level. This means only standard English is appropriate. Do not use slang or contractions—no

can'ts or *don'ts*. Completely formal writing requires one to write in the third person (as we just did in this sentence).
Formal: One can observe . . . ; this writer believes . . . .
Informal: We can observe . . . ; you can see . . . .

Informal: You get considerable leeway in informal writing. Some slang is acceptable, depending upon the tolerance of your audience, and you may be able to use a few contractions. This textbook is written on an informal level.

Colloquial: Since *colloquial* means the language of everyday speech of educated people, both contractions and slang are all right. But there is not much call for colloquial writing in your college courses, and it would be devastatingly inappropriate in most business writing. Use with proper caution.

Nonstandard: Most nonstandard phrasing (like *it don't*) will get you into big trouble in writing. Unfortunately, dialectical expressions are also considered nonstandard. Some dictionaries even label nonstandard constructions as *illiterate,* which seems harsh to us, but you should be advised that many people are unalterably prejudiced against nonstandard English. *Avoid it in writing.*

If you are in doubt about any terms that do not appear in this glossary, consult your trusty collegiate dictionary—but be sure it is of recent vintage. Even the best of dictionaries will be out of date on usage within ten years.

a/an

Use *a* before words beginning with consonant sounds; use *an* before words beginning with vowel sounds (*a, e, i, o, u*).

a martini	an Irish coffee
a tree toad	an armadillo
a hostile motorist	an hour exam (the *h* is silent)
a hopeful speech	an honest decision (the *h* is silent)
a one-car accident	an only child
(*o* sounds like *w*)	

accept/except

Accept, a verb, means "to receive or to agree with."

We *accept* your excuse with reluctance.

Except as a preposition means "but or excluding."

Everyone's coming *except* Dinsdale.

Except as a verb is not used much but means "to leave out."

> The Dean agreed to *except* the foreign language requirement since I have lived in France.

advice/advise

When you *advise* someone, you are giving *advice*.

> *vb.*
> We *advise* you to stop smoking.
>   *n.*
> Mavis refuses to follow our good *advice*.

affect/effect

The verb *affect* means "to influence." The noun *effect* means "the result of some influence."

> *n.*   *vb.*
> The *effect* on my lungs from smoking should *affect* my decision to quit.
>   *vb.*
> Smoking adversely *affects* our health.
>   *n.*
> LeRoy cultivates a seedy appearance for *effect*.

Just to confuse things further, *effect* can also be a verb meaning "to bring about." And *affect* can be a verb meaning "to cultivate an effect" or a noun meaning "emotional response."

> *vb.*
> We need to *effect* (bring about) some changes in the system.
> *vb.*
> Clyde *affects* (cultivates) a seedy appearance.
>   *n.*
> Psychologists say that inappropriate *affect* (emotional response) is a feature of schizophrenia.

These last three meanings are seldom confused with the more widely used words above. Concentrate on getting those first common meanings straight.

ain't

Still colloquial usage. Do not use it unless you are writing dialog or trying to get a laugh.

allude/refer

To *allude* means "to *refer* indirectly or briefly."

> Mark *alluded* to some previous shady dealings on the mayor's part but concentrated his attack on the present scandal.

Refer is more direct.

> Mark then *referred* to the mayor's illegal Swiss bank account.

allusion/illusion

An *allusion* is an indirect reference.

> This line of poetry contains an *allusion* to Dante's *Inferno*.

An *illusion* is a deception or fantasy.

> Seymour clung to the *illusion* that he looked like Robert Redford.

almost/most

Do not write *most all;* standard usage still requires *almost all.*

> Jocasta drank *almost* all of the Kool-Aid.
> Melvin sloshed down *most* of the iced tea.

a lot/alot

Even though *alike* is one word, *a lot* remains two.

> Misspellings can cause you *a lot* of trouble.

already/all ready

Already means "before, previously, or so soon."

> Jennifer has *already* downed three martinis.

All ready means prepared.

> Seymour is *all ready* to deliver his temperance lecture.

all right/alright

Usage is divided on this term, and *alright* is gaining acceptance. But to be safe, stick with *all right*. You could argue that since we have *all ready/already* and *all together/altogether,* we should be allowed *all right/alright*. But many will disagree:

> Alright is definitely not all right with everybody yet.

altogether/all together

Altogether means "entirely, thoroughly."

> Clarence's analysis is altogether absurd.

All together means "as a group."

> Let's sing it all together from the top.

a.m./p.m.   See *Abbreviation,* number 1C, in the "Revising Index," Chapter 13.

ambiguous/ambivalent

If something is *ambiguous,* it can be interpreted in several different ways.

> When Clyde mentioned the word "faithful," Marcella gave Jeannie a significant, but ambiguous, glance.

Ambiguous can also mean "uncertain or doubtful."

> The test results proved ambiguous.

But if you feel *ambivalent* about something, you are of two minds, having conflicting thoughts or feelings.

> Juanita has felt ambivalent toward Morris ever since he joined the Hell's Angels.

among/between

Use *among* when referring in general terms to more than two.

> Maureen found it difficult to choose from *among* so many delectable goodies.

Use *between* when referring to only two.

> She finally narrowed it down to a choice *between* the raspberry tart and the lemon meringue pie.

You can also use *between* when naming several persons or things individually.

> Elspeth vacillates *between* the key lime pie, the Bavarian cream, and the baked Alaska.

amount/number

In formal writing to be sure to use *amount* to refer to things in a mass or in bulk; use *number* to refer to things that can be counted.

> Andrew bought a sizable *amount* of peanut butter from which Dave made a considerable *number* of cookies for the bake sale.

analyzation

Do not use it. The word is *analysis*, and tacking on an extra syllable will not make it any grander.

> Luis offered a brilliant *analysis* of entropy in *Winnie the Pooh*.

and

Be careful not to write *an* when you mean *and*.

> *Careless:* I'm going to go out *an* get a pizza.
> *Correct:* I'm going to go out *and* get a pizza.

And do not get lazy and use the symbol &. Write the word out, except when taking notes.

any more/anymore

Some authorities consider only the first expression acceptable. But recent dictionaries cite *anymore* (one word) as standard English.

anyways/anywheres

Nonstandard. Use *anyway* and *anywhere*.

apprise/appraise

To *apprise* means to "inform or serve notice."

> Eloise said the officer neglected to *apprise* her of her constitutional rights.

To *appraise* means to "evaluate or judge."

> Egbert *appraised* the situation carefully and caught the next plane for Venezuela.

as

Do not use *as* to mean *because.*

> *Informal:*   Egbert returned from Venezuela, *as* the charges were dropped.
> *Improved:*   Egbert returned from Venezuela *because* the charges were dropped.

as/like

Hardly anyone takes serious umbrage over the confusion of *as* and *like* anymore, but in formal writing you might well observe the distinction. *As* is a conjunction; hence it introduces clauses.

> This pie tastes good *as* lemon pie should.

Like is a preposition; thus is introduces phrases.

> This pie tastes *like* artificial lemon.

as to

Many people feel that this phrase does nothing but clutter your sentence; they consider it a borrowing from the worst and wordiest of legalese. You can probably substitute the single word *about*.

Awkward: Melvin explained the rules *as to* registration.
Improved: Melvin explained the rules *about* registration.

author

Do not use it as a verb.

Colloquial: Ann authors our monthly newsletter.
Improved: Ann writes our monthly newsletter.

awhile/a while

Written as one word, *awhile* is an adverb.

Spot frolicked *awhile* with Bowser.

A while is an article plus a noun.

After *a while* Spot got bored and chased Bowser home.

bad/badly See *Adjective/Adverb Confusion*, page 372.

being as/being that

Do not use either one. Write *because* or *since*.

beside/besides

Do not use *beside* (at the side of) if you mean *besides* (in addition to).

He leadeth me *beside* the still waters.
Bumper has a math exam tomorrow *besides* his physics test.

better/best

Use *better* when comparing two people or things.

> Mickey is a *better* dancer than Melvin.

Use *best* when comparing more than two.

> Mickey is the *best* dancer in the place.

This rule holds true for all comparative adjectives: *prettier/prettiest; littler/littlest; happier/happiest; sadder/saddest; bigger/biggest,* etc.

between/among   See *among/between.*

busted

Do not write busted if you mean *broke.*

> *Colloquial:*   Chris *busted* his leg skiing.
> *Standard:*   Chris *broke* his leg skiing.
> *Colloquial:*   Lulu's balloon got *busted.*
> *Standard:*   Lulu's balloon *burst.*

There are a number of slang meanings for *busted;* do not use these in formal writing.

> *Slang:*   Norman got *busted* at the demonstration.
> Sergeant Snafu got *busted* to private.
> Sedgewick is flat *busted.* (no money)
> Maribelle is flat-*busted.* (no bosom)

can/may

Few people even recognize the distinction between these two words anymore, but in formal usage *can* means "to have the ability."

> Percy *can* sleep for twelve hours straight.

May is used to suggest a possibility or to request (or grant) permission.

> Percy *may* be awake by now.
> *May* I wake him, if he's not?
> Yes, you *may.*

can't help but/cannot help but

Technically, this expression is a double negative; hence some people object to it in formal writing.

> *Informal:*   I can't help but question Melvin's intentions.
> *Formal:*   I cannot help questioning Melvin's intentions.

center on/center around

As a matter of logic, you cannot *center around* anything. Always use *center on.*

> *Illogical:*   Our difficulty *centers around* Elin's refusal to sleep in the bathtub.
> *Improved:*   Our difficulty *centers on* Elin's refusal to sleep in the bathtub.

choose/chose

Choose (rhymes with ooze) means a decision is being made right now.

> I find it hard to *choose* from a long menu.

Chose (rhymes with toes) means a choice has already been made.

> I finally *chose* the eggplant surprise.

compare/contrast

These words overlap in meaning. When you *contrast* two things, you are making a comparison. But as most instructors use the terms on examinations or in writing assignments, *compare* generally means to focus on similarities; *contrast* means to focus on differences.

> *Compare* the music of the Beatles and the Rolling Stones.
> *Contrast* the music of Lawrence Welk and the Sex Pistols.

complected

Nonstandard. Use *complexioned.*

> Marilyn always longed to be sultry and dark *complexioned.*

complement/compliment

A *complement* is something that completes.

> Her purple scarf *complemented* her lavender sweater.

A *compliment* is a word of praise.

> She got many *compliments* on her purple scarf.

continual/continuous

Careful writers will make a distinction. *Continual* means "repeatedly."

> Carlos was *continually* late to class.

Continuous means "without interruption."

> We suffered *continuous* freezing weather for almost three months.

could of/should of/would of

Nonstandard. Use *could have, should have, would have.*

> I *should have (not should of)* stopped at the grocery store.

deduce/infer/imply

Deduce and *infer* mean essentially the same thing—to reach a conclusion through reasoning.

> Theodore *deduced* (or *inferred*) that Juanita was angry with him when she poured a pitcher of water over his head.

Do not confuse these words with *imply*, which means "to state indirectly or hint."

> Juanita had *implied* several times earlier in the evening that she was displeased.

differ from/differ with

To *differ from* means "to be different."

> Victoria and Steve *differ from* each other in their choice of records.

To *differ with* means "to disagree."

> Victoria and Steve *differ with* each other on the issue of free speech.

different from/different than

To be safe, stick with *different from* in formal writing.

> Turtles are *different from* terrapins in several ways.

You can save words, though, by introducing a clause with *different than;* this usage is now widely accepted.

> *Wordy:*   Your hair looks *different from* the way I remembered.
> *Improved:* Your hair looks *different than* I remembered.

disinterested/uninterested

The distinction between these words is extremely important. Do not confuse them. *Disinterested* means "impartial."

> We need a totally *disinterested* person to judge the debate.

Uninterested means "not interested."

> Albert is totally *uninterested* in the moral tension of Renaissance drama.

dominant/dominate

Dominant is an adjective or a noun.

> George has *dominant* parents.
> Brown eyes are genetically *dominant.*

Dominate is always a verb.

> George's parents *dominate* him.

effect/affect   See *affect/effect*.

enthuse

Now acceptable in speech, but since the term still offends many people, avoid it in writing. Stick with *enthusiastic*.

Colloquial: Arnie *enthuses* endlessly about the benefits of jogging.
Standard: Arnie is *enthusiastic* about the benefits of jogging.

etc.

Do not use this abbreviation (meaning "and so on") unless you have a list in which the other examples are obvious (like large cities: Paris, London, Rome, etc.). Do not ever write *and etc.*, because *etc.* means *and* so forth; thus you are saying it twice.

everyday/every day

Use *everyday* as an adjective to modify a noun or pronoun:

Josh is wearing his *everyday* clothes,

Use *every day* to mean *daily:*

It rains here almost *every day*.

except/accept   See *accept/except*.

farther/further

Either word is acceptable to mean distance.

I can't walk a step *farther*, yet we have two miles *further* to go.

To indicate something additional, use *further*.

The judge would hear no *further* arguments.

fewer/less

The distinction between these words is disappearing, but if you value precision, use *fewer* to refer to things that can be counted.

> Marvin catches *fewer* colds than Marlene.

Use *less* to refer to qualities or things that cannot be counted.

> Stanley has *less* patience than Travis.
> We have had *less* rain than usual this fall.

former/latter

Unless you are a skillful writer, do not use these terms. Too often readers must look back in order to remember which was the former (the first mentioned) and which the latter (the last mentioned). For greater clarity, repeat the nouns.

got/gotten

Both words are acceptable as past participles of the verb *to get.*

> Maurice *has got* an attractive haircut.
> Maurice *has gotten* an attractive haircut.

hanged/hung   See *hung/hanged.*

he or she/his or her

In order to include women in the language, many socially conscious people deliberately use *he or she* (instead of simply *he*) or *his or her* (instead of simply *his,* as grammarians have decreed correct for over a century now.)[1] Equally as many people, though, still consider the double pronoun awkward, as indeed it can be if used ineptly, like this:

> *Awkward:*   The student must have his or her schedule signed by an advisor before he or she proceeds to pick up his or her class cards.

[1] For an enlightening historical study explaining how the male bias in our language became so pronounced, see Julia P. Stanley, "Sexist Grammar," *College English,* 39 (March 1978), 800–811. Stanley contends that "The usage of *man, mankind,* and *he* in the early grammars of English was not generic in any sense of that term, however one might wish to construe it" (p. 801), and supplies the evidence to prove her point.

But that sentence can be easily revised to eliminate the excess pronouns.

> *Improved:* The student must have his or her schedule signed by an advisor before picking up class cards.

Better yet, that sentence can be recast in the plural to eliminate the problem altogether.

> *Improved:* Students must have their schedules signed by an advisor before picking up class cards.

Notice that the *idea* in the previous example was plural all along, even though the first two versions were written in the singular. We are taught early on to write singular even when we mean plural. We write sentences like this:

> A child should memorize *his* multiplication tables.

Really we mean *all* children should memorize *their* multiplication tables. We need to kick that singular habit and cultivate the plural, since our language has perfectly good nonsexist pronouns in the plural—*they, their, them.*

If you cannot avoid using the singular—and sometimes you can't—try to eliminate unnecessary pronouns.

> *Avoid:* The winner should pick up *his* prize in person.
> *Better:* The winner should pick up the prize in person.

If you cannot eliminate the pronoun, an occasional *his or her*—or *her or his*—is quite acceptable in current usage. See also *man/person.*

hisself

Nonstandard. Do not use it unless writing dialect.

hopefully

Almost everybody now accepts *hopefully* as a sentence modifier.

> *Hopefully* we can get the contract signed today.

But if you are writing for a conservative audience, you will do well to use *hopefully* only as an adverb meaning "in a hopeful manner":

> I signed the contract *hopefully*, thinking my life would improve.
> We *hope* to get the contract signed today.

hung/hanged

If you are talking about hanging pictures or hanging out, the verb *hang* has these principal parts: *hang, hung, hung, hanging*. But if you are referring to people hanging by the neck, the verb goes *hang, hanged, hanged, hanging*.

> Some people felt that Melvin should have been *hanged,* drawn, and quartered for forgetting to put gas in the car.

illusion   See *allusion/illusion*.

imply/infer   See *deduce/infer/imply*.

in/into/in to

To be precise, use *in* to show location; use *into* to indicate motion.

> I was *in* the back seat when our car crashed *into* the train.

Often we use *in* not as a preposition (see previous example) but as an adverb functioning almost as part of a verb: *to go in, to sleep in, to give in.* With these fused verb/adverb constructions, keep *to* as a separate word.

> *adv.*
> Do not give *in* to pressure.
> *prep.*
> Do not play *into* their hands.

irregardless

Most people still steadfastly refuse to accept *irregardless* as standard English. Do not use it; say *regardless* or *nonetheless*.

is when/is where

Do not use *is when*.

> *Avoid:*   In tragedy, catharsis *is when* the audience feels purged of pity and
> fear.
> *Improved:*   In tragedy, catharsis involves purging pity and fear from the audi-
> ence.

Use *is where* only when you mean a place:

> That *is where* I lost my keys.

> *Avoid:*   An accident *is where* someone gets careless.
> *Improved:*   Accidents *occur when* people get careless.

its/it's

Do not confuse these two terms. Memorize the two definitions if you
have trouble with them, and when you proofread, check to be sure you
have not confused them accidently. *Its* is a possessive pronoun.

> The dog chomped *its* own tail.

It's is a contraction of *it is*.

> *It's* not an exceptionally smart dog.

If you never can keep the two straight, quit using the contradiction. If
you always write *it is*, then all you have to remember is, no apostrophe
in *its*.

kind of/sort of

Colloquial when used to mean *rather* or *somewhat*.

> *Colloquial:*   Melvin is *sort of* snarly today.
> *Standard:*   Melvin is *somewhat* touchy today.

The phrases can be used in standard English, but not as adverbs.

> *Standard:*   What *kind of* junk food does Myrtle like?

Be careful, though, to avoid wordiness.

> *Wordy:*   Myrtle prefers a less salty sort of snack.
> *Improved:*   Myrtle prefers a less salty snack.

Never use *kind of a* or *sort of a* in writing.

> *Avoid:*   Grandpa is kind of a grouch today.
> *Improved:*   Gramps is grouchy today.

latter/former   See *former/latter.*

lay/lie

To lay means to put or place; *to lie* means to recline. Be sure you know the principal parts; then decide which verb you need: to place—*lay, laid, laid, laying;* to recline—*lie, lay, lain, lying.* Remember that *lay* requires a direct object: you always *lay* something. But you never *lie* anything: you just *lie down,* or *lie quietly,* or *lie under a tree,* or *lie on a couch.* Notice the difference:

> *No object:*   Selma *lies* in the hammock.
> *Direct object:*   Selma *lays* her weary body in the hammock.

If you absolutely cannot keep these verbs straight in your mind, choose another word.

> Selma *lounges* in the hammock.
> Selma *plops* her weary body in the hammock.

The verb *lie* meaning "to tell a falsehood" causes no problems since its principal parts are *lie, lied, lied, lying.* Hardly anyone past the age of five would say "Selma *lied* down in the hammock." Similarly, the slang meaning of *lay* never confuses people. Nobody ever asks, "Did you get *lain* last night?"

lead/led

Pronunciation causes the confusion here. *Lead* (rhymes with *bed*) means a heavy, grayish metal.

> Our airy hopes sank like *lead.*

Lead (rhymes with *seed*) is present tense of the verb meaning to guide.

> He *leads* me beside the still waters.

Led (rhymes with *bed*) is the past tense of the verb *lead*.

> LeRoy *led* the march last year, but he vows he will not *lead* it again.

leave/let

Standard usage allows either "*Leave* me alone" (meaning "go away") or "*Let* me alone" (meaning "stop bothering me"). But since *let* really means *to allow*, "*Leave* me give you some advice" is definitely nonstandard. Use "*Let* me give you some advice before you *leave*."

lend/loan

You may now correctly ask a loved one either to *lend* you some socks or *loan* you some socks. Only a traditionalist would be likely to object today to *loan* as a verb.

less/fewer   See *fewer/less.*

lie/lay   See *lay/lie.*

like/as   See *as/like.*

likely/liable

Although these words are virtually interchangeable today, the careful writer will use *likely* to mean "quite possibly" and *liable* to suggest responsibility.

> Your roommate is *likely* to be upset since she is *liable* for damages.

lose/loose

Another problem in pronunciation and spelling. *Lose* (rhymes with *ooze*) means to fail to keep something.

> *vb.*   *vb.*
> If we *lose* our right to protest, we will ultimately *lose* our freedom.

Loose (rhymes with *goose*) means not tight.

> *adj.*
> The noose is too *loose* on your lasso.

man/person

The generic *man* (as the term is called) is supposed to include both sexes—all human beings. But unfortunately the same word, *man*, also means simply a male human being; thus the term is ambiguous. Sometimes it includes both sexes; sometimes it does not—and sometimes nobody can tell whether it does or doesn't. Also, *man* is another word, like the generic *he*, that eclipses the female. To avoid this subtle sexism, use *person* or *people* when you mean a person or people, not just males.

> *Sexist:*   We want to hire the best *man* we can get for the job.
> *Fair:*   We want to hire the best *person* we can get for the job.

A number of compound words using the word *man* can be avoided with little difficulty.

Avoid	Prefer
chairman	chairperson, chair, moderator
congressman	representative, senator
councilman	council member
fireman	fire fighter
foreman	supervisor
mailman	mail carrier
mankind	humanity
manpower	work force
manmade	artificial, manufactured
policeman	police officer
salesman	salesperson

The tough one to replace is *manhole*. But did you ever stop to think that it could just as well be called a *streethole?*
See also *he or she/his or her.*

may/can   See *can/may*.

most/almost   See *almost/most*.

Ms.

Accepted by most and preferred by many, the term *Ms.* (rhymes with *his*) allows us to address women without indicating (or even knowing) their marital status, as the term *Mr.* has always done for men.

myself

Properly used, *myself* is either an intensive (I am going to fix the faucet *myself*) or a reflexive pronoun (I cut *myself* shaving). Do not use *myself* as a subject or an object in writing.

> *Colloquial:*   Jocasta and *myself* are going to be partners.
> *Preferred:*   Jocasta and *I* are going to be partners.
>
> *Colloquial:*   Will you play tennis with Jocasta and *myself*?
> *Preferred:*   Will you play tennis with Jocasta and *me*?

number/amount   See *amount/number*.

orientated/oriented

The word *orientated* means "facing the east." Do not use this term if you mean *oriented*.

> That college is *oriented* in the liberal tradition.

Orientation is the correct form of the noun:

> Freshman *orientation* begins in August.

prescribe/proscribe

Because these words have almost opposite meanings, you will badly confuse your readers if you use the wrong one. *Prescribe* means to recommend or to establish rules, while *proscribe* means to prohibit or denounce.

> The legislature *proscribes* the use of certain drugs unless *prescribed* by a physician.

principal/principle

Although we have numerous meanings for *principal*, the word *principle* basically means a rule: a person of high moral *principle*, a primary *principle* of physics. You can remember the *-le* spelling by association with the *-le* ending on *rule*. All other uses will end with *-al*: a high school *principal*, the *principal* on a loan, a *principal* cause or effect, the *principal* (main character) in a film or play.

probable/probably

The adjective *probable* (sounds at the end like *capable*) and the adverb *probably* (ends with a long *e* sound, like *capably*) both mean likely.

> The *probable* involvement of the CIA in the revolution *probably* caused the rebels to lose.

proved/proven

Either form is acceptable as the past participle of the verb *to prove*.

> Carlyle's innocence *was proved* in court.
> Carlyle's innocence *was proven* in court.

quite/quiet

Be careful not to confuse these words. *Quite*, an adverb, means *entirely, truly; quiet* means the opposite of *loud*.

> Carol was *quite* ready to yell, "*Quiet*, please!"

quotes

As a verb, *quotes* is standard English.

> Louella *quotes* Shakespeare even in bed.

But as a shortening of *quotation* or *quotation marks*, the term *quotes* is still considered colloquial.

> *Avoid:* You no longer need to put *quotes* around slang.

raise/rear

You never *rear* chickens; you just *raise* them. But nowadays you can either *rear* or *raise* children.

real/really

Do not use *real* as an adverb in writing.

> *Colloquial:* Charlie saw a *real* interesting movie.
> *Standard:* Charlie saw a *really* interesting movie.

But *really* (like *very*) is a limp, overworked word. Either leave it out or find a more emphatic word.

> *Improved:* Charlie saw an interesting movie.
> Charlie saw an extremely interesting movie.

reason is because

Because many readers expect a noun or adjective as complement of the *to be* verb (*am, is, was, were,* etc.), you should write "The reason is that. . . .," or rephrase your sentence.

> *Avoid:* The reason we are swamped with trash is because I forgot to put the garbage out.
> *Better:* The reason we are swamped with trash is that I forgot to put the garbage out.
> *Better:* We are swamped with trash because I forgot to put the garbage out.

refer See *allude/refer.*

rise/raise

You never *rise* anything, but you always *raise* something. Prices *rise*, spirits *rise*, curtains *rise*, but you *raise* cain, or *raise* corn, or *raise* prices.

> Taxes are *rising* because Congress has *raised* the defense budget again.

If you cannot keep these verbs straight, avoid them.

Taxes are going up.
Congress keeps increasing taxes.

shall/will

A few years back, "I *shall*" expressed simple future tense, while "I *will*" was considered emphatic. Current usage has erased this distinction. Most people use *will* consistently and rely on other means of gaining emphasis.

she or he   See *he or she/his or her.*

should of   See *could of/should of/would of.*

sit/set

The principal parts of these two verbs are as follows:

sit	sat	sat	sitting
set	set	set	setting

You seldom *sit* anything and you always *set* something (with these exceptions, which are never confused: the sun *sets*, jello and concrete *set*, hens *set*). We *sit* down or we *sit* a spell; we *set* a glass down or we *set* a time or we *set* the table.

One notable exception: the verb *sit* can mean "to cause to be seated." Thus, it is quite correct to write:

The teacher sat Buffy down and gave her a lecture.

sort of/kind of   See *kind of/sort of.*

split infinitives

Split infinitives are now acceptable in standard English, but try not to rend them asunder. A single adverb between *to* and the verb (*to hastily plan* a party) will not offend most readers, but purists still find any split infinitive objectionable. Know thy audience. (For a longer discussion, see *Split Infinitive* in the "Revising Index," Chapter 13.)

supposed to/used to

Since we never hear the -*d* sound in these phrases when we talk, the -*d* is easy to forget in writing. Whenever you write either term, be sure to add the -*d*.

than/then   See then/than.

their/there/they're

Do not confuse these words. *Their* is a possessive adjective or pronoun.

> *Their* dog is friendly. That dog is *theirs*.

There is an adverb or an expletive.

> *There* she goes. *There* is no problem.

They're is a contraction of *they are*.

> *They're* gone.

If you have trouble spelling *their,* remember that all three (*they're/there/their*) start with *the.*

theirselves

Do not use it unless writing dialect. The accepted term is *themselves.*

then/than

These words have quite different meanings. *Then* usually suggests a time.

> First we'll pick up the ice; *then* we'll get the ice cream salt.

Than usually suggests a comparison.

> No one talks faster *than* Michael.
> Claudia would rather talk *than* eat.

thusly

Do not use it: always write simply *thus*.

to/too/two

To is usually a preposition, sometimes an adverb, and also introduces an infinitive.

> to the depths, push the door to, to swing

Too is an adverb.

> Too much noise.
> Selma is going too.

Two is the number.

> two paychecks, two miles

try and/try to

Although we frequently say, "I'm going to *try and* get this job done," the usage is still colloquial. In writing stick with *try to*.

> I am going to try to get this job done.

two   See *to/too/two*.

uninterested/disinterested   See *disinterested/uninterested*.

used to/supposed to   See *supposed to/used to*.

very

Avoid this colorless, exhausted word. Find one more exact and expressive (extremely, considerably, fully, entirely, completely, utterly) or else leave it out. See also *real/really*.

weather/whether

Do not confuse these words. *Weather* is what goes on outside; *whether* introduces an alternative.

> I can't decide *whether* the *weather* will be suitable for a picnic.

who/which/that

Use *who* to refer to people (or animals you are personifying).

> The person *who* lost three keys. . . .
> Lenin, *who* is Susie's cat, ...

Use *which* to refer to animals or nonliving things.

> The earth *which* blooms in spring. . . .
> The cat *which* lives at Susie's. . . .

Use *that* to refer either to people or things.

> The person *that* lost these keys. . . .
> The earth *that* blooms in spring. . . .
> The cat *that* lives at Susie's. . . .

If you are in doubt about whether to use *who* or *whom*, see *Case of Pronouns*, number 5, in the "Revising Index," Chapter 13.

will/shall   See *shall/will*.

would of   See *could of/should of/would of*.

you (indefinite)

In informal writing, you may always address your readers as *you* (as we have done in this sentence). Somewhat questionable, though, is the use of *you* to mean just anyone (the *indefinite you*):

> In France if *you* buy a loaf of bread, *you* get it without a wrapper.

If writing on a formal level, you should use the third person singular *one*.

> In France if *one* buys a loaf of bread, *one* gets it without a wrapper.

your/you're

Your is a possessive adjective or pronoun.

> This is *your* book; this book is *yours*.

You're is a contraction of *you are*.

> Let me know when *you're* leaving.

COMPREHENSIVE EXERCISES   14-1

A. Words frequently confused
The following sentences contain words that sound alike but mean different things, like *quite/quiet, its/it's,* and *sit/set*. In each sentence, choose the appropriate term from the words in parentheses.

1. I have been (lead/led) astray again.
2. Tristan is plumper (then/than) a teddy bear.
3. (Its/It's) not the money; (its/it's) the (principal/principle) of the thing.
4. Those most in need of (advice/advise) seldom welcome it.
5. Horace can't study if his room is (to/too) (quiet/quite).
6. The automobile is a (principal/principle) offender in contributing to air pollution.
7. Our spirits (rose/raised) with the sun.
8. They had a frisky time when (there/their) goose got (lose/loose).
9. Let's (lie/lay) down and talk this over.
10. That (continual/continuous) drip from the faucet is driving me to drink.
11. You ought to (appraise/apprise) the situation carefully before you decide (weather/whether) to file a complaint.
12. (You're/Your) decision could (affect/effect) your career.
13. If you (choose/chose) to file, you should not harbor the (illusion/allusion) that all (you're/your) problems will be solved.
14. Why don't we (sit/set) this one out?
15. (Your/you're) going to be sent to Lower Slobovia if you (accept/except) this job.
16. Virgil tends to (dominant/dominate) the conversation with his (continual/continuous) complaints about the IRS.
17. I could (infer/imply) from his complaints that he owes back taxes.

18. If the (weather/whether) improves, (then/than) we will plant the garden.
19. Any news program will usually (appraise/apprise) you of a late frost.
20. Snow peas will not be (affected/effected) by a light frost.
21. I (advice/advise) you to pick them young.
22. The dean has (lain/laid) down firm rules concerning class attendance.
23. I (chose/choose) strawberry last time, and it was all right, (accept/except) there weren't any strawberries in it.
24. Sherman was (quiet/quite) outraged by Marvin's (illusion/allusion) to his bald spot.
25. How did that dog (lose/loose) (its/it's) tail?
26. Many people mistakenly think (their/they're) being witty when they (dominant/dominate) the conversation.
27. Please (set/sit) that plant over (their/there) near the window.
28. Whenever I (lie/lay) down for a nap, the children outside (rise/raise) cain.
29. Stanley is a person of firm, moral (principle/principal) who should (rise/raise) to national prominence.
30. He (implied/inferred) that using artificial chocolate (affects/effects) the taste of the cookies.
31. Which would you rather (loose/lose)—your mind or your heart?
32. In his paper, Clovis (inferred/implied) that Milton is a crashing bore, but *Paradise Lost* (affects/effects) me deeply.
33. A large (amount/number) of students love English courses.
34. There are few differences (among/between) trashy romantic novels.
35. The (principle/principal) cause of indigestion is overeating.

B. Assorted matters of usage

Most of the sentences below contain examples of questionable usage. Revise those sentences that need changing in order to be acceptable as standard English. Some contain multiple mistakes.

1. My roommate and myself moved in an apartment.
2. We need to quickly, thoroughly, and painstakingly perform the analyzation of that substance again.
3. Did Everett author that report all by hisself?
4. Having been raised on a farm, Henrietta is disinterested in urban entertainments.
5. George baked a considerable amount of cookies.
6. You could of busted the lawnmower on that huge rock.
7. For once, try and do what you're suppose to.
8. Hopefully, we are already to go now.
9. I'm going to put quotes around this slang, irregardless of what the book says.
10. Most everyone which is liable to come has all ready got here.
11. A banquet is where you eat alot of food and can't help but be bored by the speeches.
12. If we go altogether, we should be alright.
13. A person may buy his or her ticket from his or her union representative.

14. You would of had less problems if you would of centered around the main issue better.
15. The real reason I'm not coming is because I'm not interested anyways.
16. My ideas are all together different than those of the speaker.
17. If you live in Rome, you should do like the Romans do.
18. Clarence and Claudia got theirselves involved in a accident all ready on their new motorcycle.
19. Clarence use to enthuse about the virtues of being safety conscious.
20. Now his safety record ain't any different from anybody else's.
21. Can I loan you my motorcycle?
22. If you turn the key, thusly, the engine shall start.
23. Where is the monkey wrench at?
24. Being as you are between a rock and a hard place, you don't have much choice anymore, do you?
25. In areas where muggers, rapists, etc., abound, a large dog really is man's best friend.
26. You tore my heart out and stomped on it: now what am I suppose to do?
27. The main reason we overeat is because food is so delicious.
28. If I'd known you were coming, I would of left.
29. Sally and Samantha both wrote poems about air pollution; Sally's was best.
30. Charmain use to scrub the bathtub every day.

Appendix

Spelling

In the past people were considerably more relaxed about correct spelling than we are today. William Shakespeare, demonstrating his boundless creativity, spelled his own last name at least thirteen different ways. John Donne wrote "sun," "sonne," or "sunne," just as it struck his fancy. But along about the eighteenth century, Dr. Samuel Johnson decided things were out of hand. He took it upon himself to establish a standard for the less learned and brought out his famous dictionary. The language has refused to hold still, even for the stern-minded Dr. Johnson, but people have been trying to tame it ever since.

Today educated people are expected to be able to spell according to the accepted standard. Nobody encourages a lot of creativity in this area. So if you didn't learn to spell somewhere back in grade school, you've got a problem.

TRY PROOFREADING

Spelling is intimately tied up with proofreading. A quick read-through will not catch careless spelling errors, and it will not make you stop and look up words that just do not look right the way you wrote them. It will do you no good to shrug and say, "Oh, I'm a terrible speller," as though it were the same as "Oh, I'm a hemophiliac." If you know your spelling is weak, leave it alone on the rough draft—worrying about it could really cramp your style—but do look up all those words before you type the finished copy or hand in your in-class theme.

SPELLING BY RULES

Memorizing and applying spelling rules can be almost as challenging as remembering the spelling of individual words. But many people profit by knowing at least a few spelling rules, so four groups of common spelling rules follow. Three of these groups concern suffixes (ending like *-s, -ing, -able*), since those rules are a little more consistent than most.

Doubling or Not Doubling

Pattern A. Double the final consonant if it's in an accented syllable with a short vowel sound.

> forgot, forgotten, forgettable
> fog, foggy
> pad, padding
> regret, regretted

Pattern B. Do not double the final consonant if the vowel sound in its syllable is long.

> write, writer, writing
> eat, eaten
> relate, related
> rail, railing

Pattern C. Do not double the final consonant if its syllable is unaccented.

> counsel, counselor
> question, questionable

Dropping or Not Dropping

Pattern A. Drop the final *-e* before *-ing, -able,* or other suffixes beginning with vowels.

> please, pleasing
> store, storage
> sense, sensible

but:

> hoe, hoeing

Pattern B.   Retain the final *-e* before suffixes beginning with consonants.

> awe, awesome
> hope, hopeful
> live, lively
> tone, toneless

Pattern C.   If the final *-e* is preceded by a *u*, the *e* is usually dropped.

> true, truly
> argue, argument

Pattern D.   If the final *-e* makes a *c* or *g* before it soft (makes the *c* sound like *s* or makes the *g* sound like *j*), it's usually retained.

> outrage, outrageous
> notice, noticeable

Changing or Not Changing

Pattern A.   The final *-y* after a consonant changes to *i* before all suffixes except *-ing*.

> fly, flies, flying
> forty, forties
> apply, applied, applying

Pattern B.   The final *-y* after a vowel stays *y*.

> play, played
> alloy, alloys
> trolley, trolleys

but:

> lay, laid
> pay, paid
> say, said

Pattern C.   The final *-y* stays *y* in proper nouns.

> two Marys
> the Raffertys

EI or IE

Pattern A. When *i* and *e* are used together, put the *i* before the *e* in most cases.

> friend
> believe
> thief
> fierce
> niece

Pattern B. When the *i* and *e* combination follows the letter *c*, put the first *e* first.

> deceit
> conceive
> receive

Pattern C. When the *i* and *e* combination sounds like a long *a* (as in *day*), put the *e* first.

> vein
> freight

This jingle is one way many people remember the rules about *ie* and *ei:*

> i before e, except after c,
> Or when sounded as a
> As in *neighbor* and *weigh.*

One of the problems with this spelling rule is that there are many exceptions, and several of them are common. Memorization seems to be your only recourse. Here is a list of some common exceptions to the preceding *ei/ie* rules:

Pattern A Exceptions		Pattern B Exceptions
counterfeit	neither	financier
either	seize	species
foreign	sleight	
forfeit	sovereign	
height	stein	
heir	surfeit	
leisure	weird	

The Apostrophe Problem

Some people classify the myriad misuses of the apostrophe as spelling errors. Remember that apostrophes show possession (dog's puppies) or contraction (can't), but they don't belong in plain old plurals (pigs, radishes, submarines). Look up *Apostrophe* in the "Index of Mechanics, Punctuation, Grammar, and Style" and study its proper use.

SPELLING BY ROTE

Reading the preceding section on spelling rules may have led you to a conclusion: you can't spell most English words by sounding them out. *Sensible* or *sensable? Independant* or *independent? Desperate* or *desparate?* The truth is you'll just have to memorize how most words are spelled. Here are some methods you can use to help you identify problem words and learn them by heart:

1. Learn the differences between similar words. Lots of people have trouble with pairs like *accept* and *except, affect* and *effect, loose* and *lose.* We explain these differences in the "Glossary of Usage," so if you feel shaky on which of two similar words is right, look there.
2. Make a list of words you misspell. Make it up from the errors you find while proofreading, the spelling mistakes your instructors mark, and the list of frequently misspelled words at the end of this appendix. Neatly print some of these words, spelled correctly, on a piece of paper and tape it to your mirror. Maybe looking at it every morning will make the correct spellings as familiar as your own face.
3. Once you've looked up the correct spellings of your problem words, you can sometimes make up little devices to help you remember them. It helps some people to think, "You can't believe a lie," to remind themselves that *believe* has the word *lie* in it. And once you've got that one down, all you have to remember is that *receive* is the other way. If you have trouble remembering whether it's *their* or *thier*, try remembering that all three words that sound like that—*there, they're,* and *their*—begin with the word *the.* Some of these devices can get more elaborate than the spelling of the words themselves, but if devices do the trick for you, no one's going to complain.
4. You may feel that you're a hopeless case. There are dozens of learn-to-spell books written just for people like you. Ask at the local bookstore or check out some of the study guides listed at the end of "Reading and Writing in College Classes," and work through whichever one suits you best.

EXERCISE A-1

1. In each of the following groups, one word is misspelled. Find that word and look in the dictionary for its correct spelling.
   a. sandwich, tradgedy, hallucination, forever
   b. precede, proceed, superceed, recede
   c. predict, perform, personal, prespective
   d. managable, flying, tries, allowable
   e. February, experience, suprise, library
   f. dependant, arrangement, irresistible
   g. livelihood, maintainence, pronunciation
   h. desparate, separate, marriage
   i. disappear, accomodate, occurrence
   j. deceive, believe, recieve, inveigle
   k. malice, catagory, experience
   l. familiar, suspicious, athelete
   m. lonliness, management, mischief
   n. sacrifice, freindly, original
   o. ingrediant, successful, rhythm
   p. pathetic, dismal, wierd
   q. perceive, strict, writting
   r. restaraunt, conscious, neighbor

2. Add two suffixes each (-ing, -able, -s, -er, -ance, -ful, -ness, etc.) to the following words and then check your spelling with a dictionary.

a. fog	i. rebel	q. manage
b. ignore	j. battle	r. hope
c. change	k. plan	s. rally
d. advise	l. travel	t. play
e. happy	m. pad	u. thought
f. practice	n. prefer	v. write
g. hate	o. ponder	w. focus
h. alley	p. occur	

---

500 COMMONLY MISSPELLED WORDS

A

absence	accompaniment	admission
abundance	accomplish	adolescence
academic	accurately	advantageous
acceptable	achievement	advertisement
accessible	acquaintance	aesthetic
accessory	acquire	afraid
accidentally	actually	aggravate
accommodate	adequately	aggressive

alcoholic
allegiance
amateur
analysis
analyze
ancient
announcement
anticipated
anxious
apologized
apparatus
apparent
appearance
appreciate
appropriate
approximate
architectural
argument
arrangement
article
artificial
aspirin
assistance
athlete
athletic
atrocious
attendance
attitude
audible
audience
available
average
avoidance
awkward

B

bankruptcy
barbiturate
basically
beautiful
beginning
behavior
beige
believe
beneficial
biased
bicycle

bizarre
bouillon
bourgeoisie
broccoli
bruise
budget
bureaucratic
buoyancy
business

C

caffeine
calendar
calmly
cancellation
capacity
capitalism
carburetor
cashier
casual
catastrophe
category
caterpillar
cautious
ceiling
ceremony
certainly
chaos
characteristic
chauvinism
chiefly
children
chocolate
cigarette
circumstance
citizen
clique
coincidence
college
comfortable
commercial
committee
compatible
competence
competition
competitive
conceited

conceivable
conceive
concentrate
condemn
condescend
conscience
conscientious
conscious
consistent
contemporary
continuous
controlled
controversial
convenience
correspondence
counselor
courageous
credibility
crises
criticism
criticize
cruelty
curiosity
cynicism

D

daughter
debatable
deceive
deficiency
definitely
definition
delicious
democracy
dependent
descend
description
desperate
determine
detriment
devastation
developed
dialogue
diaper
different
difficult
dilemma

disappoint

disastrous

disciple

discipline

discrimination

discussion

disguise

disgusted

dominant

doubtful

E

efficient

eliminate

embarrass

emphasize

encourage

enough

environment

especially

exaggerate

excellence

except

excite

exercise

existence

experience

experiment

explanation

extremely

F

familiar

fascinate

field

finally

foreigners

forty

fourth

friendliness

fruitful

fulfill

G

garbage

gasoline

gauge

gauze

generally

generosity

generous

genuine

ghetto

glamorous

gorgeous

gossiping

government

grammar

grateful

grocery

guarantee

guerilla

guidance

guitar

gynecology

H

habitual

hallucinate

happiness

harangue

harass

height

hereditary

heroic

heroin

hilarious

hospitalization

humorous

hundred

hypocrisy

hypocrite

hysterical

I

icicle

icy

imaginary

immaculate

immediately

importance

incidentally

indefinite

independence

individually

inevitable

infinite

ingenious

ingredient

initiative

inquisitive

insistence

inspector

intellect

intelligence

interest

interference

interpretation

interrogate

interrupt

irrelevant

irresistible

irritable

J

jealousy

journey

judgment

judgement

justice

juvenile

K

karate

knowledgeable

L

laboratory

language

lascivious

laughter

leisurely

license

likelihood

literature

loneliness

ludicrous

luxurious

M

magazine

magnificent

maintenance

malice

management

maneuver

margarine

marijuana
marriage
material
mechanics
medicine
menace
menstruation
meticulous
militant
millionaire
mimeograph
miniature
mischief
miserable
misspell
mortgage
moustache
mouthful
mysterious

N

narrative
national
naturally
nauseous
necessary
neighbor
neither
neurotic
neutral
nuclear
nuisance
numerous

O

obedience
obey
oblivious
obnoxious
obscene
obsession
occasion
occurred
occurrence
opinion
opponent
opportunity
opposite

optimism
organization
original

P

pamphlet
parallel
paralyzed
particular
pathetic
peculiar
perceive
performance
permanent
persistent
personnel
pesticide
pharmacy
phenomenon
philosophical
physical
picturesque
piece
pigeon
pitiful
pleasant
pneumonia
poetry
political
possession
possible
practical
precede
predominant
preferred
prejudice
presence
prestige
prevalent
primitive
privilege
probably
procedure
proceed
process
professor
prominent

proportion
prosecutor
psychiatrist
psychic
psychoanalysis
psychology
pursue

Q

quantity
quarter
quotient

R

referring
relevance
relieve
remember
reminisce
renaissance
repetition
responsible
restaurant
rhyme
rhythm
roommate
route

S

sabotage
sacrifice
sadistic
satisfied
scenario
schedule
science
scrupulous
secondary
secretary
segregated
seize
separate
sergeant
serious
sesame
several
sherbet
sheriff

shriek
significance
silhouette
similar
simultaneous
skeleton
skepticism
skiing
skillful
society
solemn
sophomore
souvenir
spaghetti
special
specific
stadium
stamina
stereotype
stomach
straight
strength
strict
strychnine
studying
subconscious
submissive
subtle
succeed
successful
sufficiency

suicide
superficial
surprise
surrounding
susceptible
suspicious
syllable
sympathize
symptom
synchronize
synonymous
synthetic

T

tactful
tantalize
technical
technique
temperament
temperature
tenant
tendency
therapeutic
therefore
thief
thorough
tolerance
tomorrow
tragedy
traveler
traveller
tyranny

U

umbrella
undoubtedly
unnecessary
usually

V

vacancy
vacation
vacuum
valuable
vegetable
vehicle
vengeance
versatile
vicious
view
villain
vitamin

W

weird
wield
wrestle
writing

Y

yield

Z

zealous
zinc
zodiac
zucchini

Acknowledgments

Jerry Adler, excerpt from "So What Are Street Smarts?" *Newsweek*, 7 June 1982. Copyright © 1982 by Newsweek, Inc. Condensed from *Newsweek*. All rights reserved. Reprinted by permission.

Joseph Arena, excerpt from "A Strike for Bowling," *Newsweek*, 28 June 1982. Copyright © 1982 by Newsweek, Inc. Condensed from *Newsweek*. All rights reserved. Reprinted by permission.

Barbara Currier Bell, excerpt from "A Few Words on Choosing Your Dictionary," *The New York Times*, Sunday, 25 April 1982. Copyright © 1982 by The New York Times Company. Reprinted by permission.

Peg Bracken, excerpt from *The I Hate to Cook Book*, 1960. Reprinted by permission of Harcourt, Brace, Jovanovich, Inc.

Stephen Brill, excerpt from "The Traffic (Legal and Illegal) in Guns," *Harper's*, Sept. 1977. Copyright © 1977 by Stephen Brill. Reprinted by permission of The Sterling Lord Agency, Inc.

Gwendolyn Brooks, excerpt from "We Real Cool: The Pool Players. Seven at the Golden Shovel" from *The World of Gwendolyn Brooks* by Gwendolyn Brooks. Copyright © 1959 by Gwendolyn Brooks. Reprinted by permission of Harper & Row, Publishers, Inc.

Norma Cousins, excerpt from *Anatomy of an Illness*. Copyright © 1979 by W. W. Norton & Company, Inc. Used by permission of the publisher.

Vina Deloria, Jr., excerpt from "This Country Was a Lot Better Off When the Indians Were Running It," *The New York Times*, 8 March 1979. Copyright 1979 by The New York Times Company. Reprinted by permission.

Joan Didion, excerpt from "The Howard Hughes Underground," *Saturday Evening Post*, Sept. 1967. Copyright © by Joan Didion. Reprinted by permission of William Morris Agency, Inc., on behalf of the author.

Edith Efron, excerpt from "The Soaps—Anything but 99 44/100 Per Cent Pure," *TV Guide® Magazine*, 9 March 1965. Copyright 1965 by Triangle Publications. Reprinted with permission from *TV Guide® Magazine*.

T. S. Eliot, excerpts from "The Love Song of J. Alfred Prufrock," from *Collected Poems 1909–1962* by T. S. Eliot. Copyright 1936 by Harcourt, Brace, Jovanovich, Inc. Copyright © 1963, 1964 by T. S. Eliot, permission of Harcourt, Brace, Jovanovich, Inc. and Faber and Faber Ltd. Reprinted by permission of the publisher.

Blake Fleetwood, excerpt from "The Tax Police," *Saturday Review*, May 1980. Copyright © 1980, Saturday Review Magazine Co. Reprinted by permission.

Robert Frost, excerpt from "Desert Places," *The Poetry of Robert Frost*, edited by Edward Connery Lathem. Copyright 1936 by Robert Frost. Copyright © 1964 by Lesley Frost Ballantine. Copyright © 1969 by Holt, Rinehart and Winston. Reprinted by permission of Holt, Rinehart and Winston, Publishers.

Christopher Hitchens, excerpt from "The Faded Laurel Crown," *Harper's Magazine* Nov. 1977. Copyright © 1977 by *Harper's Magazine*. All rights reserved. Reprinted from the November 1977 issue by special permission.

Adam Hochschild, excerpt from "True Prep: The Ties That Bond," *Mother Jones,* May 1982. Reprinted with permission from *Mother Jones* magazine; copyright © 1982, Foundation for National Progress.

A. E. Housman, excerpt from "A Shropshire Lad," *The Collected Poems of A. E. Houseman.* Copyright 1939, 1940, © 1965 by Holt, Rinehart and Winston. Copyright © 1967, 1968 by Robert E. Symons. Reprinted by permission of Holt, Rinehart and Winston, Publishers.

Mark Kane, excerpt from "The Tomato: Still Champion," *Organic Gardening.* Copyright © 1982. Reprinted from *Organic Gardening,* Emmaus, PA. 18049, March 1982, with the permission of Rodale Press, Inc.

Joyce Carol Oates, excerpt from "How I Contemplated the World from the Detroit House of Correction and Began My Life Over Again," *The Wheel of Love,* 1970. Reprinted by permission of Vanguard Press, Publishers.

George Orwell, excerpt from *Such, Such Were the Joys, 1945.* Reprinted by permission of Harcourt, Brace, Jovanovich, Inc.

Sylvia Plath, excerpt from "Lady Lazarus," *Ariel.* Copyright © 1963 by Ted Hughes. Reprinted by permission of Harper & Row Publishers, Inc.

Michael Pousner, excerpt from "The New Urban Riots," *Newsweek,* 27 June 1977. Copyright 1977 by Newsweek, Inc. Condensed from *Newsweek.* All rights reserved. Reprinted by permission.

J. F. Powers, excerpt from "The Forks," *Prince of Darkness and Other Stories.* Copyright 1947 by J. F. Powers. Reprinted by permission of the author.

A. Philip Randolph, excerpt from "Why Should We March?" in *The Black Man and the Promise of America, 1963,* edited by Lettie J. Austin et al. Reprinted by permission of the author.

Al Reinert, excerpt from "Doctor Jack Makes His Rounds," *Esquire,* May 1975. Reprinted by permission.

Edwin Arlington Robinson, "Richard Cory" in *The Children of the Night.* Copyright © under the Berne Convention. Reprinted with permission of Charles Scribner's Sons.

Saint Geraud, "Hair Poem," *The Naomi Poems: Corpse and Beans.* Copyright © 1968 by William Knott. Reprinted by permission of Allyn and Bacon, Inc.

Anne Sexton, excerpt from "For Eleanor Boylan Talking with God," in *All My Pretty Ones.* Reprinted by permission of Houghton Mifflin Company.

Robert Shrum, excerpt from "The Imperial Congress," *New Times,* 18 March 1977. Reprinted by permission of New Times Publishing Co.

Paul Simon, "Richard Cory." Copyright © 1966 by Paul Simon. Used by permission.

Jean Stafford, excerpt from "Souvenirs of Survival," *Mademoiselle,* Feb. 1960. Copyright © 1960 by Jean Stafford. Reprinted by permission of Russell & Volkening, Inc., as agents for the author.

Judith Strassner, excerpt from "Grapes of Wrath: 1977," *New Times,* 1 April 1977. Reprinted by permission of New Times Publishing Co.

Horace Sutton, excerpt from "You Can't Live in New York," *Saturday Evening Post,* 11 March 1961. Copyright © the Curtis Publishing Company. Reprinted from the *Saturday Evening Post.*

Judy Syfers, excerpt from "Why I want a Wife," from *Radical Feminism,* 1973, edited by Anne Koedt et al. Copyright 1971 by Judy Syfers. Reprinted by permission of the author.

Studs Terkel, excerpts from *Hard Times: An Oral History of the Great Depression.* Copyright © 1970. Reprinted by permission of Pantheon Books, a Division of Random House, Inc.

James Thurber, an excerpt from "Look Out for Turkey Wort," (Letters to E. B. White). Copyright © 1981 by Helen Thurber. From *Selected Letters of James Thurber,* published by Little, Brown, Atlantic Monthly Press. Reprinted with permission.

Lester C. Thurow, "Hanging on a Cliff," *Newsweek,* 19 April 1982. Copyright © 1982 by Newsweek, Inc. Condensed from *Newsweek.* All rights reserved. Reprinted by permission.

Mark Twain, excerpts from *Mark Twain's Autobiography, Volume II.* Copyright 1924 by Clara Gabrilowitsch. Excerpt from "The War Prayer," in *Europe and Elsewhere.* Copyright 1923, 1951 by the Mark Twain Company. Excerpt from "Disgraceful Persecution of a Boy" in *Sketches New and Old* by Mark Twain. Reprinted by permission of Harper and Row, Publishers.

Peter Ustinov, excerpt from *Dear Me.* Copyright © Pavlov, S. A. 1977. Reprinted by permission of Little, Brown and Company in association with the Atlantic Monthly Press.

Gore Vidal, excerpts from "The State of the Union," from *Matters of Fact and of Fiction: Essays 1973–1976.* First appeared in *Esquire,* May 1975. Copyright © 1973, 1974, 1975, 1976, by Gore Vidal. Reprinted by permission of Random House, Inc. Excerpt from "Paradise Regained," from *The New York Review of Books,* 20 Dec. 1979. Copyright © 1979, Nyrev, Inc. Reprinted with permission from *The New York Review of Books*.

Robert Ward, excerpt from "The Mt. Kisco Sting." *New Times*, 4 March 1977. Copyright © 1977 by Robert Ward. Reprinted by permission of New Times Publishing Co.

Harry E. Waters, excerpt from "The TV Fun House," *Newsweek*, 15 May 1978. Copyright 1978 by Newsweek, Inc. Condensed from *Newsweek*. All rights reserved. Reprinted by permission.

Eudora Welty, excerpt from "Petrified Man," in *A Curtain of Green and Other Stories*. Copyright © 1939. Renewed 1967 by Eudora Welty. Reprinted by permission of Harcourt, Brace, Jovanovich, Publishers, Inc.

Dereck Williamson, excerpt from *The Complete Book of Pitfalls*. Copyright © 1971 by Derek Williamson. Reprinted by permission of the author. Excerpt from "The Mudbacks," *Saturday Review*, June 1971. Copyright © 1971, Saturday Review Magazine Company. Reprinted by permission.

Edmund Wilson, excerpt from "Hull House in 1932," from *The American Earthquake* by Edmund Wilson. Copyright © 1958 by Edmund Wilson. Reprinted with the permission of Farrar, Straus & Giroux, Inc.

William Butler Yeats, excerpt from "Long-Legged Fly," from *Collected Poems* of William Butler Yeats. Copyright 1940 by Georgie Yeats, renewed 1968 by Bertha Georgie Yeats, Michael Butler Yeats, and Anne Yeats. Reprinted by permission of the MacMillan Publishing Company, Inc.

Edward Young, excerpt from *The Fifth Passenger*. Copyright © 1963 by Edward Young, reprinted by permission of Curtis Brown Ltd., London.

William Zinsser, excerpt from "Why Johnny's Teachers Can't Write," *New York Times Magazine*, 12 Nov. 1978. Copyright © 1978 by the New York Times Company. Reprinted by permission.

Ed Zuckerman, excerpt from "The Killer Bees," *Rolling Stone*, 28 July 1977. Copyright by Straight Arrow Publishers, Inc. © 1977. All rights reserved. Reprinted by permission.

Index